PROGRAMMING STANDARD PASCAL

R. C. Holt
J. N. P. Hume

Department of Computer Science
University of Toronto

RESTON PUBLISHING COMPANY, INC., Reston, Virginia
A Prentice-Hall Company

Library of Congress Cataloging in Publication Data

Holt, Richard C
    Programming standard Pascal.

    Includes index.
    1. PASCAL (Computer program language) I. Hume,
J. N. P., joint author. II. Title.
QA76.73.P2H64   001.64'24   80-456
ISBN 0-8359-5691-1
ISBN 0-8359-5690-3 pbk.

©1980 by
RESTON PUBLISHING COMPANY, INC., Reston, Virginia 22090
A Prentice-Hall Company

10   9   8   7   6   5   4   3   2

Printed in the United States of America.

PREFACE

This book is intended to form the basis of an introductory course in computing. No particular mathematical background beyond basic arithmetic is assumed; examples are taken largely from everyday life. In this way, the focus is on programming and problem solving, rather than on mathematics. It is our strong conviction that the foundation of computer programming must be carefully laid. Bad habits once begun are hard to change. Even for those who do not continue to study computer science, an experience in the systematic analysis of problems from the statement of "what is to be done" to the final algorithm for "doing it" can be very helpful in encouraging logical thinking.

The programming language presented here is Pascal, a high-level language that encourages good programming style. The language Pascal was devised by Niklaus Wirth and his book "Pascal User Manual and Report" with Kathleen Jensen contains the definition of what is called Standard Pascal. One of the great advantages of Pascal over other high-level languages is that it is not a language with a very large number of language constructs. It is possible because of this to implement it even on very small computer systems from minicomputers to microcomputers. This book can be used with any Pascal compiler that supports Standard Pascal, such as UCSD Pascal and Pascal 6000.

In this book, Standard Pascal is introduced in a series of subsets that we call PS/1, PS/2, PS/3, and so on. The PS stands for Pascal Subsets. The book is about structured programming and that is what we hope a student will be learning by following this step-by-step presentation of Standard Pascal subsets.

Just as a program provides a list of instructions to the computer to achieve some well-defined goal, the methodology of structured programming provides a list of instructions to persons who write programs to achieve well-defined goals. The goals of

structured   programming   are   to   get   a   programming   job   done
correctly and in such a form that later modifications can be done
easily.   This means that programs must be understood by people
other than their authors.

As each Pascal subset is learned, new possibilities open up.
Even from the first subset PS/1, it is possible to write programs
that   do   calculations and print.   By the time the subset PS/5 is
reached,   a   student   has   learned   how   to   handle   alphabetic
information,   as   well   as   to   do   numerical   calculations   and
structure the control flow of the program.

Structured   programming   is especially important when working
on larger programs; a detailed discussion of the techniques of
modular   programming   and   top-down   design   accompanies   the
introduction of Pascal subprograms in PS/6.

Many   examples   in   the book are from data processing, and in
PS/8 the ability to handle files and records is introduced.
General   concepts   of data structures, searching, and sorting fit
well into this important area that touches all our lives.

The   book   includes   examples   of scientific calculations and
numerical methods and a chapter comparing various high-level
languages.   It   ends   with   a   discussion   of the operation of a
computer and the translation of a high-level programming language
into machine language.

At   all   times   we   have   tried   to present things in easy to
understand stages, offering a large number of program examples
and   exercises   to   be   done by the student. Each chapter has a
summary of the important concepts introduced in it.

The   subsets PS/1, PS/2, PS/3, ..., referred to as a group by
the name PS/k, are based on subsets for PL/1 called SP/k designed
by Richard Holt and David Wortman of the University of Toronto.

This   book   was   prepared   using   a   text editing system on a
computer.   Each program was tested using a Pascal compiler.   The
job of transcribing the authors' pencil scrawls into the computer
was done with great care and patience by Inge Weber.   The book
has ˙been class tested. We are indebted to many people but rather
than mentioning a lot of names here we have sprinkled through the
book names of people who have helped us.

The   time taken to write a book comes at the expense of other
activities.   Since most of the time was in the evenings or
weekends we must end with grateful thanks to our wives Marie and
Patricia.

R.C. Holt

J.N.P. Hume

CONTENTS

1. INTRODUCTION TO STRUCTURED PROGRAMMING   1

        WHAT IS PROGRAMMING?   1
        WHAT IS STRUCTURED PROGRAMMING?   2
        WHAT IS PASCAL?   3
        WHAT IS PS/k?   4
        WHY LEARN JUST A SUBSET?   4
        CORRECTNESS OF PROGRAMS   5
        SUMMARY   6

2. THE COMPUTER   7

        PARTS THAT MAKE THE WHOLE   7
        CODED INFORMATION   8
        MEMORY   9
        ARITHMETIC UNIT   12
        CONTROL UNIT   13
        INPUT AND OUTPUT   14
        PROGRAM TRANSLATION   16
        SUMMARY   17

3. PS/1: PROGRAMS THAT CALCULATE AND OUTPUT   19

        CHARACTERS   19
        NUMBERS   21
        CHARACTER STRINGS   22
        EXPRESSIONS   23
        EXAMPLES OF ARITHMETIC EXPRESSIONS   24
        PRINTING   24
        FORMATTING AND PRINTING   26
        THE PROGRAM   27
        CONTROL CARDS   28
        AN EXAMPLE PROGRAM   29
        SUMMARY   29
        EXERCISES   31

4. PS/2: VARIABLES, CONSTANTS, AND ASSIGNMENTS   33

     VARIABLES   33
     DECLARATIONS   34
     ASSIGNMENT STATEMENTS   35
     TRACING EXECUTION   37
     INPUT OF DATA   39
     CONVERSION BETWEEN INTEGER AND REAL   40
     COMMENTS   41
     AN EXAMPLE JOB   41
     LABELING OF OUTPUT   43
     PROGRAM TESTING   45
     COMMON ERRORS IN PROGRAMS   47
     SUMMARY   48
     EXERCISES   50

5. PS/3: CONTROL FLOW   53

     COUNTED LOOPS   53
     CONDITIONS   54
     BOOLEAN VARIABLES   55
     CONDITIONAL LOOPS   56
     READING INPUT   57
     EXAMPLES OF LOOPS   60
     BRANCHES IN CONTROL FLOW   64
     THREE-WAY BRANCHES   65
     CASE STATEMENTS   67
     EXAMPLE IF STATEMENTS   68
     PARAGRAPHING THE PROGRAM   69
     SUMMARY   70
     EXERCISES   72

6. STRUCTURING CONTROL FLOW   77

     BASIC STRUCTURE OF LOOPS   77
     FLOW CHARTS   79
     PROBLEMS WITH LOOPS   81
     NESTED LOOPS   81
     AN EXAMPLE PROGRAM   83
     LOOPS WITH MULTIPLE CONDITIONS   85
     IF STATEMENTS WITH MULTIPLE CONDITIONS   86
     SUMMARY   87
     EXERCISES   88

7. PS/4: ARRAYS   91

     DECLARATION OF ARRAYS   91
     TWO-DIMENSIONAL ARRAYS   93
     AN EXAMPLE PROGRAM   94
     SUBRANGE TYPES   96
     NAMED TYPES   97
     ARRAYS OF ARRAYS   97
     ARRAYS AS DATA STRUCTURES   98
     OTHER DATA STRUCTURES   99
     SUMMARY   100
     EXERCISES   101

8. PS/5: ALPHABETIC INFORMATION HANDLING 103

  CHARACTER STRINGS 103
  READING AND PRINTING CHARACTERS 104
  READING AND PRINTING LINES 106
  DETECTING END-OF-FILE 107
  USING EOF WHEN READING NUMBERS 108
  USING STRINGS OF CHARACTERS 110
  COMPARISON OF STRINGS FOR RECOGNITION 110
  SEQUENCING STRINGS 112
  HANDLING ARRAYS OF STRINGS 113
  AN EXAMPLE PROGRAM 115
  CONVERTING BETWEEN CHARACTERS AND NUMBERS 117
  CHAR AS A SCALAR TYPE 118
  ENUMERATED TYPES 121
  SUMMARY 123
  EXERCISES 125

9. STRUCTURING YOUR ATTACK ON THE PROBLEM 129

  STEP-BY-STEP REFINEMENT 129
  TREE STRUCTURE TO PROBLEM SOLUTION 130
  CHOOSING DATA STRUCTURES 131
  GROWING THE SOLUTION TREE 131
  DEVELOPING AN ALGORITHM 132
  THE COMPLETE PROGRAM 134
  ASSESSING EFFICIENCY 135
  A BETTER ALGORITHM 136
  BETTER ALGORITHMS 137
  SUMMARY 138
  EXERCISES 139

10. THE COMPUTER CAN READ ENGLISH 143

  WORD RECOGNITION 144
  WORDS WITH PUNCTUATION 147
  WORD STATISTICS 148
  READING PASCAL 150
  SUMMARY 150
  EXERCISES 151

11. PS/6: SUBPROGRAMS 153

  PROCEDURES 153
  FUNCTIONS 155
  NESTING AND SUBPROGRAMS 157
  ACTUAL PARAMETERS AND FORMAL PARAMETERS 159
  ARRAY VARIABLES AND CONSTANTS
      AS ACTUAL PARAMETERS 161
  GLOBAL AND LOCAL VARIABLES 162
  SUMMARY 163
  EXERCISES 166

12. MODULAR PROGRAMMING   169

    A PROBLEM IN BUSINESS DATA PROCESSING   169
    DIVIDING THE PROGRAM INTO PARTS   171
    COMMUNICATION AMONG MODULES   171
    WRITING THE MODULES   173
    THE COMPLETE PROGRAM   175
    USING MODULES   176
    MODIFYING A PROGRAM   177
    SUMMARY   178
    EXERCISES   178

13. SEARCHING AND SORTING   181

    LINEAR SEARCH   181
    TIME TAKEN FOR SEARCH   183
    BINARY SEARCH   183
    A PROCEDURE FOR BINARY SEARCH   184
    SEARCHING BY ADDRESS CALCULATION   187
    SORTING   188
    SORTING BY MERGING   188
    EFFICIENCY OF SORTING METHODS   189
    SUMMARY   190
    EXERCISES   191

14. MAKING SURE THE PROGRAM WORKS   193

    SOLVING THE RIGHT PROBLEM   193
    DEFENSIVE PROGRAMMING   194
    ATTITUDE AND WORK HABITS   194
    PROVING PROGRAM CORRECTNESS   194
    PROGRAMMING STYLE   195
    USE OF COMMENTS AND IDENTIFIERS   195
    TESTING   197
    DEBUGGING   199
    SUMMARY   201
    EXERCISES   202

15. PS/7: FILES AND RECORDS   203

    RECORDS   203
    MOVING RECORDS   204
    ARRAYS OF RECORDS   205
    INPUT AND OUTPUT OF RECORDS   206
    FILES IN SECONDARY MEMORY   208
    FILE MAINTENANCE   210
    PASCAL TEXT FILES   212
    SUMMARY   212
    EXERCISES   215

16. DATA STRUCTURES   217

    LINKED LISTS   217
    INSERTING INTO A LINKED LIST   219
    MEMORY MANAGEMENT WITH LISTS   219
    PROCEDURE FOR INSERTING INTO A LINKED LIST   220
    DELETING FROM A LINKED LIST   223
    RECORDS AND NODES   223

STACKS   224
RECURSIVE PROCEDURES   225
QUEUES   226
TREES   228
ADDING TO A TREE   229
DELETING FROM A TREE   230
PRINTING A TREE IN ORDER   231
SUMMARY   232
EXERCISES   233

17. PS/8: POINTERS AND FILE BUFFERS   237

POINTERS   237
MEMORY MANAGEMENT WITH POINTERS   239
DANGLING POINTERS   240
USING POINTERS   241
FILE BUFFERS   242
FILE MERGE USING BUFFERS   243
SUMMARY   245
EXERCISES   246

18. SCIENTIFIC CALCULATIONS   247

EVALUATING FORMULAS   248
PREDECLARED FUNCTIONS   249
GRAPHING A FUNCTION   250
A PROCEDURE FOR PLOTTING GRAPHS   252
USING THE GRAPH PROCEDURE   254
FITTING A CURVE TO A SET OF POINTS   255
SOLVING POLYNOMIAL EQUATIONS   256
SOLVING LINEAR EQUATIONS   258
COMPUTING AREAS   258
SUMMARY   259
EXERCISES   261

19. NUMERICAL METHODS   263

EVALUATION OF A POLYNOMIAL   263
ROUND-OFF ERRORS   265
LOSS OF SIGNIFICANT FIGURES   265
EVALUATION OF INFINITE SERIES   266
ROOT FINDING   269
PROCEDURE FOR ROOT FINDING   270
NUMERICAL INTEGRATION   271
LINEAR EQUATIONS USING ARRAYS   273
LEAST SQUARES APPROXIMATION   274
MATHEMATICAL SOFTWARE   275
SUMMARY   276
EXERCISES   278

20. PROGRAMMING IN OTHER LANGUAGES   281

PL/1 AND FORTRAN 77   282
ALGOL 60   286
COBOL   287

SUMMARY   289
EXERCISES   290

21. ASSEMBLY LANGUAGE AND MACHINE LANGUAGE   291

MACHINE INSTRUCTIONS   291
INSTRUCTIONS FOR A VERY SIMPLE COMPUTER   293
TRANSLATION OF A PASCAL PROGRAM   294
MNEMONIC NAMES AND MACHINE LANGUAGE   294
STORING MACHINE INSTRUCTIONS IN WORDS   296
A COMPLETE MACHINE LANGUAGE PROGRAM   297
SIMULATING A COMPUTER   299
USES OF SIMULATORS   301
SUMMARY   302
EXERCISES   303

22. PROGRAMMING LANGUAGE COMPILERS   305

A SIMPLE HIGH-LEVEL LANGUAGE   305
SYNTAX RULES   306
USING SYNTAX RULES TO PRODUCE A PROGRAM   308
ACTIONS OF THE COMPILER   311
SCANNING WORDS AND CHARACTERS   313
COMPILING ASSIGNMENT STATEMENTS   314
COMPILING WRITELN STATEMENTS   315
COMPILING WHILE AND END   316
THE COMPILER   318
RUNNING THE COMPILED PROGRAM   323
SUMMARY   325
EXERCISES   326

APPENDIX 1: SPECIFICATIONS FOR THE PS/k LANGUAGE   329

APPENDIX 2: SYNTAX OF PS/k   349

APPENDIX 3: PREDECLARED PASCAL FUNCTIONS   353

APPENDIX 4: SUMMARY OF PASCAL INPUT/OUTPUT FEATURES 355

APPENDIX 5: COLLATING SEQUENCE   359

APPENDIX 6: SYNTAX DIAGRAMS FOR FULL PASCAL   363

INDEX   367

Chapter 1
INTRODUCTION TO STRUCTURED PROGRAMMING

We hope that it is no secret that the book has to do with computers and particularly with the use of computers rather than their design or construction. To use computers you must learn how to speak their language or a language that they can understand. We do not actually speak to computers yet, although we may some day; we write messages to them. The reason we write these messages is to instruct the computer about some work we would like it to do for us. And that brings us to programming.

WHAT IS PROGRAMMING?

Programming is writing instructions for a computer in a language that it can understand so that it can do something for you. You will be learning to write programs in one particular programming language called Pascal. When these instructions are entered into a computer directly by means of a keyboard input terminal or are put on to some medium that a computer can read such as punched cards and then fed into the machine, they go into the part of the computer called its memory and are recorded there for as long as they are needed. The instructions could then be executed if they were in the language the computer understands directly, the language called machine language. If they are in another language such as Pascal they must first be translated, and a program in machine language compiled from the original or source program. After compilation the program can be executed.

Computers can really only do a very small number of different basic things. For example, an instruction which says, STAND ON YOUR HEAD, will get you nowhere. The repertoire of instructions that any computer understands usually includes the ability to move numbers from one place to another in its memory, to add, subtract, multiply, and divide. They can, in short, do all kinds of <u>arithmetic</u> <u>calculations</u> and they can do these operations at rates of up to a million a second. Computers are extremely fast calculating machines. But they can do more; they can also handle alphabetic information, both moving it around in their memory and comparing different pieces of information to see if they are the same. To include both numbers and alphabetic information we say that computers are <u>data</u> <u>processors</u> or more generally <u>information</u> <u>processors</u>.

When we write programs we write a sequence of instructions that we want executed one after another. But you can see that the computer could execute our programs very rapidly if each instruction were executed only once. A program of a thousand instructions might take only a thousandth of a second. One of the instructions we can include in our programs is an instruction which causes the use of other instructions to be repeated over and over. In this way the computer is capable of repetitious work; it tirelessly executes the same set of instructions again and again. Naturally the data that it is operating on must change with each repetition or it would accomplish nothing.

Perhaps you have heard also that computers can make <u>decisions</u>. In a sense they can. These so-called decisions are fairly simple. The instructions read something like this:

```
IF JOHN IS OVER 16 THEN PLACE HIM ON THE HOCKEY TEAM
        ELSE PLACE HIM ON THE SOCCER TEAM
```

Depending on the <u>condition</u> of John's age, the computer could place his name on one or other of two different sports teams. It can <u>decide</u> which one if you tell it the decision criterion, in our example being over sixteen or not.

Perhaps these first few hints will give you a clue to what programming is about.

WHAT IS STRUCTURED PROGRAMMING?

Certain phrases get to be popular at certain times; they are fashionable. The phrase, "structured programming" is one that has become fashionable. It is used to describe both a number of techniques for writing programs as well as a more general methodology. Just as programs provide a list of instructions to the computer to achieve some well-defined goal, the methodology of structured programming provides a list of instructions to persons who write programs to achieve some well-defined goals. The goals of structured programming are, first, to get the job done. This deals with <u>how</u> to get the job done and how to get it done <u>correctly</u>. The second goal is concerned with having it done so that other people can see how it is done, both for their education and in case these other people later have to make changes in the original programs.

Computer programs can be very simple and straightforward but many applications require that very large programs be written. The very size of these programs makes them complicated and difficult to understand. But if they are well-structured, then the complexity can be controlled. Controlling complexity can be accomplished in many different ways and all of these are of interest in the cause of structured programming. The fact that structured programming is the "new philosophy" encourages us to keep track of everything that will help us to be better programmers. We will be cataloguing many of the elements of structured programming as we go along, but first we must look at the particular programming language you will learn.

WHAT IS PASCAL?

Pascal is a language that has been developed to be independent of the particular computer on which it is run and oriented to the problems that persons might want done. We say that Pascal is a high-level language because it was designed to be relatively easy to learn. As a problem-oriented language it is concerned with problems of numerical calculations such as occur in scientific and engineering applications as well as with alphabetic information handling required by business and humanities applications.

Pascal is a reasonably extensive language, so that although each part is easy to learn, it requires considerable study to master. Many different computer installations, ranging in size from large computers to microcomputers, have the facilities to accept programs written in Pascal. This means that they have a Pascal compiler that will translate programs written in Pascal into the language of the particular machine that they have. Also many programs have already been written in Pascal; in some installations a standard language is adopted, and Pascal is sometimes that standard language.

It has been the experience over the past years that a high-level language lasts much longer than machine languages, which change every five years or so. This is because once an investment has been made in programs for a range of applications, an installation does not want to have to reprogram when a new computer is acquired. What is needed is a new compiler for the high-level language and all the old programs can be reused.

Because of the long life-span of programs in high-level languages it becomes more and more important that they can be adapted to changes in the application rather than completely reconstructed.

A high-level language has the advantage that well-constructed and well-documented programs in the language can be readily modified. Our aim is to teach you how to write such programs.

To start your learning of Pascal we will study subsets of the
full Pascal language called PS/k.

WHAT IS PS/k?

The PS in the name PS/k stands for "Pascal Subset". There
really is a series of subsets beginning at PS/1, then PS/2, and
going on up. The first subset contains a small number of the
language features of Pascal, but enough so that you can actually
write a complete program and try it out on a computer right away.
The next subset, PS/2, contains all of PS/1 as well as some
additional features that enlarge your possibilities. Each subset
is nested inside the next higher one so that you gradually build
a larger and larger vocabulary in the Pascal language. At each
stage, as the special features of a new subset are introduced,
examples are worked out to explore the increased power that is
available.

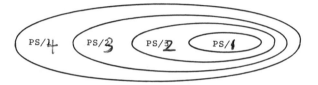

THE PS/k SUBSETS

In a sense, the step-by-step approach to learning Pascal is
structured and reflects the attitude to programming that we hope
you learn.

There is no substitute for practice in learning to program,
so as soon as possible and as often as possible, submit your
knowledge to the test by creating your own programs.

WHY LEARN JUST A SUBSET?

The Pascal language is reasonably extensive; some features
are only used rarely or by a few programmers. If you know
exactly what you are doing, then these features may provide a
faster way to program; otherwise they are better left to the
experts. A beginner cannot really use all the features of the
complete Pascal language and will get lost in the complexity of
the language description. With a small subset it is much easier
to pick up the language and then get on with the real job of
learning programming.

But perhaps most important, the PS/k language has been selected from the Pascal language so as to provide the basic features that encourage the user to produce well-structured programs. This is why it is so appropriate as a means of learning structured programming.

CORRECTNESS OF PROGRAMS

One of the maddening things about computers is that they do exactly what you tell them to do rather than what you want them to do. To get correct results your program has to be correct. When an answer is printed out by a computer you must know whether or not it is correct. You cannot assume, as people often do, that because it was given by a computer it must be right. It is the right answer for the particular program and data you provided because computers now are really very reliable and rarely make mistakes. But is your program correct? Are your input data correct?

One way of checking whether any particular answer is correct is to get the answer by some other means and compare it with the printed answer. This means that you must work out the answer by hand, perhaps using a hand calculator to help you. When you do work by hand you probably do not concentrate on exactly how you are getting the answer but you know you are correct (assuming you do not make foolish errors). But this seems rather pointless. You wanted the computer to do some work for you to save you the effort and now you must do the work anyway to test whether your computer program is correct. Where is the benefit of all this? The labor saving comes when you get the computer to use your program to work out a similar problem for you. For example, a program to compute telephone bills can be checked for correctness by comparing the results with hand computation for a number of representative customers and then it can be used on millions of others without detailed checking. What we are checking is the method of the calculation.

We must be sure that our representative sample of test cases includes all the various exceptional circumstances that can occur in practice, and this is a great difficulty. Suppose that there were five different things that could be exceptional about a telephone customer. A single customer might have any number of exceptional features simultaneously. So the number of different types of customers might be 32, ranging from those with no exceptional features to those with all five. To test all these combinations takes a lot of time, so usually, we test only a few of the combinations and hope all is well.

Because exhaustive testing of all possible cases to be handled by a program is too large a job, many programs are not thoroughly tested and ultimately give incorrect results when an unusual combination of circumstances is encountered in practice. You must try to test your programs as well as possible and at the same time realize that with large programs the job becomes very difficult. This has led many computer scientists to advocate the need to <u>prove</u> programs correct by various techniques other than exhaustive testing. These techniques rely partly on reading and studying the program to make sure it directs the computer to do the right calculation. Certainly the well-structured program will be easier to prove correct.

CHAPTER 1 <u>SUMMARY</u>

The purpose of this book is to introduce computer programming. We have begun in this chapter by presenting the following programming terminology.

Program (or computer program) - a list of instructions for a computer to follow. We say the computer "executes" instructions.

Programming - writing instructions telling a computer to perform certain data manipulations.

Programming language - used to direct the computer to do work for us.

Pascal - a popular programming language. PL/1, Fortran, Cobol, Basic and APL are some other popular programming languages.

PS/k - the programming language used in this book. PS/k is a subset of the Pascal programming language, meaning that every PS/k program is also a Pascal program, but some Pascal programs are not PS/k programs. PS/k is itself composed of subsets PS/1, PS/2 and so on. This book teaches PS/1, then PS/2, and so on up to PS/8.

High-level language - a programming language that is designed to be convenient for writing programs. Pascal is a high-level language.

Structured programming - a method of programming that helps us write correct programs that can be understood by others. The PS/k language has been designed to encourage structured programming. This book teaches a structured approach to programming.

Correctness of programs - the validity of programs should be checked. This can be attempted by comparing test results produced by the computer with the results of calculations made in another way, e.g., by using a hand calculator. Although the ideal is to try to prove a program correct by mathematical means, it is often extremely helpful to read and study the program to see that your intentions will be carried out.

Chapter 2
THE COMPUTER

"The time has come," the walrus said, "to talk of many things" - Lewis Carroll.

And the things we want to talk about in this chapter have to do with getting to know a little bit about computers and how they are organized. A computer is a complex object composed of wires, transistors, and so on, but we will not be trying to follow wiring diagrams and worrying about how to build a computer. What we will be interested in is the various main parts of a computer and what the function of each is. In this way your programming will be more intelligent; you will understand a little of what is going on inside the computer.

PARTS THAT MAKE THE WHOLE

We have already mentioned a number of things about computers. They have a <u>memory</u> where numbers and alphabetic information can be recorded. They can add, subtract, multiply, and divide. This means they have a part called the <u>arithmetic unit</u>. They can read information off certain media, like punched cards, and print results on printers. The printer may print a whole line at a time or just one character at a time, like a typewriter. We say they have an <u>input</u> (for example, a card reader) and an <u>output</u> (a printer). The input-output unit is often referred to as the I/O. Computers execute instructions in sequence. The part of the machine that does this is called the <u>control unit</u>. The arithmetic unit and the control unit are usually grouped together in a computer and called the <u>central processing unit</u> or CPU. So then the computer is thought of as having three parts, memory, I/O and CPU.

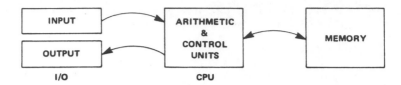

MAIN PARTS OF A COMPUTER

We will look at these different parts in turn and see how they work but first we must see how numbers and alphabetic information can be represented in a computer.

CODED INFORMATION

You are all familiar with the way that information used to travel over telegraph wires in the form of Morse Code. Perhaps you know that each letter or number is coded as a pattern of dots and dashes. For example, the letter A is a dot followed by a dash, E is one dot, V is three dots and a dash. The letters are separated from each other by a pause with no dots or dashes. The famous signal SOS is

                    ...   ---   ...

This is an easy one to remember in emergencies. The Morse Code was designed so that the signal could activate some noise-making device and the listener could then translate the coded message back into letters. Modern teletype machines can send messages much faster because the machines themselves can be used to decode the messages. For these, a character is represented by a pattern of pulses, each pattern being of the same length. Instead of dots and dashes, which are two different lengths of electric pulses, they use one basic time interval and in that time interval have either a pulse or a pause. Each character requires 5 basic time intervals and is represented by a sequence of pulses and pauses. We often write down a pulse as a 1 and a pause as 0, and then the pattern for B is 10011, I is 01100, L is 01001. The word BILL would be transmitted as

            10011011000100101001

Strings of ones and zeros like this can be associated with numbers in the binary system. In the decimal system the number 342 means

        $3 \times 10^2 + 4 \times 10^1 + 2 \times 10^0$

where 10^2 stands for 10 squared, 10^1 for 10 to the first power, that is 10, and 10^0 for 10 to the power zero, which has a value 1. In the binary system of numbers 1101 means

$$1 \times 2^3 + 1 \times 2^2 + 0 \times 2^1 + 1 \times 2^0$$

In the <u>decimal</u> <u>system</u> this binary number has a value 8+4+0+1:=13. We say that this number in the decimal system requires 2 <u>decimal</u> <u>digits</u> to represent it. In the binary system it requires 4 <u>binary</u> <u>digits</u>. We call a binary digit a <u>bit</u>. So the binary number representing the word BILL has 20 bits, each letter requiring 5 bits. Sometimes we take the number of bits required to represent a character as a group and call it a <u>byte</u>. Then the word representing BILL has four bytes. In a computer we must have a way of recording these bits, and usually the memory is arranged into <u>words</u>, each capable of holding a whole number of bytes.

In some machines a single letter is represented by a byte of six bits and the word length is 6 bytes or 36 bits. Most minicomputers and microcomputers have 2 bytes in a word and 8 bits in each byte. There are many different combinations of byte length and word length in different computers. This is something the machine designer must decide.

MEMORY

Most machines record letters and numbers in the binary form because it is possible to have recording devices that can record, read, and hold such information. Most recording devices involve a recording something like that on the tape of a magnetic tape recorder. There is a big difference, though, in the recording. On audio tape we have a magnetic recording that varies in intensity with the volume of the sound recorded. The frequency of the variations gives the pitch of the sound. For a computer, the recordings vary between two levels of intensity which you might think of as "on" and "off". If in a particular region there is an "on" recording it could indicate the binary digit one and if "off" the digit zero. So on a strip of magnetic tape there would be designated areas that are to hold each bit of information.

BITS RECORDED ON MAGNETIC TAPE

Binary digits can thus be recorded on reels of magnetic tape. In a similar way they can be recorded on tracks of a magnetic disk and these disks can be stacked one above the other on a spindle that is kept constantly spinning. To read or record information on a magnetic disk the recording/reading head moves to the correct track of the correct disk.

MAGNETIC DISK MEMORY

This kind of memory is called a magnetic disk pack and is commonly used when large amounts of information are to be stored in the computer and requested randomly. If information is to be retrieved in a particular sequence or order then a magnetic tape reel can be used to store it. Tape reels and disk packs can be removed from the machine and stored if you need to keep information for long periods of time. Smaller disk memories can be used where individual disks are inserted into the reader by the user. These disks are often limp and are called floppy disks. Tape reels on regular audio-type cassettes can also be used as secondary memory.

Neither tape nor disks are as fast to read and write as another type of magnetic recording on the surface of a constantly spinning cylinder called a drum.

MAGNETIC DRUM MEMORY

All these devices require the movement of objects, a reel of tape, a spinning disk or drum, and sometimes read/write heads. These mechanical devices can never give really high-speed access to information. We need memory devices with no moving parts so we can perform operations at rates of the order of a million a second. The only things that move in a really high-speed memory device are the electric signals. As you know, electric signals can move very rapidly, at nearly the speed of light. A very common form of high-speed memory used before the advent of large scale integrated circuits were developed was the magnetic core memory. A magnetic core is a tiny doughnut-shaped piece of material that can be magnetized. When magnetized it is like a bar magnet bent around in a circle.

MAGNETIC CORE

There are two directions in which a core can be magnetized, clockwise and counter-clockwise, and these can represent the two binary digits. To form a memory the cores are threaded on to wires in two directions just like a fly screen, with a core around every intersection of the wires. When signals pass through the wires they can record information in the cores or read out information from the cores, and it can all happen extremely rapidly.

MAGNETIC CORE MEMORY

If the main memory of the computer is made of magnetic cores grouped into words, to find any particular word you need to know where it is located in the array of cores. You need to know its address. Every word (which, remember, is just a group of bits, one bit in each core) has its own address which is a number. An address may, for example, be 125. Words that are neighbors in the array have consecutive addresses, such as 125 and 126, just like houses on a street. The addresses themselves do not have to be stored in the computer. You can tell what address a word has from its location in the array. This is not always possible for houses on the street because the numbering is not completely systematic.

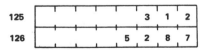

THE CONTENTS OF WORDS IN MEMORY

Since the development of microminiaturized electronic circuits on silicon chips, high-speed memory devices can be produced using this solid state technology. Magnetic core memories are now largely replaced by integrated circuits, but the idea of memory address is the same.

ARITHMETIC UNIT

All computers have a part where arithmetic can take place. This is the <u>arithmetic unit</u>. When a new number is written in a memory location, the old number stored there is automatically erased, just as any old recording is erased as a new recording is made on a magnetic tape recorder. Just reading a number, like playing an audio recording, does not damage the recording no matter how often you do it. If you want to combine numbers, say add them, it is usually done in a special location in the arithmetic unit called the <u>accumulator</u>. On some machines, the size of the accumulator is the same as the size of a word in memory. Words, or rather the information stored in memory locations, can be loaded into the accumulator. In a simple machine language, the instruction

        LOAD 125

would cause the number recorded in location 125 to be placed in the accumulator. Whatever was recorded in the accumulator before would be erased before the load takes place. If we want to add another number we would write

        ADD 126

This would add the number stored in 126 to what was already in the accumulator and the sum of the two numbers would then be in the accumulator. This total could be recorded in the memory for later use by the instruction

        STORE 127

The result of the addition would now be in location 127 but would also remain in the accumulator.

The accumulator can also be used for subtraction, multiplication, and division. In a high-level language like Pascal you never need to think about the accumulator. You merely indicate that you want numbers in two locations, say A and B, to be added and name the location, say C, where you want the answer to be stored. You write this all in one statement, namely

        C:=A+B

This Pascal statement says: add the number stored in location A to the number stored in location B and place the result in location C. In the machine all location addresses are numbers. In Pascal we give the locations names which are called <u>identifiers</u>. The compiler changes these names to numerical locations and changes the single instruction

        C:=A+B

to the three machine instructions.

```
LOAD   A
ADD    B
STORE  C
```

CONTROL UNIT

You have just seen examples of machine language instructions. They each consist of two parts: the operation part, for example LOAD, and the address part, A. Each part can be coded as a binary number, then the whole instruction will just be a string of bits. Suppose that you have a machine with a word length of 36 bits. Then an instruction might be itself stored in such a word with, say, 18 bits for the operation part and 18 bits for the address part. With 18 bits you can represent binary numbers that go from 1 up to 2 to the power 18, which is 262,144. You can refer to any one of over a quarter of a million different memory locations.

Consecutive instructions in a machine language program are stored in consecutive locations in the memory and are to be executed one after the other. The control unit does two things. It uses a special location called the instruction pointer to keep track of what instruction is currently being executed. It places the instruction to be executed in a special location called the control register. In the control register the instruction is decoded and signals are issued to the different parts of the computer so that the operation requested is actually carried out. As each instruction is executed, the instruction pointer is increased by one to give the address of the next instruction in the program. This next instruction is then fetched from the memory, placed in the control register, and executed. This process continues, with instructions being executed sequentially unless a special instruction is encountered, which resets the instruction pointer and causes a jump from the normal sequence to a different part of the program.

In brief, the control unit controls the sequence of execution of instructions and determines the effect that execution has on the information stored in the memory.

Computers were originally referred to as stored program calculators because the instructions as well as the numbers or characters they operate on are stored in the memory. They were also referred to as sequential machines, because normally they followed a sequence of instructions one after another unless a jump instruction directed them to do otherwise.

We have said that the memory of a computer can be contained on a single silicon chip. This is true also of the parts of the computer that make up the central processing unit. If the CPU is all on a single chip we call the computer a microprocessor.

INPUT AND OUTPUT

We have spoken of having both data and instructions in the memory of the machine and changing the data by the execution of instructions. But how do we get data or instructions into the computer, and how do we get data out of the machine after it has been operated on? That is the function of the <u>input and output units</u>. We must have instructions that cause the machine to <u>read</u> information into its memory and to <u>print</u> information out from its memory. And we must have parts of the computer, the input and output units, that respond to these instructions. Most small computers use individual input/output terminals at which information can be entered through a keyboard and output is produced as a display on a cathode ray tube (CRT) screen. Sometimes there is also a printer for obtaining <u>hard copy</u> of what can be seen on the screen. This same type of terminal may be attached, perhaps by a telephone line, to a larger computer as one of many terminals sharing the time of the computer. We say that this is a <u>time sharing</u> arrangement for a number of simultaneous users. Because each user enters his program and data directly into the terminal and receives the results rapidly, the system is often said to be an <u>interactive</u> system. However if the system requires the complete program and data to be entered before compilation and execution begins it is usually known as <u>batch processing</u>.

Batch processing can also be done very effectively by having each user prepare the program and data <u>off-line</u> and then submit it to an input device for processing. The turnaround time between submission and processing must be rapid if programs are being developed but can be slower if planned production runs are being made. One input device commonly used is a punched card reader. You are all familiar with the standard punched card with 80 columns in which punching can take place.

80-COLUMN PUNCHED CARD

For digits, a single hole is made in a column in the position corresponding to the digits 0 to 9. Each alphabetic character requires two holes in a column, one in a digit position and the other in one of the three positions at the top of the card called the 0,11, and 12 positions. Special characters like dollar signs require that three holes be punched in a column. The actual representations in terms of punched holes for each character or digit can be fixed into a card punch <u>keyboard</u> so that when the key on the keyboard for the character is pressed, the correct punching occurs on the card. Many <u>keypunches</u> also interpret the punching by printing the corresponding characters at the top of the card above the column where the punching is. This is so that you can read what is punched on the card. The machine can only read the punching.

Sometimes cards are prepared by marking them with a soft black pencil in certain designated areas. These marks are then read by a reader that senses their presence, just as the punched card reader senses holes. On mark sense cards digits require a single mark, alphabetic characters and special characters require two marks in the same column. Some keywords in the Pascal language can be obtained by marks in the first column or at the top of other columns.

When a mistake is made in punching cards, the card is to be ejected from the punch and removed. A second attempt is then made to produce a correctly punched card. One of the good things about cards is that they can individually be replaced or removed and new cards inserted in a <u>card deck</u> without having to repunch the entire deck. Since instructions are placed in sequence, usually one to a card, this sequence must be maintained. If you drop a deck of cards they can get out of sequence and it is difficult to get them arranged correctly again. Keep an elastic band around your card decks to prevent accidents. The elastic is removed as they are placed into the card reader then replaced immediately after they are read.

The keyboard of a card punch or online computer input terminal is similar to that of a standard typewriter, so it helps if you can type. But hunt-and-peck methods will get you there too. In addition to the ordinary typewriter keys, there are special keys for indicating the end of the input for that card or line. In all our examples we will think of a one to one correspondence between individual punched cards and lines of input on a CRT screen, and between printed lines and output lines on the screen. Most CRT displays permit 80 characters to a line.

The hard copy output units can be line-at-a-time printers or typewriters. The typewriters are the same as those used for input with online terminals. When card decks are the form of input, the output usually comes on the fast printers. Printers can have very high speeds. A speed of 1000 lines a minute is common, but some printers go faster. Most printers are slower.

Across a printed page there are often positions to print 120, 132 or more characters although some printers print only 72 characters on a line. The paper is continuous but may be divided by perforations into pages, each capable of holding about 60 lines of printing. Your output will probably be limited to a few pages for each run on the computer. Because users' jobs on a high-speed printer are run one after another each must be careful to put an identification on the program so that the appropriate output can be claimed. You have to tear the pages apart by hand as the machine feeds paper continuously, piling the printer output on the other side of the printer from the blank paper supply.

PROGRAM TRANSLATION

We have said that three machine language instructions, namely,

```
LOAD  A
ADD   B
STORE C
```

correspond to what is written in Pascal as

C:=A+B

Instructions in the high-level language Pascal are very much simpler to write than instructions in machine language. For one thing, you do not have to be aware of the accumulator; for another, the notation is very similar to the one used in simple mathematical expressions and should be easy for you to get used to. The Pascal language is more powerful in that a single Pascal instruction can correspond to many machine language instructions. We will see later that if you are working in a high-level language, the machine can detect when you make certain kinds of mistakes in your program.

In summary, high-level languages are designed to suit <u>you</u> rather than suit a computer. And in being that way they make the job of programming less difficult.

A Pascal program cannot execute directly on a computer but must be translated into the language for the particular computer you have. This is accomplished after the Pascal program has been read in, or loaded into, the memory. The translation is performed by another program, called the compiler, that is already stored in the computer memory. The compiler reads your Pascal program and produces the appropriate sequence of machine language instructions from your Pascal statements. After compilation, execution of the machine language program begins automatically, provided you have not made any errors in your Pascal program that the compiler can detect but cannot repair. The kind of errors that are detectable are mostly in the <u>form</u> of

the statements. If they are not proper or grammatical statements
in the Pascal language the compiler will report an error to you
in your printout. Errors in grammar are called <u>syntax</u> <u>errors</u>.
In English you know there is an error in the sentence,

>   THE BOYS IS WALKING.

A machine can spot this kind of error but it cannot easily spot
an error in meaning. It might never determine that the sentence,

>   THE HOUSE IS WALKING.

is not a meaningful sentence; it would accept it as syntactically
correct.

Well, that is enough of an introduction now; let us get down
to actually writing programs.

CHAPTER 2 <u>SUMMARY</u>

In this chapter we presented the main parts of a computer and
showed how information is stored in the memory. We explained
briefly how a high-level language such as Pascal is translated,
or compiled, to machine language before being executed by a
computer. The following important terms were introduced.

Memory - the part of a computer that stores information, such
  as data or a program. Magnetic tapes, disks, and drums
  are called secondary memory; they require mechanical
  motion to access information stored on them. Main
  memory can be immediately accessed by the computer; main
  memory may be composed of magnetic cores but is usually
  in the form of a microminiaturized circuit on a silicon
  chip. We say the memory is a solid state one. The
  computer can transfer information between secondary
  memory and main memory.

CPU (central processing unit) - composed of the arithmetic
  unit and the control unit. The arithmetic unit carries
  out operations such as addition and multiplication. The
  control unit directs other parts of the computer,
  including the arithmetic unit, to carry out a sequence
  of instructions that is in the main memory.

Input and output - ways of getting information into and out
  of a computer. The punch card, or IBM card, can be used
  to prepare input for a computer. An input device called
  a card reader is used to sense the holes in punch cards
  and transmit the encoded information to the main memory.
  An output device called a printer takes information from
  main memory and prints it on paper.

     An   input/output   terminal   suitable   for   use   by
individual users is often a keyboard and a cathode ray
tube display screen attached directly (or perhaps by
telephone line) to the computer. We say this is online
with the computer.

Coded   information - before information can be entered into a
     computer, it must be coded in a convenient form for the
     computer's circuitry.   The circuitry recognizes "off"
     and "on" which we can think of as 0 and 1. The smallest
     unit of information is a binary digit, 0 or 1, called a
     bit.   Letters are represented in a computer by a
     sequence of bits, called a byte. Bytes are arranged
     into words, typically four bytes to the word. The main
     memory of the computer is a sequence of words. These
     words can hold data and programs.

Translation (or compilation) - before a program written in a
     language like Pascal can be executed by a computer, it
     must be translated into machine language. The program
     as written in Pascal is called the source program.   The
     translated program is placed in words in the main memory
     and is executed by the computer's CPU.

Chapter 3
PS/1: PROGRAMS THAT CALCULATE AND OUTPUT

This is the chapter where we set the stage for programming and you meet the cast of characters in the play. Nothing very much is going to happen in this first subset, PS/1, but you will be able to go through the motions of writing a complete program, submitting it to a computer and having it executed. This will let you get used to the mechanics of running a keyboard input-output terminal or, if you are handling cards, learn how to arrange a card deck, and find out what you must do with it to get it read by the computer. Also you will see what kind of output to expect. Things will happen, though what the computer is actually doing for you will not be very exciting yet. But remember you will go through the same motions as are necessary when your programs do have more content.

CHARACTERS

We will be learning the programming language Pascal a little bit at a time. Any language consists of words and the words are made up of <u>symbols</u> that we call <u>characters</u>. These characters are put together in <u>strings</u>. In English the word

ELEPHANT

is a string of characters of length eight. It contains only seven different characters, the character E being used twice. We can tell that it is a word because it has a blank in front of it and one at the end. In a way the blank is also a character, but a <u>special character</u> for separating words. We sometimes denote the blank by b when we print programs in this book so that you can see how many blanks are present.

In English, we group words into sentences and we can tell the end of a sentence because of a special mark, the period. We also have a different kind of sentence that ends with a question mark, don't we? In addition to periods and question marks, we have other punctuation marks which serve to make sentences in the language easier to read. They also serve to remove ambiguity in a sentence. There is some doubt about the meaning of the sentence,

THE STUDENT CLAIMS THE TEACHER UNDERSTANDS.

The doubt is removed if it is written with commas, as,

THE STUDENT, CLAIMS THE TEACHER, UNDERSTANDS.

It is important that statements in a programming language be unambiguous, so punctuation is used a great deal. Instead of a sentence, the basic unit in the main part of a program is a statement. Statements are separated by semicolons. This serves to separate them just as periods separate sentences in English. The comma is used to separate items in any list of similar items, and parentheses are used to enclose things that belong together.

We will have words in Pascal that are made up of letters of the alphabet and might also have digits in them. When we are writing a Pascal program we want it to be understandable. So we choose words like English words. We use words like NAME, COST, INCOME, TAX, INVOICE, SUM, or words like PAGE1, TABLE6, ITEM35, and so on. Most of these words are invented by you. You are not allowed to use words that do not at least have one letter at the beginning. If the Pascal compiler sees a digit at the beginning of a word it assumes that it is a number. For example, 317 is taken as a number. This means that words like 3RDPAGE are illegal and will not be accepted by the Pascal compiler.

Before we leave characters we should perhaps list them. A character is a letter, or a digit, or a special character. The letters are

A B C D E F G H I J K L M N O P Q R S T U V W X Y Z
a b c d e f g h i j k l m n o p q r s t u v w x y z

In this book we will use capital letters only in our programs. In general, lower case letters may be used instead of upper case letters. Matching upper and lower case letters are equivalent.

The digits are

0 1 2 3 4 5 6 7 8 9

The special characters are

: + - * / ( ) = , . ' [ ] < > ; | | |

b   blank

Pairs of special characters are often used as <u>special</u> <u>symbols</u> in
the language. For example, each of the following pairs has a
fixed meaning

:= <> <= >= ..

Various other special characters are often available on different
computer systems.

NUMBERS

Computers can do arithmetic calculations and they can do them
extremely rapidly. When you learned arithmetic you first learned
to handle numbers that are whole numbers, or integers. You
learned that 5+6=11 and 2x3=6. In Pascal numbers like 2, 3, 512,
809, and 46281 are called <u>integer</u> <u>constants</u>. Any string of
digits is an integer constant. You will remember that we will be
storing numbers in the computer and representing them as a string
of bits in some coded representation. The largest integer we can
represent will be limited by the length of the string of bits
that are in a word in our computer. Word lengths vary from one
computer to another and different Pascal compilers have different
maximum lengths for the digit strings that represent integer
numbers. You will be safe in expecting at least four decimal
digits to be within the maximum.

If you have integers requiring longer digit strings, for
instance the population of the world, you must use the other form
of numbers which is the <u>real</u> form.

If you have a large number like

635,642,000

you can write it as

6.35642×10^{8}

Perhaps you recognize this as what is called scientific notation.
In Pascal the form of a <u>real</u> <u>constant</u> such as our example is

6.35642E8

The first part is called the <u>fraction</u> <u>part</u>, the second part the
<u>exponent</u>. The exponent part is written using the letter E
followed by the power of 10 that is to multiply the fraction
part. Maybe you learned this notation before in a science course
where very big numbers, like the mass of the moon, often occur.
<u>Real</u> notation is also used for numbers that are not integers.
These are either <u>fractions</u> or <u>mixed</u> <u>numbers</u>. We write either of
these in decimal notation where a point called the decimal point

separates the integer from the fraction part. Examples of fractions are

   .5   .0075   .0000023

Mixed numbers are

   5.27   889.6   6.0216

When we write fractions or mixed numbers in exponent notation we usually standardize the form by putting the first non-zero digit followed by a decimal point then the remaining digits. Then the power of 10 is computed to make it right. The fraction .0000023 is written as 2.3×10^{6}. In Pascal this then is 2.3E-6. It could also be written as 0.23E-5, or 23.0E-7, or even as 23E-7.

   An integer constant must <u>not</u> have a decimal point. A real constant can be written either as a mixed number with at least one digit to the left of the decimal point <u>and</u> one digit to the right, e.g. 0.02, or in the exponent form. In the exponent form it usually has a decimal point (with exceptions like the example 23E-7) and <u>must</u> have an exponent part. There must be digits on both sides of the decimal point. The exponent part is the letter E followed by an optional plus or minus sign followed by one or more digits.

CHARACTER STRINGS

   We have said that computers can handle both numbers and strings of characters. We have seen that there are two forms for numbers, integers and reals.

   A character string can consist of any of the characters that we have specified: letters, digits and special characters. Very often, when printing the results of a computer calculation, we want the results labeled. What we want is to print a string of characters on the page. In the statement that specifies what we want the computer to print, we include the actual string that we want printed enclosed in single quotation marks. These strings enclosed in quotation marks are called <u>literals</u> or <u>character string constants</u>.

   Examples of literals are

   'BILL JONES', 'BALANCE IN ACCOUNT', 'X='

If the literal you want to use contains a quotation mark or an apostrophe, which is the same character, then you must put two quotes rather than a single quote. For example, the literal corresponding to the short form of 'CANNOT' is 'CAN''T'.

EXPRESSIONS

One of the important concepts we have in Pascal is that of an
expression. The way that we explain what a word like expression
means is basically to give examples and then generalize these
examples.

First of all 32, 5, 6.1E2 and 58.1E6 are all expressions. So
the general statement is that integer constants and real
constants are expressions. So are literals like

'THIS IS AN EXPRESSION'

Any expression may be enclosed in parentheses and still be an
expression. For example (32) and (6.1E2) are also expressions.
The expressions that are integer or real constants can be
combined into compound expressions using the signs of arithmetic
for adding, subtracting, multiplying, and dividing. These
expressions are called arithmetic expressions. We use the
standard signs for adding and subtracting, namely the plus and
minus. For multiplication we use the asterisk (*) because there
is no times sign. For division we use the slant or slash symbol
(/). Examples of arithmetic expressions are

2+3, 5.2E1*7.8E5, 6E0/2E0, 10-15

Integer and real values may be combined in a single expression,
and when they are the result is a real value. For example,
2+3.0E1 has the value 3.2E1.

If two numbers are to be divided using the slant operator,
the result will be a real value even if both numbers are
integers. For example, 6/2 gives the real result

3.0E0

Two integers may be divided to produce an integer value using
the operator DIV. For example, 5 DIV 2 would give the integer 2.
The result is truncated. If you want to find the remainder in an
integer division, use the operator MOD. The result of 5 MOD 2 is
the integer 1, the remainder when 5 is divided by 2.

Here is a very complicated arithmetic expression

2*5+8-3*5/2+6

In evaluating this you have to know what to do first because you
really can only add, subtract, multiply or divide numbers two at
a time. The rule is to do the multiplications and divisions
first, then the additions and subtractions. Also you start at
the left-hand side of the expression and work to the right. We
are using here rules of precedence, that the operations multiply
and divide have precedence over add and subtract. Parentheses

can be used to guide the sequence of evaluation.   For example,
you write 3*(5+8) instead of 3*5+8 if you want the addition to
take place before the multiplication. Expressions in parentheses
take precedence.

EXAMPLES OF ARITHMETIC EXPRESSIONS

   The following examples illustrate the rules for performing
arithmetic in the Pascal programming language.

72+16   Value is 88.

8*5+7   Value is 47. Note that * means multiply.

2+10*4   Value is 42. Note that multiplication is done before
                  addition.

(2+10)*4   Value is 48. The parentheses cause the addition to
                  be done before the multiplication.

1/3   This division will produce the real value
                  3.33333E-01. We can use integers and real values
                  with / and we always get a real value as the result.

72E0+16E0   Value is 88E0, which can be written in other forms
                  such as 8.8E1 and 8.80000E+01.

(9.83E0+16.82E0)/2.935E0

                  This expression is equivalent to the following
                  $$\frac{9.83+16.82}{2.935}$$
                  Real numbers may be written in the exponent
                  form or as mixed numbers. The parentheses were
                  used so the division would apply to the sum
                  of 9.83E0 and 16.82E0 (and not just to 16.82E0).

17 DIV 5   Value is 3. Note that only the integer part of the
                  quotient is given. DIV accepts only integers (not
                  real values) and gives an integer result.

17 MOD 5   Value is 2. This is the remainder when 17 is
                  divided by 5. MOD accepts only integers (not
                  real values) and gives an integer result.

PRINTING

   Our main purpose in subset number one is to introduce you to
Pascal and to get you to write your first program.   The program
is not going to do very much but it has to do something so that

you can see that it is working. The most it can do is to print
numbers or character strings on the printer (or output them on
the CRT display). Then you can see that some action is taking
place. When we mention a print line it is the same thing as a
line on a CRT display.

The statement that we will use in the program is like this

WRITELN (3, 5.1E1, 'BILL');

Printing produced by the WRITELN statement is placed in
successive fields across the print line. The print line has
spaces for a certain number of characters. The items that are in
parentheses after the WRITELN are placed one to a field going
from left to right and then a new line is started. Literals are
printed, without the quotation marks, in a field the same size as
the length of the literal. The size of fields reserved for
integers and real numbers varies from one Pascal compiler to
another. We will assume a compiler in which integers are printed
right-justified in a field of width 10 character positions and
real numbers are printed, in the exponent form, in a field of
width 14 character positions. For example, the number −378.52
would be printed as

b−3.785200E+02

One digit always appears to the left of the decimal point. The b
indicates that one blank character position is to the left of the
sign. A blank will not precede an integer if it takes up all 10
character positions reserved for it.

Since literals are printed in fields whose size is the same
as the length of the literal, a literal should begin with a blank
so that a space will separate it from other items that are
printed.

A blank line can be left by using

WRITELN(' ');

since here the literal consists only of a blank. Actually the
statement

WRITELN;

will produce the same result.

Expressions other than integer and real constants and
literals may also be placed in a WRITELN statement. The
statement

WRITELN(2+3, 4/2);

will result in a 5 being printed in the first field and
2.000000E+00 in the second. An interesting statement might be

```
WRITELN(' 2+3=',2+3);
```

it would print

2+3=   5

There would be 9 spaces between the equal sign and the 5 in the
actual printing. Note that the quotes around the literal are not
printed.

In all the examples of a WRITELN statement we have shown a
semicolon at the end. This is necessary to separate it from the
next statement in the program but is not used if the statement
happens to be the last of a list of statements.

If you do not want to finish a printed line in an output
statement you use WRITE instead of WRITELN. The list of
statements

```
WRITE(3);
WRITE(5.1E1);
WRITELN(' BILL');
```

accomplishes exactly the same result as the single statement

```
WRITELN(3,5.1E1,' BILL');
```

The WRITE statement is like WRITELN except it does not cause a
new line to be started after its items are printed.

FORMATTING AND PRINTING

You can control the spacing of the printing precisely by
putting formatting numbers into a WRITE or WRITELN statement.
Suppose you bought 13 fattening chocolates, weighing together 0.6
kilograms at $6.87 per kilogram. You could calculate and print
the cost by

```
WRITE(' I BOUGHT', 13, 'GOODIES FOR', 0.6*6.87, 'DOLLARS')
```

This prints the following

I BOUGHT   13GOODIES FOR   4.12200E+00DOLLARS

The spacing is very poor. And the form of the REAL number
unfortunately has an exponent.

We can fix these problems this way

```
WRITE(' I BOUGHT', 13:3, 'GOODIES FOR':12, 0.6*6.87:5:2,' DOLLARS')
```

Now the spacing and form of REAL number is better:

```
    I BOUGHT 13 GOODIES FOR 4.12 DOLLARS
```

In the WRITE statement, the 3 after the 13 means print the 13 in
a field of 3 characters, instead of the default field size of 10.
The 12 following 'GOODIES FOR' means to use a field width of 12.
Since 'GOODIES FOR' has only 11 characters, there is one more
blank added on the left, which separates it from the printed 13.
Following 0.6*6.87 is 5:2 which means print the answer in five
columns, using 2 digits to the right of the decimal point. The
blank before DOLLARS was inserted by inserting a blank in
'DOLLARS' to make ' DOLLARS', but we could just have well used
'DOLLARS':8.

The following methods of formatting can be used. Blanks are
used to pad on the left to the given width.

literal:width   Print the literal string in width columns

integer value:width   Print the integer value in width columns

real value:width:fractional digits
                Print the REAL value in width columns with
                "fractional digits" to the right of the decimal point
                without the exponent part

real value:width   Print the REAL value in width columns with
                the exponent part.

A new page of printing can be started by placing the statement

    PAGE

in the program.

                    THE PROGRAM

Now that you know two statements that will give some action,
you must learn what is necessary to make a complete program.
Then you can try the computer for yourself. All programs begin
with a line like this

    PROGRAM OPUS1 (INPUT,OUTPUT);

The name OPUS1 is one we made up to describe the very first
complete program. (OPUS is Latin for "work"). You must make up
an identifier you like yourself. It must start with a letter and
have no special characters. The rest of the first line is
rigidly specified for all Pascal programs that require only the
card reader and printer. It begins with the keyword PROGRAM and,
after the name OPUS1 that you have invented, the words INPUT and
OUTPUT separated by a comma and enclosed in parentheses. This
first line is terminated by a semicolon.

Now comes the big moment for a complete program.

```
PROGRAM OPUS1 (INPUT,OUTPUT);
   BEGIN
      WRITELN(' 2+3=',2+3)
   END.
```

There it is, our opus number one, a complete Pascal program. The body of the program starts with the keyword BEGIN and finishes with the keyword END followed by a period. In between the BEGIN and END is a list of statements separated by semicolons.   Since our list consists of only one statement, the WRITELN statement, it does not have a semicolon after it.

But wait, one little thing is still needed, namely, two control cards. On one you identify yourself, so that the output printing can be returned to you, and not someone else, and also you tell the computer what compiler to use.

CONTROL CARDS

In this book we will show Pascal programs with control cards (or control lines). Many computer systems require control cards with programs to know how to handle a particular program. Other computer systems separate the control into command lines which are typed into a typewriter terminal, to tell the system how to handle a program. If your system uses command lines instead of control cards, you should just ignore the control cards in our examples.

The beginning control card that is used is different in different installations. The one we use is of the form

$JOB   'PAT HUME'

The $ sign is punched in column 1 of the card followed immediately, starting in column 2, by the word JOB.   Inside the quotation marks you put your own name, which then appears on your output exactly as you wrote it.   Often control cards are prepunched with things like $JOB on them and you must add your own name. In our examples we will just use a $JOB card and you can find out what is required by your own compiler.

When you punch the cards for the program use columns 2-80 of the card. Column 1 is reserved for the special $ sign which indicates control cards.   You need not start the punching of a statement in column 2. Any number of blanks can be left before the first word or between words. Later on we will be showing you how to indent the statements in your program to make it easier to read.

There is another control card required at the end. In our installation it has $DATA in the first five columns.

AN EXAMPLE PROGRAM

The following is a complete job for the computer. This job illustrates the use of the WRITELN statement.

```
1   $JOB    'RIC HOLT'
2     PROGRAM ZIGZAG (INPUT,OUTPUT);
3       BEGIN
4           WRITELN(' Z    G','Z    G');
5           WRITELN('  I  A ','I A':5);
6           WRITELN('   GZ  ','GZ':4)
7       END.
8   $DATA
```

The program causes the following pattern to be printed.

```
Z    GZ    G
 I  A  I  A
  GZ    GZ
```

As you can see, the top line of the pattern is printed by the WRITELN statement numbered 4. This statement causes its first literal, ' Z   G', to be printed in the first field of the print line and its second literal, again 'Z   G', to be printed in the second field of the print line. Note that the first character to be printed in the line is a blank. Statements 5 and 6 cause the printing of the second and third lines of the pattern. Line 6 could be replaced by the following two statements without changing the printed pattern:

```
WRITE('   GZ  ');
WRITELN('GZ':4)
```

The two statements are equivalent to statement 6 because the first one does not end the line.

CHAPTER 3 SUMMARY

In this chapter, we explained how to write very simple computer programs. These programs are written in a small subset of the Pascal language which is called PS/1. The following important terms were presented.

Character - is a letter (ABC...Z), digit (012...9) or special character +*/.;:, etc.

Integer constant - is an integer (whole number) such as 78 and 2931. There may be a minus sign in front of the integer. An integer constant should not be preceded by a dollar sign and must not contain commas or a decimal point. The following should not be used: $25 25,311.

Real constant - is a number such as 3.14159E0 (equal to 3.14159x10^0 or simply 3.14159). A real constant in the exponent form consists of a fraction (3.14159) and an exponent part (E0). A real constant in the mixed number form consists of a decimal point and must have at least one digit to the left of it and at least one on the right.

Literal (or character string constant) - is a sequence of characters enclosed in quotes, such as 'WHY NOT?'.

Arithmetic expression - composed of either a single number or a collection of numbers combined using addition, subtraction, multiplication, division and modulo (+, -, *, /, DIV and MOD). Parentheses may enclose parts of the expression.

Rules of precedence - specify the order for applying +,-, * and / to compute the value of an arithmetic expression. Parenthesized expressions are evaluated first. Proceeding from left to right, * and / are applied first and then + and -.

WRITE - means "print". The WRITE statement prepares expressions (literals or arithmetic expressions) for printing. A line is not actually completed until a WRITELN is executed.

WRITE - integers, real values and string literals such as -24, 2.7E3 and 'HELLO' are printed using a statement of the form

--▷WRITE(list of expressions separated by commas)

The line is not actually written until a WRITELN is executed. The values are printed on paper or written to another device such as a computer typewriter terminal.

WRITELN - this is similar to WRITE but also completes the current line so the next line can be started. The parenthesized list of values is optional for WRITELN.

Field - WRITE and WRITELN cause values to be written (printed) in fields across a line. We will assume that an integer is given a field of 10 print columns, a real value is given 14 columns and a literal is given its actual width, but this varies from compiler to compiler.

Formatted writing - the width of a field can be given explicitly in a WRITE or WRITELN statement. For example

```
-15:5        produces   bb-15
'FRED':7     produces   bbbFRED
4E1:5:1      produces   b40.0
```

where b stands for blank.

Carriage control characters - in some computer systems the first character of each line is used for controlling the printer's carriage, for example, to make it double-space or skip to a new page. In examples in this book we try to print a blank character for carriage control at the beginning of each line because that works on all computer systems, but you may find this blank is not needed at your computer system.

Output (or printout) - printing, or display on a cathode ray tube screen, which the computer does at your request. The WRITELN statement produces output from the computer.

CHAPTER 3 EXERCISES

1. What will the following program cause the computer to print?

```
PROGRAM LETTER (INPUT,OUTPUT);
  BEGIN
    WRITELN(' *   *');
    WRITELN(' ** **');
    WRITELN(' * * *');
    WRITELN(' *   *')
  END.
```

Can you rearrange the lines in this program to print a different letter?

2. Write programs to print the following:

(a)
```
    SEESEE        YOU   YOU      PEAPEAPEA
SEE     SEE       YOU   YOU      PEA     PEA
SEE               YOU   YOU      PEA     PEA
SEE               YOU   YOU      PEAPEAPEA
SEE               YOU   YOU      PEA
SEE               YOU   YOU      PEA
SEE.    SEE       YOU   YOU      PEA
    SEESEE        YOUYOUYOU      PEA
```

(b)
```
T
TR                M          SQUARE
TRI               A O        Q   R          A
TRIA              I   N      U   A        R M
TRIAN           DIAMOND      A   U        Y   I
TRIANG            I   N      R   Q      PYRAMID
TRIANGL           A O        ERAUQS
TRIANGLE          M
```

(c)

```
    T  T
    I  I
    C  C                                        PLUS
TICTACTOE    Z   G   Z   G                       PLUS
    A  A        I  A    I  A               PLUSPLUSPLUS
    C  C          GZ       GZ              PLUSPLUSPLUS
TICTACTOE                                        PLUS
    O  O                                         PLUS
    E  E
```

(d)

```
    H         STAIR         CH  EC  KE  RS
  O P           S              CH  EC  KE  RS
    S           T           CH  EC  KE  RS
    C           E              CH  EC  KE  RS
  O T           P           CH  EC  KE  RS
    C         STAIR            CH  EC  KE  RS
    H           S           CH  EC  KE  RS
                T              CH  EC  KE  RS
                E
                P
```

3. What do the following cause the computer to print?

    (a) WRITELN(2,' PLUS',3,' IS',2+3);
    (b) WRITELN(' 23424+19872+36218=',
           23424+19872+36218);
    (c) WRITELN(' 2 FORMULAS:',2+3*5,(2+3)*5);
    (d) WRITELN(' SUBTRACTION',20-10-5,20-(10-5));

4. Write statements to calculate and print the following:

    (a) The sum of 52181 and 10032.
    (b) 9213 take away 7918.
    (c) The sum of 9213, 487, 921, 2013 and 514.
    (d) The product of 21 times the sum of 816, 5 and 203.
    (c) 343 plus 916 all multiplied by 82.
    (f) 3.14159 (pi) times 8.94 divided by 2.
    (g) 3.14159 times the square of 8.94 (Note: X^2 can be written as X*X).

Chapter 4
PS/2: VARIABLES, CONSTANTS, AND ASSIGNMENTS

In this subset you will learn how to read numerical information into the computer, how to perform arithmetic calculations on the numbers you read in, and how to print the answers out. You will learn, as well, how to make your programs understandable to others (as well as to yourself) by careful choice of words that you can make up and by comments that you can add to your program. The principal concept to learn in this subset is the idea of a variable.

VARIABLES

We have said that a computer has a memory and that in the memory there are locations where information can be stored. Each location has its own unique address. In a high-level language like Pascal we do not ever refer to an actual machine address. Instead we use a name to identify a particular location. It is like referring to a house by the name of the owner rather than by its street address. We use the word variable to stand for the memory location. It is named by an identifier.

The identifier for a variable must begin with a letter and contain no blanks or special characters. If you think of the variable as the store location and its name as the identifier then you will realize that the value of the variable will be the actual information that is stored in the memory location. Locations are arranged to hold only one type of information or data. We speak of the data type of a variable. A variable may hold integers, in which case we say it is an integer variable. It could also be a real variable or a character variable. If a variable is an integer variable its value can be any integer. The value may be changed from time to time in the program but its type can never change; once an integer variable, always an integer variable.

Examples of variable identifiers are

ACCTNO, TAX, TOTAL, MARK

They are similar to the identifier we used to name a program.

It is very important to choose identifiers that relate to the kind of information that is stored in the corresponding locations. Well-chosen identifiers make a program easier to understand.

DECLARATIONS

We must make the words we want to use as variable identifiers known to the compiler and associate them with memory locations suitable for the particular data type they will hold. This is accomplished by means of "declarations" that are placed in the program immediately following the PROGRAM heading.

We will not, at the moment, show how character variables can be declared but look only at integer and real variables. To declare that SUM is to be an integer variable we write

VAR SUM: INTEGER;

The identifier is after the keyword VAR and followed by a colon and the keyword INTEGER, then a semicolon. This establishes SUM as having the type INTEGER. To declare DISTANCE to be a real variable use

VAR DISTANCE: REAL;

If a number of integer variables are required they are all listed after the VAR separated by commas, for example

VAR SUM,MARK,NUMBER: INTEGER;

Both integer and real variables are put into a single declaration as in the following

VAR SUM: INTEGER;
    DISTANCE,SPEED: REAL;

The keyword VAR can appear only once. Putting declarations in a program is like phoning ahead for hotel reservations; when you need it, the space is there with the right name on it. Also the compiler can substitute the actual machine address whenever it encounters a variable in the program. It does this by keeping a directory showing variable identifiers and corresponding memory locations. This directory is set up as the declarations are read

by the compiler. <u>In some Pascal compilers only the first eight</u>
<u>characters of a variable identifier are recorded in the directory</u>
so no two variables should have identifiers which are identical
in the first eight characters.

You should not use as variable identifiers any of the words
that are Pascal keywords. These are PROGRAM, VAR, BEGIN, END,
and others we have not yet encountered.

ASSIGNMENT STATEMENTS

In addition to declarations, in this chapter you will be
learning two types of Pascal statements that cause things to
happen as the program is executed. We say that they are
<u>executable</u> <u>statements</u>. The WRITELN statement is an executable
statement; it causes printing to take place. One of the two new
executable types we will have is the statement that <u>reads</u> cards,
the READ statement, but first we will look at the <u>assignment</u>
<u>statement</u>.

There are no <u>keywords</u> in an assignment statement but it has a
very definite form. The form is

    identifier := expression;

There is a <u>colon followed by an equal sign</u> and on the left of
this is a single word, a variable identifier. This identifier
must have been declared to be either integer or real. On the
right hand of the colon and equal signs there is an expression.
We have looked at expressions that contained integer or real
constants; now expressions can also contain integer or real
variable identifiers. We have expressions like

    5+10/3E0   (8+9)*7

but now we can have expressions like

    SUM+1   TOTAL/1.00E2   SUM-MARK

We will not use variable identifiers in the expression of an
assignment statement to begin with but instead use a simple
expression, an integer constant. For example,

    AGE:=5;

is an assignment statement. It causes the number 5 to be stored
in the memory location called AGE. If AGE appeared in the
declaration

    VAR AGE: INTEGER;

then the number is stored as an integer and would be output by

```
    WRITELN(AGE);
```

as 5. If, on the other hand, it were declared REAL it would be
stored and printed as 5.000000E+00.

    So   far   the   expression   on   the   right-hand   side   of   the
assignment has just been an integer constant, but we can have
more complicated expressions.

```
    AGE:=1979-1966;
```

Here we are subtracting the year of birth, 1966, from the year
1979 to get the age in 1979. This instruction would assign the
value 13 to the variable AGE. We could get the same result as
follows

```
    BIRTHYEAR:=1966;
    THISYEAR:=1979;
    AGE:=THISYEAR - BIRTHYEAR;
```

Here we have two additional variables BIRTHYEAR and THISYEAR
which are given values in assignment statements and then used in
an expression on the right-hand side of another assignment
statement. We could have another statement

```
    NEXTAGE:=AGE+1;
```

which would give the age the following year to the variable
NEXTAGE. Remember, if we use identifiers in a program they must
all appear in declarations. We would need the declaration

```
    VAR AGE,BIRTHYEAR,THISYEAR,NEXTAGE: INTEGER;
```

A variable may be assigned values over and over during a program.
For example, we might have

```
    SUM:=2+3;
    WRITELN(SUM);
    SUM:=3+4;
    WRITELN(SUM);
```

and so on. Now we come to perhaps the most confusing type of
assignment statement. Suppose in a program you were making
calculations year by year and needed to keep a variable AGE that
held the value of the current age for the calculation. We might
change the value at the end of the year by the assignment:

```
    AGE:=AGE+1;
```

Now you can see that the assignment statement is certainly
not an equation, or this would be nonsense. What happens when
this statement is executed is that the value stored in the
variable AGE is added to the integer 1 and the result of the
addition stored back in the same location.

In machine language, if the memory location of AGE is 336 and if there is a constant 1 stored in location 512, then the Pascal assignment statement

    AGE:=AGE+1;

could be translated as

    LOAD 336
    ADD   512
    STORE 336

TRACING EXECUTION

We have seen that variables are associated with locations in the memory of the computer. We can assign values to variables and, during a program, we can change the values as often as we want. The values can <u>vary</u> and that is why the locations are called variables. The location stays the same but the value can change.

Sometimes it is helpful, when getting used to writing programs, to keep track of values stored in the memory locations corresponding to each variable. This can help us to understand the effect of each statement. Some statements change a value; others do not. We call this <u>tracing</u> <u>the</u> <u>execution</u> of instructions.

We do not need to know the numerical, or machine address of the locations. As far as we are concerned the identifier is the address of the variable. For example, if before execution of

    AGE:=AGE+1;

the value stored in the variable AGE was 13 then, after execution, the value stored in the variable AGE would be 14.

We will trace now a slightly more complicated program by writing the values of all the variables involved after each instruction is executed. Here we will use some meaningless names like X,Y, and Z because the program has no particular meaning. We just want to learn to trace execution. We will write the tracing on the right-hand side of the page and the program on the left.   The labels over the right-hand side give the names of the locations; their values are listed under the names, opposite each instruction. When the value of a particular variable has not yet been assigned we will write a dash.

```
LINE                                            X      Y      Z
 1    PROGRAM TRACE (INPUT,OUTPUT);
 2       VAR X,Y,Z: INTEGER;                     -      -      -
 3       BEGIN                                   -      -      -
 4          X:=5;                                5      -      -
 5          Y:=7;                                5      7      -
 6          Z:=X+Y;                              5      7     12
 7          X:=X+5;                             10      7     12
 8          X:=Z;                               12      7     12
 9          Y:=Z;                               12     12     12
10          X:=X+Y+Z;                           36     12     12
11          Y:=Y*Z;                             36    144     12
12          Z:=(X+Y)DIV 12;                     36    144     15
13          X:=X MOD 5;                          1    144     15
14          WRITELN(X,Y,Z)                       1    144     15
15       END.                                    1    144     15
```

The lines of the program are numbered so that we can make
reference to them. You will have found that the computer numbers
the lines in your program so that it can refer to errors in
specific lines.

First notice that the locations X,Y, and Z do not get
established until the declaration VAR. They have no values
assigned at this point. All is straightforward until line 7 when
X appears on both sides of the assignment statement. The values
shown at the right are, remember, the values after execution of
the statement on that line. In line 12 note that since a
division between two integers is to take place and the result
assigned to an integer variable that the operator DIV must be
used. When the division yields an integer the answer is exact
but if there is a remainder on division the fractional part of
the division is dropped. We say it is truncated. To get the
fractional part of the result in a division we must use the
operator / and store the answer in a REAL variable location. If
the remainder in an integer division is desired the MOD operator
can be used.

The output statement in line 14 is different from the output
statements in PS/1 because now we can include the names of
variables in the list. We have

WRITELN(X,Y,Z)

The machine can tell the difference between variable identifiers
and literals because identifiers have no quotes. There is no
possible confusion between numbers and identifiers because an
identifier may not begin with a digit. You can see now why
Pascal has this rule.

In this example we showed a division with truncation.
Sometimes we want to round off the results of a division, say in

determining costs to the nearest cent. If COST is the value in cents of a 2-kilogram package of soap flakes then the cost of one kilogram to the nearest cent COSTKG is produced by using the function ROUND

```
COSTKG:=ROUND(COST/2);
```

The variable COSTKG has been declared to be integer so it will accept only whole number values. If you do not want to round off a REAL value but would rather truncate the fractional part, you should use the function TRUNC as in

```
COSTKG:=TRUNC(COST/2);
```

Since COST is an INTEGER variable, for this example we can get truncation more easily using COST DIV 2 instead of TRUNC(COST/2).

INPUT OF DATA

Now we will learn how to read data into the computer. We did not learn this at the same time as we learned to print data because the idea of a variable is essential to input. It is not essential to output because we can have numbers and literals, that is, integer and real constants and constant character strings. If we use

```
READ(X,Y,Z);
```

we will read three numbers off a card and store them in the three variables X, Y, and Z. The card with the three numbers is called a data card and is placed in the card deck immediately following the $DATA control card. We need to have a $DATA control card whether or not there are any data cards. On the data card, the numbers need not be arranged in any set fields, but must be separated from each other by at least one blank. Here is a sample program, including control cards, that reads information in and prints it out.

```
$JOB    'PAT HUME'
 PROGRAM INOUT (INPUT,OUTPUT);
    VAR X,Y,Z: INTEGER;
    BEGIN
       READ(X,Y);
       Z:=X+Y;
       WRITELN(Z,Y,X)
    END.
$DATA
 5  7
```

The printed output for this program would appear in the first three fields and would be

```
    12        7        5
```

On input, the first number on the data card, namely 5, is associated with the first variable X and stored in that location. The number 7 is stored in location Y.

When punching real numbers for input, you do not have to put any more significant figures than necessary in either the fraction or exponent; you need not punch

2.000000E+00

You can have only 2.0E0 or 2E0. If the exponent is zero, you may omit it completely. Thus numbers like

35.8   3.14159   0.025

are all acceptable as real numbers.

CONVERSION BETWEEN INTEGER AND REAL

Conversions from integer to real form will occur automatically whenever the variable that is to hold the number is of type real. If a data item is on a card as an integer and is read into a location defined by a variable that has been declared as REAL, then it will be converted to real. However it is not permitted to assign a real value, either in an assignment statement or by a read, to an integer variable. The real value must first be transformed into an integer using either the ROUND or TRUNC function.

```
$JOB    'RIC HOLT'
 PROGRAM CONVERT (INPUT,OUTPUT);
    VAR X,Y: INTEGER;
        Z: REAL;
    BEGIN
       READ(X,Y,Z);
       WRITELN(X,Y,Z);
       READ(X,Y,Z);
       WRITELN(X,Y,Z)
    END.
$DATA
 22   36   25   2   181   5E4
```

The output for this program will have two lines with the printing

```
        22          36  2.500000E+01
         2         181  5.000000E+04
```

Within a program it is often necessary to convert from a real value to an integer. For example, suppose that AVERAGEMARK is a real variable holding the average mark in a term examination. You would like the average to the nearest mark. Declare another variable AVERAGE as integer and write in the program

AVERAGE := ROUND(AVERAGEMARK);

AVERAGE will then be an integer, the rounded average mark.

COMMENTS

One of the main aims of structured programming is that your programs be easily understood by yourself and by others. Choosing variable names that suggest what is being stored is an excellent way to make programs readable. We have shown several programs with just X,Y, and Z as variable names. This is because these are meant to show you what happens in assignment statements and READ and WRITELN statements and are not about real applications. It is not advisable to use such meaningless names. We want your programs to look more like English than like algebra when you are finished.

One other thing that you can do to make a program understandable is to include comments in English along with the program. We have been providing comments to some of our examples in the accompanying text but you can write comments right into the program. To accomplish this, simply enclose the comments inside a pair of symbols that will act like brackets; in that way the comment is not mistaken for a program statement. The symbols you use are (* to begin and *) to end the comment. For example,

(* THIS IS A COMMENT *)

could be placed anywhere in the program where blanks can occur. To be sensible it is best to have comments occur at the ends of lines or on separate lines.

When the special characters | and | are available, they are used to enclose comments rather than (* and *). For example,

| THIS IS A COMMENT |

Comments must not have *) (or | as the case may be) in them, or be put in the data. From now on we will be including comments in our examples.

AN EXAMPLE JOB

We now give a job (control cards, program and data values) which illustrates the use of variables, assignment statements, READ statements, and comments. The program reads in the length, width and height of a box (as given in inches) and then prints the area of the base of the box (in square centimeters) and the volume of the box (in cubic centimeters). Lines 1 and 19 are control cards, lines 2-18 are the program and line 20 gives the data.

```
 1   $JOB    'MARIE GUINDON'
 2    PROGRAM CONVERT(INPUT,OUTPUT);
 3      (* READ BOX LENGTH, WIDTH AND HEIGHT IN INCHES *)
 4      (* THEN CONVERT TO CENTIMETERS AND CALCULATE *)
 5      (* THE BOX'S BASE AREA AND VOLUME. *)
 6      CONST CMPERINCH=2.54;
 7      VAR LENGTH,WIDTH,HEIGHT,AREA,VOLUME: REAL;
 8      BEGIN
 9         READ(LENGTH,WIDTH);
10         LENGTH:=CMPERINCH*LENGTH;
11         WIDTH:=CMPERINCH*WIDTH;
12         AREA:=LENGTH*WIDTH;
13         WRITELN(' AREA=  ',AREA);
14         READ(HEIGHT);
15         HEIGHT:=CMPERINCH*HEIGHT;
16         VOLUME:=HEIGHT*AREA;
17         WRITELN(' VOLUME=',VOLUME)
18      END.
19   $DATA
20      2.6   1.2   6.92
```

This program will print the following

```
AREA=        2.01290E+01
VOLUME=      3.53803E+02
```

where the area is in square centimeters and the volume is in cubic centimeters. The area and volume printed depend on the three values on the data cards; the data values 2.6, 1.2 and 6.92 could be replaced by the dimensions of a different box.

Line 2 marks the beginning of the program; it causes no action on the part of the computer. Lines 3, 4 and 5 are intended for you, the reader of the program, and are ignored by the computer.

Line 6 of the program is a definition of a constant. The constant identified by the name CMPERINCH is given the value 2.54. Constants differ from variables in that they maintain the same value throughout the program's execution. Definitions of constants must precede the declaration (VAR) of variables. Line 7 sets up memory locations for variables called LENGTH, WIDTH, HEIGHT, AREA, and VOLUME. These variables have the REAL type, instead of the INTEGER type, because they have non-integer values (such as 2.6). Line 9 causes the data values 2.6 and 1.2 to be read into variables LENGTH and WIDTH.

Line 10 takes the value 2.6E0 from the LENGTH variable, multiplies it by the constant CMPERINCH and then returns the result to LENGTH. Line 11 is similar to line 10.

Line 12 takes the values in LENGTH and WIDTH, multiplies them together, and places the result in AREA. Line 13 then prints:

AREA=   2.01290E+01

As of line 13, the variables HEIGHT and VOLUME have not been used. An attempt to print HEIGHT or VOLUME in line 13 would be an error because those variables have not yet been given a value.

Since the READ statement of line 9 uses up the first two data values, 2.6 and 1.2, the READ statement of line 14 reads the value 6.92 into HEIGHT. The computer does not know that 6.92 represents the height of a box. It only knows that it is instructed to read the next data value into the variable named HEIGHT.

Line 15 converts to centimeters, line 16 computes the volume and line 17 prints the volume. Notice that this statement has no semicolon after it since it is the last in a list of statements before END. As a matter of fact no real problem is created if you do put a semicolon here since a null statement (that is, no statement at all) is a legitimate statement in Pascal. You can just assume that there is an invisible null statement after the semicolon before END. We will not take advantage of this rather wierd situation because there will be places where a semicolon too many would cause an error condition. Line 18 is the end of the program and tells the computer to stop working on this program. Notice that END has a period after it.

This job would print the same thing if we made the following changes.

(1) Replace line 9 by the two assignment statements:

    LENGTH:=2.6;
    WIDTH:=1.2;

(2) Replace line 14 by the assignment statement:

    HEIGHT:=6.92;

(3) Delete line 20, the data values.

These three changes result in a program which is given the dimensions of the box by assignment statements rather than by input statements (READ statements). The advantage of the original program, which uses READ statements, is that the program will work for a new box simply by replacing the data card, line 20.

LABELING OF OUTPUT

Just as comments help to make a program more understandable, output that is properly identified by labeling is self-

explanatory. What you are trying to do is to prepare documents
that need no further explanation from you when you show your
computer printout to others.

    The compiler lists your program, including comments, but the
output data should also be labeled so the reader is in no doubt
about what the numbers are, without reading the program. Very
often you present results without showing how you got them, that
is, you do not include the program.

    There are two basic ways to label results. If different
values of the same set of variables are listed in columns on the
output, then a label can be placed at the top of each column.
For example, the output for comparing costs of boxes of soap
flakes might be

```
    COST    WEIGHT(KG)   COST/KG
    125          1         125
    200          2         100
    260          3          87
```

There is no reason to use exactly the same labels as the variable
names, since the literals printed at the top of the columns can
be longer and contain blanks. They are printed independently.
The program that produces this table might be

```
$JOB     'JOHN ZAHORJAN'
 PROGRAM SOAP (INPUT,OUTPUT);
    (*COMPUTE AND TABULATE COST PER KG*)
    VAR COST,WEIGHT,COSTKG: INTEGER;
    BEGIN

        (* PRINT HEADINGS OF TABLE *)
        WRITELN('     COST ',' WEIGHT(KG)','  COST/KG');

        (* PROCESS DATA FOR FIRST BOX *)
        READ(COST,WEIGHT);
        COSTKG:=ROUND(COST/WEIGHT);
        WRITELN(COST,WEIGHT,COSTKG);

        (* PROCESS DATA FOR SECOND BOX *)
        READ(COST,WEIGHT);
        COSTKG:=ROUND(COST/WEIGHT);
        WRITELN(COST,WEIGHT,COSTKG);

        (* PROCESS DATA FOR THIRD BOX *)
        READ(COST,WEIGHT);
        COSTKG:=ROUND(COST/WEIGHT);
        WRITELN(COST,WEIGHT,COSTKG)
    END.
```

```
$DATA
    125    1
    200    2
    260    3
```

You can see how comments can be inserted, how the column headings are printed, and how each line of the table is calculated and printed. Each output statement is WRITELN (not WRITE) so each one causes a new line to be started after printing the three numbers. In the program we have repeated three statements, without change, one set of three for each box. If we had 100 boxes, this would have been a little monotonous. When we want to repeat statements we do <u>not</u> do it this way; a more convenient way is possible with a new Pascal statement that will cause this kind of repetition. But that comes in the next subset, PS/3.

A second kind of output labeling was already used in the previous example but can be illustrated by a program segment

```
COST:=5;
WRITELN('COST=',COST);
```

This would result in the printing

```
COST=        5
```

This method is easier when just a few numbers are being printed.

PROGRAM TESTING

It is easy to make mistakes in programming. The first thing you should do to test a program is to read over your program carefully to spot errors. It is valuable to trace the execution yourself before you submit it to the computer. Your goal should always be to produce programs that you <u>know</u> are correct without testing, but this is not always possible. You could ask someone else to read it too. If he cannot understand your program it may show that your program is poorly written or has errors. Next you put your program on cards and proofread your cards to see that they match your intentions. Check that the control cards are present. Next you submit your deck.

If you have made errors in your program that involve the form of statements, the compiler spots these during compilation and reports them on the output. It refers to an error of a certain type in line so and so of the program. It has been careful to give numbers to each line so that it can make these references. Errors in form are called <u>syntax errors</u>. Examples of common syntax errors are

1. leaving out the semicolon between statements

2. forgetting the END with its period
3. misspelling a keyword

In a way, a syntax error is a good error since it is detected for you by the computer. But it is frustrating to have to correct it and resubmit the job. It wastes time. Some people say that having syntax errors is a symptom of sloppy programming and a sure indication that there are other errors.

<u>When there are simple syntax errors, most compilers attempt to repair them and go on.</u> Their repairs are just guesses at what you intended and some of the guesses are pretty wild. They always give the programmer a warning if a repair has been attempted. Some errors cannot be repaired and, as a result, no execution takes place. Your printout has only the program listing and error messages. Very sad! Back to the drawing board. Be sure to proofread the entire listing of your program, looking for unreported errors.

If there are no unrepairable syntax errors, execution can take place right after compilation. This does not, however, mean that all is well.

If answers are printed, they should be checked against hand calculated answers. If they agree, it is possible that your program is correct. If they disagree it is possible that your hand calculations are incorrect or that your program has errors. The errors now are usually of a kind called <u>semantic errors</u>. You are asking for a calculation that you did not mean to ask for. It has a different <u>meaning</u> from your intentions. For instance, you are adding two numbers and you meant to subtract them.

To find semantic errors you must look at the program again and try to trace what it must be doing rather than what you — thought it would do. To help in the tracing it is sometimes necessary to insert additional WRITELN instructions between other statements and print out the current value of variables that are changing. In this way you can follow the machine's activity. These extra WRITELN instructions can be removed after the errors have been found.

Sometimes there is no output printing from the WRITELN instructions that give the final results. This might happen in many ways, for instance, if you ask in the READ statements for more data items than you have on the data cards without testing for the end of the file. The computer will tell you it reached the END OF FILE so the error is spotted. It is important that the data items match the variables in the READ statements, or answers can be ridiculous.

Care must be taken about the INTEGER and REAL distinction between numbers as the computer converts from integer to real automatically and will not warn you if things are going wrong.

COMMON ERRORS IN PROGRAMS

When you try running a program on a computer, the computer may detect <u>errors</u> in your program. As a result, <u>error messages</u> will be printed. Since the computer does not understand the purpose of your program, its error messages are limited to describing the specific illegalities which it detects. Unfortunately, the computer's error messages usually do not tell you how to correct your program so that it will solve the problem you have in mind.

In order to help you avoid such errors, we list some of the errors which commonly occur in students' programs.

<u>Missing semicolons</u> - Do not forget to put semicolons between statements and no semicolon after the last statement of a list. No semicolon follows a list containing a single statement.

<u>Missing parentheses</u> - Do not forget the parentheses required around the list of items in a READ or WRITE statement.

<u>Missing first line of program</u> - Every Pascal program must have a line of the form

        PROGRAM identifier (INPUT,OUTPUT);

<u>Missing END.</u> at the end of the program.

<u>Missing $DATA</u>

<u>Missing quotes</u>, especially the last quote. Consider the following erroneous statement:

        WRITELN('INVOICE);

This statement is missing a quote between the E and the right parenthesis. After printing an error message, the compiler may try to repair the error by concluding that you want it to print
        INVOICE);
rather than
        INVOICE

<u>Uninitialized variables</u> - When a variable is declared, a memory location, or cell, is set aside, but no special value is placed in the cell. That is, the cell is not yet initialized. A variable must be given a value, via an assignment statement or a READ statement, before an attempt is made to use the value of the variable in a WRITELN statement or in an expression.

<u>Undeclared variables</u> - Before a variable is used in a statement (assignment, READ or WRITELN) the variable must be declared.

The declaration of variables must precede all statements. Definition of constants precedes the declaration of variables.

Mistaking I for 1 - The characters I and 1 look similar, but are entirely different to the computer.

Mistaking O for 0 - The characters O(oh) and 0(zero) look similar, but are entirely different to the computer.

CHAPTER 4 SUMMARY

This chapter introduced variables, as they are used in programming languages. Essentially, a variable is a memory location, or cell, which can hold a value. Suppose X is the name of a variable; then X denotes a cell. If X is a variable having the INTEGER type, then the cell for X can hold an integer value such as 9, 291, 0 or -11.

The following important terms were discussed in this chapter.

Identifier - can be used as the name of a variable or constant. An identifier must begin with a letter; this letter can be followed by additional letters or digits. The following are examples of identifiers: X, I, WIDTH, INCOMETAX and A1. In many Pascal compilers only the first 8 characters of an identifier are used, so that no two identifiers in a program should have the same first 8 characters.

Type - Each variable has a type; in this chapter we introduced the INTEGER and REAL types. The type of a variable is determined by its declaration.

Variable declaration - establishes variables for use in a program. For example, the declaration

        VAR I: INTEGER;

creates a variable called I which can be given integer values.

Constant definition - establishes named constants for use in a program. For example, the definition

        CONST PI=3.14159;
          CONVERT=2.54;

creates named constants PI and CONVERT. Definition of constants occurs immediately after the PROGRAM heading; this is followed by the declaration of variables before the BEGIN that precedes any WRITELN, READ or assignment statements.

VAR - the keyword instructing the computer to create variables. A declaration can be of the form:

⟶ VAR list of identifiers separated by commas: type;

The type must be INTEGER or REAL for the PS/2 subset. The declaration can be extended for further variables, for example:

```
VAR I: INTEGER;
    X,Y: REAL;
    J,K: INTEGER;
```

We sometimes express the form of the declaration of variables by writing

```
VAR variable|,variable|:type;
    |variable|,variable|:type;|
```

where the curly brackets indicate that what is contained in them can appear zero or more times.

Assignment - means a value is assigned to a variable. For example, the following is an assignment statement which gives the value 52 to the variable I:

```
I:=52;
```

Truncation - throwing away the fractional part of a number. When a real number is to be assigned to a variable with the INTEGER type, the variable can be given the truncated value by using the TRUNC function. If X is real and Y integer

```
Y:=TRUNC(X);
```

will assign the integral part of the value of the real variable X to the integer variable Y.

Rounding - changing a real number to the nearest integer. If X is real and Y integer

```
Y:=ROUND(X);
```

assigns the value of X, rounded off, to the integer variable Y.

Number conversion - changing an integer number to a real number or vice versa. Conversion from real to integer requires either truncation or rounding of the result. Integer values are converted automatically to real when assigned to (or read into) a real variable location.   *NOTE*

Data (or input data) - values which a program can read. The data values follow $DATA.

READ - means "Read data." The READ statement reads data values into a list of variables.

READ statement - this statement is of the form:

    ——▷ READ(list of variable names separated by commas);

Reading will automatically proceed to the next data card when the values of one card have all been read.

Comments - information in a program which is intended to assist a person reading the program. The following is a comment which could appear in a Pascal program:

    (* THIS PROGRAM PRINTS GAS BILLS *)

Comments do not affect the execution of a program.

Documentation - written explanation of a program. Comments are used in a program to document its actions.

Keyword - a word, such as PROGRAM or BEGIN, which is an inherent part of the programming language. Keywords must not be used as identifiers.

Errors - improper parts of, or actions of, a program. For example, the statement

    WRITELN('HELLO';

has an error in that a right parenthesis is missing. If the computer detects an error in your program, it will print an "error message".

CHAPTER 4 EXERCISES

1. Suppose that I, J and K are variables with the integer type and they presently have the values 5, 7 and 10. What will be printed as a result of the following statements?

```
WRITELN(I,I+1,I+J,I+J*K);
K:=I+J;
WRITELN(K);
J:=J+1;
WRITELN(J);
I:=3*I+J;
WRITELN(I);
```

2. RADIUS, DIAMETER, CIRCUMFERENCE and AREA are REAL variables. A value has been read into RADIUS via a READ statement. Write statements which do each of the following.

(a) Give to DIAMETER the product of 2 and RADIUS.

    (b) Give to CIRCUMFERENCE the product of pi (3.14159) and
       DIAMETER.
    (c) Give to AREA the product of pi and RADIUS squared.
       (RADIUS squared can be written as RADIUS*RADIUS.)
    (d) Print the values of RADIUS, DIAMETER, CIRCUMFERENCE
       and AREA.

3. Suppose I is a variable with the INTEGER type. I has already
been given a value via an assignment statement. Write statements
to do the following.

    (a) Without changing I, print out twice the value of I.
    (b) Increase I by 1.
    (c) Double the value of I.
    (d) Decrease I by 5.

4. M, N and P are variables with the integer type. What will the
following statements cause the computer to print?

```
M:=43;
N:=211;
P:=M;
M:=N;
N:=P;
WRITELN(M,N);
```

5.(a) What will be printed by the following job?

```
 1  $JOB     'ANN MORLEY'
 2   PROGRAM PAIRS(INPUT,OUTPUT);
 3      VAR FIRST,SECOND: INTEGER;
 4      BEGIN
 5         READ(FIRST,SECOND);
 6         WRITELN(FIRST+SECOND);
 7         READ(FIRST,SECOND);
 8         WRITELN(FIRST+SECOND)
 9      END.
10  $DATA
11     22   247   -16
12     528
```

(b) Which lines of this job are control cards? Which are program
and which are input data?

6. (a) What will be printed by the following job?

```
 1   $JOB     'FRED LEE'
 2    (* CALCULATE TERM MARK *)
 3    PROGRAM COMBINE(INPUT,OUTPUT);
 4       VAR GRADE1,GRADE2: REAL;
 5           MARK: INTEGER;
 6       BEGIN
 7           READ(GRADE1,GRADE2);
 8           MARK:=ROUND((GRADE1+GRADE2)/2);
 9           WRITELN(GRADE1,GRADE2,MARK)
10       END.
11   $DATA
12      81.7
13      85.9
```

(b) Which lines of this job are control cards; which are program and which are input data?

7. Trace the execution of the following program. That is, give the values of the variables LENGTH, WIDTH, and ABOUT and give any output after each line of the program.

```
    $JOB     'JOE MURPHY'
     PROGRAM AREA(INPUT,OUTPUT);
        VAR SIZE,LENGTH,WIDTH: REAL;
            ABOUT: INTEGER;
        (* READ SIZES AND CONVERT FEET TO YARDS *)
        BEGIN
            READ(SIZE);
            WIDTH:=SIZE/3;
            READ(SIZE);
            LENGTH:=SIZE/3;
            ABOUT:=ROUND(WIDTH*LENGTH);
            WRITELN(' LENGTH AND WIDTH ARE',LENGTH,WIDTH);
            WRITELN(' AREA IS:',LENGTH*WIDTH,
               ' THIS IS ABOUT',ABOUT,' (SQUARE YARDS)')
        END.
    $DATA
      9.60   15.9
```

8. Write a program which reads three values and prints their average, rounded to the nearest whole number. For example, if 20, 16 and 25 follow the $DATA card then your program should print 20. Make up your own data for your program.

9. Write a program which reads a weight given in pounds and then prints out the weight in (1) pounds, (2) ounces, (3) kilograms and (4) grams. Note: 16 ounces equal one pound, 2.2046 pounds equal one kilogram and 1000 grams equal one kilogram. Use named constants in your program.

Chapter 5
PS/3: CONTROL FLOW

In the first two subsets of Pascal we have learned to write programs with statements that cause the computer to read cards and assign values to variables, evaluate arithmetic expressions and assign the values to variables, and print results with labels. In all programs the statements were executed in sequence until the END was reached, at which time the program was terminated. In this subset we will learn two ways in which the order of executing statements may be altered. One involves the repetitious use of statements; the other involves alternate paths in the flow of statements. The first is called a loop, the second a branch. We speak of the flow of control since it is the control unit of the computer that determines which statement is to be executed next by the computer.

COUNTED LOOPS

The normal flow of control in a program is in a straight line. So far, in the statements that are bracketed in the list between the BEGIN and the END, one statement is executed after another. We can, however, give a statement that will cause the statement that follows it to be repeated. In the last chapter, in the example where we were reading information about boxes of soap flakes, we had to write the statements over and over to get repetitions. A statement that will produce repetition is the counted FOR loop. For our example we could have written

```
FOR I:=1 TO 3 DO
   BEGIN
      READ(COST,WEIGHT);
      COSTKG:=ROUND(COST/WEIGHT);
      WRITELN(COST,WEIGHT,COSTKG)
   END;
```

The three statements that we had to repeat three times are prefaced by

```
FOR I:=1 TO 3 DO
    BEGIN
```

and followed by END;

The three statements bracketed by BEGIN and END act as a single compound statement. The variable I is an index, which must be declared as an integer variable, and which counts the number of repetitions. First the index I is set to 1, then the compound statement is executed. After the execution, control is sent back to the FOR. At this time the index I is increased by 1, making it 2. The compound statement is again executed and, then, back we go to the FOR. This time I becomes 3 and a third execution of the compound statement in the FOR loop takes place. When control returns to the FOR this time, I is found be equal to the final value 3 so control goes out of the loop to the next statement after the compound statement.

A counted or indexed FOR loop is used whenever we know exactly how many repetitions we want to take place. We do not need to start the count at 1. We could, for example, have

```
FOR COUNT:=12 TO 24 DO
```

Here we have called the index COUNT and are starting at 12 and going up to, and to include, 24. In these statements we have counted forward by 1. We can also count backwards by -1. If we write

```
FOR COUNT:=10 DOWNTO 1 DO
    statement
```

it will cause the "statement" to be executed with COUNT taking the values 10, 9, 8, ..., 1.

The other kinds of loop statements are the WHILE...DO statement and the REPEAT...UNTIL statement but we cannot introduce them until we look at conditions. The WHILE...DO is a loop statement that causes repetition as long as a certain condition is true. The condition concerned is written at the beginning of the loop after the word WHILE. The REPEAT...UNTIL is a loop statement that causes repetition until a certain condition is true. The condition is written at the end of the loop after the word UNTIL.

CONDITIONS

There are expressions in Pascal that are called relational expressions and these have values that are either true or false. The following is a list of relational expressions with their value written on the same line. The symbol > means is greater than, < means is less than, the equal sign means is equal to, and the sign <> means is not equal to.

relational expression	value
5=2+3	true
7>5	true
2<6	true
5+3<2+1	false
6<>10	true
5>5	false
5>=5	true

You can see how these work. These are sometimes called Boolean expressions after the logician George Boole.

There are compound conditions formed by taking two single conditions and putting either the Boolean (logical) operator AND or the Boolean operator OR between them. When conditions are compounded in this way, each simple condition should have parentheses around it. This is because Boolean operators have higher precedence than relational operators.

With AND both conditions must be true or else the compound condition is false. For example,

   (8>7) AND (6<3)

is false since (6<3) is false. With OR, if either or both of the single conditions is true, the compound condition is true. For example, (8>7) OR (6<3) is true since (8>7) is true. It is possible to have multiple compoundings. For example,

   ((8>7) AND (2=1+1)) AND ((6>7) OR (5>1))

is true. The parentheses here show the sequence of the operations. There is a rule of precedence if there are no parentheses, namely, the AND operator has higher precedence than the OR operator. This means that AND operations are done before OR operations.

A Boolean operator that requires only one condition is the NOT operator. The condition

   NOT(5>6)

is true since 5 is not greater than 6.

BOOLEAN VARIABLES

If you want to assign a Boolean value to a variable, it must be typed by a declaration as BOOLEAN. BOOLEAN is a variable type

just like REAL and INTEGER. But a Boolean variable can only have
one of two values, namely TRUE or FALSE. Boolean variables can
not be read but can be assigned Boolean values, or printed. They
are printed in a 10 character field like integers.   They cannot
be used in numeric expressions.   For example, if you want a
Boolean variable SWITCH assigned the value true you must include
the declaration and the assignment.

    VAR SWITCH: BOOLEAN;
    SWITCH:=TRUE;

The variable SWITCH may be used in a condition.

CONDITIONAL LOOPS

    We have introduced the notion of a condition; now we will
actually use it. One of the major uses of conditions is in the
conditional loop.   There are two of these the REPEAT...UNTIL
condition and the WHILE condition DO loop. We will look first at
the WHILE...DO loop. The form of this loop is

    WHILE condition DO
        statement

The repetition of "statement" which is called the body of the
loop is to take place as long as the condition stated after the
word WHILE is true. Once it is false, the control goes to the
next statement after the loop. If you want to have a number of
statements in the body of a loop you must make them into a
compound statement using BEGIN and END.

    So far we have discussed only conditions involving integer
constants. These are always true or false. The condition in the
WHILE loop cannot be like this, because if it were always true we
would loop forever and if always false we would not loop at all.
The condition must involve a variable whose value changes during
the looping.

    In the following example a WHILE...DO loop is used to
accomplish what the counted FOR loop did for the soap flakes
boxes.


```
1   I:=1;
2   WHILE I<=3 DO
3      BEGIN
4          READ(COST,WEIGHT);
5          COSTKG:=ROUND(COST/WEIGHT);
6          WRITELN(COST,WEIGHT,COSTKG);
7          I:=I+1
8      END;
9   WRITELN(I);
```

In statement 1 the value of the variable I appearing in the condition is set initially to 1, then we enter the loop. This stage is called <u>initialization</u>. In line 2 we begin the loop. The condition after the WHILE is true since I is 1, which is less than 3. Thus the compound statement starting with BEGIN and going down to END is executed. This compound statement constitutes the <u>body</u> of the loop. In the body, statement 7 <u>alters</u> the value of the variable appearing in the condition. This means that it is changing each time around the loop. At the end of the first execution of the loop it becomes 1+1=2. After the compound statement has been executed, control returns to the start of the loop. The condition is then examined and since it is true (2<=3), the body is executed a second time. It will be true also on the third time but on the fourth round, I will be 4 and (4<=3) is false. When I is printed by statement 9 it is 4. This printing is not part of the original example, but was included here to show you what happens to the index I.

The <u>various phases of a WHILE...DO loop</u> are

*Phase 1. <u>Initialization,</u> especially of the variable in the <u>condition</u>

*Phase 2. <u>Test</u> condition and if true then go to the next statement which is the body of the loop, if false go to the statement following the body

*Phase 3. <u>Execute</u> the statement that constitutes the body of the loop <u>which includes altering the variable in the</u> <u>condition</u>

Phase 4. <u>Return to phase 2</u>.

Phase 1 is necessary to give the variable appearing in the condition an initial value. Since the body of the loop must alter the variable in the condition in addition to taking some other action, it almost always is a compound statement.

Before we introduce the REPEAT...UNTIL loop we will compare the use of the WHILE...DO conditional loop and the FOR...DO counted loop.

<u>READING INPUT</u>

As an example of looping we will look at reading data from cards and printing it out, assuming that each card produces one line of printing. The only real problem will be to stop when you reach the last card. There are two distinct ways of doing this. One is to count the cards by hand, prepare a card with this count

on it, and place it in front of the data cards.   Then   we   use   a
counted   FOR   loop to read them.   The second method is to place a
card at the end of the data cards with a piece of   data   that   is
impossible   as a real entry.   We call it a <u>dummy</u> <u>card</u>.   Sometimes
it is called an <u>end-of-file</u> <u>marker</u>.   In a later subset, PS/5,   we
will see how the EOF end of file predeclared function can be used
to detect the last card when no end-of-file marker is supplied in
the data.

   We   will   now   examine   the two methods in turn.   Suppose, to
talk specifically, that each data card has on it a student number
and   a   grade   received in an examination.   To illustrate we will
have only three data cards, but you can see how it will work with
more.

<u>Method</u> 1. Counting the cards

```
$JOB     'GORDY PROCTOR'
 PROGRAM MARKS1 (INPUT,OUTPUT);
    VAR STUDENTNUMBER,MARK,COUNT,I: INTEGER;
    BEGIN
       WRITELN(' STUDENT':10, 'MARK':10);
       READ(COUNT);
       FOR I:=1 TO COUNT DO
          BEGIN
             READ(STUDENTNUMBER,MARK);
             WRITELN(STUDENTNUMBER,MARK)
          END
    END.
$DATA
   3
   1026    86
   2051    90
   3163    71
```

Notice that we took the trouble to label the output.   Perhaps the
two ENDs, one after the other, seem strange.   The   first   belongs
to   the   compound   statement   in   the FOR loop, the second to the
BEGIN prefacing all statements.   The machine can   keep   track   of
these   just   as   you   can   tell which right parenthesis goes with
which left one in this example:

   (2+5*(2+6))

   In   the   second   method   we   will place a dummy card with two
zeros on it at the end of the deck.

<u>Method 2</u>. Testing for the dummy card

```
$JOB     'JIM CORDY'
 PROGRAM MARKS2 (INPUT,OUTPUT);
   VAR STUDENTNUMBER,MARK: INTEGER;
   BEGIN
      WRITELN(' STUDENT':10, 'MARK':10);
      READ(STUDENTNUMBER,MARK);
      WHILE STUDENTNUMBER <> 0 DO
         BEGIN
            WRITELN(STUDENTNUMBER,MARK);
            READ(STUDENTNUMBER,MARK)
         END
   END.
$DATA
   1026    86
   2051    90
   3163    71
      0     0
```

In this example you will notice that the <u>initialization</u> involves <u>reading the first card outside the loop</u>, in order to get a value for the variable STUDENTNUMBER appearing in the condition of the WHILE...DO. In the WHILE...DO line the symbol <> means "not equal". Since the first card has already been read, it must be printed before a new card is read. This means that the sequence is WRITELN then READ, rather than the way it is in method 1. As soon as the new card has been read, we return to the WHILE where the condition is tested.

Methods 1 and 2 for dealing with a variable number of items, like cards, are used again and again in programming. The WHILE is more difficult to program but probably more useful, since if there are many cards, it is better for the user to stick in an end-of-file card than to count cards.

EXAMPLES OF LOOPS

We will now give example programs to illustrate details about loops. The examples each draw a zigzag. Here is the first example:

FOR DO

```
1    PROGRAM WIGGLE(INPUT,OUTPUT);
2        VAR J: INTEGER;
3        BEGIN
4            FOR J:=1 TO 3 DO
5                BEGIN
6                    WRITELN('        *');
7                    WRITELN('         *');
8                    WRITELN('          *');
9                    WRITELN('           *')
10               END
11       END.
```

This program, appropriately called WIGGLE, prints the following pattern:

The WIGGLE program causes the body of the loop, lines 5 through 10, to be executed three times. The variable J is 1 during the time the first four stars are printed. J is 2 during the time the next four stars are printed, and J is 3 while the last four stars are printed. After the last star is printed, J is set to 4 and since J then exceeds the limiting value, 3, of the loop, the loop is terminated.

Notice that in this program the variable J is used for only one purpose: to see that the loop is repeated the desired number of times. Line 4 means, essentially, "Repeat this loop three times." If we replaced line 4 by the following line

        FOR J:=9 TO 11 DO

then the program would still print the same pattern. The only difference is that J would have the values 9, 10, and 11 during the printing of the stars and would end up with the value of 12. Although this replacement for line 4 does not change the pattern printed, it should not be used because it makes the program more confusing for people to understand. This is because people more

naturally think of "repeat this loop three times" as running
through the loop with values 1, 2, and 3, rather than values 9,
10, and 11.

   Here is one more possible replacement for line 4 which does
not change the printed pattern:

       FOR J:=3 DOWNTO 1 DO

In this case, J will be 3 while the first four stars are printed,
then J will be 2 while the next four stars are printed, and then
J will be 1 while the last four stars are printed. Finally, J
will end up with the value of zero. This illustrates the fact
that if the step size, which is -1 here, is negative, then the
loop will count backwards to smaller values. Again, for this
example program, the original version of line 4 is preferable
because it is easier to understand its meaning at a glance.

   Once a FOR loop finishes, there is some confusion about the
final value of the counting variable. For example, in the WIGGLE
program, does J end up as 3 (the final value) or does it end up
as 4 (getting ready for the next time through but finding that 4
exceeds the limit 3). The Pascal language side steps this
question by leaving the value of J "undefined" after the loop,
meaning that the final value may be different depending on what
compiler you are using. You should avoid this confusion by
following this advice.

   ✳When a FOR loop has finished, do not use the final value of
    the counting variable.

   There is another possible source of confusion in FOR loops.
For example, what happens in WIGGLE if we set the counting
variable J to 15 by an assignment statement in the loop body?
The result is that J is not in the range 1 to 3. The FOR loop no
longer means: repeat for J equal to 1 then 2 then 3. To avoid
this confusion, Pascal has this rule:

   ✳Inside a counted FOR loop, the program must not not alter the
    value of the counting variable.

   We will now rewrite our WIGGLE program using WHILE...DO
instead of a counted FOR. We will call our new program WAGGLE.
(Did you know that in German "wiggle waggle" means "waddle" like
a duck? Well it does.)

```
1    PROGRAM WAGGLE(INPUT,OUTPUT);
2       VAR J: INTEGER;
3       BEGIN
4          J:=1;
5          WHILE J<=3 DO
6             BEGIN
7                WRITELN('          *');
8                WRITELN('           *');
9                WRITELN('            *');
10               WRITELN('           *');
11               J:=J+1
12            END
13      END.
```

WHILE - DO

This WAGGLE program works like our previous WIGGLE program. Lines 4, 5, and 11 of WAGGLE are equivalent to line 4 of WIGGLE. Since it is easier to see that line 4 of WIGGLE means, "Repeat this loop three times," the WIGGLE version is preferable. We will, however, use WAGGLE to illustrate a few more points about loops.

In the WAGGLE program, consider moving line 11, which is

        J:=J+1;

up to between lines 6 and 7. This change does not alter the printed pattern. It simply changes the point at which J has its value increased. J will have the value 2 while the first four stars are printed, then 3 while the next four stars are printed and finally 4 while the last four stars are printed. J ends up with the value of 4. Even though J is set to 4 before the last four stars are printed, the loop is not stopped. This is because J is not compared to the limit value 3 until control returns to line 5. This illustrates the fact that in a WHILE...DO loop, the condition is tested only once - at the top - each time through the loop.

Now let us look back at the WAGGLE program. Suppose that you prepared this program for the computer and mistakenly made line 11 into

        J:=J-1;

The mistake is that the plus sign was changed to a minus sign. Such a small mistake! Surely the computer will understand that a plus was wanted! But it will not do so. The computer has a habit of doing what we <u>tell</u> it to do rather than what we <u>want</u> it to do. Given the WAGGLE program, with the mistake, the computer will do the following. With J set to 1 it will print the first four stars. Then, as a result of the erroneous line 11, it will set J to 0 and will print another four stars. Then it will set J to -1 and print four more stars. Then it will set J to -2 and print four more stars and so on and so on. In theory, it will <u>never stop</u> printing stars because the condition J<=3 will always be

true. This is called an infinite loop. Luckily, the computer
will eventually stop this looping when your program has printed
too much or has executed too many statements. When it stops your
program, it will print an error message complaining about the
excessive printing or running of your program. Unfortunately,
the error message will not tell you that you should have had a
plus sign instead of a minus sign, because the computer will not
know what you were thinking when you prepared the program.

AN ALTERNATIVE CONDITIONAL LOOP

There is another conditional loop in Pascal besides the
WHILE...DO loop. We can use REPEAT...UNTIL instead of WHILE...DO
when we know that the loop is always executed at least once.
Remember that WHILE...DO allows zero repetitions, when the
condition is false when first tested. The REPEAT...UNTIL loop
has this form.

```
REPEAT
    list of statements separated by semicolons
UNTIL condition
```

In this loop no BEGIN...END is necessary if the body of the loop
contains more than one statement. The test of the condition does
not occur until the end of the loop so that all REPEAT...UNTIL
loops are executed at least once. We will use WHILE...DO loops
for most examples but here is a program that shows how a file of
cards could be read using REPEAT...UNTIL.

Method 2. Testing dummy card, at least one non-dummy

```
$JOB    'DAVE ELLIOTT'
 PROGRAM MARKS3A(INPUT,OUTPUT);
    VAR STUDENTNUMBER,MARK:INTEGER;
    BEGIN
        WRITELN(' STUDENT':10, 'MARK':10);
        READ(STUDENTNUMBER,MARK);
        REPEAT
            WRITELN(STUDENTNUMBER,MARK);
            READLN(STUDENTNUMBER,MARK)
        UNTIL STUDENTNUMBER=0
    END.
$DATA
 1026    86
 2051    90
 3163    71
    0     0
```

This program would not work if there were no student marks at
all.

BRANCHES IN CONTROL FLOW

We have learned how to change from a flow of control in a straight line, or <u>sequential</u> control, to flow in a loop, either counted or conditional. Now we must look at a different kind of structure in the sequence of control. This structure is called selection or branching. It is a little like a fork in the road where there are two paths that can be followed. The road branches into two roads. When you come to a fork in a road you must <u>decide</u> which of the two branches you will take. Your decision is based on where you are heading. Suppose one sign at the fork gives the name of your destination and the other road sign gives some other name. Suppose your destination is Toronto; an instruction for deciding which branch to take might be

```
IF LEFTBRANCHSIGN='TORONTO' THEN
    take the left branch
ELSE
    take the right branch
```

We have written this decision in exactly the form you use in Pascal for branching in the sequence of control. The main difference is that the part we have written as "take the left branch" must be replaced by a Pascal statement to do something. The same is true of the other branch which follows the keyword ELSE.

Suppose that there is a variable called CLASSA which contains the number of students in a class called A. Students are to be assigned to Class A if their mark in computer science (CSMARK) is over 80; otherwise they are to be assigned to Class B (CLASSB). The Pascal statement which decides which class to place the student in, and counts the number going into each class, is

```
IF CSMARK>80 THEN
    CLASSA:=CLASSA+1
ELSE
    CLASSB:=CLASSB+1;
```

<u>The IF...THEN...ELSE statement</u> causes control to split into <u>two paths</u> but, unlike forks in roads, you will notice that it immediately comes back together again. This means that we are never in any doubt about what happens; after the execution of one or the other of the two branches, the control returns to the normal sequence. One way of looking at the IF...THEN...ELSE statement is that <u>it provides two possibilities</u>, only one of which is to be <u>selected</u>, depending on whether the condition following the IF is true or false. After one or the other path is executed the normal control sequence is resumed.

If you want to execute two or more statements in either the THEN branch or the ELSE branch, you must enclose them with BEGIN in front and END afterwards. For example, consider the program segment

```
IF X>Y THEN
   BEGIN
      X:=Y+1;
      Y:=5
   END
ELSE
   BEGIN
      Y:=X+1;
      X:=3
   END;
```

We will not try to give any meaning to this example. It just shows how the BEGIN and END must be used when more than one statement follows either the THEN or the ELSE.

You must always have one statement, or a compound statement bracketed by BEGIN...END after the THEN. If there is nothing that you want to do in the ELSE branch you must leave out the word ELSE entirely. For instance, you may have the statement which would eliminate the balance in a bank account if it were less than 10 cents.

```
IF BALANCE<10 THEN
   BALANCE:=0;
```

Here there is no ELSE statement, but this just means that if the balance is larger than 10 cents we do not make it zero.

A program error will occur if a semicolon is placed preceding the keyword ELSE. Sometimes a superfluous semicolon will not do any harm but here it will.

THREE-WAY BRANCHES

We have seen how a sequential control structure can be split up into two branches and then brought together again. What do we write if we have a situation where more than two branches are required? We will do a three-way branch and then you will see how any number of branches can be achieved. This can also be viewed as selecting one of three alternatives.

As an example, we will write a program that counts votes in an election. Suppose that there are three political parties called Conservative (right), Radicals (left) and Mugwumps (middle-roaders) and that to vote for one of these parties you punch a 1, or a 2, or a 3 respectively on a card. Here is the program that reads the vote cards and counts each party and the total. The last card has -1 on it.

```
$JOB     'MARJORIE DUNLOP'
 PROGRAM VOTING (INPUT,OUTPUT);
    CONST CONSERVATIVE=1;
        RADICAL=2;
        MUGWUMP=3;
    VAR VOTE,RIGHT,LEFT,MIDDLE,COUNT: INTEGER;
    BEGIN
        RIGHT:=0;
        LEFT:=0;
        MIDDLE:=0;
        READ(VOTE);          ← for End of file
        WHILE VOTE<>-1 DO
            BEGIN
                IF VOTE=CONSERVATIVE THEN
                    RIGHT:=RIGHT+1
                ELSE
                    IF VOTE=RADICAL THEN
                        LEFT:=LEFT+1
                    ELSE
                        IF VOTE=MUGWUMP THEN
                            MIDDLE:=MIDDLE+1;
                READ(VOTE)
            END;
        COUNT:=RIGHT+LEFT+MIDDLE;
        WRITELN(' CONSERV.':10,'RADICAL':10,'MUGWUMP':10,'TOTAL':1Q);
        WRITELN(RIGHT,LEFT,MIDDLE,COUNT)
    END.
$DATA
(vote cards with either 1, or 2, or 3 on them)
-1 (dummy value for end-of-file)
```

In this program we have two different things happening. One is a three-way branch, which is accomplished by a series of three IF...THEN statements, one for each value of VOTE. This means that an invalid vote does not get counted anywhere. If we wanted notification that there was an invalid vote we could have inserted the following in the program right before READ(VOTE) at the end of the loop body.

```
ELSE
    WRITELN(' INVALID VOTE',VOTE);
```

This then makes it a four-way branch.

The minimum program needed for a three-way branch would be one IF...THEN...ELSE statement nested inside another:

```
IF VOTE=CONSERVATIVE THEN
    RIGHT:=RIGHT+1
ELSE
    IF VOTE=RADICAL THEN
```

```
      LEFT:=LEFT+1
   ELSE
      MIDDLE:=MIDDLE+1;
```

If there are any invalid votes, they are given to the MUGWUMP party.

There is no fixed way of doing the job. Here is another try at it.

```
IF VOTE<MUGWUMP THEN
   IF VOTE<RADICAL THEN
      RIGHT:=RIGHT+1
   ELSE
      LEFT:=LEFT+1
ELSE
   MIDDLE:=MIDDLE+1;
```

Again we have nesting of two IF...THEN...ELSE statements, but in a different sequence. It is good practice not to have a second IF...THEN...ELSE nested after the THEN; it is preferable to have it in the ELSE branch. Notice that we put the ELSE that goes with an IF vertically beneath it so that the nesting of the statements is clear. In the next section we will show how three-way and higher branches can be handled using a CASE statement.

CASE STATEMENTS

If there are more than two alternatives in a selection process it is easier to use a CASE statement. The form of this statement is

```
CASE expression OF
   case-label1: statement1;
   case-label2: statement2;
      ...
   case-labelN: statementN
END;
```

Instead of the nested IF statement in the VOTING program we could have this CASE statement

```
CASE VOTE OF
   CONSERVATIVE: RIGHT:=RIGHT+1;
   RADICAL: LEFT:=LEFT+1;
   MUGWUMP: MIDDLE:=MIDDLE+1
END;
```

The value of the variable VOTE can be the same as one of the three named constants: CONSERVATIVE, RADICAL or MUGWUMP, and depending on its value the correspondingly labelled statement is executed. For example, if VOTE=2 (RADICAL) then we execute LEFT:=LEFT+1. The label of a statement is separated from the statement itself by a colon. Each label must be an integer

constant, for example 3 or MUGWUMP. Notice that there is an END
terminating the CASE statement and that there is no semicolon
just preceding END.

The CASE statement expects to select exactly one of the
statements, so the selecting value, VOTE in this example, must
have one of the values of the case labels. If we are not sure
that VOTE is 1,2 or 3, we can expand the program to

```
IF VOTE has the value 1, 2 or 3 THEN
    CASE VOTE OF
        (Same as in previous CASE statement)
    END
ELSE
    WRITELN(' INVALID VOTE',VOTE);
```

The only thing missing is that we have not written "VOTE has the
value of 1,2 or 3" in Pascal. We will see how this can be done
using AND and OR in the next chapter.

Each alternative in the CASE must be a single statement. If
we want a list of statements, we must enclose them in
BEGIN...END, as is done in IF statements.

A particular alternative in a CASE statement can have more
than one label. Suppose the Conservative and Mugwump parties
form a coalition and we wish to count their votes together in the
variable COALITION. We could use this CASE statement.

```
CASE VOTE OF
    CONSERVATIVE,MUGWUMP: COALITION:=COALITION+1;
    RADICAL: LEFT:=LEFT+1
END
```

Of course we would need to declare COALITION as an integer
variable.

EXAMPLE IF STATEMENTS

We will now give a series of examples of IF statements which
might be used in a government program for handling income tax.
Let us suppose that the program is to write notices to people
telling them whether they owe tax or they are to receive a tax
refund. The amount of tax is calculated and then the following
is executed.

```
IF TAX > 0 THEN
    WRITELN(' TAX DUE IS',TAX,' DOLLARS')
ELSE
    WRITELN(' REFUND IS',-TAX,' DOLLARS');
```

Notice that it was necessary to change the sign of "tax" when printing the refund.

Unfortunately, our program, like too many programs, is not quite right. If the calculated tax is exactly zero, then the program will print REFUND IS 0 DOLLARS. We could fix this problem by the following.

```
IF TAX > 0 THEN
    WRITELN(' TAX DUE IS',TAX,' DOLLARS')
ELSE
    IF TAX = 0 THEN
        WRITELN(' YOU OWE NOTHING')
    ELSE
        WRITELN(' REFUND IS',-TAX,' DOLLARS');
```

We have used a nested IF statement to solve the problem, that is, an IF statement which is inside an IF statement. In general, we can nest any kind of statement inside an IF statement including assignment statements, READ and WRITELN statements, FOR statements, and IF statements.

Now suppose that when the tax is due we wish to tell the taxpayer where to send his check. We can expand the program as follows:

```
IF TAX > 0 THEN
    BEGIN
        WRITELN(' TAX DUE IS',TAX,' DOLLARS');
        WRITELN(' SEND CHECK TO DISTRICT OFFICE')
    END
ELSE
    IF TAX =0 THEN
        WRITELN(' YOU OWE NOTHING')
    ELSE
        WRITELN(' REFUND IS',-TAX,' DOLLARS');
```

Since we wanted more than one statement to be executed when TAX > 0 we had to group them together using the construct:

```
BEGIN...END
```

This construct acts like a set of parentheses and makes our two statements appear as one compound statement. Notice that no BEGIN...END is necessary after the ELSE because what follows is a single IF...THEN...ELSE statement.

PARAGRAPHING THE PROGRAM

In order to follow the structure of the nesting of IF...THEN...ELSE statements we have indented the program so that the IF and ELSE that belong to each other are lined up vertically. The statements following the THEN and the ELSE are

indented. This is called <u>paragraphing</u> the program, and is
analogous to the way we indent paragraphs of prose to indicate
grouping of thoughts. Paragraphing makes a valuable contribution
to understandability and is a <u>must</u> in structured programming.

Also, if you examine the programs with FOR loops you will see
that the loop body has been indented starting right after the
FOR.   In the next chapter we will be examining the situation
where FOR loops are nested, and then we will use two levels of
indentation.   We indent the statement bracketed by BEGIN and END
to show the scope of the compound statement.

There are no set rules about how much indentation you should
use, or exactly how, for instance, an IF...THEN...ELSE statement
should be indented; but it is clear that <u>being systematic is an
enormous help.</u>

CHAPTER 5 SUMMARY

In this chapter we introduced statements which allow for (a)
repetition of statements and (b) selection between different
possibilities.   We introduced <u>conditions</u> which are used to
terminate the repetition of statements and to choose between
different possibilities.   Comparisons and Boolean operators are
used in specifying conditions. The following important terms
were discussed in this chapter.

Loop   - a programming language construct which causes repeated
      execution of statements. In PS/k, loops are either counted
      FOR loops or conditional loops.

<u>Counted FOR loop</u> - has the following <u>form</u>:

   → FOR variable := start TO limit DO
       statement

The variable, called the counting variable, must have the
INTEGER type. Each of "start," and "limit" can be
expressions; these expressions are evaluated before the
repetition starts and are not affected by the statement of
the loop body. Counting proceeds by 1s from the start up to
and including the limit. If start is not less than or equal
to limit no execution of the loop body will take place.
Counting backwards by -1 is accomplished by using the <u>form</u>

   → FOR variable:=start DOWNTO limit DO
       statement

Limit must be less than or equal to start or else the loop
will not be executed at all.

<u>WHILE loop</u> - has the following <u>form</u>:

—▷ WHILE condition DO
        statement

The condition is tested at the beginning of each pass through
the loop. If it is found to be true, the statement of the
loop body is executed and then the condition is again tested.
When the condition finally is found to be false, control is
passed   to   the   statement   which   follows   the   loop body
statement. Any variables which appear in the condition must
be given values before the loop begins. The loop body is
executed zero or more times.

REPEAT loop - has the following form

    —▷ REPEAT
            statements separated by semicolons
        UNTIL condition

Similar   to   WHILE   loop   except that the condition is tested
after the execution of the statements; repetition continues
until the condition is found to be true. The loop body is
executed one or more times.

Loop body - the statement that appears inside a loop. If you
want to have several statements in the body of a FOR...DO
loop or a WHILE...DO loop they must be made into a compound
statement. To do this the statements are bracketed by BEGIN
and END and separated from each other by semicolons.

Comparisons - used in conditions. For example, comparisons can
be used in a condition to determine how many times to execute
a loop body. The following are used to specify comparisons.

        <   less than
        >   greater than
        <=   less than or equal
        >=   greater than or equal
        =   equal
        <>   not equal

Conditions - are either true or false. Conditions can be made up
    of comparisons and the following three Boolean operators.

        AND
        OR
        NOT

End-of-file (or end-of-data) detection - When a loop is reading a
    series of data items, it must determine when the last data
    item has been read. This can be accomplished by first
    reading in the number of items to be read and then counting
    the items in the series as they are read. It can also be
    accomplished by following the last data item by a special

dummy card which contains special, or dummy data. The
program knows to stop when it reads the dummy data.

IF statement - has the following form:

   ⟶ IF condition THEN
        statement
     [ELSE
        statement]

The square brackets are shown around the ELSE clause to show
that it can be omitted. If the condition is true, the first
statement is executed. If the condition is false, the second
statement, if present, is executed. In either case, control
then goes to next statement after the ELSE clause - or if the
ELSE clause is omitted, to the next statement after the THEN
clause. Any statement, including another IF statement, can
appear as a part of an IF statement. If more than one
statement is required after the THEN or ELSE they must be
bracketed by BEGIN...END into a compound statement. Note
that there can be no semicolon preceding the ELSE.

CASE statement - when there are more than two alternatives in a
selection statement, a CASE statement can be more direct than
a set of nested IF...THEN...ELSE statements. It has the form

   ⟶ CASE expression OF
        case-label1: statement1;
        case-label2: statement2;
          ...
        case-labelN: statementN
    END

When the CASE statement is encountered in a program the
expression is evaluated and the statement executed whose
case-label matches that value. The expression must match one
of the labels or the meaning of the CASE statement is
undefined (depends on the particular compiler). Each case
label is an integer constant. Several case labels separated
by commas can label a single choice.

Paragraphing - indenting a program so that its structure is
easily seen by people. The statements inside loops and
inside IF statements are indented to make the overall program
organization obvious. The computer ignores paragraphing when
translating and executing programs.

CHAPTER 5 EXERCISES

1. Suppose I and J are variables with values 6 and 12. Which of
the following conditions are true?

(a)   2*I<=J

```
(b)    2*I-1<J
(c)    (I<=6) AND (J<=6)
(d)    (I<=6) OR (J<=6)
(e)    (I>0) AND (I<=10)
(f)    (I<=12) OR (J<=12)
(g)    (I>25) OR ((I<50) AND (J<50))
(h)    (I<>4) AND (I<>5)
(i)    (I<4) OR (I>5)
(j)    NOT(I>6)
```

2.   The   following program predicts the population of a family of
wallalumps over a 2-year period, based on the   assumption   of   an
initial   population   of   2   and   a   doubling of population each 2
months.   What does the program print?

```
 PROGRAM EXPLODE (INPUT,OUTPUT);
    VAR MONTH,POPULATION: INTEGER;
    BEGIN
       POPULATION:=2;
       WRITELN('    MONTH',' POPULATION');
       FOR MONTH:=0 TO 24 DO
          BEGIN
             WRITELN(MONTH,POPULATION);
             POPULATION:=2*POPULATION
          END
    END.
```

3.   Suppose   you   have hidden away 50 dollars to be used for some
future emergency.   Assuming an inflation rate of 12 per cent   per
year,   write   a program to compute how much money, to the nearest
dollar, you would need at the end of each of the next 15 years to
be   equivalent   to the buying power of 50 dollars at the time you
hid it.

4.   Trace the following program.   That is, give the values of the
variables together with any output after the   execution   of   each
statement.

```
      $JOB      'F.G.WONG'
 1    PROGRAM CLASS (INPUT,OUTPUT);
 2       VAR NUMBER,GRADE,SUM: INTEGER;
 3       BEGIN
 4          SUM:=0;
 5          READ(GRADE);
 6          NUMBER:=0;
 7          WHILE GRADE<>-1 DO
 8             BEGIN
 9                IF(GRADE>=0) AND (GRADE<=100) THEN
10                   BEGIN
11                      SUM:=SUM+GRADE;
12                      NUMBER:=NUMBER+1
13                   END
14                ELSE
15                   WRITELN(' **ERROR:GRADE=',GRADE);
16                READ(GRADE)
17             END;
18          WRITELN(' AVERAGE IS',SUM/NUMBER)
19       END.
      $DATA
       95   110   85   -1   75
```

5. Write a program that reads the following data cards and calculates the average of (a) each of the two columns of data, and (b) each row of the data. You should either precede the data with a number giving the count of the following data cards or add a dummy card following these data cards or rely on the normal end-of-file mark.

92	88
75	62
81	75
80	80
55	60
64	60
81	80

6. Write a program which reads in a sequence of grades (0 to 100) and prints out the average grade (rounded to the nearest whole number), the number of grades and the number of failing grades (failing is less than 50). Assume that a "dummy" grade of 999 will follow the last grade. See that your output is clearly labelled. Answer the following questions:

(a) What will happen if the grade 74 is mispunched as 7 4?

(b) What will happen if the dummy grade 999 is left off? (You can try this.)

(c) What will your program do if there are no grades, i.e., if 999 is the only data item?

(d) What will happen if the two grades 62 and 93 are mispunched as 6293?

Test your program using the following data:

```
85  74  44  62  93
41  69  73 999
```

7. Write a program which determines the unit price (cents per ounce) of different boxes of laundry soap. Round the unit price to the nearest penny. Each box will be described by a card of the form:

pounds	ounces	price
5	0	125

This box of soap has a rounded unit price of 2 cents per ounce. Make up about 10 data cards describing soap boxes; if you like, use real examples from a supermarket. You are to precede these cards with one data card containing a single integer giving the number of soap box cards. Do not use a dummy card to mark the end of the data. Print a nicely labelled table giving weights, prices in cents and unit costs. Answer the following questions:

(a) What would your program do if the above example data card were mispunched as

```
50    125
```

(b) Would it be possible to make your program "smart enough" to detect some kinds of mispunched data? How or why not?

Chapter 6
STRUCTURING CONTROL FLOW

In the last chapter we introduced the two kinds of statements that cause an alteration from the linear flow of control in a program. One kind caused <u>looping</u>, the counted FOR, the WHILE...DO and the REPEAT...UNTIL; the other caused <u>branching</u>, or selective execution, the IF...THEN...ELSE and the CASE statement. Learning to handle these two kinds of instructions is absolutely essential to programming. And learning to handle them in a systematic way is essential to structured programming.

BASIC STRUCTURE OF LOOPS

It is hard to appreciate, when you first learn a concept like loops, that all loops are basically the same. They consist of a sequence of statements in the program that:

1. Initialize the values of certain variables that are to be used in the loop. These consist of assigning values to

   (a) variables that appear in the condition of a WHILE condition DO or a REPEAT...UNTIL condition.

   (b) variables that appear in the body of the loop on the right-hand side of assignment statements.

2. Indicate that a loop is to commence. If it is a WHILE...DO give the condition that is to control the number of repetitions. If it is a counted FOR loop give the number of repetitions. If it is a REPEAT loop the control on the number of repetitions is not given until the end of the loop body. Each of the three types of loops has a <u>control phrase that determines the number of repetitions.</u>

(a) A counted loop's repetition is controlled by the control phrase after the FOR, for example

FOR I:=1 TO 20 DO

(b) In the conditional WHILE...DO loop, the control phrase is, for example

WHILE I <= 20 DO

The condition should contain at least one variable.

(c) In the conditional REPEAT...UNTIL loop the control phrase is at the end of the loop, for example

UNTIL J>5

3. Give the list of statements, called the body of the loop, that are to be executed each time the loop is repeated. Both the FOR and WHILE loops must have a single statement which may be BEGIN...END as the body. If the loop is a conditional loop, then within the body of the loop there must be some statements that assign new values to the variables appearing in the condition. Usually there is only one variable and its value may be changed by either

(a) an assignment statement or

(b) a READ statement.

4. At the end of the loop control is returned to the beginning.

5. Give the next statement to be executed once the looping has been carried out the required numbers of times. Control goes from the beginning of the loop to this statement when

(a) the condition of the WHILE is false or

(b) the value of the index controlling the counted FOR loop has already reached the value indicated after the word TO.

Control passes directly from the end of a REPEAT...UNTIL loop to the next statement when the condition after the UNTIL is true.

It is to be noted very carefully that there is no exit from the loop, except from one fixed location (either the beginning or the end depending on the kind of loop it is), and this exit always goes to the statement immediately after the end of the loop. It is never possible to go somewhere else in a program. In this way we keep track of control flow and never have the possibility of getting confused about its path. The complete language Pascal offers a statement for altering the path of control called the GOTO statement. It permits you to send control to statements with "labels" in your program. Since computer scientists came to recognize the importance of proper structuring in a program, the freedom offered by the GOTO statement has been recognized as not in keeping with the idea of structures in control flow. For this reason we will <u>never</u> use it. It is <u>not</u> a member of any subset of PS/k. You will find that a Standard Pascal compiler will not prevent you from using a GOTO. Even so, you should not use it.

For many good programmers it has long become a habit to restrict the use of the GOTO to that of leaving the body of a loop somewhere in the middle and exiting to the statement following the end of the loop. An exit inside the body is usually related to a second condition. This second condition can be incorporated in the condition following the WHILE or UNTIL by having a compound condition. We will look at examples of this later in the chapter.

FLOW CHARTS

A flow chart is a diagram made up of boxes of various shapes, rectangular, circular, diamond and so on, connected by lines with directional arrows on the lines. The boxes contain a description of the statements of a program and the directed lines indicate the flow of control among the statements. The main purpose of drawing a flow chart is to exhibit the flow of control clearly, so that it is evident both to the programmer and to a reader who might want to alter the program.

A method of programming that preceded the present method of structured programming found that drawing a flow chart helped in the programming process. It was suggested that a first step in writing any program was to draw a flow chart. It was a way of controlling complexity.

When we limit ourselves to the two standard forms of altering control flow, the loop and the selection constructs, there is little need to draw these flow charts. In a sense, <u>especially if</u> <u>it is properly paragraphed, the program is its own flow chart; it</u> <u>is built of completely standard building blocks.</u>

Perhaps it would be helpful to show what the flow charts of our two basic building blocks would be like in case you wanted to draw a flow chart for your whole program.

Here is the flow chart for an IF...THEN...ELSE statement.

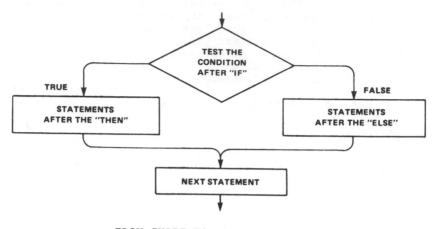

FLOW CHART FOR IF...THEN...ELSE

The flow chart for a CASE statement would be similar except that there are more than two alternative paths.

For the WHILE loop that we described, the flow chart would be as shown. The various phases are numbered.

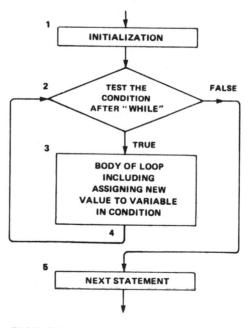

FLOW CHART FOR CONDITIONAL LOOP

The flow chart for the counted FOR would be similar except that box 2 would initialize the index to its first value, increment it by the required amount and then test to see if the loop has been executed the specified number of times. A REPEAT...UNTIL loop is similar also.

With these basic diagrams and the ordinary straight line sequence representing the compound statement, flow charts for all PS/k programs can be built. In a way, because they are so obviously related to the program, they do not really need to be drawn. Any one of the rectangular boxes in these diagrams may be replaced by a sequence of rectangular boxes, or either one of the two basic diagrams themselves. An important thing to notice is that into each of these elementary blocks there is a single entrance and, from each, a single exit. This is critical to maintaining good structure.

PROBLEMS WITH LOOPS

Certain errors are very common with loops. With counted loops the likelihood of errors is much smaller, since the initialization and alteration of the index are done by the FOR itself. You can, however, forget to initialize a variable that is used in the body of the loop. Another problem comes if by chance the index that is used to count the loop is altered in the loop body. This is strictly illegal in Pascal. The letters I, J, and K are often used as indexes, and you must be careful not to use them again before a previous use is finished. This can happen when one FOR loop is nested inside another and the index I is used by mistake for both loops. You might write

FOR I:=1 TO N DO

and forget to initialize N. You should trace the execution of all loops by hand to see if the first iteration is working correctly. Then you should also check the last one.

NESTED LOOPS

We will now look at the more complicated loops. In the following example, subsidiary output has been inserted for testing purposes. The program sums the marks of students in 4 subjects and prints these with the average, to the nearest mark. There are a number of cards, one for each student. A card with the total number of students precedes the mark cards.

```
$JOB     'BOB CHERNIAK'
 PROGRAM CLASS (INPUT,OUTPUT);
    (* A SAMPLE PROGRAM WITH NESTED LOOPS *)
    VAR NUMBEROFSTUDENTS,I,J,SUM,AVERAGE,
        MARK,STUDENTNUMBER: INTEGER;
    BEGIN
       READ(NUMBEROFSTUDENTS);
       FOR I:=1 TO NUMBEROFSTUDENTS DO
          BEGIN
             SUM:=0;
             READ(STUDENTNUMBER);
             FOR J:=1 TO 4 DO
                BEGIN
                   READ(MARK);
                   SUM:=SUM+MARK;
                   WRITELN(MARK,SUM)
                END;
             AVERAGE:=ROUND(SUM/4);
             WRITELN(STUDENTNUMBER,AVERAGE)
          END
    END.
$DATA
 3
 205    55    60    65    70
 208    83    81    96    90
 209    72    68    78    81
```

The program is being tested with the extra printing of

```
    WRITELN(MARK,SUM);
```

Here is the output produced by the computer in addition to the usual program listing:

```
       55        55
       60       115
       65       180
       70       250
      205        63
       83        83
       81       164
       96       260
       90       350
      208        88
       72        72
       68       140
       78       218
       81       299
      209        75
```

Since we were now satisfied that all was well, we removed the card with WRITELN(MARK,SUM) and ran the program with the full

number of data cards. You will notice that when we have one FOR
loop nested inside another we use two levels of indentation to
indicate the control structure.

AN EXAMPLE PROGRAM

We will illustrate some details about loops with another
program. Like some of our previous examples, this program prints
a zigzag. However, our new program is smarter than the old ones
in that it can print out different sizes of and numbers of zigs
and zags, depending on the input data.

```
$JOB     'IRA GREENBLATT'
 PROGRAM PICKZIG (INPUT,OUTPUT);
    VAR MAJOR,MINOR,
        HOWMANY,HOWBIG: INTEGER;
    BEGIN
       READ(HOWMANY,HOWBIG);
       FOR MAJOR:=1 TO HOWMANY DO
          BEGIN
             WRITELN(' ****');
             FOR MINOR:=1 TO HOWBIG DO
                WRITELN(' *');
             WRITELN(' ****');
             FOR MINOR:=1 to HOWBIG DO
                WRITELN('    *')
          END
    END.
$DATA
  3  2
```

This program, given the data values 3 and 2, prints the following
pattern. We have shown in parentheses values of MAJOR and MINOR
during the printing of each of the single star lines.

```
                                          (MAJOR,MINOR)
****
*                                            (1,1)
*                                            (1,2)
****
    *                                        (1,1)
    *                                        (1,2)
****
*                                            (2,1)
*                                            (2,2)
****
    *                                        (2,1)
    *                                        (2,2)
****
*                                            (3,1)
*                                            (3,2)
****
    *                                        (3,1)
    *                                        (3,2)
```

The first data value, 3, caused the sub-pattern

```
        ****
        *
        *
        ****
            *
            *
```

to be printed three times. The second data value, 2, was used in determining the height of this sub-pattern.

   As you can see in the program, there are two separate loops inside the main FOR loop. Both of these loops use the variable MINOR as a counting variable. There is no difficulty using MINOR in this way. Each time one of these two loops is entered, MINOR is set back to have the value 1.

   We can change the pattern printed by changing the data card. For example, the following pattern is printed for data values 1 and 1.

```
                                          (MAJOR,MINOR)
****
*                                            (1,1)
****
    *                                        (1,1)
```

In this case, the loops are each executed only once.

We can shrink the pattern down to nothing at all by using the data values 0 and 1. When the first data value is zero, then the limit value HOWMANY is also zero and is less than MAJOR's starting value 1. As a result, the main loop is executed zero times. Since the main loop is not executed, the second data value, 1, has no effect. We could supply data values 0 and 2 instead of 0 and 1 and would still get the same pattern, namely, no pattern at all.

Now let us switch things around so the second data value is zero, but the first is not. For data values 2 and 0, the pattern becomes

```
        ****
        ****
        ****
        ****
```

In this case the main loop is executed twice, but the two inside loops were each executed zero times.

The data values were used by this program to determine the pattern to print. You could write other programs which print different pictures for different data.

LOOPS WITH MULTIPLE CONDITIONS

Sometimes we must terminate a loop if something happens that is unusual. One of the conditions controlling the loop is the standard one; the other is the unusual one. All loops with double-headed conditions must be WHILE...DO or REPEAT...UNTIL loops, since the counted loop does not allow for the possibility of a second condition. We have seen that compound conditions can be formed from two or more simple conditions using the AND and OR Boolean operators.

As an example, we will write a program to look for a certain number in a list of numbers on cards. If you find it in the list, print the position it occupies in the list; if it is not in the list, print NOT IN LIST. The list will be positive integers terminated by an end-of-file marker -1.

```
$JOB     'MARY SEEDHOUSE'
 PROGRAM HUNT (INPUT,OUTPUT);
    VAR NUMBER,LISTNO,I: INTEGER;
    BEGIN
        READ(NUMBER);
        READ(LISTNO);
        I:=1;
        WHILE (LISTNO<>NUMBER) AND (LISTNO <> -1) DO
            BEGIN
                I:=I+1;
                READ(LISTNO)
            END;
        IF LISTNO=NUMBER THEN
            WRITELN(' I=',I)
        ELSE
            WRITELN(' NOT IN LIST')
    END.
$DATA
 35
 12    16    25    35    40
 51   -1
```

The output for the program with this data is

```
        I=    4
```

Notice that in the body of the loop the variable LISTNO in the condition can be changed by the READ(LISTNO) statement; it is initialized outside the loop. Since an index I is required to give the position of the number in the list, it must be incremented in the statement I:=I+1 and initialized to 1 outside the loop.

IF STATEMENTS WITH MULTIPLE CONDITIONS

Just as the conditional loop can have multiple conditions, so also can IF statements. These can be used very effectively to avoid nesting of IF statements. Suppose you want to count people in a list who fall into a particular age group, say 18-65, as ADULTS. The following program will count the number in the category ADULT in the list. The list of ages is terminated by a -1.

```
$JOB     'ANGIE BAUER'
 PROGRAM WORKERS (INPUT,OUTPUT);
    CONST DUMMY=-1;
    VAR ADULT,AGE: INTEGER;
    BEGIN
       READ(AGE);
       ADULT:=0;
       WHILE AGE<>DUMMY DO
          BEGIN
             IF (AGE>=18) AND (AGE<=65) THEN
                ADULT:=ADULT+1;
             READ(AGE)
          END;
       WRITELN(' NUMBER OF ADULTS=',ADULT)
    END.
$DATA
 16 25 31 12 28 69 -1
```

The output is NUMBER OF ADULTS= 3.   The IF with the compound
condition could have been replaced by   the   more   awkward
construction with a nested IF statement:

```
    IF AGE>=18 THEN
       IF AGE<=65 THEN
          ADULT:=ADULT+1;
```

but this is not advisable.

CHAPTER 6 <u>SUMMARY</u>

     In this chapter we have taken a closer look at the loop and
selection constructs. We discussed flow charts and the GOTO
statement as they relate to the PS/k subset of Pascal. We
presented more complex examples of loops and conditions.   The
following important terms were discussed.

Flow chart - a graphic representation of a program. A flow chart
     consists of boxes of various shapes interconnected by arrows
     indicating flow of control. PS/k programs can be represented
     by flow charts.

Exit from a loop - means stopping the execution of a loop. Exit
     from a WHILE...DO loop occurs at the beginning of the loop
     when the loop's condition is found to be false. Exit from a
     REPEAT...UNTIL loop occurs at the end of the loop when the
     condition is found to be true.

GOTO statement (not in PS/k) - transfers control to another part
     of a program. The GOTO statement is available in full Pascal
     and is sometimes used to exit from a loop by transferring
     control to the statement following the loop. Careless use of

GOTO statements leads to complex program structures which are difficult to understand and to make correct.

Nested statements - means statements inside statements. For example, FOR loops can be nested inside FOR loops.

Multiple conditions - conditions which use the AND and OR Boolean operators.

CHAPTER 6 EXERCISES

We will base all the exercises for this chapter on the same problem, which we now describe. A meteorologist keeps records of the weather for each month as a deck of punched cards. The first card of the deck gives the number of days of the month.

The following cards give the rainfall, low temperature, high temperature and pollution count for each day of the month. For example, the data for a month could be as follows:

```
31
  0   33   37   3
1.2   34   39   3
  0   35   40   0.5
  0   34   38   2
etc.
```

Each of the following exercises requires writing a program which reads one month's weather and answers some questions about the month's weather. To make things easier for you, answers for the first two exercises are given.

1. Find the first rainy day of the month. (The following program finds the required day and is a solution for this exercise.)

```
PROGRAM WETDAY (INPUT,OUTPUT);
   VAR RAIN,LOW,HIGH,POLLUTION: REAL;
      DAY,MONTHLENGTH: INTEGER;
   BEGIN
      READ(MONTHLENGTH);
      DAY:=0;
      RAIN:=0;
      WHILE (RAIN=0) AND (DAY<MONTHLENGTH) DO
         BEGIN
            READ(RAIN,LOW,HIGH,POLLUTION);
            DAY:=DAY+1
         END;
      IF RAIN>0 THEN
         WRITELN(' DAY',DAY,' WAS RAINY')
      ELSE
         WRITELN(' NO RAINY DAYS')
   END.
```

2. See if the data cards for the days of the month are reasonable. Verify that the rainfall does not exceed 100 and is not negative. Verify that the temperature lies between -100 and 200 and that the high is at least as large as the low. Verify that the pollution count is neither above 25 nor below zero. (The following program validates the month's data and is a solution for this exercise.)

```
PROGRAM VERIFY (INPUT,OUTPUT);
    VAR RAIN,LOW,HIGH,POLLUTION: REAL;
        DAY,MONTHLENGTH: INTEGER;
    BEGIN
        READ(MONTHLENGTH);
        FOR DAY:=1 TO MONTHLENGTH DO
            BEGIN
                READ(RAIN,LOW,HIGH,POLLUTION);
                IF(RAIN<0)OR(RAIN>100)THEN
                    WRITELN(' DAY',DAY,' HAS WRONG RAIN:',RAIN);
                IF(LOW< -100)OR(LOW>HIGH)OR(HIGH>200)THEN
                    WRITELN(' DAY',DAY,
                        ' HAS WRONG TEMPERATURES:',LOW,HIGH);
                IF(POLLUTION<0)OR(POLLUTION>25)THEN
                    WRITELN(' DAY',DAY,
                        ' HAS WRONG POLLUTION:',POLLUTION)
            END
    END.
```

3. What was the warmest day of the month, based on the high?

4. What was the first rainy day having a high temperature above 38?

5. What were the days of the month with more than a 5-degree difference between the high and low temperatures?

6. What were the two warmest days of the month?

7. Did the pollution count ever exceed 5 on a day when the temperature stayed above 35?

8. What three consecutive days had the most total rainfall?

9. Was it true that every rainless day following a rainy day had a lower pollution count than the rainy day?

10. Using the first 10 days' data, "predict" the weather for the 11th day. Compare (either by hand or within the program) the prediction with the data for the 11th day.

Chapter 7
PS/4: ARRAYS

So far in our programming, each memory location for data had
its own special name; each variable had a unique identifier.   In
this chapter we will introduce the idea that groups of data will
share a common name and be differentiated from each other by
numbering each one uniquely.

DECLARATION OF ARRAYS

Suppose, for example, that we had a list of 50 integers and
we wanted the sum of all the numbers. Rather than giving each
one of 50 memory locations holding the list a different name, we
give the list, or array, a name, say NUMBER, and distinguish the
various members of the array by giving each a unique index.   The
index is most often an integer. The first element in the array
is called NUMBER[1], the second NUMBER[2] and so on up to
NUMBER[50]. To declare such an array of variables we use the
declaration

    VAR NUMBER: ARRAY[1..50] OF INTEGER;

Each element of the array NUMBER is an INTEGER type variable.   In
the declaration, after the keyword ARRAY we give, in square
brackets, the range of the index, namely from 1 to 50. Here is
the program that reads 50 integers into the array, adds them up,
and prints the sum:

```
PROGRAM SUMLIST(INPUT,OUTPUT);
   VAR NUMBER: ARRAY[1..50] OF INTEGER;
      SUM,I: INTEGER;
   BEGIN
      (* READ IN NUMBERS *)
      FOR I:=1 TO 50 DO
         READ(NUMBER[I]);
      (* ADD NUMBERS *)
      SUM:=0;
      FOR I:= 1 TO 50 DO
         SUM:=SUM+NUMBER[I];
      WRITELN(SUM)
   END.
```

The declaration of the array NUMBER indicates that the index has
a range from 1 to 50 and that the elements of the array are
integers. In the FOR loops, reference to NUMBER[I] refers in
turn to NUMBER[1], NUMBER[2] to NUMBER[50]. This is what makes
the array such a powerful programming tool; we need not refer to
each element separately in the program but only to the general
element NUMBER[I].

In this example, it is not necessary to read all the numbers
and then add them up; we did it that way just to show what is
necessary for reading or summing a list. We could have written
only one loop, combining the two operations.

```
(* READ AND ADD NUMBERS *)
SUM:=0;
FOR I:=1 TO 50 DO
   BEGIN
      READ(NUMBER[I]);
      SUM:=SUM+NUMBER[I]
   END;
WRITELN(SUM)
```

If reading and adding the numbers is all that is required we
could do it without an array at all as in this program:

```
PROGRAM ADDUP(INPUT,OUTPUT);
   VAR NUMBER,SUM,I: INTEGER;
   BEGIN
      SUM:=0;
      FOR I:=1 TO 50 DO
         BEGIN
            READ(NUMBER);
            SUM:=SUM+NUMBER
         END;
      WRITELN(SUM)
   END.
```

We should not use an array if we do not need one.

Usually, there is more to be done that requires having the list still present. For instance we could think of dividing each member of a list by the sum and multiplying by 100 before we wrote them out. This would express each entry as a percentage of the group. To do this we would add these statements to our original program:

```
FOR I:=1 TO 50 DO
   BEGIN
      NUMBER[I]:=ROUND(NUMBER[I]*100/SUM);
      WRITELN(NUMBER[I])
   END;
```

In the FOR loop the statements with the index I result in each member of the list being operated on and changed to a percentage then printed.

TWO-DIMENSIONAL ARRAYS

It is possible to have arrays that correspond to entries in a table rather than just a single list. For instance, a table of distances between 4 cities might be

	1	2	3	4
1	0	20	38	56
2	20	0	12	30
3	38	12	0	15
4	56	30	15	0

We could call this array DISTANCE. DISTANCE[1,4] is 56 and DISTANCE[3,4] is 15. The first number in the parentheses refers to the row in the table, the second to the column. You can see that DISTANCE[3,1] has the same value as DISTANCE[1,3]; the table is symmetric, in this case, about the diagonal line running from top left to bottom right. All entries on this diagonal are zero; the distance from a city to itself is zero.

We must learn how to declare such a two-dimensional array. All that is necessary is to write

VAR DISTANCE: ARRAY[1..4,1..4] OF INTEGER;

Here, in square brackets after the keyword ARRAY, we have the ranges of two indexes separated by a comma. The first index is the number of rows, the second the number of columns. As an example, we will read in this table and store it in the memory. On each input data card we will punch one row of the data:

```
PROGRAM READTABLE(INPUT,OUTPUT);
   VAR DISTANCE: ARRAY[1..4,1..4] OF INTEGER;
       I,J: INTEGER;
   BEGIN
      FOR I:=1 TO 4 DO
         BEGIN
            FOR J:=1 TO 4 DO
               READ(DISTANCE[I,J]);
            READLN
         END
   END.
```

In this program there is one FOR loop nested inside another. We have used two indexes, I to give the row number, J to give the column number. When I=1 the inner loop has J go from 1 to 4. This means the elements of the array on the first card are stored in these variables:

    DISTANCE[1,1] DISTANCE[1,2] DISTANCE[1,3] DISTANCE[1,4]

These are the elements in row 1 of the table. In giving the name of each element of a two-dimensional array you write, in square brackets separated by a comma, the values of the two indexes. It is just customary to think of a table in such a way that the first index is the row number, the second the column number. Since our table is symmetric it does not matter if we interchange rows and columns, because we get exactly the same result. For most tables it does matter, and you must be careful. A table like this is called a matrix by mathematicians.

AN EXAMPLE PROGRAM

    We will illustrate the use of two-dimensional arrays in terms of a set of data collected by a consumers' group. This group has been alarmed about the recent rapid rise in price of processed wallalumps. They sampled grocery store prices of processed wallalumps on a monthly basis throughout 1978, 1979 and 1980 and observed that prices varied from 75 cents to 155 cents as the following table shows:

                                Month

	1	2	3	4	5	6	7	8	9	10	11	12
1978	87	89	89	89	85	85	85	75	90	100	100	100
1979	95	95	95	95	90	90	85	90	100	110	120	110
1980	110	110	115	115	115	100	100	110	120	140	145	155

These 36 prices were made available on data cards and a program was needed to analyze the price changes.

The following program reads in the data and determines the average price for 1979:

```
PROGRAM COST (INPUT,OUTPUT);
    VAR PRICE: ARRAY[1978..1980, 1..12] OF INTEGER;
        MONTH,YEAR,TOTAL: INTEGER;
    BEGIN
        FOR YEAR:=1978 TO 1980 DO
            (* READ IN PRICES FOR ONE YEAR *)
            FOR MONTH:=1 TO 12 DO
                READ(PRICE[YEAR,MONTH]);
        (* DETERMINE THE AVERAGE PRICE IN 1979 *)
        TOTAL:=0;
        FOR MONTH:=1 TO 12 DO
            TOTAL:=TOTAL+PRICE[1979,MONTH];
        WRITELN(' AVERAGE 1979 PRICE:', ROUND(TOTAL/12))
        (* ADD STATEMENTS HERE TO CALCULATE OTHER AVERAGES *)
    END.
```

In this program, the array PRICE is declared so it can have a first index which can range from 1978 to 1980 and a second index which can range from 1 to 12. Effectively, the PRICE array is a table in which entries can be looked up by month and year. The first part of the program uses the data to fill up the PRICE array. The second part of the program sums up the prices for each month during 1979 and calculates the average 1979 price.

We could as well calculate the average price for a particular month. For example, the following calculates the average price in February:

```
TOTAL:=0;
FOR YEAR:=1978 TO 1980 DO
    TOTAL:=TOTAL+PRICE[YEAR,2];
WRITELN(' AVERAGE FEB. PRICE:',ROUND(TOTAL/3));
```

We could calculate the average price for the entire three-year period as follows.

```
TOTAL:=0;
FOR YEAR:=1978 TO 1980 DO
    FOR MONTH:=1 TO 12 DO
        TOTAL:=TOTAL+PRICE[YEAR,MONTH];
WRITELN(' OVERALL AVERAGE:',ROUND(TOTAL/36));
```

This example has illustrated the use of two-dimensional arrays. It is possible to use arrays with three and more dimensions. For example, our consumers' group might want to record prices for five grades of processed wallalumps (that makes one dimension), for three years (that makes two dimensions), for each month (that makes three dimensions). The array declaration

```
VAR PRICE: ARRAY[1..5, 1978..1980, 1..12] OF INTEGER;
```

would set up a table to hold all this data.

SUBRANGE TYPES

When we are programming we often find that we are using a particular limited set of values. In the wallalump example, we were interested in the values 1978, 1979 and 1980, because those are the years of the survey. The variable YEAR is declared as an INTEGER, but it only holds the values 1978 to 1980. The first index of the PRICE array is restricted to be 1978 to 1980. We say 1978 to 1980 is a subrange of the integers and in Pascal we write this subrange as 1978..1980. The two dots can be read as "to".

Instead of declaring YEAR to be an INTEGER, we could be more precise and declare it as a subrange. The declaration becomes

```
VAR PRICE: ARRAY[1978..1980, 1..12] OF INTEGER;
    MONTH: 1..12;
    YEAR: 1978..1980;
    TOTAL: INTEGER;
```

As you can see MONTH has been declared to have only values 1 to 12. We call 1..12 a subrange type; it is a subset of the type called INTEGER.

This change in the declaration does not effect the program, it still calculates and prints the same thing. But the new declaration is better than the old because it tells someone reading the program a lot about the MONTH and YEAR variables. Without looking beyond the declaration we know the small set of values that will be given to the two variables. This means it is easier to read and understand the program; when programs start getting long and complex, it is important to keep them as understandable as possible. Besides helping the reader, the new declaration may help the compiler to do a better job in translating the program; since it knows more about MONTH and YEAR, it may be able to produce a faster or smaller machine language program from the Pascal program. And when we use ranges the computer can help us locate errors; for example, if YEAR has a range of 1978..1980 but is accidently assigned the value 93482, the computer can warn us of the problem.

We do not declare TOTAL to be a subrange because we do not know much about its values. They are read from the data and do not fit neatly into subranges, like the twelve months of the year do.

For this Pascal subset, PS/4, each array index must be an integer subrange, such as 1..12. In the next subset we will see that there are subranges of other types that can be an array index, for example, 'A'..'D', means the subrange of characters that are 'A', 'B', 'C' and 'D'.

NAMED TYPES

You probably noticed that the declaration of the PRICE array contains the same subranges 1978..1980 and 1..12 used for YEAR and MONTH. Rather than repeating these subrange types, we can give them names.

```
TYPE MONTHTYPE=1..12;
     YEARSPAN=1978..1980;
VAR PRICE: ARRAY[YEARSPAN,MONTHTYPE] OF INTEGER;
     MONTH: MONTHTYPE;
     YEAR: YEARSPAN;
     TOTAL: INTEGER;
```

MONTHTYPE and YEARSPAN are named types. It is useful to name a type, such as a subrange, when it will be used in many declarations. This small example does not have very many declarations, but you can see the idea.

In general any type can be given a name and this type name can be used in following declarations. For example, we could give a name to the type ARRAY[YEARSPAN,MONTHTYPE] OF INTEGER and then declare PRICE using this type name.

In a Pascal program we give declarations in this order: the named constants, the named types and then the variables. For example, here are our declarations again, this time with names given to the beginning and ending years.

```
CONST FIRSTYEAR=1978;
      LASTYEAR=1980;
TYPE MONTHTYPE=1..12;
     YEARSPAN= FIRSTYEAR..LASTYEAR;
VAR ..(as before)..
```

Suppose we modify our program to use FIRSTYEAR where it uses 1978, LASTYEAR where it uses 1980, LASTYEAR-FIRSTYEAR+1 where it uses 3 and 12*(LASTYEAR-FIRSTYEAR+1) where it uses 36. Our program still works as before. But now it can be easily changed to handle another year's data, by simply changing the definition of LASTYEAR to

```
LASTYEAR=1981;
```

This sort of flexibility is important because it makes it easier to keep programs up to date.

ARRAYS OF ARRAYS

Pascal allows us to have arrays of any type including INTEGER and REAL. Since any array itself is a type, we can have an array whose parts are another array. This sounds confusing but an

example should make it clear. If we have a year's data, say
month by month prices, then we can place these in an array:

```
TYPE YEARSDATA=ARRAY[1..12] OF INTEGER;
VAR THISYEAR: YEARSDATA;
```

The twelve prices for one year can be recorded in the THISYEAR
array. But if we are interested in three years, we can use

```
TYPE YEARSDATA=ARRAY[1..12] OF INTEGER;
VAR PERIOD: ARRAY[1978..1980] OF YEARSDATA;
```

PERIOD contains all the data for the three years and PERIOD[1979]
contains the data just for 1979. The data for February 1979 is
held in PERIOD[1979][2]. This is equivalent to our old variable
called PRICE where the same data was in PRICE[1979,2]. In the
case of PERIOD[1979][2] we use the first index [1979] to pick a
year's array of data and the second [2] to pick a month within
the year. With PRICE[1979,2] we choose the year and month at the
same time with the index pair [1979,2].

The only advantage of using the PERIOD array instead of PRICE
is that with PERIOD we can deal with an entire year at a time.
Pascal allows arrays to be assigned, so if we want to set the
prices in 1980 to be the same as those in 1979, we can change all
12 month values by writing the assignment

```
PERIOD[1980]:=PERIOD[1979];
```

With PRICE we would have to write a loop to copy the 12 values
one at a time. Although arrays can be assigned, they cannot be
compared,   so   we   are   <u>not</u>   allowed   to   write
PERIOD[1978]=PERIOD[1979] to test if the 1978 prices are the same
month by month, as the 1979 prices.

ARRAYS AS DATA STRUCTURES

We have spoken of structured programming and shown how
control flow is structured in a program. Now we can speak of the
structure   of   data. Giving variables identifiers that are
meaningful has been the only way we could systematize data so
far. But with arrays we find that data can be structured or
organized into one-dimensional forms called lists, or two-
dimensional forms called tables. We can use even higher-
dimensional arrays when we need them.

When we approach a problem and want to solve it by creating a
computer program we must decide on the data structures we will
use. We must decide in particular whether or not we need to
establish arrays for any of the data, or whether single variables
will serve us well enough.

> ✳ Arrays will be useful whenever we must store groups of
> similar pieces of information. They are not necessary when small
> amounts of information come in, are processed, and then go out.

OTHER DATA STRUCTURES

Just so that you do not think that single variables and
arrays are the only kind of data structures we can have, we will
mention a few others.

One common structure is the <u>tree</u> structure. The easiest way
to think of a tree is to imagine a family tree. At the risk of
being called chauvinists we will show only the male members in
the tree and talk of fathers and sons. This keeps it simple.

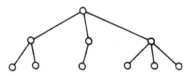

TREE STRUCTURE

The diagram shows a man with three sons. The first son has two
sons, the second one son, the third three. The grandfather is
the <u>root</u> of the tree. The tree is of course growing upside down.
The lines joining the relatives are called <u>branches</u>; the people
themselves are <u>nodes</u>.

The data we might store could be the names of the people, and
the tree structure would have to be stored also. The way it is
done is to have <u>links</u> or <u>pointers</u> stored with the data to give
the structure. Each father entry requires a link to each of his
sons.

A list can also be arranged with elements and links instead
of in an array. This means that some of the information stored
is used to describe the data structure and some to give the data.
With arrays, the structure is given by the fact that one element
follows right next to the preceding element. It does not need a
link.

Later we will be investigating other data structures in
detail. Often we will use the array structures to implement
structures like trees or lists with links from one element to
another.

CHAPTER 7 SUMMARY

This chapter has introduced array variables, which are used for manipulating quantities of similar data. An array is made up of a number of elements, each of which acts as a simple, non-array variable. The following terms are used in describing arrays and their uses.

Array declaration - <u>sets aside memory space for an array</u>. For example, the declaration

        VAR COST: ARRAY[1..4] OF REAL;

sets aside space for the array elements COST[1], COST[2], COST[3] and COST[4]. Each of these elements can be used like a simple, non-array REAL variable.

Array index (sometimes called array subscript) - used to designate a particular element of an array. For example, in COST[I], the variable I is an array index. An array index can be any arithmetic expression that has an integer value.

Array bounds - the range over which array indexes may vary. For example, given the declaration

        VAR PRICE:ARRAY[1978..1980, 1..12] OF INTEGER;

an array element of PRICE can be specified by PRICE[Y,M], where M can range from 1 to 12 and Y can range from 1978 to 1980.

Out-of-bounds index - an array index which is outside the bounds specified in the array's declaration. This is an error.

Subrange type - a type such as 1978..1980 that specifies a subrange of another type. 1978..1980 is a subrange of the type INTEGER.

Named type - any type, for example, 1..12, can be given a name and then used in declarations. INTEGER, REAL and BOOLEAN are predeclared named types.

Multiply-dimensioned arrays - arrays requiring more than one index, such as the PRICE array given above.

Arrays of arrays - these are similar to multidimensioned arrays. Each index is written in its own square bracket, for example PERIOD[1978][2] rather than PRICE[1978,2].

CHAPTER 7 EXERCISES

1. Write a program that will read in the length of a one-dimensional array then read the array itself. It is then to replace each element of the array by the sum of all elements up to and including that element and then output the resulting array.

2. Set the values of the elements of a two-dimensional integer array that has the same number of rows as columns so that the diagonal elements are all +1 and the off-diagonal elements −1. Read in an integer giving the size of a subset of the array and print out the subset array one row to a line. You should limit the size to a maximum of 8x8.

3. In mathematics, two one-dimensional arrays of equal length may be multiplied together. The product (sometimes called the scalar product of two vectors) is the sum of the products of corresponding elements in the two arrays. If one array is named A and the other B then the scalar product is the sum for I going from 1 to the length of the array of terms of the form

    A[I]*B[I]

Write a program to find the scalar product of two one-dimensional arrays. Read in the length of the arrays as a variable.

4. In mathematics, two matrices may be multiplied together if the number of columns of the first matrix is equal to the number of rows of the second. The product is a matrix. If we have a matrix A with L rows and M columns and a matrix B with M rows and N columns the elements of the product matrix C are given by the relation

    C[I,J] = sum for K going from 1 to M of A[I,K]*B[K,J]

Write a program that reads values of L,M,N then reads in matrices A and B computes matrix C and prints it out. Limit the values of L,M, and N to be 8 or less and use two-dimensional integer arrays to represent the matrices.

Chapter 8
PS/5: ALPHABETIC
INFORMATION HANDLING

We have said that computers can handle alphabetic information as well as perform numerical calculations. But most of the emphasis so far, except for labeling our tables of numerical output, has had very little to do with alphabetic data handling. It is true that we have been dealing with words, like identifiers, but these have been in the Pascal programs rather than being handled by them as data. We have, in fact, never had anything but numbers, either real or integer, on the data cards following the $DATA control card. In this chapter we will learn how to read in alphabetic data from data cards, how to move it from one place to another in the memory of the computer, how to join different pieces of information together, and how to separate out a part of a large piece of information.

CHARACTER STRINGS

The term "alphabetic information" that we used in the last section is really not general enough to describe what we will learn to handle in this subset of Pascal. It is true that we will be able to handle what you normally mean by alphabetic information, things like people's names

SARAH MARIE WOOD

but we also want to handle things like street addresses. For example, an address like

2156 CYPRESS AVENUE

includes digits as well as letters of the alphabet. This kind of information we call alphanumeric or alphameric for short. But that is not all; we want to handle any kind of English text with

words, numbers, and punctuation marks, like commas, semicolons,
and question marks.

THIS TEXT CONTAINS 7 WORDS; DOESN'T IT?

We have defined a word as being a string of one or more
characters preceded and followed by a blank or a punctuation
mark, other than an apostrophe. This definition makes 7 a word.

The information we want to handle is any string of characters
that may be letters, digits, punctuations marks or blanks.   We
tend to think of a blank as being not a character, but a string
of blanks is quite different from a string with no characters at
all. We call the special string with no characters at all a null
string. We often write b for the blank character so that you can
count how many blank characters are in a string.

HEREbISbAbCHARACTERbSTRINGbSHOWINGbTHEbBLANKSbEXPLICITLY.

In Chapter 3 we introduced the characters in the Pascal
language. In that listing there are more than we have referred
to so far in this chapter.   The list of special characters
includes symbols we need for arithmetic operations +, -, /, *,
as well as for making comparisons in logical conditions >, <, =.
Then often we used parentheses of two kinds, not to mention the
characters like ; : and , .

One reason we want to be able to handle strings of any of
these characters is to be able to work with Pascal programs
themselves as data.   This is the kind of job a compiler must do,
and a programming language like Pascal should be suitable for
writing a compiler program.

READING AND PRINTING CHARACTERS

We can use variables that hold characters in much the same
way that we have been using variables to hold integer and real
numbers.   If we need to store a letter, which is a character, we
can make the declaration

VAR LETTER: CHAR;

CHAR is a new type. We can put the value which is letter H into
the LETTER variable by the assignment statement

LETTER:='H';

We now write out the value of LETTER by

WRITE(LETTER);

This causes the 'H' to be printed. Here is a program that prints
HI.

```
PROGRAM FRIENDLY(INPUT,OUTPUT);
   VAR LETTER: CHAR;
   BEGIN
      LETTER:='H';
      WRITE(LETTER);
      LETTER:='I';
      WRITE(LETTER)
   END.
```

This is a rather clumsy way to do the same thing that is done by the statement WRITE('HI'). But CHAR variables provide us with the ability to read and manipulate character values.

We can read in the data character by character and print it out. We can use READ(LETTER) to read the next character in the data into LETTER. Reading a character is not like reading a number in that blanks are not automatically skipped. This is because a blank is a legitimate character just like other characters such as Q and *.

Here is a program that reads and prints characters until it finds a period.

```
$JOB  'ALAN ROSSELET'
 PROGRAM ECHO(INPUT,OUTPUT);
    VAR CHARVALUE: CHAR;
    BEGIN
       REPEAT
          READ(CHARVALUE);
          WRITE(CHARVALUE)
       UNTIL CHARVALUE='.'
    END.
$DATA
 HOW DO YOU DO.
```

This program prints its input data, namely

    HOW DO YOU DO.

Notice that the characters such as blank and period are treated the same way as letters. In the UNTIL test, CHARVALUE is compared to period. A single character, such as 'Q' or '.' can be assigned or compared to a CHAR variable. But a string with more that one character, such as 'ABC' would not be allowed.

Now if you think about it, HOW DO YOU DO is really a question and deserves a question mark at the end not a period. So we will modify our program to put on the question mark.

```
$JOB  'KIRSTEN DOUGLAS'
 (* PRINT LINE TO PERIOD, CHANGE PERIOD TO '?' *)
 PROGRAM QUESTION(INPUT,OUTPUT);
    VAR LINE: ARRAY[1..80] OF CHAR;
       LENGTH,I: 0..80;
    BEGIN
       LENGTH:=0;
       REPEAT (* READ INTO LINE ARRAY *)
          LENGTH:=LENGTH+1;
          READ(LINE[LENGTH])
       UNTIL LINE[LENGTH]='.';
       LINE[LENGTH]:='?'; (* MAKE QUESTION *)
       FOR I:=1 TO LENGTH DO
          WRITE(LINE[I]);
       WRITELN;  (* FINISH LINE *)
       WRITELN(' THE LENGTH WAS',LENGTH:4)
    END.
$DATA
 HOW DO YOU DO.
```

As you can see, this program does more things than the first
version did. This one prints.

```
   HOW DO YOU DO?
   THE LENGTH WAS   15
```

There was a blank in front of HOW, so the length is 15 instead of
14 as you might have thought.

   Although it was not necessary for this example, we read all
the characters into an array before printing any. The program
shows how an array of characters can be used to hold a line of
text. We have assumed that the line is at most 80 characters
long, as is certainly the case if they fit on a single punch
card. Often we have a string of characters stored in an array
with a separate variable, LENGTH in this case, to keep track of
how many characters are of interest.

                    READING AND PRINTING LINES

   In this book we often talk of the data as being punched on
cards. This is because traditionally many computer systems have
used punch cards (IBM cards) to hold both programs and data. But
more and more this is changing, especially with minicomputers and
microcomputers, where data and programs more likely are stored on
magnetic tapes or disks.

   Fortunately we do not need to be concerned with whether we
are reading from cards or tape or disk because the same Pascal
statement READ works for them all. But the terminology sometimes
gets confusing, and in this chapter we will often talk of input
lines instead of data cards because Pascal has special features
called READLN (read line) and EOLN (end of line).

In the last example we were able to find the end of the string of characters because it ended with a period. But usually there is not a predictable character at the end of a line. If we knew the number of characters in the line of data, we could have our program count them to determine the end. In some computer installations the input data is on cards and is guaranteed to contain exactly 80 characters per line. In such a situation, the program can read a line by counting the 80 characters.

But we should avoid counting this way for two reasons. First, even in installations that use cards, it is common to trim off some or all of the blanks on the right side, so the length is usually less than 80. Second, if the data is typed into a computer terminal, each line is ended when "carriage return" is typed, and lines are of varying lengths.

Pascal provides a way to determine if the end of the line has been reached, by EOLN, the end-of-line predeclared function. Usually EOLN is false, but becomes true when there are no more characters to be read on a line. Here we use it to read and print a line while counting the characters.

```
LENGTH:=0;
WHILE NOT EOLN DO
   BEGIN
      LENGTH:=LENGTH+1;
      READ(CHARVALUE);
      WRITE(CHARVALUE)
   END;
WRITELN;
WRITELN(' THE LENGTH WAS',LENGTH)
```

This works even when there are zero characters on the line, which is the case with terminal input when "carriage return" is the first thing typed on the line.

DETECTING END-OF-FILE

Now that we have Pascal statements to read and print a single line, we can enclose them in a loop to read all the input data lines (or cards).

```
$JOB  'WENDY PIITZ'
 (* PRINT THE DATA AND COUNT THE LINES *)
 PROGRAM COPY(INPUT,OUTPUT);
    VAR LINECOUNT: INTEGER;
        CHARVALUE: CHAR;
    BEGIN
        LINECOUNT:=0;
        WHILE NOT EOF DO
            BEGIN
                LINECOUNT:=LINECOUNT+1;
                WHILE NOT EOLN DO
                    BEGIN
                        READ(CHARVALUE);
                        WRITE(CHARVALUE)
                    END;
                READLN;  (* GET READY TO READ NEXT DATA LINE *)
                WRITELN  (* CLOSE OFF PRESENT PRINTED LINE *)
            END;
        WRITELN;
        WRITELN(LINECOUNT,' LINES READ')
    END.
$DATA
MAN IS NATURALLY CREDULOUS AND INCREDULOUS,
TIMID AND RASH. (BLAISE PASCAL 1660)
```

NOTE

We have used two new Pascal features in this example, EOF and READLN.

* EOF is a predeclared function that is much like EOLN, but tells when the end-of-file has been reached. Usually EOF is false, but when there are no more characters in the file of data it becomes true. Notice that our program works correctly even when there are no lines of data because EOF is tested before any reading or printing is done.

* READLN is used when we want to begin reading the next line of data. When EOLN becomes true, then READLN is called so the first character of the next line can be read. If EOLN is not true, which means that there are more characters on the current data line, then READLN skips the rest of the characters on the present line and then goes to the next line.

USING EOF WHEN READING NUMBERS

Up to now, when we have read lists of numbers, we have detected the end of the list by either counting numbers or having a dummy number such as -1 at the end. Instead of using a dummy number, we can use EOF, but we have to be careful. This example is supposed to compute the sum of a list of numbers:

```
(* THIS DOES NOT WORK CORRECTLY *)
SUM:=0;
WHILE NOT EOF DO
    BEGIN
        READ(NUMBER);
        SUM:=SUM+NUMBER
    END;
```

The EOF test is not right because there may be blanks after the last number. If so, EOF remains false, because more characters (blanks) can be read, and we try to read another number. But there is no number to read. This is an error and will be handled differently by various computer installations. We want our program to be correct on any installation, so we will rewrite it.

We will assume that there is at least one number (not zero numbers); this simplifies the program. We also assume that there is a single number on each line (or card) and that there are no blank lines following the line containing the last number.

```
(* READ AND SUM ONE OR MORE NUMBERS *)
SUM:=0;
REPEAT
    READLN(NUMBER);
    SUM:=SUM+NUMBER
UNTIL EOF
```

When READLN has parameters such as NUMBER, it first reads in the values, just like READ, and then skips to the beginning of the next data line. So READLN(NUMBER) is equivalent to READ(NUMBER) followed by READLN.

Since the last number is on the last data line, READLN for the last number skips any blanks following the number and causes EOF to become true.

You have to be careful when using READLN. For example, if there are three numbers on a line and READLN(NUMBER) reads the first one then the other two will be skipped. We could use READLN(N1,N2,N3) instead to correctly read the three numbers into N1, N2 and N3. Or we could equivalently use

```
READ(N1);
READ(N2);
READ(N3);
READLN
```

What all this means is that EOF can be used to detect the last number, but it is not as simple as we might hope. And when the list might contain zero numbers it is very tricky.

USING STRINGS OF CHARACTERS

We have seen how a line of data can be read a character at a time into the LINE variable declared by the type ARRAY[1..80] OF CHAR. Since arrays can be assigned, if we had another variable declared like LINE, we could assign one to the other, and move the whole string. But we cannot compare these arrays or print them out except a character at a time. We can print the whole string of characters HELLO simply by using WRITE('HELLO'). But we do not yet have a way to print a whole string when it is in an array.

In Pascal we use <u>packed</u> arrays of characters when we want to compare or print the whole array, for example

```
PROGRAM AMICABLE(INPUT,OUTPUT);
    VAR GREETING: PACKED ARRAY[1..9] OF CHAR;
    BEGIN
        GREETING:=' GOOD-BY ';   (* BLANKS BEFORE AND AFTER *)
        WRITELN(GREETING)
    END.
```

The literal string ' GOOD-BY ' is 9 characters long, including both blanks, so we can assign it to GREETING. We can use a packed array like an ordinary one. GREETING[1] holds a blank, GREETING[2] holds a G and so on. If we put this before the WRITE:

GREETING[9]:='E';

then GOOD-BYE is printed with an E on the end.

We are allowed to assign or compare a literal string such as ' GOOD-BY ' to a packed character array only if the number of characters is exactly the same, 9 in this case. Note that this literal string contains two blanks as well as a hyphen.

The range of a packed character array must begin with 1, as in 1..9, and must end with 2 or more.

COMPARISON OF STRINGS FOR RECOGNITION

To compare two strings they should be <u>of the same length</u> and <u>be stored as PACKED ARRAYs</u>. We need to be able to compare one string with another for two purposes, to recognize them and to put them in order. To <u>recognize</u> a string we see if it is the same as some other string. String comparisons are made in Boolean conditions since their result is either true or false; the strings are the same or they are not. Here is a program that

reads and prints words until it reaches the word STOP.   Remember
that to compare an array representing a string with a literal
string the array must not only be the same length as the literal
but be declared as a PACKED ARRAY since in fact literal strings
are stored as packed arrays.

We will assume that each word we read has at most 10
characters and will chop any longer than that to 10.

MEC
ASLAN 12

```
$JOB  'JOHN GUTTAG'
 (* READ AND PRINT WORDS UNTIL 'STOP' IS FOUND *)
 PROGRAM READING(INPUT,OUTPUT);
    CONST MAXLENGTH=10;
    VAR WORD: PACKED ARRAY[1..MAXLENGTH] OF CHAR;
        LENGTH: 0..MAXLENGTH;   ← subrange
        COUNT: INTEGER;
    BEGIN
        COUNT:=0;
        REPEAT
            COUNT:=COUNT+1;
            LENGTH:=0;
            WHILE(NOT EOLN)AND(LENGTH<MAXLENGTH) DO
                BEGIN
                    LENGTH:=LENGTH+1;
                    READ(WORD[LENGTH])
                END;
            READLN;
            WHILE LENGTH<MAXLENGTH DO          } Blank fill up to max length
                BEGIN
                    LENGTH:=LENGTH+1;
                    WORD[LENGTH]:=' '
                END;
            WRITELN(WORD)
        UNTIL WORD='STOP      ';
        WRITELN(COUNT:5,' WORDS READ')
    END.
$DATA
SOUP
SLOW
SIP
STOP
SIT
```

The output will be

```
SOUP
SLOW
SIP
STOP
    4 WORDS READ
```

We had to put six blanks in the STOP to make it 10 characters long so we could compare it to WORD. After reading each word we had to fill in the rest of the WORD array with blanks. Otherwise the WRITELN would print unpredictable characters to the right of each word, and the comparison with 'STOP   ' would not work. If there were no word STOP in the data the computer would inform you of an end-of-file error, as your program would just run off the end of the list of words without testing for EOF.

This example shows that packed characters can be printed and compared as a whole. But Pascal provides no way to read the whole array at once so we must do it a character at a time.

SEQUENCING STRINGS

The other use of string comparisons is to sequence strings, to put them in order. Usually we speak of alphabetic order for alphabetic strings.

ABCDEFGHIJKLMNOPQRSTUVWXYZ

The alphabet and digits have the normal order among themselves: 0 comes before 9, A comes before Z. The operators > and < are used to compare the strings. The two strings being compared must be of equal length. The following program reads in 10 names and prints out the one that is the last alphabetically. To do this we must be able to compare each string that is read in with the string that is presently the last alphabetically and replace the current final name if the latest one is greater alphabetically.

The names to be examined are put one to a card starting in column 1.

```
$JOB   'LAURIE JOHNSTON'
 (* PRINT ALPHABETICALLY LAST NAME IN DATA *)
 PROGRAM LAST(INPUT,OUTPUT);
    CONST MAXLENGTH=15;
       BLANKS='               ';
       ALPHABETICFIRST='AAAAAAAAAAAAAAA';
    VAR NAME,FINAL: PACKED ARRAY[1..MAXLENGTH] OF CHAR;
       LENGTH: 0..MAXLENGTH;
    BEGIN
       FINAL:=ALPHABETICFIRST;
       WHILE NOT EOF DO
          BEGIN
             NAME:=BLANKS;
             LENGTH:=0;
             WHILE(NOT EOLN)AND(LENGTH<MAXLENGTH) DO
                BEGIN
                   LENGTH:=LENGTH+1;
                   READ(NAME[LENGTH])
                END;
             READLN;
             IF NAME>FINAL THEN
                FINAL:=NAME
          END;
       WRITELN(' ALPHABETICALLY LAST IS: ',FINAL)
    END.
$DATA
HORNING
TSICHRITZIS
WORTMAN
GOTLIEB
```

This program will output

```
ALPHABETICALLY LAST IS: WORTMAN
```

Notice the way that the blanks are placed in the array NAME before the characters are read in. This effectively pads the name read in, on the right with blanks, to bring it to the standard length of 15 characters.

HANDLING ARRAYS OF STRINGS

Suppose you wanted to read in a list of names of 50 students and print them out in reverse order, that is, last first. We would need to read in the entire list before we could begin the printing. This means we must have a memory location for each name. We must be able to reserve this space by a declaration. We would need an array of memory locations each one of which is a packed array of characters. It is an array of string variables. For the list of names of students we would use the following:

```
TYPE NAMETYPE=PACKED ARRAY[1..20] OF CHAR;
VAR STUDENT: ARRAY[1..50] OF NAMETYPE
```

Each student's name is stored in a character string variable whose length is 20.

We are now ready for the program that reverses the order of a list of names. Here the array index is an integer variable I.

```
$JOB     'LES MEZEI'
 (* READ 50 NAMES AND PRINT IN REVERSE ORDER *)
 PROGRAM REVERSE (INPUT,OUTPUT);
    CONST MAXLENGTH=20;
       MAXNAMES=50;
    TYPE NAMETYPE=PACKED ARRAY[1..MAXLENGTH] OF CHAR;
    VAR STUDENT: ARRAY[1..MAXNAMES] OF NAMETYPE;
       I: 1..MAXNAMES;
       J: 0..MAXLENGTH;
       BLANKS,NAMETEMP: NAMETYPE;
    BEGIN
       (* READ LIST OF NAMES *)
       FOR J:=1 TO MAXLENGTH DO
          BLANKS[J]:=' ';
       FOR I:=1 TO MAXNAMES DO
          BEGIN
             J:=0;
             NAMETEMP:=BLANKS;
             WHILE (NOT EOLN) AND (J<MAXLENGTH) DO
                BEGIN
                   J:=J+1;
                   READ(NAMETEMP[J])
                END;
             READLN;
             STUDENT[I]:=NAMETEMP
          END;
       (*PRINT REVERSED LIST *)
       FOR I:=MAXNAMES DOWNTO 1 DO        } note from 50 down
          WRITELN(STUDENT[I])
    END.
$DATA
 (list of 50 names, one to a line)
```

Again you can see what a powerful programming tool the indexed variable can be. The index I that is counting the loop is used to refer to the different members of the list. In the first FOR loop the names are read in character by character and padded on the right with blanks; the first is stored in the variable STUDENT[1], the second in STUDENT[2], and so on. In contrast, the first iteration of the printing loop outputs STUDENT[50], the next STUDENT[49], and so on. Note again that we must read strings character by character but can print them as a unit.

We have set NAMETEMP to blanks, read each character in a name
into NAMETEMP[J] and then assigned all of NAMETEMP to STUDENT[I].
We could eliminate NAMETEMP and use STUDENT directly. We would
set STUDENT[I] to blanks and read each character directly into
STUDENT[I][J], where STUDENT[I][J] means character number J of
the string STUDENT[I].

AN EXAMPLE PROGRAM

Sometimes a table has different types of information in
different columns. To use a two-dimensional array we must have
every element of the same type. Instead we use a number of one-
dimensional arrays, one for each column of the table. We will
now give an example in which the table is the timetable for
teachers in a high school. The timetable has been prepared as a
deck of cards. Each card has a teacher's name left-justified in
columns 1 to 14, a period (1 to 6) and a room number.

The cards look like the following:

(teacher)	(period)	(room)
MS. WEBER	1	216
MRS. THOMPSON	6	214
MRS. JACOBS	1	103
MS. WEBER	4	200
MRS. REID	2	216
...		

A program is needed to print out the timetable in order of
periods. First, all teachers with their classrooms for the first
period should be printed; then all teachers with their classrooms
for period 2 and so on up to period 6. The output from the
program should begin this way:

```
PERIOD          1
MS. WEBER       216
MRS. JACOBS     103
   ...
```

The following program produces this output:

```
 1 (* PRINT TIMETABLE PERIOD BY PERIOD *)
 2 PROGRAM PERIODS(INPUT,OUTPUT);
 3    CONST MAXLENGTH=17;
 4       MAXENTRIES=50;
 5       LASTPERIOD=6;
 6    TYPE NAMETYPE=PACKED ARRAY[1..MAXLENGTH] OF CHAR;
 7    VAR TEACHER: ARRAY[1..MAXENTRIES] OF NAMETYPE;
 8        PERIOD: ARRAY[1..MAXENTRIES] OF 1..LASTPERIOD;
 9        ROOM: ARRAY[1..MAXENTRIES] OF INTEGER;
10        THISPERIOD: 1..LASTPERIOD;
11        I,HOWMANY: 0..MAXENTRIES;
12        N: 1..MAXLENGTH;
13    BEGIN
14       (* READ TIMETABLE *)
15       HOWMANY:=0;
16       WHILE NOT EOF DO
17          BEGIN
18             HOWMANY:=HOWMANY+1;
19             FOR N:=1 TO MAXLENGTH DO
20                READ(TEACHER[HOWMANY][N]);
21             READLN(PERIOD[HOWMANY],ROOM[HOWMANY])
22          END;
23       (* PRINT TIMETABLE BY PERIODS *)
24       FOR THISPERIOD:=1 TO LASTPERIOD DO
25          BEGIN
26             WRITELN(' PERIOD            ',THISPERIOD);
27             FOR I:=1 TO HOWMANY DO
28                IF PERIOD[I]=THISPERIOD THEN
29                   WRITELN('  ',TEACHER[I],ROOM[I])
30          END
31    END.
```

The first loop in this program reads in the cards representing the timetable. Note that because the alphabetic information of the teachers' names is followed by the integer information we do not have to be looking for the end-of-line mark as we read the character string. Nor do we need to pad the name with blanks; the blanks will be read from the card.

Our program is able to read in a timetable consisting of <u>at most 50 cards</u>. If there are more than 50 cards in the timetable, then line 18 will eventually set HOWMANY to 51; this value of HOWMANY will be used in lines 20 and 21 as an index for the TEACHER, PERIOD and ROOM arrays. This would be an error, because the declarations specify that 50 is the largest allowed array index. The problem is that the index is <u>out of bounds</u> in line 18 when I exceeds 50. You should try to take care that array indexes in your programs stay within their declared bounds.

The next three sections discuss more advanced programming ideas, namely number conversion, scalar types and enumerated types. Some readers may choose to skip these sections altogether or return to them later.

CONVERTING BETWEEN CHARACTERS AND NUMBERS

When a program prints a number using WRITE, the number is converted to the characters that are printed. And READ takes characters on an input line (card) and converts them into a number. These conversions are automatic in that the programmer does not need to worry about how they are done. But sometimes it is necessary to do these conversions explicitly, as the following example shows.

Suppose there are numbers packed together on the input cards. To save space no blanks appear between the numbers. We can tell where one number ends and the next begins only because we know the length of each number. In the case of printing the highschool time table, we might have data in the form

1216MS. WEBER

The first "1" means period 1 then the next three digits mean room 216 and next comes the teacher's name. Pascal does not provide an automatic method of reading numbers packed together like this; but we can write a program that does the job.

We will use the predeclared function ORD that changes a character value to a number value. Each character has a unique "ordinal" value, for example on most minicomputers and microcomputers we have

```
ORD('A') = 65
ORD('B') = 66
...
ORD('0') = 48
ORD('1') = 49
...
```

Appendix 5 gives common values of ORD as determined by the collating sequences on various computers. Unfortunately all computers do not use the same collating sequence. On most computers the letters 'A' to 'Z' have increasing but not necessarily contiguous ORD values, and the digits '0' to '9' have increasing, contiguous values.

If we have a character variable C then we can read the first digit of a line and convert it to a number this way

```
READ(C);   (* READ CHARACTER GIVING PERIOD *)
PERIOD:=ORD(C)-ORD('0')
```

We assign the integer variable PERIOD the ordinal value of C as adjusted by the ordinal value of the character zero. This adjustment is necessary because for example ORD('3') does not equal 3, but ORD('3')-ORD('0') equals 3.

Once we have read the digit for the period, we can read the next three digits for the room number this way.

```
ROOM:=0;
FOR I:=1 TO 3 DO
   BEGIN
      READ(C);
      ROOM:=10*ROOM+ORD(C)-ORD('0')
   END;
```

This starts with ROOM=0 and reads the character '2', for room
216. The first time through the loop 10*ROOM equals zero and so
ROOM takes the numeric value 2. The next digit '1' is read, and
ROOM is assigned the value 21. Finally the '6' is read and ROOM
ends as 216. The loop successively uses multiplication by 10 to
slide left the previously read digits in calculating the value of
ROOM.

In a similar but reverse manner, number values can be
converted to strings of characters. The predeclared function CHR
does the opposite of ORD; it changes a number to a character.
For example, if CHR(C) has the numeric value N then CHR(N) is
character C. If we have a number N whose value is in the range 0
to 9, we can convert it to the corresponding character this way.

```
C:=CHR(N+ORD('0'))
```

Note that before taking the CHR we must adjust N by the ordinal
of character zero.

If the number N is larger than 9, we can convert it to a
character string a digit at a time.

```
VAR D: ARRAY [1..10] OF CHAR;
...
FOR PLACE:=10 DOWNTO 1 DO
   BEGIN
      D[PLACE]:=CHR((N MOD 10)+ORD('0'));
      N:=N DIV 10
   END
```

This uses the MOD operator to find the rightmost digit of N and
puts this digit into the D array. The D array is successively
filled up from the right while N successively loses its rightmost
digit because of the division by 10.

CHAR AS A SCALAR TYPE

We have seen that integers can be used to control FOR loops,
to choose alternatives within case statements, and to index
arrays. For example, we can have

```
VAR I: 1..3;
   A: ARRAY[1..3] OF INTEGER;
...
FOR I:=1 TO 3 DO
   A[I]:=0;
...
CASE I OF
   1: statement1;
   2: statement2;
   3: statement3
END
```

Because of these uses we say integers are a <u>scalar</u> <u>type</u>.

The type CHAR is also a scalar type and we can have

```
VAR L: 'A'...'C';
   A: ARRAY['A'...'C'] OF INTEGER;
...
FOR L:='A' TO 'C' DO
   A[L]:=0;
...
CASE L OF
   'A': statement1;
   'B': statement2;
   'C': statement3
END
```

The variable L can take values 'A', 'B' or 'C'. Similarly array
A and the CASE statement can be indexed by values 'A', 'B' or
'C'.

We will give an example in which each data card gives a
student's name and a grade of A, B or C. The program reads the
names and grades. It prints a sentence about each student's work
and reports the number of A grades, B grades and C grades.

```
(* READ AND TABULATE GRADES *)
PROGRAM GRADING(INPUT,OUTPUT);
   CONST NAMELENGTH=11;
   VAR CLASSSIZE,STUDENT: INTEGER;
      I: 1..NAMELENGTH;
      NAME: PACKED ARRAY [1..NAMELENGTH] OF CHAR;
      GRADE: 'A'..'C';
      COUNT: ARRAY['A'..'C'] OF INTEGER;
   BEGIN
      FOR GRADE:='A' TO 'C' DO
         COUNT[GRADE]:=0;
      READLN(CLASSSIZE);
      FOR STUDENT:=1 TO CLASSSIZE DO
         BEGIN
            FOR I:=1 TO NAMELENGTH DO
               READ(NAME[I]);
            READLN(GRADE);
            WRITE(NAME);
            CASE GRADE OF
               'A': WRITELN('DID EXCELLENT WORK.');
               'B': WRITELN('DID GOOD WORK.');
               'C': WRITELN('DID FAIR WORK.')
            END;
            COUNT[GRADE]:=COUNT[GRADE]+1
         END;
      WRITELN;
      FOR GRADE:='A' TO 'C' DO
         WRITELN(COUNT[GRADE],' STUDENT(S) WITH MARK ',GRADE)
   END.
$DATA
3
 R. MARTY  B
 R. SCHILD A
 M. GREEN  B
```

For the data shown this program prints

```
R. MARTY  DID GOOD WORK.
R. SCHILD DID EXCELLENT WORK.
M. GREEN  DID GOOD WORK.

   1 STUDENT(S) WITH MARK A
   2 STUDENT(S) WITH MARK B
   0 STUDENT(S) WITH MARK C
```

Unfortunately, the letters 'A' to 'Z' are not contiguous
values on some computers, notably computers using the IBM
standard EBCDIC collating sequence (see Appendix 5). On such
computers the loop

```
    FOR L:='A' TO 'Z' DO ...
```

executes more than 26 iterations, because of the non-printable
characters appearing in the middle of the alphabet. But many
computers including most minicomputers and microcomputers use the

ASCII collating sequence in which the letters are contiguous, so
the loop would execute 26 times, once for each letter. Although
we haven't shown it, many computer systems also allow lower case
letters 'a' to 'z' and these can be used as character values.

    We have seen that CHAR values can be used much like INTEGER
values, because both CHAR and INTEGER are scalar types.   But
arithmetic is not allowed for CHAR values. For example, if L is
of type 'A'..'Z', this is not legal:

    L:=L+1;

This statement seems to mean to set L to the next character. We
can use the predeclared function SUCC to change L this way.

    L:=SUCC(L);

For example, if L was '1', it becomes '2' or if L was 'A', it
becomes 'B'. Besides the successor function SUCC, there is a
predecessor function PRED. For example:

    L:=PRED(L);

sets L to the preceding character value. Conceptually, SUCC adds
one and PRED subtracts one. If I is an INTEGER then SUCC(I)
actually means I+1 and PRED(I) means I-1.

                        ENUMERATED TYPES

    Sometimes we are interested in a particular small set of
items, for example, the 12 months of the year. It is customary
to represent the months as numbers, for example, January becomes
1, February becomes 2 and so on. Numbering members of a set in
this way is rather artificial although sometimes convenient.
Pascal provides a way of avoiding this numbering. We can define
a type which has the twelve months as values.

    TYPE MONTHTYPE=(JAN,FEB,MAR,APR,MAY,JUNE,
                    JULY,AUG,SEPT,OCT,NOV,DEC);
    VAR MONTH: MONTHTYPE;

Given these declarations, we can assign any month value to MONTH,
for example,

    MONTH:=FEB;

We can write a FOR loop to be executed for each month, for
example:

    FOR MONTH:=JAN TO DEC DO ...

and we can select case alternatives using months, for example

```
CASE MONTH OF
   SEPT,OCT,NOV,DEC: WRITELN('FIRST TERM');
   JAN,FEB,MAR,APR: WRITELN('SECOND TERM');
   MAY,JUNE,JULY,AUG: WRITELN('SUMMER TERM')
END
```

We say that MONTHTYPE is an <u>enumerated type</u> because we give the names for (we enumerate) each value of the type, in this example, JAN through DEC. Enumerated types are scalar types and we can use them for array indexes as well as for CASE selection and FOR loop counters. Values of enumerated types can be compared (=, <>, >, <, >=, <=) and assigned.

In the last chapter we had an example of a two dimensional array to hold the prices of wallalumps each month for a period of three years. That example can be re-written to use our new definition of MONTHTYPE. In each FOR loop we must change "1 TO 12" to be "JAN TO DEC". Each month number must be changed to the month name, for example, 2 is changed to FEB.

<u>We can have subranges of enumerated types</u>, for example

```
VAR SUMMER: MAY..AUG;
```

SUMMER can take on the values MAY, JUNE, JULY and AUG. Like CHAR values, enumerated values can be used with ORD, SUCC, and PRED, for example:

```
ORD(JAN)=0
ORD(FEB)=1
...
SUCC(JAN)=FEB
PRED(FEB)=JAN
```

Essentially, CHAR is a predefined enumerated type whose values are the characters. Similarly, Boolean is a predeclared enumerated type whose values are FALSE and TRUE. Unfortunately there is no way to READ or WRITE programmer-defined enumerated types.

In principle, we never need to define new enumerated types because we can use integers instead. And we can name integer values, for example, we could define

```
CONST JAN:=0;
   FEB:=1;
   ...
   DEC:=11;
```

But defining a new enumerated type offers the following advantages. First, it tells the reader of the program something about its purpose and so helps understandability. For example, when we see SEPT instead of 9 we immediately know that we are dealing with a month. Second, enumerated values are restricted in use, for example, if through some accident we write 3*SEPT, the compiler will tell us that this is nonsense. Similarly if we accidently write

    YEAR:=SEPT

where year is an integer, the compiler will catch the error. This extra help from the compiler is possible because enumerated types provide new, distinct sets of values.

    There are many uses of enumerated values; here is a list of some obvious enumerated types

    TYPE RATING=(PRIME,ACCEPTABLE,REJECT);
       NOTES=(DOH,RE,MI,FA,SO,LA,TI);
       DAYS=(SUN,MON,TUES,WED,THURS,FRI,SAT);
       SHOEWIDTH=(AAA,AA,A,B,C,D,DD,DDD);
       SHIRTSIZE=(SMALL,MEDIUM,LARGE,XLARGE);
       STAFFCLASS=(HOURLY,SALARIED,OFFICER);

CHAPTER 8 SUMMARY

    In this chapter we have given methods of manipulating single characters and strings of characters. The following important terms were presented.

CHAR - variables of type CHAR have characters as their values. Character values can be assigned, compared, read and written. When a CHAR variable is read, preceding blanks are not skipped, because a blank is a legitimate character.

EOLN - this is a predeclared function that becomes true when there are no more characters on the present input line (card). When EOLN becomes true, READLN should be called to prepare for reading the next line.

READLN - this is a predeclared procedure that reads the remaining characters, if any, on the present line and prepares for the reading of the next line. If READLN has a parameter, as in READLN(N), the parameter value is read before READLN takes effect.

EOF - this is a predeclared function that becomes true when there are no more characters that can be read.

PACKED - when an ARRAY [1..n] OF CHAR is PACKED, where n is at least 2, it can be compared, assigned or written as a unit. Literal strings, such as 'HI' are considered to be packed arrays of characters. Two packed arrays can be compared or assigned only if they have the same length.

Length of a string - The number of characters in a string. If the length of a string to be stored in an array is

less than the size of the array the string can be left-
justified in the array and padded on the right with
blanks. Its length then becomes equal to the size of
the array and it can be compared with other strings of
the same length.

String comparisons - used to test character strings for
equality and for ordering. Strings of equal length can
be compared using the following operators:

        <   comes before (less than)
        >   comes after (greater than)
        <=   comes before or is equal (less than or equal)
        >=   comes after or is equal (greater than or equal)
        =   equal
        <>   not equal

In this chapter we also presented more advanced features, namely
number conversion, characters as scalar types and enumerated
types. These important terms were discussed:

ORD - this is a predeclared function that changes each
    character value to a distinct number. (ORD also accepts
    enumerated values and produces numbers.)

CHR - this is a predeclared function that is the inverse of
    ORD. If C is a character then CHR(ORD(C))=C.

Scalar type - these can have subranges and can be array
    indexes, CASE selector expressions and FOR loop
    counters. The following are scalar types: INTEGER,
    CHAR, BOOLEAN and programmer-defined enumerated types.
    (Technically, REAL is a a scalar type but it cannot be
    used for these purposes.)

SUCC - this is a predeclared function that takes a value of a
    scalar type and produces the next value, for example,
    SUCC('A')='B'.

PRED - is like SUCC but produces the preceding value.

Enumerated type - a type whose values are given by listing
    their names (by enumerating them). Here is a type whose
    values are RED, WHITE and BLUE:

        TYPE FLAGCOLORS=(RED, WHITE, BLUE);

CHAPTER 8 EXERCISES

1. Which of the following comparisons of strings are true?

    (a)   'DAVID BARNARD' = 'DAVID BARNARD'
    (b)   'E. WONG   ' = 'EDMUND WONG'
    (c)   'MARK FOX ' = 'MARK FOX'
    (d)   'JOHNSTON' > 'JOHNSON '
    (e)   '416 ELM ST   ' < '414 ELM STREET'
    (f)   'HUME,PAT' >= 'HOLT,RIC'
    (g)   'ALLEN' <> 'ALAN '

2. Read in a phrase P from a single card, such as

ONE SWALLOW DOES'NT MAKE A SUMMER

or
    AN OUNCE OF PREVENTION IS WORTH A POUND OF CURE

Write statements to accomplish each of the following.

    (a) Find the first blank in P and set its location into the integer variable FIRSTBLANK.

    (b) Set the integer variable LASTWORD to the location of the beginning of the last word in P.

    (c) Change P by adding a period at the end of the phrase.

    (d) Change P by replacing its first word by the character '1'.

    (e) Change P by extending it on the right by the phrase THEY SAY.

    (f) Set the integer variable COUNT to the number of words in P. You can assume that each word, except the last word, is followed by a single blank.

3. Write a program which looks up Nancy Wong's telephone number and prints it. You are given a set of data cards, each containing a name and a phone number. For example, the first card of this deck might be

    JOHN ABEL   443-2162

4. Write a program that checks to see that the "I before E except after C" rule in spelling is followed. Your program should read some text which appears as a series of strings. It should search for I and E appearing next to each other. If the combination is EI and is not immediately preceded by a C, then the string should be printed together with an appropriate warning

message. Similar action should be taken if C immediately precedes IE.

5. Write a program that will accept names of persons (first and last) punched one to a data card in the form

        LOUISA MOLYNEUX

and print out

        MOLYNEUX, L.

Make sure your program will work for names already abbreviated to initials. Arrange that the program will work for a number of cards on each run.

6. Write a program which reads text and determines the percentage of words having three letters. For simplicity, use text without any punctuation.

7. What does the following program print?

```
PROGRAM FLOWERS (INPUT,OUTPUT);
    TYPE STRING6=PACKED ARRAY[1..6] OF CHAR;
    VAR POEM: ARRAY[1..2] OF STRING6;
        PART,SAYITAGAIN: INTEGER;
    BEGIN
        POEM[1]:='A ROSE';
        POEM[2]:='  IS  ';
        FOR SAYITAGAIN:=1 TO 3 DO
            FOR PART:=1 TO 2 DO
                WRITELN(POEM[PART]);
        WRITELN(POEM[1])
    END.
```

8. What does this program print?

```
$JOB     'DIANNE KITCHEN'
 PROGRAM POLISH(INPUT,OUTPUT);
    TYPE NAMETYPE= PACKED ARRAY[1..9] OF CHAR;
    VAR NAME: ARRAY[1..20] OF NAMETYPE;
        PRICE: ARRAY[1..20] OF INTEGER;
        I,J,P,N: INTEGER;
        NAMETEMP: NAMETYPE;
    BEGIN
       READLN(N);
       FOR I:=1 TO N DO
          BEGIN
             FOR J:=1 TO 9 DO
                READ(NAMETEMP[J]);
             NAME[I]:=NAMETEMP;
             READLN(PRICE[I])
          END;
       READLN(P);
       FOR I:=1 TO N DO
          IF PRICE[I]>P THEN
             WRITELN(NAME[I])
    END.
$DATA
    3
JOHNSONS  518
LEMON OIL 211
DOMINO    341
    300
```

9. Write a program which reads yesterday's and today's stock-market selling prices and prints lists of rapidly rising and rapidly falling stocks. A typical data card will look like this:

   GENERAL ELECTRIC 93.50 81.00

The card gives you the company's name followed by yesterday's price, followed by today's price. Your program should print a list of companies whose stock declined by more than 10 per cent, and then a list of companies whose stock rose by more than 10 per cent.

10. You work for the Police Department and you are to write a program to try to determine criminals' identities based on victims' descriptions of the criminals. The police have cards describing known criminals. These cards have the form

    name   height   weight

Here is an example:

   JOEY MACLUNK 67   125

There is another set of cards giving descriptions of criminals participating in unsolved crimes. Here is such a deck:

```
14 DEC:  SHOP LIFTING       72     190
 9 NOV:  PURSE SNATCHING     66     130
 6 NOV:  BICYCLE THIEVERY    67     135
```

The two numbers give the criminal's estimated height and weight. Write a program which first reads in the deck describing the unsolved crimes. Then it reads the file cards giving the known criminals' names and descriptions. Each known criminal's height and weight should be compared with the corresponding measurements for each unsolved crime. If the height is within 2 inches and the weight is within 10 pounds, your program should print a message saying the criminal is a possible suspect for the crime. (Note: Joey MacLunk is not a real person!)

11. Write a program that uses ORD to find the value of 10 numbers on an input card. Each number takes up a field of three columns. Each is right-justified in its field and may have a minus sign. The first and second columns of a field may be blank.

12. Write a program that reads a positive number and formats it into an array of 10 characters, in this way.

$ZZ,ZZ9.99

Each Z means zero suppression, so the dollar sign moves right (leaving blanks to the left) until a non-zero is found. The comma is printed only if it has a non-zero digit to its left. Each position given here as 9 is printed as a digit even if it is zero. For example

```
210732  is  formatted  as  $2,107.32
 67150  is  formatted  as    $671.50
     4  is  formatted  as      $0.04
```

You should use the CHR function to do the number conversion.

Chapter 9
STRUCTURING YOUR ATTACK
ON THE PROBLEM

STEP-BY-STEP REFINEMENT

Most of the examples of programming so far have been short examples. Nevertheless we have emphasized <u>some</u> of the aspects of good programming. These were:

1. Choosing meaningful words as identifiers.

2. Placing comments in the program to increase the understandability.

3. Paragraphing loops and selection statements to reveal the structure of control flow.

4. Choosing appropriate data structures.

5. Reading programs and tracing execution by hand, to strive for correctness before machine testing.

All of these are important even in small programs, but it is only when we attempt larger programs that our good habits will really start to pay off.

And when we work on larger programs we will find that we have something else to structure, and that is our attack on the problem. To solve a problem we must move from a statement of what the problem to be solved is, to a solution, which is a well-structured program for a computer. The language of our program will be Pascal.

The original statement of a problem will be in English, with perhaps some mathematical statements. The solution will be in Pascal. What we will look at in this chapter is the way we move from one of these to the other. We will be discussing a method whereby we go step by step from one to the other. This systematic method we will refer to as <u>step</u>-<u>by</u>-<u>step</u> <u>refinement</u>. Sometimes we say that we are starting at the top, the English-language statement of the problem, and moving down in steps to the bottom level, which is the Pascal program for the solution. We speak of the <u>top</u>-<u>down</u> <u>approach</u> to problem solution.

<u>TREE STRUCTURE TO PROBLEM SOLUTION</u>

To illustrate the technique of structuring the solution to a problem by the step-by-step refinement, or the top-down approach, we need a problem as an example. We need a problem that is large or difficult enough to show the technique, but not so large as to be too long to follow. If a program is too long and involved we will use another technique that divides the job into modules and does one module at a time. This is called <u>modular</u> <u>programming</u>. It is another form of structured programming. But it must wait until we have learned PS/6.

The example we choose is sorting a list of names alphabetically. We will now start the solution by trying to form a tree which represents the structure of our attack. The root of the tree is the statement of the problem. In the first move we show how this is divided into three branches:

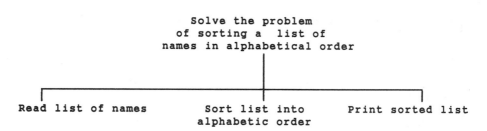

```
                    Solve the problem
                 of sorting a  list of
               names in alphabetical order
                           |
                           |
        _____|_____
       |                   |                   |
Read list of names     Sort list into      Print sorted list
                       alphabetic order
```

At each of the three nodes that descend from the root we have an English statement. These statements are still "what-to-do" statements, not "how-to-do-it." <u>A statement of how to do something or other is called an algorithm for doing it.</u> A set of instructions for assembling a hi-fi amplifier is an algorithm for making a hi-fi amplifier. A cake recipe in a cookbook is an algorithm for making a cake. The problem of making a cake is solved by following the recipe.

We will be moving down each branch of the solution tree replacing a statement of "what to do" by an algorithm for doing it. The algorithms will not necessarily be in the Pascal language. We will use a mixture of English and Pascal at each node until in the nodes farthest from the tree root we have a Pascal program.

CHOOSING DATA STRUCTURES

Before we try to add more branches to the solution tree, we should decide on some data structures for the problem of sorting the list of names. We need not make all the decisions at this stage, but we can make a start.

We will use an array of character strings called NAME to hold the list of names to be sorted. The length of this list we will call N and we will allow names up to 30 characters in length. Because we want to compare the names to sort them, we will store each name in a packed array of 30 characters. This we define as type NAMETYPE. What we are deciding on is really the declarations for the Pascal program, and for now we have decided that we need

```
CONST NAMELENGTH=30;
   MAXLIST=100;
TYPE NAMETYPE=PACKED ARRAY[1..NAMELENGTH] OF CHAR;
VAR NAME: ARRAY[1..MAXLIST] OF NAMETYPE;
   TEMP: NAMETYPE;
   I,N: 0..MAXLIST;
   J: 1..NAMELENGTH;
```

In these declarations we are allowing a maximum size for the list of 100 names. The actual list will have N names, and we must read this number in as part of the input. We will put one name on each card left-justified in the first 30 columns. For indexing the list we clearly will need an index I. We will, as well, need a J for indexing a name as we read it in a character at a time. To compare names they must all be of equal length. We will assume for the moment that we will keep the sorted list in the same locations as the original list. The names will have to be rearranged, and this means some swapping will be needed. We will use the variable TEMP with type NAMETYPE to do this swapping.

GROWING THE SOLUTION TREE

Having decided on at least some of the data structures, we are prepared to continue the process of structuring the solution tree. We can see how to develop the left and right branches now, even as far as transforming them into Pascal program segments. We must read in the names character by character. The middle branch can be refined a little by saying that sorting will be accomplished by element swapping. Here is the tree now:

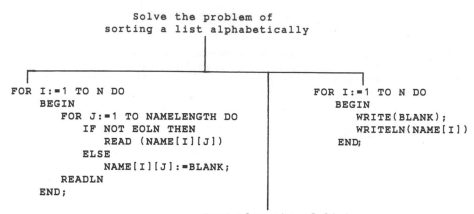

```
                    Solve the problem of
                  sorting a list alphabetically
```

```
FOR I:=1 TO N DO                          FOR I:=1 TO N DO
    BEGIN                                     BEGIN
        FOR J:=1 TO NAMELENGTH DO               WRITE(BLANK);
            IF NOT EOLN THEN                     WRITELN(NAME[I])
                READ (NAME[I][J])           END;
            ELSE
                NAME[I][J]:=BLANK;
        READLN
    END;
```

```
                      Swap elements of list
                       NAME until sorted
```

At this stage we must obviously face up to designing an algorithm
for producing a sorted list by swapping.

DEVELOPING AN ALGORITHM

    We want the names to be in the sorted list so that each name
has a larger value than the name ahead of it in the list.

    In the sorted list

        HOLT
        HORNING
        HULL
        HUME

we see that each name is alphabetically greater than the one
preceding it.

    In our solution tree one branch must be developed further;
this is, "Swap elements of list NAME until sorted." We have seen
from the example that a sorted list has the largest value in the
last position. This is also true of the list if an element is
removed from the end. The new last element is the largest one of
the smaller list. So our next refinement in the solution is to
arrange the list in this way. We write:

    "Do with LAST varying from N to second,
        swap elements so largest is in LAST"

In the list of four names, LAST begins with a value of 4, and the
names are swapped so HUME is in position 4. Then last is set to
3 and the names are swapped so HULL is in position 3. Then last
is set to 2 and HORNING is placed in position 2. The only

remaining name, HOLT, is left in position 1, and the list is alphabetized.

The first part of this can be written in Pascal as

```
FOR LAST:=N DOWNTO 2 DO
```

But we must still refine the part,

"Swap elements so largest is in LAST"

We will now refine this part; it becomes

```
"FOR I varying from first TO (LAST-1)
    IF element[I] > element[I+1] THEN
    swap elements"
```

The first two parts of this can now become Pascal; this produces

```
FOR I:=1 TO LAST-1 DO
    IF NAME[I] > NAME[I+1] THEN
        swap elements;
```

We must now refine the statement "swap elements". It is

```
TEMP:=NAME[I];
NAME[I]:=NAME[I+1];
NAME[I+1]:=TEMP;
```

Because these three statements go after a THEN, we must precede them by BEGIN and follow them by END.

Now we can assemble the complete program.

THE COMPLETE PROGRAM

```
$JOB     'RICK BUNT'
 PROGRAM SORT (INPUT,OUTPUT);
    (* SORT LIST OF N NAMES ALPHABETICALLY *)
    CONST BLANK=' ';
       NAMELENGTH=30;
       MAXLIST=100;
    TYPE NAMETYPE=PACKED ARRAY[1..NAMELENGTH] OF CHAR;
    VAR NAME: ARRAY [1..MAXLIST] OF NAMETYPE;
       TEMP: NAMETYPE;
       I,N,LAST: 0..MAXLIST;
       J: 1..NAMELENGTH;
    BEGIN
       (* READ NAME LIST *)
       READLN(N);
       FOR I:=1 TO N DO
          BEGIN
             FOR J:=1 TO NAMELENGTH DO
                IF NOT EOLN THEN
                   READ(NAME[I][J])
                ELSE
                   NAME[I][J]:=BLANK;
             READLN
          END;
       (* SWAP ELEMENTS OF LIST UNTIL SORTED *)
       (* LOOP WITH LAST VARYING FROM N TO SECOND *)
       (* SWAP ELEMENTS SO LARGEST VALUE IS IN LAST *)
       FOR LAST:=N DOWNTO 2 DO
          (* WITH I VARYING FROM FIRST TO LAST-1 *)
          (* IF ELEMENT[I] > ELEMENT[I+1] *)
          (* SWAP THESE ELEMENTS *)
          FOR I:=1 TO LAST-1 DO
             IF NAME[I] > NAME[I+1] THEN
                BEGIN
                   TEMP:=NAME[I];
                   NAME[I]:=NAME[I+1];
                   NAME[I+1]:=TEMP
                END;
       (* PRINT NAME LIST *)
       FOR I:=1 TO N DO
          BEGIN
             WRITE(BLANK);
             WRITELN(NAME[I])
          END
    END.
$DATA
 5
ANDREWS
CAMERON
ALLEN
BAKER
DAWSON
```

Notice that the English parts of the solution tree remain as comments in the final program. Comments are not added after a program is written, so that it can be understood at a later date, but are an integral part of the program construction process.

ASSESSING EFFICIENCY

In this approach to problem solution we have moved step by step to refine the statement of the problem in English into a program in a language that is acceptable to a computer, namely Pascal. In the process, as we constructed the solution tree, we gradually replaced statements of what is to be done by statements of how it is to be done; we devised an algorithm for performing the process. The algorithm was expressed in English, or a mixture of English and Pascal. Then finally we had a Pascal program.

Nowhere during this process have we spoken about the efficiency of the method that we have chosen, that is, the efficiency of our algorithm. This is because the issue of efficiency complicates the solution. Since in structured programming we are trying to control complexity, we have in this first attempt eliminated efficiency from our considerations.

This means that to now add the refinement of a more efficient algorithm will require us to back up to an earlier point in the solution tree and redo certain portions. In the step-by-step refinement method of problem solution we do not always move from the top down in the solution tree. In that sense, then, the top-down approach is slightly different. In it you would move always in the one direction. In practice this would be impractical, as afterthoughts must always be allowed to improve a method of solution. The only reason to reject afterthoughts is that the work in incorporating them is not justified, considering the gain that would result.

In our particular example you can see that it is possible, at a certain stage, that the list might be sorted and that there is no need to keep on to the bitter end. What we should incorporate is a way of recognizing that the list is sorted so that the mechanical sorting process can stop.

A BETTER ALGORITHM

What we must do is to back up in the solution tree to the point where we had in the middle branch the words, "Swap elements of NAME until sorted." We have translated this essentially by the statement, "Swap elements of NAME in such a way that at the end of the swapping process the list is sure to be sorted."

We are going to change now to the statement, "Swap elements of NAME in such a way that at the end of the swapping process the list would be sorted, and stop either when the list <u>is</u> sorted or when the normal end of the swapping process is reached." You can see that we are going to have a loop now with two conditions. The condition of the swapping process's being finished is the same as what we have now. What we must add is the second condition

"list is not sorted"

But how do we know when the list is sorted? We must devise a method to test whether or not the list is sorted. You will notice that if the inner loop does not swap any names, the list <u>must</u> be sorted. We should have a Boolean flag called SORTED that can be set to TRUE to indicate that the list is sorted or FALSE to indicate that the list is not sorted.

The outer loop would then begin

WHILE(NOT SORTED) AND (LAST>=2)DO

We would have to initialize this loop by having these instructions precede it.

SORTED:=FALSE;
LAST:=N;

These set the flag SORTED to FALSE so that the loop will begin properly and start the count. Inside the loop we must perform the adjustment in the index LAST by -1. Since we are now using a WHILE loop instead of a counted FOR loop, we must do our own counting. This would mean we need the instruction

LAST:=LAST-1

just before the end of the loop. We want SORTED to be changed to TRUE if <u>no</u> swapping takes place in the inner FOR loop. This can be accomplished if we set it to TRUE just before we enter the inner loop and return it to FALSE if any swapping does take place. The altered part of the program is as follows. The variable SORTED must be declared as BOOLEAN.

```
(* SWAP ELEMENTS OF LIST UNTIL *)
(* EITHER SWAPPING PROCESS IS COMPLETED *)
(* OR THE LIST IS SORTED AS INDICATED *)
(* BY THE FLAG 'SORTED' BEING TRUE *)
SORTED:=FALSE;
LAST:=N;
WHILE(NOT SORTED)AND(LAST>=2)DO
    BEGIN
        SORTED:=TRUE;
        FOR I:=1 TO LAST-1 DO
            IF NAME[I] > NAME[I+1] THEN
                BEGIN
                    SORTED:=FALSE;
                    TEMP:=NAME[I];
                    NAME[I]:=NAME[I+1];
                    NAME[I+1]:=TEMP
                END;
        LAST:=LAST-1
    END;
(* PRINT NAME LIST *)
  (as before)
```

BETTER ALGORITHMS

In our example we could see that an improvement in the efficiency of the sorting algorithm could be achieved, and we backed up the solution tree and redid a portion to incorporate the improvement. This was an easier job than trying to think about efficiency in the first place. This is why in the step-by-step refinement method we do not consider efficiency at first. In a way we were lucky that our algorithm could be modified so readily. We might have done the swapping in an entirely different way, in which we would not be able to detect a sorted list by the absence of swapping on any iteration of the process.

To see how this might be, suppose that to sort this list each element were compared with the first element. If it were smaller, the two would be swapped. With the smallest in the first position the list would be shortened by one and the process repeated. The difficulty here is that the fact that no swapping occurs in any round only means that the smallest is already in the first position, not that the list is sorted. We have no way of seeing that the list is sorted unless we compare each list member with its next-door neighbor. And this is what we did in our sorting method.

So our method is more suited to this particular improvement than a method that involves swapping by comparison of each element with one particular element. If we had started this way we would have had to revise completely. To say that efficiency considerations are left until after a first algorithm is programmed produces disadvantages. For many standard processes like sorting, various algorithms have been explored, their efficiencies evaluated, and a best algorithm determined. The method we have developed is certainly not the best that has been devised.

This best, or optimal, algorithm often depends on the problem itself. For instance, one algorithm may be best for short lists, another for long lists. Establishing "the" best method is very difficult and depends on circumstances. Always try to pick a "good" algorithm if you are programming a standard process. At least avoid "bad" algorithms. Very often, programs are already written using good algorithms and you can use them directly in your own program. But that is something we will discuss in the subset PS/6. We can create programs from modules that are already made for us. Then one of the branches of your solution tree is filled by a prefabricated module. We need only learn how to hook it up to our own program. We can also create modules of our own. This technique is called modular programming and it is an additional way to conquer problem solving, by dividing the problem into parts.

CHAPTER 9 SUMMARY

In previous chapters we concentrated primarily on learning a programming language; we have covered variables, loops, character strings, arrays and so on. In this chapter, the focus has been on using a programming language to solve problems.

The method of problem solving which we described is based on the idea of dividing the problem into parts - the divide-and-conquer strategy. Each of these parts in turn is divided into smaller parts. This continues until eventually the solution to the problem has been broken into small parts which can be written in a programming language like Pascal. We will review this method of problem solving using the following terms:

Top-down approach to programming. When using a computer to solve a problem, you should start by understanding the problem thoroughly. You start at the "top" by figuring out what your program is supposed to do. Next you split your prospective program into parts, for example, into a reading phase, a computation phase, and a printing phase. These phases represent the next level in the design of your program. You may continue by defining the data which these phases use for passing information among themselves, and then by writing Pascal statements for each of the phases. The Pascal statements are the bottom level of your design; they make up a program which should solve your problem. In larger programs, there may be many intermediate levels between the top - understanding the problem completely - and the bottom - a program which solves the problem. (Beware:top-down program design does not mean writing PROGRAM name(INPUT,OUTPUT); at the top of the page, followed by declarations, followed by statements! The top level in top-down design means gaining an understanding of the problem to be solved, rather than writing the first line of Pascal.)

Step-by-step refinement. When you are writing a program, you should start with an overall understanding of the program's purpose. You should proceed step by step toward the writing of this program. These steps should each refine the proposed program into a more detailed method of solving the problem. The last step refines the method to the level where the computer can carry out the required operations. This means that the final refinement results in a program which can be executed by the computer. As you can see, the idea behind top-down programming is step-by-step refinement leading from the problem statement to the final program.

Tree structures to problem solution. In this chapter we have illustrated top-down programming by drawing pictures of trees. The root, or base, of the tree is labelled by the statement of the problem. Once the problem has been refined into subproblems, we have our tree grow a branch for each subproblem. In turn, each subproblem can be divided, resulting in sub-branches, and so on. When you are actually solving problems, you will probably not actually draw such a tree. However, you may well use the idea behind drawing this tree, namely, step-by-step refinement leading from problem statement to problem solution.

Use of comments. One of the purposes of comments, (*...*), in a program is to remind us of the structure of the program. This means that comments are used to remind us that a particular sequence of Pascal statements has been written to solve one particular part of the problem.

CHAPTER 9 EXERCISES

1. You are to have the computer read a list of names and print the names in reverse order. In your top-down approach to writing your program, you first decided your program should have the overall form:

(a) Read in all of the names;

(b) Print the names in reverse order;

Next, you decided that the names will be passed from part (a) to part (b) via an array declared by

VAR NAME: ARRAY[1..50] OF STRING10;

where we have preceding this the type definition

TYPE STRING10 = PACKED ARRAY[1..10] OF CHAR;

The index of the last valid name read into this array will be passed to part (b) in a INTEGER variable called HOWMANY. Making no changes to this overall form, you must now complete the program. Include comments at the appropriate places to record the purpose of the two parts of your program. Answer the following questions about your completed program.

- Can you think of another way to write part (a) of your program without changing part (b)? How?

- Can you think of another way to write part (b) of your program without changing part (a)? How?

2. The school office wants a list of all A students and a list of all B students. There is a punched card for each student giving his name left-justified in the first 20 columns followed by a space then the grade in the next 2 columns, for example:

DAVE TILBROOK A-

Each grade is A,B,C,D or F, which may be followed by + or -. The school's programmer has designed the following three possible structures for a program to read these cards and print the two required lists.

First program structure:
(a) Read names and grades and save all of them in arrays;
(b) Print names having A grades;
(c) Print names having B grades;

Second program structure:
(a) Read names and grades and save only those with A's or B's in arrays;
(b) Print names having A grades;
(c) Print names having B grades;

Third program structure:
(a) Read names and grades, printing names with As and saving only names with Bs.
(b) Print names having Bs.

Suppose the final program will have room in arrays to save at most 100 students' names. What advantage does the second program structure have over the first one? What advantages does the third program structure have over the second one? You do not need to write a program to answer these questions.

3. A company wants to know the percentage of its sales due to each salesman. Each salesman has a card giving his identification number and the dollar value of his sales. The top-down design of a program to print the desired percentages has resulted in this program structure:

(a) Read in salesmen's numbers and sales and add up total sales;
(b) Calculate each salesman's percentage of the total sales;

(c) Print the salesmens' numbers and percentages.

Parts (a) and (c) have been written in Pascal. You are to write part (b) in Pascal, add declarations and complete the program. Here is part (a) written in Pascal:

```
(* READ IN SALESMEN AND SALES AND ADD UP TOTAL SALES *)
TOTALSALES:=0;
I:=1;
WHILE NOT EOF DO
    BEGIN
        READLN(SALESMAN[I],SALES[I]);
        TOTALSALES:=TOTALSALES+SALES[I];
        I:=I+1
    END;
N:=I-1;
```

Here is part (c) written in Pascal:

```
(* PRINT SALESMEN'S NUMBERS AND PERCENTAGES *)
WRITELN('    SALESMAN','    PERCENT');
FOR I:=1 TO N DO
    WRITELN(SALESMAN[I],PERCENT[I]);
```

You are to complete the program without changing parts (a) and (c).

Chapter 10
THE COMPUTER CAN
READ ENGLISH

In the subset PS/4 you learned how to handle character strings. You learned how to compare strings, either for the purpose of recognizing particular strings or for putting various strings in order. But there are more things that you can do with strings. In this chapter we will show how to create the illusion that the computer does things that we normally associate with people; we might say that it is "intelligent". We say it has an artificial intelligence, since it is of course <u>not</u> human, and thinking is what humans do. The field of artificial intelligence in computer science concerns itself with getting the computer to perform acts that we think of as the province of humans. Of course, when we see how it is done, we realize it is just a mechanical process. It has to be mechanical or a machine could not do it. But if you do not know how the "trick" is performed, it does seem as if the machine can "think".

The field of artificial intelligence is involved with many different activities of man as imitated by machine, but one of the most interesting is the way that a machine is made to deal with statements made in <u>natural language</u>. We call a language, like English, a natural language because it evolved over a period of time through use. A language like Pascal is a <u>formal language</u>. It has been defined, it is unambiguous and it is really very limited. Trying to get computers to deal with natural language is a major task. We would like to be able to write questions in natural language and have the computer provide answers to our questions from a bank of information. This is a goal in information retrieval systems.

We have not yet got very far along the way towards question-answering systems in natural language, but it is clear there are basic "skills" the computer must have before it can cope with this. One of these skills is the ability to read.

WORD RECOGNITION

When you first learn how to read you must learn to recognize
words. To do this you must recognize what a word is. You learn
the basic characters, the letters, then you learn that a word is
a string of characters with a blank in front and a blank after it
and no blanks in between. We are now going to write a program
that will input a line of text and split it up into words.   To
simplify   the job, we will begin our problem without any
punctuation marks in the text. As an example,

        HEREbISbAbTEXTb

where we have used b to represent a blank. The method of dealing
with problem solving by simplification is very helpful. Solve a
simpler problem before you try a harder one. We will learn to
cope with punctuation marks later. We will use character arrays
such as TEXT defined by

        VAR TEXT: ARRAY[1..80] OF CHAR;

We will not use a PACKED ARRAY here because we will not compare
or write TEXT as a unit. Indexing an array, as in TEXT[I], is
less efficient on some computers when the array is packed,
because the computer must extract, or unpack the character from a
collection of characters (from a computer "word"). But on many
computers the unpacking is very efficient and on these we do not
worry about efficiency when using PACKED.

    Our solution tree for this problem is:

                Read text a word at a time
                              |
    ┌─────────────────────────┴──────────────────┐
                              WHILE (any text is left)DO
    Read line of text   Split off and print next word
      and determine its length

All the parts are straightforward except "Split off and print
next word." We will refine it further:

```
                    Split off and print next word
                                   |
                                   |
      ┌────────────────────────────┴────────────────────────────┐
Find next letter of TEXT                    WHILE(letter not a blank)DO
                                                BEGIN
                                                    Add letter to word;
                                                    Get next letter
                                                END;
```

To determine the next letter of the text we use a pointer which
indicates the position in the text string that you are currently
working on.   We will call this pointer COLUMN. The next letter
will be TEXT[COLUMN]. To add a letter to WORD we use another
pointer called LETTER.

    WORD[LETTER]:=next letter

We are ready now for the program:

```
$JOB      'JULIE SANDORFI'
 PROGRAM READING (INPUT,OUTPUT);
    (* READ TEXT A WORD AT A TIME *)
    CONST BLANK=' ';
        MAXCOL=80;
        MAXCOLPLUS1=81;
    TYPE LINETYPE=ARRAY[1..MAXCOLPLUS1] OF CHAR;
    VAR TEXT,WORD: LINETYPE;
        LETTER,LENGTHLINE,LENGTHWORD,I: 0..MAXCOL;
        COLUMN: 1..MAXCOLPLUS1;
    BEGIN
        TEXT[MAXCOLPLUS1]:=BLANK; (* UNUSED DUMMY AT END *)
        WHILE NOT EOF DO
            BEGIN
                (* READ LINE OF TEXT AND DETERMINE ITS LENGTH *)
                COLUMN:=1;
                WHILE(NOT EOLN) AND (COLUMN<=MAXCOL) DO
                    BEGIN
                        READ(TEXT[COLUMN]);
                        COLUMN:=COLUMN+1
                    END;
                READLN;
                LENGTHLINE:=COLUMN-1;
                COLUMN:=1;
                WHILE COLUMN<=LENGTHLINE DO
                    BEGIN
                        (* SPLIT OFF AND PRINT NEXT WORD *)
                        WHILE(COLUMN<=LENGTHLINE)AND(TEXT[COLUMN]=BLANK) DO
                            COLUMN:=COLUMN+1;
                        LETTER:=1;
                        WHILE(COLUMN<=LENGTHLINE)AND(TEXT[COLUMN]<>BLANK) DO
                            BEGIN
                                WORD[LETTER]:=TEXT[COLUMN];
                                LETTER:=LETTER+1;
                                COLUMN:=COLUMN+1
                            END;
                        LENGTHWORD:=LETTER-1;
                        IF LENGTHWORD<>0 THEN
                            BEGIN
                                FOR I:=1 TO LENGTHWORD DO
                                    WRITE(WORD[I]);
                                WRITELN
                            END
                    END
            END
    END.
```

This program has been somewhat complicated because several blanks
might separate words and there might be trailing blanks after the
last word on a line. These trailing blanks cause the program to
determine that LENGTHWORD=0, so we avoid printing when this is
true.   We made the TEXT array one column longer than the maximum
allowed line width because the WHILE test to see if TEXT[COLUMN]
is blank is sometimes made when COLUMN is one beyond MAXCOL. The

array index must not have a value outside the declared   range   of
the index for TEXT.

WORDS WITH PUNCTUATION

We   want   now   to   modify   the   previous   program to do the same
thing when there are punctuation marks present, that is, find the
words in a text and print them out one by one. We usually try to
build on the   previous   work   so   that   we   do   not   need   to   do
everything   from   scratch.   If we could reduce the text with the
punctuation marks to one without such marks, we   could   then   use
the old program. The solution tree would be:

```
                      Read a text with
                      punctuation marks
        ┌───────────────────┴────────────────────┐
   Eliminate                               Read a text without
   punctuation marks                       punctuation marks
```

Our problem is to eliminate punctuation marks from text.   This is
accomplished as the text is read by this program segment:

```
WHILE NOT EOLN DO
   BEGIN
      Read a character;
      IF character is a letter or blank THEN
         Advance column index
   END;
```

The program for this will be:

```
      WHILE NOT EOLN DO
         BEGIN
            READ(TEXT[COLUMN]);
            IF(TEXT[COLUMN]=' ')OR
                 ((TEXT[COLUMN]>='A')AND(TEXT[COLUMN]<='Z'))THEN
               COLUMN:=COLUMN+1
         END;
```

After this has been executed, TEXT can be separated into words as
in the previous program since all the punctuation marks have been
removed.

This book is set by a computer so that the words in any line are both left- and right- justified; there is one non-blank character in the leftmost and one in the rightmost position of each line of text. This is accomplished by inserting extra blanks between words so that some have two or three blanks instead of one. It is a job that used to require a skilled linotype operator. You will notice that for this book the computer never hyphenates words, and this may mean that some lines have rather a lot of blanks. This happens when the first word of the next line is a long one. We will speak more of <u>text editors</u> a little later.

WORD STATISTICS

We have learned to read words of a text, recognize certain words such as STOP, replace words and to treat words in a list in different ways as we did with the list of names. Another important use of a computer in dealing with words involves keeping statistics about the lengths of words. Different authors have different patterns of use of words and this shows up in the frequency with which they use words of different lengths. Some authors use a lot of long words; others rarely do.

In this section we will read a text and from it prepare a frequency distribution of word lengths. To add a little extra interest to this problem, we will display the results in graphic form. For instance, we will have a display like this for output:

```
LENGTH OF WORD        FREQUENCY
      1               ***
      2               ******
      3               ********
      4               *****
```

This display, called a histogram, represents the result of analyzing the frequency of different word lengths in a text. It shows that there were 3 one-letter words, 6 two-letter words, 8 three-letter words, and 5 four-letter words.

We will not read the entire line of text this time before breaking it into words but will read a word at a time. We will presume that there are no punctuation marks, just words with blanks between them.

```
$JOB 'PHYLLIS GOTLIEB'
 PROGRAM DISPLAY(INPUT,OUTPUT);
    (* DETERMINE FREQUENCIES OF WORD LENGTHS (UP TO 20) *)
    CONST MAXLENGTH=20;
    VAR FREQUENCY: ARRAY[1..MAXLENGTH] OF INTEGER;
        LENGTH,I,J: INTEGER;
        CH: CHAR;
    BEGIN
        FOR I:=1 TO MAXLENGTH DO
            FREQUENCY[I]:=0;
        WRITELN(' LENGTH OF WORD','       FREQUENCY');
        WHILE NOT EOF DO
            BEGIN
                CH:=' '; (* INITIALIZE TO START LOOP *)
                WHILE(NOT EOLN)AND(CH=' ')DO (* SKIP LEADING BLANKS *)
                    READ(CH);
                IF CH <> ' ' THEN    (* IF LINE HAS A WORD THEN *)
                    BEGIN
                        LENGTH:=1;
                        WHILE (NOT EOLN) AND (CH <> ' ')DO
                            BEGIN
                                READ(CH);
                                LENGTH:=LENGTH+1
                            END;
                        IF CH=' ' THEN
                            LENGTH:=LENGTH-1; (* IGNORE TRAILING BLANK *)
                        IF LENGTH<=MAXLENGTH THEN
                            FREQUENCY[LENGTH]:=FREQUENCY[LENGTH]+1
                    END;
                IF EOLN THEN
                    READLN
            END;
        FOR I:=1 TO MAXLENGTH DO
            BEGIN
                WRITE(I,'          ');
                FOR J:=1 TO FREQUENCY[I] DO
                    WRITE('*');
                WRITELN
            END
    END.
$DATA
 ROSES ARE RED
 VIOLETS ARE BLUE
 HONEY IS SWEET
 AND SO ARE YOU
```

The output for this is

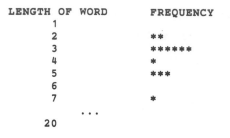

```
LENGTH OF WORD      FREQUENCY
        1
        2           **
        3           ******
        4           *
        5           ***
        6
        7           *
            . . .
       20
```

READING PASCAL

We have been reading English text and performing operations on it, or as the result of it. All these operations, we see, are absolutely mechanical but give you the impression that the computer is capable of doing things we think of as "intelligent work". One of the fields of artificial intelligence that has been explored is the translation from one language to another. The translation of one natural language into another, such as English to French, has had only qualified success. It works, but not well when the text is ambiguous or difficult. The translations are not good literature, to say the least.

But computers are being used for language translation every day, for the translation of programming languages into machine languages. The reason this is possible is that programming languages are well defined and quite limited.

Your Pascal programs are translated by the compiler program into machine language programs before execution. A Pascal program is made up of keywords and identifiers such as FOR, READ and WHILE and special symbols such as semicolon and colon. A translator for Pascal first reads in the characters of the Pascal program and separates them into keywords, identifiers and special symbols. It can tell which keyword it has read by comparing the word it has read to the known keywords. When a statement keyword such as WHILE is recognized, the translator knows it is to produce machine language for a loop. The last chapter of this book discusses how this is done.

CHAPTER 10 SUMMARY

In this chapter we have shown how the computer can, in a sense, understand English. The computer can recognize words by scanning for their beginnings and endings. Typically, words in English are surrounded by blanks or special characters; programs can be written which separate out words by searching for these characters. Due to the great speed of computers, they sometimes have the appearance of being intelligent, in spite of the fact that their basic mode of operation is very simplistic, such as seeing if a given character is a blank. Pascal compilers have been developed to read text which looks somewhat like English; the text which they have been designed to read is Pascal programs.

CHAPTER 10 EXERCISES

1. A <u>palindrome</u> is a word or phrase which is spelled the same backwards and forwards. The following are examples of word palindromes: "I", "mom", "deed" and "level". Blanks and punctuation are ignored in phrase palindromes, for example, "Madam, in Eden I'm Adam" and "A man, a plan, a canal, Panama". Write a program which reads a string and determines if it is a palindrome.

2. You are to write a program which will help in reviewing a script to determine its suitability for television screening. Your program is to give a list of the frequency of use of the following unacceptable words:

PHOOEY SHUCKS JEEPERS GOLLY

Make up a few lines of script to test out your program.

3. You are employed by an English teacher who insists that "and" should not be preceded by a comma. Hence, "Crosby, Stills, Nash and Young" is acceptable, but "Merril, Fynch, and Lynn" is not. Write a program which reads lines of text, searches for unacceptable commas, removes them, and makes stern remarks such as the English teacher would make about errors.

4. Write a program which reads text and then prints it so that its left and right margins are vertical. First the program is to read the number of characters to print per line. Whenever enough words for one line have been collected, blanks are inserted between words to expand the line to the desired width. Then the expanded line is printed.

Chapter 11
PS/6: SUBPROGRAMS

In this subset we will be introducing the idea of subprograms other than the main program that has constituted all programs so far. The purpose of having subsidiary programs or subprograms is so that a larger program can be divided into parts. In this way we "divide and conquer" a complicated problem. Sometimes a part of the solution of one problem can be used in many different problems, and making it into a subprogram creates a module or building block which can be used in many programs.

PROCEDURES

There are two kinds of subprograms in Pascal: procedures and functions. Essentially, procedures allow you to invent new Pascal statements, while functions allow you to invent new operations. We will give an example of a procedure first.

Suppose we wish to determine the larger of two INTEGER numbers. We could write a procedure to find the larger one; this is done in the following procedure declaration:

```
PROCEDURE LARGER(FIRST,SECOND: INTEGER; VAR RESULT: INTEGER);
    BEGIN
        IF FIRST>SECOND THEN
            RESULT:=FIRST
        ELSE
            RESULT:=SECOND
    END;
```

The heading of the procedure declaration is the keyword PROCEDURE, followed by the name of the procedure, LARGER, followed in parentheses by a list of <u>formal parameters</u> with their types. There are two kinds of formal parameters: <u>value parameters</u> and <u>variable parameters</u>. A variable parameter is sometimes called a VAR parameter because it is declared using the keyword VAR in the formal parameter list. Variable parameters are used to feed information into a subprogram and also to feed information back out. Value parameters can only feed information into the subprogram.

    The body of the procedure is a compound statement prefaced by BEGIN and terminated by END. Note that the <u>END of a procedure has a semicolon after it.</u> To use this procedure in a main program its declaration is included immediately after any variable declarations of the main program. Here is an example

```
$JOB    'STEWART LEE'
 PROGRAM BEST (INPUT,OUTPUT);
    VAR DATA1,DATA2,MAXIMUM: INTEGER;

    (* THIS IS THE DECLARATION OF THE PROCEDURE *)
    PROCEDURE LARGER(FIRST,SECOND: INTEGER; VAR RESULT: INTEGER);
       BEGIN
          IF FIRST>SECOND THEN
             RESULT:=FIRST
          ELSE
             RESULT:=SECOND
       END;

    (* THIS IS THE BODY OF THE MAIN PROGRAM *)
    BEGIN
       READ(DATA1,DATA2);
       LARGER(DATA1,DATA2,MAXIMUM);
       WRITELN(' THE LARGER IS',MAXIMUM)
    END.
$DATA
 5  31
```

We have included a blank line before and after the procedure declaration but this is not necessary.

    When the LARGER procedure is called, via the <u>procedure statement</u> in the main program

```
    LARGER(DATA1,DATA2,MAXIMUM);
```

the value formal parameter FIRST takes the value of the <u>actual parameter</u> DATA1, SECOND takes the value of the actual parameter DATA2 and RESULT which is a variable formal parameter becomes another name for MAXIMUM. Inside the procedure, whenever the value of RESULT is changed, the effect is to change the value of MAXIMUM. The LARGER procedure is entered and RESULT, which is really MAXIMUM, is set to the larger of FIRST and SECOND. When the end of the LARGER procedure is reached, execution returns to the statement just beyond the procedure statement, which invoked

its use. It returns to the WRITELN statement.   Given the data
values 5 and 31, the program will print

     THE LARGER IS   31

Conceptually,   our   procedure   provides   us   with   a   new   Pascal
statement which we can use whenever we want to find the larger of
two numbers.

     This has been a very simple example; if you were writing such
a simple program as this one you would not bother to use a
procedure.

                         FUNCTIONS

     We   will   now   show how function subprograms are declared and
used. We could have found the larger number by writing a
function rather than a procedure. A function named BIGGER is
used in the following version of the program.

     Here is the declaration for a function named BIGGER:

```
FUNCTION BIGGER(FIRST,SECOND: INTEGER): INTEGER;
   BEGIN
      IF FIRST>SECOND THEN
         BIGGER:=FIRST
      ELSE
         BIGGER:=SECOND
   END;
```

The heading for a function declaration is the keyword FUNCTION
followed by the name of the function, here BIGGER, then in
parentheses the formal parameters and their type. After the
parentheses we have a colon and then the type of the function
itself. The name of the function acts like a variable which must
be assigned a value before you finish execution of the function.
In this example the variable BIGGER is assigned the value of the
value parameter FIRST or SECOND depending on which is bigger.
Functions   are   not   allowed   to have variable (VAR) formal
parameters; the single output value is assigned to the function
itself.

     Here is a program using this function.

```
$JOB      'RON BAECKER'
 PROGRAM BIGONE (INPUT,OUTPUT);
    VAR DATA1,DATA2,MAXIMUM: INTEGER;

    (* THIS IS THE FUNCTION DECLARATION *)
    FUNCTION BIGGER(FIRST,SECOND: INTEGER): INTEGER;
       BEGIN
          IF FIRST>SECOND THEN
             BIGGER:=FIRST
          ELSE
             BIGGER:=SECOND
       END;

    (* THIS IS THE BODY OF THE MAIN PROGRAM *)
    BEGIN
       READ(DATA1,DATA2);
       MAXIMUM:=BIGGER(DATA1,DATA2);
       WRITELN(' THE LARGER IS',MAXIMUM)
    END.
$DATA
 5  31
```

This job will print the same as the previous job, namely:

```
THE LARGER IS      31
```

The BIGGER subprogram is a function because it provides a value to its name, BIGGER in its declaration. Since it is a function, it must be given a type, the type of the value its name is to be assigned. The BIGGER function is entered as a result of the fact that its name appears in the assignment statement of the main program:

```
MAXIMUM:=BIGGER(DATA1,DATA2);
```

When the BIGGER function is entered, the value formal parameter FIRST is assigned the value of the actual paremeter DATA1 and SECOND the value of DATA2. Conceptually, our function provides us with a new arithmetic operation which we can use in arithmetic expressions. We could have replaced the assignment to MAXIMUM and the immediately following WRITELN statement by the statement

```
WRITELN(' THE LARGER IS',BIGGER(DATA1,DATA2));
```

This change would not affect the printed answer.

Our example subprograms LARGER and BIGGER illustrate the following differences between procedures and functions. The definition of a function must include the type of the function itself. The value assigned to BIGGER must match this type. For example, in the function called BIGGER, the value assigned to BIGGER matches the INTEGER type given in the function heading. A procedure is entered when it is invoked using its name as the first word in a statement, followed by a list of actual parameters in parentheses. A function is entered when its name appears in an expression, such as the right side of an assignment statement, followed by a list of actual parameters in parentheses.

NESTING AND SUBPROGRAMS

Once a procedure has been defined, it can be used, by name, just like any other Pascal statement. It is even possible to use statements that invoke procedures inside other procedures. We will give simple examples to show the use of nesting with procedures. The following job prints the largest of its three data values.

```
$JOB    'SCOTT GRAHAM'
 PROGRAM BIGGEST (INPUT,OUTPUT);
    VAR DATA1,DATA2,DATA3,MAXIMUM: INTEGER;
    PROCEDURE LARGER(FIRST,SECOND:INTEGER;VAR RESULT:INTEGER);
       (exactly as previous version of LARGER procedure)
       END;
    PROCEDURE LARGEST(FIRST,SECOND,THIRD:INTEGER;VAR RESULT:INTEGER);
       VAR GREATER: INTEGER;
       BEGIN
          LARGER(FIRST,SECOND,GREATER);
          LARGER(GREATER,THIRD,RESULT)
       END;

    BEGIN
       READ(DATA1,DATA2,DATA3);
       LARGEST(DATA1,DATA2,DATA3,MAXIMUM);
       WRITELN(' THE LARGEST IS',MAXIMUM)
    END.
$DATA
 5   31   27
```

This job will print:

```
    THE LARGEST IS      31
```

The procedure named LARGEST determines which of its first three value parameters is largest and assigns the largest value to its variable parameter, named RESULT. It accomplishes this by first using LARGER to assign the larger of the first two parameters to the variable GREATER, and by using LARGER again to assign the larger of GREATER and the third parameter to RESULT. The variable GREATER is declared as a variable inside the procedure LARGEST. This variable is referenced only inside the LARGEST procedure. It is a local variable and is not known to either LARGER or the main program BIGGEST. To be accessible to a program (or procedure) a variable must be either declared in that procedure or in a procedure that contains it.

The procedures LARGER and LARGEST both have parameters named
FIRST and SECOND. This causes no trouble because the parameters
of LARGER are hidden from LARGEST and vice versa. As a rule it
is good programming practice to avoid duplicate names, as they
may confuse people reading a program. However, in some cases,
such as this example, it seems natural to repeat names in
separate procedures. Since duplicate names in separate
procedures are kept separate in Pascal, this causes no
difficulty.

We will now show an example of nesting with our BIGGER
function. We will use it in the following job to print the
largest of three numbers.

```
$JOB      'HUGH DEMPSTER'
 PROGRAM BIGONE (INPUT,OUTPUT);
    VAR DATA1,DATA2,DATA3: INTEGER;
    FUNCTION BIGGER(FIRST,SECOND:INTEGER):INTEGER;
       (Exactly as previous version of BIGGER function)
       END;
    BEGIN
       READ(DATA1,DATA2,DATA3);
       WRITELN(' LARGEST IS',BIGGER(BIGGER(DATA1,DATA2),DATA3))
    END.
$DATA
 5  31  27
```

This job finds the larger of the first two data items using the
BIGGER function, and uses the BIGGER function again to compare
that value to the third data value. In the WRITELN statement,
the first actual parameter to the BIGGER function is another call
to the BIGGER function. This causes no trouble, because the
inner call to BIGGER first returns 31, which is the larger of 5
and 31. Then the outer call to BIGGER compares 31 to 27 and
returns the value of 31. Using a call to BIGGER inside a call to
BIGGER is actually no more complicated than, say,

```
((5+31)+27)
```

This expression means add 5 and 31 and add 27 to the result. By
comparison,

```
BIGGER(BIGGER(5,31),27)
```

means find the larger of 5 and 31 and then find the larger of
this and 27.

We will now show another kind of subprogram nesting. If the
procedure named LARGER is to be used only inside the procedure
named LARGEST, we can give the definition of LARGER inside
LARGEST. This is done in the following job:

```
$JOB      'LARRY LIN'
 PROGRAM BIGONE (INPUT,OUTPUT);
    VAR DATA1,DATA2,DATA3,MAXIMUM: INTEGER;

    (* DECLARATION OF LARGEST, WITH LARGER NESTED INSIDE IT *)
    PROCEDURE LARGEST(FIRST,SECOND,THIRD:INTEGER;VAR RESULT:INTEGER);
       VAR GREATER: INTEGER;
       PROCEDURE LARGER(FIRST,SECOND:INTEGER;VAR RESULT:INTEGER);
          (Exactly as previous version of LARGER procedure)
          END;
       BEGIN
          LARGER(FIRST,SECOND,GREATER);
          LARGER(GREATER,THIRD,RESULT)
       END;

    (* BODY OF MAIN PROGRAM *)
    BEGIN
       READ(DATA1,DATA2,DATA3);
       LARGEST(DATA1,DATA2,DATA3,MAXIMUM);
       WRITELN(' THE LARGEST IS',MAXIMUM)
    END.
$DATA
 5  31  27
```

The job works just like the previous job which contains a
procedure named LARGEST. The only difference is that since
LARGER has been hidden inside LARGEST, the LARGER procedure is no
longer available for use in the main program. The fact that
LARGER and LARGEST have formal parameters with the same names
does not cause trouble; each procedure will use its own local
meanings for the names FIRST, SECOND and RESULT. This example
has shown how a procedure declaration can be nested inside
another procedure declaration.

ACTUAL PARAMETERS AND FORMAL PARAMETERS

We have introduced two terms in connection with procedures
and functions: actual parameters and formal parameters. The
formal parameters are the identifiers used in the declaration of
a subprogram for information that is to be fed into a subprogram
or, in the case of procedures, to be given out. Actual
parameters are the expressions (often variables) in the calling
procedure that are to be put into correspondence with the
subprogram formal parameters. And there must be a one-to-one
correspondence between the number and type of the actual
parameters and the formal parameters.

Each formal parameter is declared to be a variable parameter
by specifying VAR or a value parameter by not specifying VAR.
Procedures can have both kinds of formal parameters but functions
can have only value parameters.

All references to variable parameters in a procedure effectively refer to the corresponding actual parameter. This is done by means of pointers to the locations that hold the actual parameters. These pointers are set automatically at the time the procedure is called. When the procedure is executing, each time the value of a variable parameter is changed the corresponding actual parameter is effectively altered.

An actual parameter corresponding to a variable formal parameter is restricted to be a variable such as GREATER and cannot be an expression or constant such as X+1 or 25. This restriction is made so that changing the actual parameter makes sense, for example, it makes sense to change the value of GREATER but we cannot change the value of 25.

Value parameters are different from variable parameters and can receive expressions and constants, as well as variables, as actual parameters. The value of the actual parameter is used to give an initial value to the formal parameter. After this initialization, there is no relation between the actual and formal parameters, and the value parameter acts just like a local variable.

Here is a diagram to show the association between formal parameters and actual parameters for the program BEST given as the first example of the use of a procedure. The directions of the arrows shows the direction of flow of the data.

```
PROCEDURE LARGER     PROGRAM BEST
     FIRST    <---    DATA1
     SECOND   <---    DATA2
     RESULT   <-->    MAXIMUM
```

FIRST and SECOND are value parameters and receive data from the program. These values are stored on entering the procedure LARGE and are the values contained in DATA1 and DATA2. RESULT is a variable parameter which is assigned a value in the procedure; this value is assigned to the variable MAXIMUM of the program BEST.

The formal parameters of a subprogram are associated with actual parameters at the time the subprogram is called, so a subprogram may be used in the same program with different sets of actual parameters in other statements. Notice that local variables are ordinary variables in the subprogram. These local variables cannot be referenced outside the subprogram. Each time the subprogram is called, these variables must have values before being used, because their values from any previous calls are discarded.

ARRAY VARIABLES AND CONSTANTS AS ACTUAL PARAMETERS

We will do another simple example to show how array variables and constants can be used as actual parameters. Suppose we write a procedure that will add the elements of an integer array, LIST, of N elements and call the total SUM. Let us name the procedure TOTAL. The type of any array variable used as a parameter must be defined in the calling program. Here is the declaration for the procedure TOTAL.

```
(* ADD THE N ELEMENTS OF LIST *)
PROCEDURE TOTAL(LIST: INTARRAY;N: INTEGER;VAR SUM: INTEGER);
   VAR I: INTEGER;
   BEGIN
      SUM:=0;
      FOR I:=1 TO N DO
         SUM:=SUM+LIST[I]
   END;
```

Now let us write a calling program for this:

```
$JOB    'LARRY LAFAVE'
 PROGRAM BILL (INPUT,OUTPUT);
    TYPE INTARRAY=ARRAY[1..10] OF INTEGER;
    VAR INVOICE: INTARRAY;
        I,GROSS: INTEGER;
    (include declaration of TOTAL procedure here)
    BEGIN
       FOR I:=1 TO 5 DO
          READ(INVOICE[I]);
       TOTAL(INVOICE,5,GROSS);
       WRITELN(' GROSS=',GROSS)
    END.
$DATA
 25  36  21  7  2
```

The output will be

```
   GROSS=       91
```

In this example, notice that the actual parameter INVOICE is in correspondence with the parameter LIST. The declaration of LIST must be of the same type as INVOICE. This type, namely INTARRAY, is defined in the main program. It is a user-defined type.

In this example, we have a constant 5 as the actual in correspondence with the value parameter N. When the procedure is entered, N is assigned the actual parameter's value, which is 5. After that N can be used or changed without any effect on the actual parameter.

When the TOTAL procedure is called, the entire INVOICE array is copied into the LIST array, because LIST is a value parameter. Copying of big arrays is inefficient and can be avoided by

declaring the array formal parameter using VAR. With VAR we have
a variable parameter instead of a value parameter, so instead of
copying all of INVOICE into LIST, a pointer to INVOICE is used
instead.   With this change, our TOTAL procedure still works as
before. References in the procedure to LIST[1] will then point
at INVOICE[1]. There is no location in the memory identified by
LIST[1], but there is for INVOICE[1], and LIST[1] simply points
to INVOICE[1].

Pascal requires that the type of each formal parameter be
given by a type identifier. For example, the following would not
be allowed

PROCEDURE TOTAL (LIST: ARRAY[1..10] OF INTEGER; etc)

We avoided this problem by using

TYPE INTARRAY=ARRAY[1..10] OF INTEGER;

in the main program and then declaring LIST to be of type
INTARRAY. In a similar way, the result type of a function must
be given by a type identifier and for functions this type cannot
be an array or record; we will talk about records in a later
chapter.

GLOBAL AND LOCAL VARIABLES

Any variable declared inside a procedure is said to be local
to that procedure. It is a local variable. Variables declared
in a main program are available by the same name to all
subprograms whose declaration is nested in the main program.   We
say that variables declared in the surrounding program are global
to the nested program. Notice that the same variable identifier
I is used in the main program BILL and also as a local variable
in the procedure TOTAL. These are treated as absolutely separate
variables.   These is no need to worry about accidental
coincidences between names of local and global variables. Inside
the procedure, the local one is used exclusively. Outside the
procedure, the one local to the procedure is not visible.

The statements inside a subprogram can use variables declared
in the surrounding program without passing them through the
parameter list.   We have not done this in any example so far,
because our purpose in having subprograms was to separate the
parts of the program completely; the only communication has been
through the list of parameters. Sometimes, if a great deal of
information is to be passed, and if the procedure is being
custom-made exclusively for your own program, it is appropriate
for the subprogram to reference variables that are declared only
in the main program. Remember we call such variables global to
the subprogram since they are declared in a surrounding program.
Variables that are declared in the subprogram are said to be

<u>local</u> to that subprogram. Sometimes we refer to the <u>scope</u> of a variable. The scope of a local variable in the subprogram is the subprogram itself. A global variable has a larger scope; its scope is the main program and the subprogram. Variables are considered local or global depending upon where they are declared; similarly user-defined constants, types and subprograms are also either local or global. A procedure can both change and read global variables but a function should only read them.

CHAPTER 11 SUMMARY

In this chapter we have introduced subprograms. Subprograms allow us to build up programs out of modules. The reasons for using subprograms in programs include the following:

1. Dividing the program into parts which can be written by different people.

2. Dividing a program into parts which can be written over a period of time.

3. Making a large program easier to understand by building it up out of conceptually simple parts.

4. Factoring out common parts of a program so they need not be written many times within a program.

5. Factoring out commonly-used logic so that it can be used in a number of different programs.

6. Separating parts of a program so they can be individually tested.

There are two kinds of subprograms in Pascal: procedures and functions. Essentially, a procedure provides a new kind of Pascal statement and a function provides a new kind of operation. The following important terms were discussed in this chapter.

Subprogram declaration - means giving the meaning of a subprogram to the computer. Subprogram declarations in Pascal must come after constant definitions, type definitions, and variable declarations. Procedures can be declared using the following form:

```
PROCEDURE identifier[([VAR] identifier|,identifier|:type
         |;[VAR] identifier|,identifier|:type|)];
   [constant declaration]
   [type declaration]
   [variable declaration]
   |subprogram declaration|
   BEGIN
      statement|;statement|
   END;
```

The curly brackets indicate zero or more repetitions of what is inside them. The square brackets indicate that the enclosed item is optional. Procedures may have no parameters whatsoever in which case the procedure's identifier has no list in parentheses following it.

Functions can be declared using the following form:

```
FUNCTION identifier[(identifier|,identifier|:type
        |;identifier|,identifier|:type|)]:type;
   [constant declaration]
   [type declaration]
   [variable declaration]
   |subprogram declaration|
   BEGIN
      statement|;statement|
   END;
```

If a function has no parameters, the parameters and their enclosing parentheses are omitted. Functions must not have any variable parameters. The function is given a value by assigning to its name in the function's body. The type of a function is given following the list of formal parameters and must be a named type.

Procedure (or function) name - follows the rules for variable identifiers.

Calling a procedure (invoking a procedure) - causing a procedure to be executed. A procedure is called by a statement of the form

        procedure name(actual parameters);

If the procedure has no formal parameters, then the actual parameters with their enclosing parentheses are omitted. A function is called by using its name, followed by a parenthesized list of actual parameters if required, in an expression. Value actual parameters may be any expressions which yield a value of the right type. VAR actual parameters must be variables.

Returning from a procedure or function - terminating the execution of a subprogram and passing control back to the calling place. When the end of a procedure is reached, there is a return to the statement just beyond the calling statement. After a function is finished it causes the returned value to be used in the expression containing the function reference.

Actual parameters - A call to a procedure or function can pass it actual parameters. These must be the same in number, sequence, and type as the formal parameters.

Formal parameters - the list of parameters that are to be used by the procedure and produced as results. Information to be used can be passed in through a value parameter; information passed out <u>must</u> go through a variable parameter. Declarations of variable parameters are prefaced by the keyword VAR. All parameters must be typed in the procedure heading. Parameters that are arrays must be given a type that is named in the calling procedure. The parameter type is given after the identifier of the parameter and separated from it by a colon.

Value parameters - those formal parameters in a procedure or function heading that are not preceded by the keyword VAR are passed to the procedure as values. The actual arguments corresponding to value parameters can be any expression that evaluates to a value of the same type as the formal parameter.

Variable parameters - those formal parameters in a procedure heading that are preceded by the keyword VAR. Assignments may be made to variable parameters in the procedure and such assignments are equivalent to assignments to the actual parameter that is in correspondence with the formal variable parameter. Functions may not have variable parameters.

Scope - of a variable is the extent of the program over which the variable is meaningful. Local variables have a meaning only within the subprogram where they are declared.

CHAPTER 11 EXERCISES

1. What does the following program print? What are the formal
parameters and actual parameters in this program?

```
PROGRAM NUMBERS (INPUT,OUTPUT);
    VAR I,MAGNITUDE: INTEGER;
    PROCEDURE ABSOLUTE(K: INTEGER; VAR L: INTEGER);
        BEGIN
            IF K>=0 THEN
                L:=K
            ELSE
                L:=-K
        END;
    BEGIN
        FOR I:=-2 TO 2 DO
            BEGIN
                ABSOLUTE(I,MAGNITUDE);
                WRITELN(MAGNITUDE)
            END
    END.
```

2. What does the following program print? What are the parameters
and arguments in this program?

```
$JOB    'TOM HULL'
 PROGRAM WEATHER (INPUT,OUTPUT);
    TYPE REALARRAY=ARRAY[1..31] OF REAL;
    VAR TEMPERATURE,RAIN: REALARRAY;
        DAY,TIME: INTEGER;
    PROCEDURE AVERAGE(VAR LIST: REALARRAY; HOWMANY: INTEGER);
        VAR TOTAL: REAL;
            I: INTEGER;
        BEGIN
            TOTAL:=0;
            FOR I:=1 TO HOWMANY DO
                TOTAL:=TOTAL+LIST[I];
            WRITELN(TOTAL/HOWMANY)
        END;
    BEGIN
        READ(TIME);
        FOR DAY:=1 TO TIME DO
            READ(TEMPERATURE[DAY],RAIN[DAY]);
        WRITE(' AVERAGE TEMPERATURE:');
        AVERAGE(TEMPERATURE,TIME);
        WRITE(' AVERAGE RAINFALL:');
        AVERAGE(RAIN,TIME)
    END.
$DATA
 5  45.0  0  47.2  0  48.0  0.3  47.5  2.1  48.0  0
```

3. Write a procedure that reads an array of names counting how many it gets and another which sorts the array of names into alphabetic order. For example, your procedure could be used in the following program:

```
PROGRAM ORDER(INPUT,OUTPUT);
    TYPE NAMETYPE=PACKED ARRAY[1..20] OF CHAR;
        LISTTYPE=ARRAY[1..100] OF NAMETYPE;
    VAR WORKERS: LISTTYPE;
        I,NUMBER: INTEGER;
    PROCEDURE READLIST(VAR COUNT: INTEGER ; VAR PEOPLE : LISTTYPE);
        (you write this part)
        END;
    PROCEDURE SORT(LENGTH: INTEGER; VAR NAMES: LISTTYPE);
        (You write this part)
        END;
    BEGIN
        READLIST(NUMBER,WORKERS);
        SORT(NUMBER,WORKERS);
        FOR I:=1 TO NUMBER DO
            WRITELN(WORKERS[I])
    END.
```

4. What does the following procedure do? Write a small program which uses this procedure.

```
PROCEDURE METRIC( VAR LENGTH: REAL);
    BEGIN
        LENGTH:=2.54*LENGTH
    END;
```

5. What does the following procedure do? Write a small program which uses this procedure.

```
FUNCTION CONVERT(VAR INCHES: REAL): REAL;
    BEGIN
        CONVERT:=2.54*INCHES
    END;
```

Chapter 12
MODULAR PROGRAMMING

In the last chapter we learned how to use subprograms in the
Pascal language. One of the important purposes of subprograms in
programming languages is to divide programs into parts - parts
that are convenient to use and easy to understand. This idea of
dividing a program into parts is called modular programming. In
this chapter we will show how a program can be divided into
convenient modules; each of these modules will be a procedure.

A PROBLEM IN BUSINESS DATA PROCESSING

We will illustrate modular programming by solving a problem
which might arise in a small business. Suppose that Acme
Automotive Supplies uses a computer to help keep track of its
customers' accounts. For each customer, there is an account
card, giving the customer's name, account number, credit limit
and balance owing to Acme.

For example, Cooks Garage has account number 14 and presently
owes $28.32 to Acme. Cooks Garage is allowed a credit limit of
$200.00; this means that if Cooks Garage is less than $200.00
behind in paying its bills to Acme, Acme will not press for
payment. This information is recorded on a punched card as
follows:

COOKS GARAGE   14   20000   2832

A field of width 15 characters is reserved at the beginning of
the card for the customer's name. Because it is the first item
on the card we can count on blanks to be present in the input if
the name is less than 15 characters. To avoid the use of decimal
points, a dollar amount such as $200.00 is given in cents as
20000.

The payments to Acme from its customers are recorded on
<u>transaction cards</u>. Each transaction card gives a customer's
account number and the amount of a payment by the customer. For
example, the card

       14   2832

records the fact that $28.32 was received from the customer with
account number 14. Since Cooks Garage corresponds to the account
number 14, this means that Cooks Garage has paid $28.32 to Acme.

The account manager for Acme needs a program to read the
account cards and the month's transaction cards and print the
accounts as they stand after the payments. For example, suppose
that corresponding to the account card

       COOKS GARAGE   14   20000   2832

there is only the one transaction card

       14   2832

The account manager would like the program to print the fact that
account number 14, for Cooks Garage, has a credit limit of 20000
and a current balance owing of 0. The program is supposed to
read data such as:

       COOKS GARAGE   14   20000   2832
       JONES REPAIR   6   5000   8240
       ...   (more account cards)
       XXX   -1   0   0   (dummy account card)
        6   1000
       14   2832
        6   1000
       ...   (more transaction cards)
       -1   0   (dummy transaction card)

The program is to print the updated accounts; a report such as
the following should be printed.

                    ACME AUTOMOTIVE SUPPLIES
                      ACCOUNTING REPORT

       CUSTOMER   ACCOUNT NO.   CREDIT LIMIT   BALANCE

       COOKS GARAGE   14   20000   0
       JONES REPAIR   6   5000   6240
            ...

The account manager says that Acme has accounts for 16 customers.
He has told us that each customer has one account card and that
an account number can be any number from 1 to 999. The
transaction records are not in any particular order, and the

number of payments by a particular customer each month varies widely - from no payment to quite a number of payments.

DIVIDING THE PROGRAM INTO PARTS

We need a program which reads the accounts, updates them using the month's transactions and prints the updated accounts. We start designing our program by dividing it into the three parts:

```
Read accounts;
Update accounts;
Print accounts
```

Since Pascal does not provide a statement, "Read accounts," we will write a Pascal procedure called READACCOUNTS. Our procedure will have the following form:

```
PROCEDURE READACCOUNTS;
    (declarations local to READACCOUNTS)
    BEGIN
        (statements)
    END;
```

Similarly, we will write Pascal procedures called UPDATEACCOUNTS and PRINTACCOUNTS. Assuming these three procedures are available, then we can write:

```
READACCOUNTS;
UPDATEACCOUNTS;
PRINTACCOUNTS
```

If our three procedures are written correctly, then this sequence of three statements will solve our business data processing problem.

We have divided our program into three parts, or modules. Now we need to provide data so the parts can communicate.

COMMUNICATION AMONG MODULES

The procedure READACCOUNTS must have a place to store the information from the account cards, so this information can be used by the procedure UPDATEACCOUNTS. Similarly, the UPDATEACCOUNTS procedure must store the updated account information, so it can be printed by the PRINTACCOUNTS procedure.

To meet these communication needs, we can declare arrays for the account numbers, customer names, credit limits and balances. The following declaration creates the desired arrays:

```
CONST MAXACCOUNTS=20;
   NAMESIZE=15;
   DUMMY=-1;  (* MARKS END OF DATA *)
TYPE RANGE=1..MAXACCOUNTS;
   NAMETYPE=PACKED ARRAY[1..NAMESIZE] OF CHAR;
VAR CUSTOMER: ARRAY[RANGE]OF NAMETYPE;
   ACCOUNTNUMBER,CREDITLIMIT,BALANCE: ARRAY[RANGE]OF INTEGER;
```

For possible future growth, we have allowed for more accounts than Acme's present 16 accounts. The upper limit of 20 for the arrays provides room for 19 accounts plus a dummy account. We checked with the account manager to verify that 15 characters are enough to record each customer's name.

We will use MAXACCOUNTS instead of 20 in our program. This is so that the present limit on the number of accounts can be easily increased by making a single change to our program, namely to the definition of MAXACCOUNTS. We will also use NAMESIZE instead of 15 and DUMMY instead of -1 so we can easily change the field size for customer's names and the end-of-file marker. This shows how CONST definitions can be used to isolate a particular limit or decision so it can be conveniently modified later. In many cases, definitions of constants, types and subprograms are used in an analogous way to facilitate program maintenance.

We will place definitions in the main procedure, making them global. This allows the procedures READACCOUNTS, UPDATEACCOUNTS and PRINTACCOUNTS to access the arrays. The overall program organization is:

```
(* READ, UPDATE AND PRINT ACCOUNTS FOR ACME *)
(*     AUTOMOTIVE SUPPLIES.                  *)
PROGRAM ACCOUNT (INPUT,OUTPUT);
   (declarations, such as for the ACCOUNTNUMBER array,
      used for communication among procedures)
   PROCEDURE READACCOUNTS;
      (declarations local to READACCOUNTS)
      BEGIN
         (statements)
      END;
   (definition for the UPDATEACCOUNTS procedure)
   (definition for the PRINTACCOUNTS procedure)
   BEGIN
      READACCOUNTS;
      UPDATEACCOUNTS;
      PRINTACCOUNTS
   END.
```

The procedure READACCOUNTS will finish by reading the dummy account card into the arrays. The procedures UPDATEACCOUNTS and PRINTACCOUNTS will recognize the end of the list of accounts when they encounter the dummy account number -1.

The three procedures communicate by changing and inspecting the arrays. First, the READACCOUNTS procedure reads the information on the account cards into four arrays. Next, the

UPDATEACCOUNTS procedure reads the transaction cards and updates the account information accordingly. This updating will modify the BALANCE array, but does not change the other three arrays. Finally, the PRINTACCOUNTS procedure prints the updated accounts. Note that this procedure does not change any of the four arrays.

WRITING THE MODULES

We are now ready to write the procedures because we have designed the overall program structure and the data to be used for communication among the three procedures.

We will start the READACCOUNTS procedure by writing a comment to explain its purpose:

```
(* READ ACCOUNT CARDS INTO THE ARRAYS CUSTOMER,      *)
(*       ACCOUNTNUMBER, CREDITLIMIT AND BALANCE       *)
```

Immediately following this comment will come the line:

```
PROCEDURE READACCOUNTS;
```

Next will come the declarations for variables that are local to the READACCOUNTS procedure. We are not ready to write these declarations, because we have not yet designed the body of the procedure.

The procedure requires a loop such as the following, which repeatedly reads account cards.

```
Loop initialization;
WHILE(There are more account cards)DO
    BEGIN
        Read another card
    END;
```

We can fill up the arrays starting with item 1, then item 2 and so on. We will declare a variable called ITEM to keep track of the number of the item. The body of the loop, "Read another card," will use READ statements to read information from the account cards. But the loop body must also get ready for the reading of the next card, and it must provide information to be tested to see if "There are more account cards." This can be accomplished by writing the loop body this way:

```
FOR J:=1 TO NAMESIZE DO
    READ(CUSTOMER[ITEM][J]);
READLN(ACCOUNTNUMBER[ITEM],CREDITLIMIT[ITEM],BALANCE[ITEM]);
ACCOUNT:=ACCOUNTNUMBER[ITEM];
ITEM:=ITEM+1;
```

We will declare ACCOUNT to be an integer variable; the loop is terminated when ACCOUNT becomes -1. We now write "Loop initialization" so that the loop is started correctly, and we have:

```
ITEM:=1;
(* SET ACCOUNT SO LOOP WILL START PROPERLY *)
ACCOUNT:=0;
WHILE ACCOUNT<>DUMMY DO
    BEGIN
        FOR J:=1 TO NAMESIZE DO
            READ(CUSTOMER[ITEM][J]);
        READLN(ACCOUNTNUMBER[ITEM],CREDITLIMIT[ITEM],
            BALANCE[ITEM]);
        ACCOUNT:=ACCOUNTNUMBER[ITEM];
        ITEM:=ITEM+1
    END
```

This sequence of Pascal statements has the meaning:

> Read in the account cards together with the dummy account card;

The variable ITEM is left having as its value one more than the number of accounts.

This completes the writing of the READACCOUNTS procedure. Putting the pieces together, it looks like this:

```
(* READ ACCOUNT CARDS INTO THE ARRAYS CUSTOMER,      *)
(*     ACCOUNTNUMBER, CREDITLIMIT AND BALANCE        *)
PROCEDURE READACCOUNTS;
    VAR ITEM,ACCOUNT,J: INTEGER;
    BEGIN
        ITEM:=1;
        (* SET ACCOUNT SO LOOP WILL START PROPERLY *)
        ACCOUNT:=0;
        WHILE ACCOUNT<>DUMMY DO
            BEGIN
                FOR J:=1 TO NAMESIZE DO
                    READ(CUSTOMER[ITEM][J]);
                READLN(ACCOUNTNUMBER[ITEM],CREDITLIMIT[ITEM],
                    BALANCE[ITEM]);
                ACCOUNT:=ACCOUNTNUMBER[ITEM];
                ITEM:=ITEM+1
            END
    END;
```

We have written the READACCOUNTS procedure using step-by-step refinement. We started by deciding the purpose of the procedure. Then we divided the procedure into pieces. Finally, we wrote the pieces in Pascal.

We will not give detailed descriptions of the writing of the UPDATEACCOUNTS and PRINTACCOUNTS procedures. Similar methods can be used in writing those two procedures.

THE COMPLETE PROGRAM

Assuming the other two procedures have been written, we can put the pieces together to make the program given here.

```
(* READ, UPDATE AND PRINT ACCOUNTS FOR ACME *)
(*     AUTOMOTIVE SUPPLIES *)
PROGRAM ACCOUNT (INPUT,OUTPUT);
   CONST MAXACCOUNTS=20;
      NAMESIZE=15;
      DUMMY=-1;  (* MARKS END OF DATA *)
   TYPE RANGE=1..MAXACCOUNTS;
      NAMETYPE=PACKED ARRAY[1..NAMESIZE] OF CHAR;
   VAR CUSTOMER: ARRAY[RANGE]OF NAMETYPE;
      ACCOUNTNUMBER,CREDITLIMIT,BALANCE: ARRAY[RANGE]OF INTEGER;

   (*READ ACCOUNT CARDS INTO THE ARRAYS CUSTOMER, *)
   (*  ACCOUNTNUMBER, CREDITLIMIT AND BALANCE *)
   PROCEDURE READACCOUNTS;
      (exactly as given previously)
      END;

   (*READ TRANSACTION CARDS AND UPDATE THE ACCOUNTS *)
   PROCEDURE UPDATEACCOUNTS;
      VAR ITEM,ACCOUNT,PAYMENT: INTEGER;
      BEGIN
         READLN(ACCOUNT,PAYMENT);
         WHILE ACCOUNT<>DUMMY DO
            BEGIN
               ITEM:=1;
               WHILE(ACCOUNTNUMBER[ITEM]<>ACCOUNT) AND
                     (ACCOUNTNUMBER[ITEM]<>DUMMY) DO
                  ITEM:=ITEM+1;
               IF ACCOUNTNUMBER[ITEM]=ACCOUNT THEN
                  BALANCE[ITEM]:=BALANCE[ITEM]-PAYMENT
               ELSE
                  WRITELN(' ERRONEOUS TRANSACTION ACCOUNT:',
                     ACCOUNT);
               READ(ACCOUNT,PAYMENT)
            END
      END;

   (* PRINT THE ACCOUNTS *)
   PROCEDURE PRINTACCOUNTS;
      VAR ITEM: INTEGER;
      BEGIN
         WRITELN('          ACME AUTOMOTIVE SUPPLIES');
         WRITELN('            ACCOUNTING REPORT');
         WRITELN;
```

```
            WRITELN(' CUSTOMER        ','ACCOUNTNO.        ',
               'CREDIT LIMIT       ','BALANCE');
            WRITELN;
            ITEM:=1;
            WHILE ACCOUNTNUMBER[ITEM]<>DUMMY DO
               BEGIN
                  WRITELN(' ',CUSTOMER[ITEM],ACCOUNTNUMBER[ITEM]:5,
                     CREDITLIMIT[ITEM]:15,BALANCE[ITEM]:15);
                  ITEM:=ITEM+1
               END
        END;

  (* MAIN PROGRAM: READ, UPDATE AND PRINT ACCOUNTS *)
  BEGIN
     READACCOUNTS;
     UPDATEACCOUNTS;
     PRINTACCOUNTS
  END.
```

In this program we used local and global variables to our advantage. The arrays are declared in the main program so they are available to the READACCOUNTS, UPDATEACCOUNTS and PRINTACCOUNTS procedures. We made some variables, such as PAYMENT, local to the procedures using them. Although we declared three variables named ITEM, they are kept separate by Pascal because they were declared in different procedures.

USING MODULES

In our example, we divided our program into three modules, namely, the READACCOUNTS, UPDATEACCOUNTS and PRINTACCOUNTS procedures.

```
  (* MAIN PROGRAM: READ, UPDATE AND PRINT ACCOUNTS *)
  BEGIN
     READACCOUNTS;
     UPDATEACCOUNTS;
     PRINTACCOUNTS
  END.
```

This main procedure is very easy to understand because it specifies the order of using the modules, without giving internal details about the modules. These details are important, but are best understood separately, in the definitions of the modules. Many of these details can be changed inside a particular module without changing either the main procedure or our understanding of the program's overall structure.

Programs that process business data typically have an organization similar to that of our example. In particular, they are often based on a set of modules which are called by a main program. For larger and more complex programs, individual modules may be composed of sub-modules, the sub-modules may be composed of sub-sub-modules, and so on.

Our example is not a large program.   Even though it is
relatively small, we have been able to make it simple by dividing
it   into distinct parts.   It is almost impossible for programmers
to write, understand or modify a large, complex program unless
the program is divided into distinct parts, each having a
relatively simple purpose.

MODIFYING A PROGRAM

It is common for programs to be changed during their
lifetimes.   Sometimes a change is required to fix errors in the
program.   Sometimes a change is required because the purpose of
the program is changed.   In our program for Acme Automotive
Supplies we used named constants so certain changes could be made
by changing a single number.   For example, we can change the
width of names by changing 15 in the definition of NAMESIZE,
instead of searching for all occurrences of 15 in the program.

Perhaps the account manager for Acme discovers that in
addition to the printing of all updated accounts, he needs a
separate list of customers whose credit limits have been
exceeded.   This is an example of exception reporting; such
reporting helps managers by listing only those items that require
action.

When a useful program is modified, we call this program
maintenance.   We do not maintain a program because it wears out!
Instead, we maintain a program when there are new requirements
for the program or there are errors in the program.

As an example of a program modification, we will take the
situation in which a credit exception report is required by the
Acme account manager.   The program must list those customers
whose balance owing is greater than their credit limit.   We
already have modules which read accounts, update them and print
them.   Given the updated accounts, we need a module which prints
the names of customers with exceeded credit.   The main procedure
is changed to this sequence of procedure statements:

```
READACCOUNTS;
UPDATEACCOUNTS;
PRINTACCOUNTS;
PRINTCREDITEXCEPTIONS;
```

Using our old program, we add a new procedure named
PRINTCREDITEXCEPTIONS and invoke this procedure.

We are able to produce a program to print credit exceptions
very easily.   This is because our old program is easy to
understand and thus easy to modify.

Since our program is modular, we can use the pieces - the
modules - to build new programs.   Suppose the Acme account
manager decides he needs a list of accounts both before and after

the update. We can easily modify our program to meet this requirement by changing the calls to:

```
READACCOUNTS;
PRINTACCOUNTS;
UPDATEACCOUNTS;
PRINTACCOUNTS;
(more procedure statements)
```

We simply use the PRINTACCOUNTS procedure twice - before and after using UPDATEACCOUNTS. No modules need to be added or changed.

CHAPTER 12 SUMMARY

In this chapter we showed how modular programming can be used in solving a simple problem in data processing. We developed a program containing three modules to solve the problem. Each of these modules was a Pascal procedure.

The overall structure of our program was designed using step-by-step refinement. Once we had stated the data processing problem to be solved, we refined the idea "solve the problem" into the three steps:

```
Read accounts;
Update accounts;
Print accounts
```

We wrote three modules to carry out these steps.

Modules should be designed to perform conceptually simple activities, and they should use their parameters and any shared variables in a straightforward manner. When a program has been carefully divided into good modules, it can be easily understood and maintained.

CHAPTER 12 EXERCISES

All the exercises for this chapter are based on the program which reads, updates and prints accounts for Acme Automotive Supplies. Each exercise asks you to modify the program; you may need to add new modules, change or improve old modules or change the main program. When making these changes, be sure that old comments are appropriately modified and new comments are added as needed.

1. Add a new procedure named PRINTCREDITEXCEPTIONS that prints each account having a balance greater than its credit limit. Write the main program so that the accounts are read and updated, then the credit exceptions are printed and then all of the accounts are printed. Test the modified program.

2. Make modifications so that the number of accounts and the number of transactions are printed before the listing of accounts. Test the modified program.

3. Make the program less vulnerable to data errors by having it check for and report the following problems:

(a) More accounts than can be stored in the arrays.

(b) Negative credit limits.

(c) Unlikely payments - negative or more than $999.99.

Test the modified program.

4. Modify the program so that it prints the total of the balances of the accounts. Test the modified program.

Chapter 13
SEARCHING AND SORTING

When a large amount of information is stored in a computer, it must be organized so that you are able to get at the information to make use of it. This problem of data retrieval is at the heart of all business operations. Records are kept of employees, customers, suppliers, inventory, in-process goods, and so on. These records are usually grouped in some way into what are called files. We might have, for example, a file of employee records, a file of customer records, an inventory file, and so on. Each file must be kept up to date.

A file that we all have access to is printed in the telephone book. It consists of a series of records of names, addresses, and telephone numbers. We say that there are three fields in each of these records: the name field, the address field, and the phone-number field. The file is in the alphabetic order of one of the three fields, the name field. We say that the name field is the key to the ordering of the file. The file is in alphabetic order on this field because that is how it can be most useful to us for data retrieval. We know someone's name and we want his phone number. We might also want his address and that too is available. The telephone company also has the same set of records, ordered using the phone-number field as the key.

In this chapter we will be investigating how a computer can search for information in a file and how records can be sorted.

LINEAR SEARCH

One way to look for data in a file is to start at the beginning and examine each record until you find the one you are looking for. This is the method people use who do not have large files. But for more than about 12 records it is not a good filing system. It will serve as an example to introduce us to the idea of searching mechanically and give us a bad method to compare our better methods to. We will create a file which consists of names

and telephone numbers but the file will not be ordered by either
name or number.

We will keep the file in two one-dimensional arrays, one
called NAME and one called NUMBER. NUMBER[I] will be the correct
telephone number for NAME[I]. We will read this file, then read
a list of names of people whose phone numbers are wanted. Here
is the program to do this job. We are assuming that our file of
names and phone numbers is punched so that the name is left-
justified in the first 20 columns followed by the phone number in
the next 8 columns.

```
$JOB 'DON MCQUARRIE'
 (* LOOK UP PHONENUMBERS IN DIRECTORY *)
 PROGRAM PHONES(INPUT,OUTPUT);
    CONST NAMEWIDTH=20;
        NUMBERWIDTH=8;
        DIRECTORYSIZE=50;
        DUMMY='*';
    TYPE NAMETYPE=PACKED ARRAY[1..NAMEWIDTH] OF CHAR;
        NUMBERTYPE=PACKED ARRAY[1..NUMBERWIDTH] OF CHAR;
        DIRECTORY=ARRAY[1..DIRECTORYSIZE] OF NAMETYPE;
        DIRECTORYINDEX=0..DIRECTORYSIZE;
    VAR NAME: DIRECTORY;
        NUMBER:ARRAY[1..DIRECTORYSIZE] OF NUMBERTYPE;
        FRIEND,BLANKS: NAMETYPE;
        FILESIZE,I: DIRECTORYINDEX;
        J: 0..NAMEWIDTH;
        K: 1..NUMBERWIDTH;
    BEGIN
        (* READ IN FILE OF NAMES AND NUMBERS *)
        I:=0;
        REPEAT
            I:=I+1;
            FOR J:=1 TO NAMEWIDTH DO
                READ(NAME[I][J]);
            FOR K:=1 TO NUMBERWIDTH DO
                READ(NUMBER[I][K]);
            READLN
        UNTIL NAME[I][1]=DUMMY;
        FILESIZE:=I-1;
        FOR J:=1 TO NAMEWIDTH DO
            BLANKS[J]:=' ';
        WHILE NOT EOF DO
            BEGIN (* LOOK UP FRIEND'S NUMBER *)
                FRIEND:=BLANKS;
                J:=0;
                WHILE (NOT EOLN) AND (J<NAMEWIDTH) DO
                    BEGIN
                        J:=J+1;
                        READ(FRIEND[J])
                    END;
                READLN;
                I:=1;
                WHILE(FRIEND<>NAME[I]) AND (I<=FILESIZE)DO
```

```
            I:=I+1;
        IF FRIEND=NAME[I] THEN
            WRITELN(FRIEND,NUMBER[I])
        ELSE
            WRITELN(FRIEND,'UNLISTED')
    END
  END.
$DATA
PERRAULT,R.          483-4865
BORODIN,A.           782-8928
COOK,S.A.            763-3900
ENRIGHT,W.H.         266-1234
*                    999-9999
BORODIN,A.
BERNSTEIN,P.
```

The output will be

```
BORODIN,A.           782-8928
BERNSTEIN,P.         UNLISTED
```

We have stored the phone number as a character string because of the dash between the first three and the last four digits.

TIME TAKEN FOR SEARCH

In the last section we developed a program for a linear search. The searching process consists of comparing the friend's name, FRIEND, with each name in the file of names NAME[1], NAME[2], NAME[3], and so on until either the name is found or the end of the file is reached. For a small file, a linear search like this one may be fast enough, but it can be time-consuming if the file is lengthy.

If there are N records in the file and the name is actually in the file, then on the average there will be N/2 comparisons. The largest number of comparisons would be N if the name were last in the file, the least number would be 1 if the name were first. A file of 1000 names would require 500 comparisons on the average. This gets to look rather formidable. It is for this reason that we do something to cut down on the effort. What we do is to sort the file into alphabetic order and then use a method of searching called binary searching. We will look at sorting later, but first we will see how much faster binary searching can be.

BINARY SEARCH

The telephone book is sorted alphabetically and the technique most of us use for looking up numbers is similar to the technique known as binary searching. We start by opening the book near where we think we will find the name we are looking for. We look at the page that is open and compare any name on it with the name being sought. If the listed name is alphabetically greater we know we must look only between the page we are at and the beginning of the book. We have eliminated the second part of the book from the search. This process is repeated in the part that might contain the name until we narrow the search down to one page.

In binary searching, instead of looking where we think we might find the name, we begin by looking at the name in the middle of the file and discard the half in which it cannot lie. This process cuts the possible number of names to be searched in half at each comparison.

A file of 16 names would require a maximum of 4 comparisons: one to cut the list to 8, another to 4, another to 2, and another to 1. Of course, we might find it earlier, but this is the most work we have to do. It is the maximum number of comparisons. With a linear search of 16 records we might have to make 16 comparisons, although 8 is the average. If we have a file of 1024 records, the binary search takes a maximum of 10 comparisons. This can be calculated by seeing how many times you must divide by 2 to get down to 1 record . Put mathematically, 1024 is equal to

$$2*2*2*2*2*2*2*2*2*2$$

Just one more comparison, making 11 altogether, will let you search a list of 2048 entries. Then 4096 can be done with 12 comparisons.   You can see how much more efficient binary searching can be when the file is a long one.

A PROCEDURE FOR BINARY SEARCH

We will now design a program for doing a binary search and write it so that it can be called as a procedure. When we write

    SEARCH(BASICFILE,KEY,SIZE,LOCATION)

we are asking for the value of LOCATION for which BASICFILE[LOCATION]=KEY, where BASICFILE is an array of items declared as of type NAMETYPE. If the KEY is not in the file, LOCATION will be set to zero.

We will develop the algorithm for the binary search in two stages as an illustration of step-by-step refinement. We will write out our proposed solution in a form that is a mixture of English and Pascal.

```
Set LOCATION to zero in case KEY is not in BASICFILE;
WHILE(there is more of the file to search) DO
    BEGIN
        Find middle of file;
        IF middle value matches KEY THEN
            BEGIN
                Set LOCATION to middle;
                Discard remainder of file
            END
        ELSE
            IF middle value comes after KEY THEN
                Discard last half of remainder of file
            ELSE
                Discard first half of remainder of file
    END;
```

It will be important to know the FIRST and LAST of the remainder of the file at any time in order to establish the MIDDLE and to discard the appropriate half. We initially set FIRST to 1 and LAST to SIZE. Then to find the middle we use

```
MIDDLE:=TRUNC((LAST+FIRST)/2);
```

It will not matter that this division is truncated as the process of finding the middle is approximate when the number of entries in the file is an even number. Refining the expression, "Discard last half of remainder of file," becomes

```
LAST:=MIDDLE-1;
```

and, "Discard first half of remainder of file," becomes

```
FIRST:=MIDDLE+1;
```

Notice that we are discarding BASICFILE[MIDDLE] as well in each case. The procedure can now be written:

```
(* LOCATE KEY USING BINARY SEARCH *)
PROCEDURE SEARCH(BASICFILE:DIRECTORY; KEY:NAMETYPE;
            SIZE:INTEGER; VAR LOCATION:DIRECTORYINDEX);
    VAR FIRST,LAST,MIDDLE: INTEGER;
    BEGIN
        (* SET LOCATION TO ZERO FOR CASE OF KEY NOT IN FILE *)
        LOCATION:=0;
        (* INITIALIZE THE SEARCH LOOP *)
        FIRST:=1;
        LAST:=SIZE;
        (* SEARCH UNTIL FILE IS EXHAUSTED *)
        WHILE FIRST<=LAST DO
            BEGIN
                MIDDLE:=(FIRST+LAST) DIV 2;
                IF BASICFILE[MIDDLE]=KEY THEN
                    BEGIN
                        LOCATION:=MIDDLE;
                        (* DISCARD ALL OF FILE *)
                        FIRST:=LAST+1
                    END
                ELSE
                    IF BASICFILE[MIDDLE]>KEY THEN
                        (* DISCARD LAST HALF *)
                        LAST:=MIDDLE-1
                    ELSE
                        (* DISCARD FIRST HALF *)
                        FIRST:=MIDDLE+1
            END
    END;
```

A program that uses this procedure can now be written. We will
use it to look up telephone numbers. We will replace the
following serial search in the PHONES program:

```
I:=1;
WHILE(FRIEND<>NAME[I]) AND (I<=FILESIZE) DO
    I:=I+1;
IF FRIEND=NAME[I] THEN ...
```

This becomes:

```
SEARCH(NAME,FRIEND,FILESIZE,I);
IF I<>0 THEN ...
```

We are assuming that the file of names is sorted alphabetically.
The procedure SEARCH should be included right after the
declaration of variables in the main program.

You will notice that the binary search program has more
instructions than the linear search that it is replacing. Each
step is more complicated, but the whole process is much faster
for a large file because fewer steps are executed.

SEARCHING BY ADDRESS CALCULATION

We have seen that the efficiency of the searching process is very much improved by having a file sorted. The next method of searching uses data organized in a way so there is "a place for everything, and everything in its place".

Suppose you had a file of N records numbered from 1 to N. If you knew the number of the record, you would immediately know the location. The number would be the index of the array that holds the file entries. Each entry would have a location where it belonged. The trouble usually is to find the location of a record when what you know is some other piece of information such as a person's name.

Files are sometimes arranged so that they are organized on serial numbers that can be calculated from some other information in the record. For example, we could take a person's name and, by transforming it in a certain definite way, change it into a serial number. This transformation often seems bizarre and meaningless, and we say the name is hash-coded into a number. When the number has been determined, the location is then definite and you can go to it without any problem.

Usually with hash coding it happens that several records have the same hash code. This means that, instead of the code providing the address of the exact record you want, what you get is the address of a location capable of containing several different records. We call such a location a bucket or bin. We then must look at the records in the bin to find the exact one we are interested in. Since the number is small they need not be sorted. A linear search is reasonable when the number of items is small.

If fixed-size bins are used to store the file, it is important to get a hash coding algorithm that will divide the original file so that roughly the same number of records is in each bin.

As an example of a hash-coding algorithm, suppose that we had 1000 bins and wanted to divide a file of 10,000 records into the bins. The file might already have associated with each record an identifying number. For example, it might be a Social Insurance number or a student number. These numbers might range from 1 to 1,000,000. One way to divide the records into bins would be to choose the last three digits of the identifying number as the hash code. Another hash code might be formed by choosing the third, fifth, and seventh digit. The purpose is to try to get a technique that gives about the same number of records in each bin. More complicated hashing algorithms may be necessary.

SORTING

We have already developed a sorting program as an example of step-by-step refinement in Chapter 9. The method we used is called a <u>bubble</u> <u>sort</u>. Each pair of neighboring elements in a file is compared and exchanged, to put the element with the larger key in the array location with the higher index. On each exchange pass, the element with the largest key gets moved into the last position. The next pass can then exclude the last position because it is already in order.

We have shown that the binary search technique is much more efficient for a large file than a linear search. In the same way, although a bubble sort is a reasonable method for a small file, it is not efficient for a large file. What we usually do to sort a large file is to divide it into a number of smaller files. Each small file is sorted by a technique such as the bubble sort, then the sorted smaller files are merged together into larger files.

We will look at an example in which two sorted files are merged into a single larger sorted file.

SORTING BY MERGING

We will develop a procedure called MERGE to merge FILE1, which has SIZE1 records ordered on the field KEYFILE1, with FILE2, which has SIZE2 records ordered on the field KEYFILE2, and store it in FILE3. We will invoke this procedure with the statement

    MERGE(KEYFILE1,SIZE1,KEYFILE2,SIZE2,KEYFILE3);

Here is the MERGE procedure:

```
(* MERGE TWO SORTED FILES *)
PROCEDURE MERGE(KEYFILE1:FILETYPE; SIZE1:INTEGER;
     KEYFILE2:FILETYPE; SIZE2:INTEGER; VAR KEYFILE3:FILETYPE);
   VAR I1,I2,I3: INTEGER;
   BEGIN
      I1:=1;
      I2:=1;
      I3:=1;
      (* MERGE UNTIL ALL OF ONE FILE IS USED *)
      WHILE(I1<=SIZE1)  AND  (I2<=SIZE2)DO
         BEGIN
            IF KEYFILE1[I1]<KEYFILE2[I2]THEN
               BEGIN
                  KEYFILE3[I3]:=KEYFILE1[I1];
                  I1:=I1+1
               END
            ELSE
               BEGIN
                  KEYFILE3[I3]:=KEYFILE2[I2];
                  I2:=I2+1
               END;
            I3:=I3+1
         END;
      (* ADD REMAINING ITEMS TO END OF NEW FILE *)
      WHILE I1<=SIZE1 DO
         BEGIN
            KEYFILE3[I3]:=KEYFILE1[I1];
            I1:=I1+1;
            I3:=I3+1
         END;
      WHILE I2<=SIZE2 DO
         BEGIN
            KEYFILE3[I3]:=KEYFILE2[I2];
            I2:=I2+1;
            I3:=I3+1
         END
   END;
```

EFFICIENCY OF SORTING METHODS

The number of comparisons required to merge the two previously sorted files in our example is SIZE1+SIZE2. To sort a file of length N by the bubble sort we can count the maximum number of comparisons that are needed. It is

$$(N-1)+(N-2)+(N-3)+\ldots+1$$

This series can be summed and the result is

$$N(N-1)/2 \quad \text{which is}$$

$$N^2/2 - N/2$$

When N is large, the number of comparisons is about $N^2/2$, since this is very large compared to N/2. We say the execution time of the algorithm varies as N^2; sorting 100 items takes 100 times the number of comparisons that sorting 10 items does. We will now make calculations to see why sorting by merging is useful for long files. To sort a file of N items, by first using a bubble sort on two files N/2 in length then merging, requires $N^2/4-N/2$ for the bubble sort and N for the merge. This makes a combination total of

$$N^2/4 + N/2 \quad \text{comparisons.}$$

Using a bubble sort on the whole file gives a result of

$$N^2/2 - N/2 \quad \text{comparisons.}$$

When N is 100, the bubble sort merge method requires 2,550 comparisons, the straight bubble sort requires 4,950 comparisons. We can keep dividing files and subfiles, sorting them by merging, with further improvements. In the limit we have a <u>successive merge</u> sort that is efficient enough to be used for large files.

                        CHAPTER 13 SUMMARY

     This chapter has presented methods of searching and sorting that are used in computer programs. These methods manipulate <u>files</u> of <u>records</u>. Each record consists of one or more <u>fields</u>.

     A search is based on a <u>key</u>, such as a person's name, that appears as one field in a record of a file. A <u>linear search</u> locates the desired record by starting at the first record and inspecting one record after another until the given key is found. A linear search is slow and should not be used for large files; a faster search method, such as binary search, should be used for large files.

     A <u>binary search</u> requires that the file be ordered according to the key field of the records. An unordered file can be ordered using one of the sorting methods given in this chapter. The binary search inspects the middle record to determine which half of the file contains the desired record. Then the middle record of the correct half is inspected, to determine which quarter of the file contains the desired record, and so on, until the record is located.

     If the key is a number that is identical to the index of the desired record then no searching is required, because the key gives the location of the record. Sometimes the key can be manipulated to create a <u>hash code</u> that locates a small set of records, called a <u>bucket</u>, that includes the desired record.

A file of records can be ordered using the bubble sort. This method repeatedly passes through the file, interchanging adjacent out-of-order records until all records are in order. The bubble sort is slow and should not be used for large files; a faster sorting method, such as sorting by merging, should be used for large files.

A file can be sorted by merging in the following manner. First the file is divided into two sub-files and each of the sub-files is sorted by some method, such as the bubble sort. Then, starting with the first records of the two sub-files, the ordered file is created by passing through the sub-files and successively picking the appropriate (smaller key or alphabetically first key) record. If the sub-files are large, they should be sorted by a fast method, such as a merge, instead of by a bubble sort.

CHAPTER 13 EXERCISES

1. The students for a particular high-school class have their names recorded on cards, for example:

ABBOT, HAROLD

These cards are arranged alphabetically. Another deck of cards contains the names of newly-entered students for the same class; these cards are also alphabetically arranged. Write a program that reads the two sets of cards and prints out all the names alphabetically. Your program should read the smaller deck first and store its names in an array. Then the alphabetized list should be printed at the same time the larger deck is read. Explain why it is better to read the smaller deck first. What is the advantage of printing the list while the second deck is being read, rather than waiting till both decks are read?

2. Do exercise 1 assuming that the large deck is alphabetized, but the small deck is not.

3. Write a program that maintains a "lost and found" service. First the program reads cards giving found objects and the finders' names and phone numbers. For example, this card

SIAMESE CAT MISS MABEL DAVIS 714-3261

means Miss Mabel Davis, having phone number 714-3261, found a Siamese cat. These cards are to be read and ordered alphabetically and then a similar set of cards for losers of objects is to be processed. If a lost object matches a found object, then the program should print the name of the object as well as the finder, the loser and their telephone numbers. Assume the loser cards are not alphabetized. Process each loser card as it is read, using a binary search.

Chapter 14
MAKING SURE THE
PROGRAM WORKS

Throughout this book, we have emphasized structured programming techniques; these include step-by-step refinement, programming without the GO TO statement, choosing good variable names and so on. These techniques make it easier to write correct programs. We have also given techniques for testing and debugging programs. In this chapter we will collect and expand upon these techniques for making sure a program works.

SOLVING THE RIGHT PROBLEM

The specifications for a program tell what the program must do to solve a problem. Before starting to write a program, the programmer needs the detailed specifications for the program. Suppose the problem is to print pay checks for the employees of a company; there is a card giving each employee's name and amount of payment. The programmer needs to know the format of the data on the cards as well as the format for the pay checks. These formats are part of the specifications for the program to print pay checks.

Sometimes the program specifications are not completely agreed upon and written down. If an employee's card indicates an amount of $0.00, this may mean that the employee is on leave and is to receive no pay check. If the programmer does not know the special significance of $0.00 - because the specifications are not complete - he may write a program that prints hundreds of worthless pay checks. All too often programs fail to handle special situations such as $0.00 correctly. If the programmer is in doubt about such a situation, he should check the specifications and make sure they are complete.

DEFENSIVE PROGRAMMING

Errors are sometimes made in the preparation of data for a program. Amounts may be mispunched on cards; more data may be supplied than anticipated. The method of handling data errors may be given in the program specifications, or it may be left to the discretion of the programmer. Sometimes a programmer can write his program so that it detects and reports bad data. This is called defensive programming. Some programs are written to accept absolutely any data; after reporting a bad data item, the program ignores the item or attempts to give it a reasonable interpretation. If a program is written assuming no data errors, bad data items may prevent the program from doing its job. It is the programmer's responsibility to make his program sufficiently defensive to solve the problem at hand.

ATTITUDE AND WORK HABITS

The quality of a computer program is determined largely by the attitudes and work habits of the programmer. Some programmers underestimate the programming task. They write programs too quickly, they do not test their programs sufficiently, and they are too willing to believe that their programs are correct.

Most programs, when first written, contain some errors. This is not surprising when you consider the vast number of possible programming errors and the fallibility of every programmer. The programmer should take the attitude that a program is not correct until it is shown to be correct.

One good method of preparing computer programs is to write them using a soft lead pencil. This allows easy corrections and improvements by erasing and replacing lines. If a major change is required, an entire page should be recopied. The program should be submitted to the computer only when the programmer feels confident that no more changes are required. This method of program preparation can save the programmer a lot of time. The savings come because it is easy to change a program when it is still on paper and fresh in the programmer's mind. Each later change requires the programmer to relearn the program before he can confidently make modifications. A few minutes of desk-checking a program can save hours of debugging time. The programmer who tries to "do it right the first time" comes out ahead, saving his own time and writing programs with fewer errors.

PROVING PROGRAM CORRECTNESS

The most effective way to make sure a program works correctly is to study the program thoroughly. It should be read again and again until the programmer is thoroughly convinced that it is right.

It helps if a second programmer reads and approves the program. Ideally, the second programmer should read the program after its author feels that it is correct, but before it is submitted to the computer. The second reader provides a new point of view and may be able to find typical errors such as incorrect loop initialization.

This process of studying programs to make sure they are correct can be called "proving program correctness". Sometimes programs are proven correct using a mathematical approach; proving that a program is correct is then similar to proving that a theorem in geometry is true. More often, programs are proven correct by a non-mathematical, common-sense approach. The program is considered to have errors until proven correct.

PROGRAMMING STYLE

A program should be easy to read and understand; otherwise the job of studying it to verify its correctness will be hopeless. The programmer should strive for a good <u>programming style</u>, remembering that other readers will be in a hurry and will be critical of sloppiness or unnecessary confusion in the program. It commonly happens that as a programmer makes a program clearer and easier to understand, he discovers ways to improve or correct the program.

It takes work to write programs that are easy to read - just as it takes work to write clear English. Good writing requires care and practice. One way of making programs readable and understandable is to give them a simple organization - so the reader can easily learn the relationship among program parts. We have previously presented step-by-step refinement and modular programming as techniques for designing programs. As well as aiding in the writing of programs, these techniques help make programs easier to read.

USE OF COMMENTS AND IDENTIFIERS

One of the rules of good programming style is this: comments and identifiers should be chosen to help make a program understandable. Comments should record the programmer's intentions for the parts of the program. It is a good idea to write comments as the program is being written.

Better programs require fewer comments, because the program written in Pascal closely reflects the intentions of the programmer. Programs become more difficult to read if they are cluttered with obvious comments such as

```
(* INCREASE N BY 1 *)
N:=N+1;
```

Comments are usually needed to record:

- <u>Overall purpose of a program</u>. What problem the program is to solve. As well, comments may be used to record the program's author and its date of writing.

- <u>Purpose of each module</u>. Similar to the comments for an overall program.

- <u>Purpose of a collection of statements</u>. Such a comment might give the purpose of a loop.

- <u>Assumptions and restrictions</u>. At certain points in a program, assumptions and restrictions may apply to variables and the data. For example, one program part may assume that another program part has set NUMBER_OF_ACCOUNTS to a positive number less than 20 to indicate the number of customer accounts.

- <u>Obscure or unusual statements</u>. As a rule, such statements should be avoided. If they are required they should be explained.

Well-chosen identifiers make a program easier to read. Each identifier should record the function of the named object. For example, an array used to save account numbers should be named ACCOUNTNUMBER and not ARRAY. A procedure used to read accounts should be named READACCOUNTS and not P1 or MARGARET.

If a variable has a very simple purpose, such as indexing through an array, a one-letter name such as I, J or N may be appropriate. This is because these letters are commonly used for indexing in mathematics. But if the index variable has some additional meaning, such as counting input data cards, a longer name may help the reader.

Avoid abbreviations, such as TBNTR for table entry. Avoid acronyms, such as SAX for sales tax. Unless abbreviations or acronyms are well known to the reader before seeing the program, they impose an extra memorization task that interferes with understanding the program.

Avoid meaningless identifiers such as A, B, C, D and TEMP1. A single-letter identifier such as D is sometimes appropriate for a simply-used variable when the name D is relevant, for example, it stands for diameter. Adding a digit such as 1 or 2 to the end of an identifier, as in TEMP1, can be confusing unless it explains the purpose of the named object.

TESTING

After the program has been written and studied to verify its correctness, it should be tested. The purpose of testing is to run the program to demonstrate that it is working properly.

The tests must be chosen with care because only a limited number of them can be run. Consider a program designed to sort any list of 100 names into alphabetic order. Certainly we could not test it exhaustively by trying every possible list of 100 names. We would be testing for years! Rather than exhaustive testing we need to design tests which try every type of situation the program is to handle.

Well-designed tests should point out any errors in the program. Ultimately, testing demonstrates errors better than it demonstrates program correctness.

When testing reveals an error, that is, a <u>bug</u>, in the program, the programmer is faced with a <u>debugging</u> task. We shall present debugging techniques later. Right now, we will give techniques for testing.

The programmer will need to study the program in order to design good tests. The tests should make each statement execute at least once - but this is not enough. Suppose the statement

    AVERAGE:=TOTAL/COUNT;

is tested and computes the desired average. This does not demonstrate that all is well; it may be that in some situations COUNT can become zero. If this statement is executed with COUNT set to zero, the statement does not make sense. So, not only should every statement be executed, but it should be executed for the type of situation it is expected to handle. Care should be taken to:

- <u>Test end conditions</u>. See that each loop is executed correctly the first time and last time through. See that indexes to arrays reach their smallest and largest possible values. Pay particular attention to indexes and counters which may take on the value zero.

- <u>Test special conditions</u>. See that data which rarely occurs is handled properly. If the program prints error messages, see that each situation requiring such a message is tested.

Designing tests to exercise all end conditions and special conditions is not easy - but it is worthwhile in terms of program reliability.

The programmer should be able to tell from test results if the program is executing correctly. Sometimes this is easy because the program prints intermediate results as it progresses. Sometimes the programmer will need to add special printing statements so he can verify that the program is running correctly. These statements can:

Print data as it is read. If there is not too much data, it may be good to have the program print the data as it is read.

Print messages to record the statements being executed. For example, a message might say READING ACCOUNTS PROCEDURE ENTERED.

Print values of variables. This allows the programmer to verify by hand that the values are correct. The best time to print variables is when modules start and when they finish, so the programmer can verify that variables were modified correctly.

Print warnings of violated assumptions. Suppose a procedure is used to set WHERE to the index of the smallest number in a list of 12 numbers. The assumption that WHERE receives a value from 1 to 12 can be tested by

```
IF (WHERE<1) OR (WHERE>12)THEN
    WRITELN(' ERROR:WHERE=',WHERE);
```

Care must be taken to design appropriate printing statements for testing. Too much printing will not be read by the programmer; too little printing will not give the programmer sufficient information about the execution of the program.

Ideally, tests should be designed before the program is submitted to the computer. With the program still fresh in his mind, the programmer can more easily invent tests that try out every statement. Sometimes a programmer discovers that parts of a program are difficult to test; a slight change in the program may overcome this difficulty. It is best to make these changes when the program is still on paper, before time has been invested in punching or mark-sensing the program and submitting it to the computer. Designing tests requires the programmer to read his program with a new point of view. It sometimes happens that this point of view uncovers errors in the program. The best time to fix these errors is when the program is still on paper.

As programs become larger, it becomes increasingly difficult to test them thoroughly. Large programs can be tested by first testing the modules individually. Then the modules are combined into larger modules and these are tested and so on. The process is called bottom-up testing. This method of testing uses specially-written test programs that call the modules with various values of parameters, shared variables and input data.

Whenever a program is modified, it should be retested. All the changed parts should be tested. In addition, it is a good idea to test the entire module containing changes, or even the entire program. The reason is that modifications often require a precise understanding of the surrounding program, and this understanding is sometimes not attained. Very commonly, program modifications introduce errors.

DEBUGGING

A program has bugs (errors) when it fails to solve the problem it is supposed to solve. When a program misbehaves we are faced with the problem of debugging - correcting the error. The program's misbehavior is a symptom of a disease and we must find a cure. Sometimes the symptom is far removed from the source of the problem; erroneous statements in one part of a program may set variables' values incorrectly and trigger a series of unpredicted actions by the program. When the symptoms appear via incorrect program output, the program may be executing in a different module. The programmer is left with a few clues: the incorrect output. He has to solve the mystery and cure the disease. Solving these debugging mysteries can take more time than writing the program.

When a program contains a bug, this means that the programmer made at least one mistake. We can categorize programmer errors as follows:

Errors in making the program machine-readable. If the program is prepared on punch cards, PROCEDURE might be mis-punched as PROCDEURE. These are keypunching errors.

Errors in using the programming language. The programmer did not understand a language construct. For example, to compare two character arrays they must be of the same length.

Errors in writing program parts. Although a particular program part was properly designed, it was not correctly written in Pascal. For example, a loop designed to read in account cards might always execute zero times because of writing the loop's terminating condition incorrectly.

Errors in program design. The program parts and their interactions might be improperly designed. The program designer might forget to provide for the initialization of variables used by some modules. He might overlook the fact that one module, say, PRINTACCOUNTS, should be called only after calling another module, say, READACCOUNTS.

Solving the wrong problem. The programmer did not understand the nature of the problem to be solved. He may have misunderstood the program specifications. Perhaps the specifications were not correct or complete.

This list of possible errors has proceeded from the least serious to the most disastrous. The first type of errors, such as keypunching errors, can be corrected easily once detected. The last type of error, misunderstanding the purpose of the program, may require scrapping the entire program and starting over again.

Some programmers are overly optimistic and immediately conclude that any bugs in their programs are not very serious. Such a programmer is quick to make little changes in his program to try to make the symptoms of the problem disappear. The wise programmer knows that program misbehavior is an indication of sloppiness and that sloppiness leads easily to disastrous errors. He takes program misbehavior as a sign that the program is sick - he gives it a checkup by studying it.

The overly optimistic programmer is forever saying, "I just found the last bug." When the wise programmer finds a bug, he looks for five more.

Many of the least serious errors, such as misspelled keywords, are automatically pointed out by error messages, because the error results in an illegal Pascal program. These errors are usually easy to fix. Some errors are particularly treacherous; they seem to defy attempts to correct them. Here is some advice - some of it repeated from earlier parts of this book - to help you track down treacherous bugs.

<u>Read all error messages</u>. In their hurry to read their program's output, some programmers fail to notice error messages. These messages may pinpoint a bug.

<u>Beware of automatic error repair</u>. Compilers try to make it easier to get programs working by "repairing" errors. For example, the programmer might carelessly write X:=2Y; the compiler might repair this to X:=2; such repairs can save time by allowing more of the program to be compiled and executed on one run. However, these repairs should not be taken as intelligent advice; remember, the compiler has no idea what problem you are trying to solve.

<u>The first error messages may help more than later ones</u>. This is because the first messages are closer to the source of the problem. Later messages may simply indicate that a previous error is still causing trouble.

<u>Beware of confusion between I and 1</u>. Some people can consistently read X:=X+I; to mean increase X by one. Errors like this can be found by reading the program character by character - as a computer does! In general, the human tendency to read what we want to be there, rather what is actually there makes debugging difficult.

<u>Beware of misspellings</u>. Some words are easily misspelled. A person who is concentrating on understanding a program may overlook RECEIPT occasionally spelled as RECIEPT.

<u>Beware of language peculiarities</u>. Pascal was designed to minimize language peculiarities, but it still has some traps for the naive programmer. Among the worst of these are:

(a) <u>Putting a semicolon after THEN</u>. The following lines of Pascal will check to see if X is greater than 2:

```
IF X > 2 THEN;
   Y:=X;
```

Whether this is true or not, Y will be set to X. The semicolon after THEN acts as a null statement, which is executed when X is greater than 2.

(b) <u>Omitting VAR for parameters returning results</u>. The following procedure is intended to change the sign of X in the statement NEGATE(X).

```
PROCEDURE NEGATE(J: REAL);
   BEGIN
      J:=-J
   END
```

Unfortunately, the programmer forgot to put VAR before the declaration of J, so J is a value parameter rather than a variable parameter. As a result, J is given a copy of X's value and this copy is negated without affecting X. The procedure should be corrected by inserting VAR before J:REAL.

If everything else fails in the debugging effort, the programmer is forced to rerun his program to gain more information about the errors. The programmer may add statements to print variables or to trace the program's execution. These statements are designed using the same techniques used in testing to show programs work properly. If the original tests had been carefully enough designed, there is a good chance they would have pinpointed the error and eliminated later time-consuming debugging.

CHAPTER 14 SUMMARY

In this chapter we have listed techniques for making sure a program works. There are a vast number of ways a program can be wrong, so the programmer should learn to be careful at all the stages of program preparation. When a programmer is too hasty to submit his program to the computer, this results in persistent bugs and excessive time spent in debugging. The following important techniques and terminology were presented in this chapter.

Program specifications - explanation of what a program is to do. This should include the forms of the input and output data and the type of calculation or data manipulation to be performed. Essentially, program specifications explain how the computer is to be used to solve a particular problem.

Programming habits - the way a programmer goes about his work. Ideally, he should take the slow but sure approach, completing his program in pencil and thoroughly studying it before submitting it to the computer.

Program correctness - studying a program to verify that it satisfies its specifications.

Programming style - if the style is good, then the program can be easily read and understood.

Use of comments and identifiers - good programming style requires that comments and identifiers be chosen to make a program understandable. Comments should record the programmer's intentions; identifiers should record the function or use of the named object.

Testing - running a program to demonstrate that it meets its specifications. Tests should be designed to try every type of situation the program is to handle. Ultimately, testing is better at demonstrating bugs than demonstrating program correctness.

Debugging - correcting errors in a program. Debugging can be the most difficult and time-consuming part of trying to make a program work. These difficulties can be minimized by using the techniques listed in this chapter.

CHAPTER 14 EXERCISES

1. In this exercise you are to use defensive programming. Modify the program given in chapter 8 so that it will handle errors in the data gracefully. The program reads a list of names and prints the list in reverse order.

2. Try to write a program that is completely correct before you submit it to the computer. Have a friend help you by studying your program for errors after you are convinced that it is free of errors. Record the time you spend preparing the program and record any programming errors you make. Your program should perform one of the following tasks:

(a) The program should read a series of integers followed by the dummy value 99999. Print the sum of the positive integers and the number of negative integers.

(b) The program should read and print a list of alphabetically ordered names. If a name is repeated in the data, it should be printed only once.

Chapter 15
PS/7: FILES AND RECORDS

So far we have spoken about files of records and discussed
the process of searching for particular records. This process
was made more efficient by having the files sorted. We then
looked at ways of sorting files of records. All sorting methods
involve moving records around in the computer memory. In our
sorting examples, we did not really deal with the situation of
sorting records that consisted of more than the one field, namely
the key field of the ordering. In our examples, then, moving the
record meant only moving this one field. In most data processing
applications, records contain a number of fields, and it is
important to be able to write statements in a program to move all
the fields as a single unit. We will be introducing the idea of
a record structure which is a group of several fields designed to
make file processing simple to program.

When large quantities of data have to be processed, it is
impossible to store files of records completely within the main
memory of the computer. It is usual to keep large files in
secondary storage such as magnetic tape or magnetic disk storage.
We must then be able to read records from such a file and write
records into it. We will be looking at the statements in Pascal
that permit us to manipulate files in secondary storage.

RECORDS

A Pascal RECORD is a collection of several fields and is
particularly suitable for records in a file. As a simple
example, suppose that we want to describe each entry in the
telephone book as a record. We would identify the entire record
by the identifier CUSTOMER and the three fields as

```
        CUSTOMER.NAME
        CUSTOMER.ADDRESS
        CUSTOMER.PHONENUMBER
```

Here is a diagram showing the fields:

CUSTOMER

NAME	ADDRESS	PHONENUMBER

The field identifiers are a composite of their own identifiers, NAME, ADDRESS, and PHONENUMBER and the whole record's identifier, CUSTOMER. The composite is constructed by putting a dot, or period, between the record name and the field name.

The record structure would be declared this way.

```
        VAR CUSTOMER:
        RECORD
            NAME: PACKED ARRAY[1..20] OF CHAR;
            ADDRESS: PACKED ARRAY[1..30] OF CHAR;
            PHONENUMBER: PACKED ARRAY[1..8] OF CHAR
        END;
```

This record structure consists of two levels of naming. At the first level we have the identifier of the record structure declared, namely CUSTOMER. The next level has three fields declared. Each of these has its own type. So it is possible to have each field with a different type. Here, all the fields are of type PACKED ARRAY..OF CHAR, but each has a different range.

A record structure is sometimes called the <u>layout</u> of a record.

MOVING RECORDS

One of the reasons for having record structures is that they make it simple to program the movement of a whole record from one place to another. When a move is to take place, the location that will receive the structure must be declared to have exactly the same set of fields. If we want to have two or more different records with the same layout we can describe the layout as a type as in

```
TYPE CUSTOMERTYPE=
    RECORD
        NAME: PACKED ARRAY[1..20] OF CHAR;
        ADDRESS: PACKED ARRAY[1..30] OF CHAR;
        PHONENUMBER: PACKED ARRAY[1..8] OF CHAR
    END;
VAR CUSTOMER,WORKSPACE: CUSTOMERTYPE;
```

The record WORKSPACE will have all the same fields, NAME, ADDRESS and PHONENUMBER. They will be referred to as WORKSPACE.NAME, WORKSPACE.ADDRESS, and so on. We say that the record structures CUSTOMER and WORKSPACE have the same record type.

To move the record CUSTOMER into the record WORKSPACE we need only write

```
        WORKSPACE := CUSTOMER;
```

This is equivalent to the group of assignment statements

```
    WORKSPACE.NAME:=CUSTOMER.NAME;
    WORKSPACE.ADDRESS:=CUSTOMER.ADDRESS;
    WORKSPACE.PHONENUMBER:=CUSTOMER.PHONENUMBER;
```

An entire record can be assigned to another by a single assignment statement only if one record has the same type as the other.

ARRAYS OF RECORDS

Just as other types such an INTEGER may form arrays, records may form arrays. Each member of the array of records has the same type. For the telephone-book records, an array of 100 such records could be declared by

```
    TELEPHONEBOOK: ARRAY[1..100] OF CUSTOMERTYPE;
```

An array of records can be used for grouping records for sorting purposes. A procedure for sorting a group of CUSTOMER records that have been declared in the main procedure will be given. The records are to be sorted on the key PHONENUMBER. The array of records called CUSTOMER will be global to the procedure. The only parameter that the procedure has is NUMBEROFRECORDS. A WORKSPACE record is declared as a local variable with the type CUSTOMERTYPE.

```
PROCEDURE SORT(NUMBEROFRECORDS: INTEGER);
    (* SORT RECORDS BY PHONENUMBER *)
    VAR WORKSPACE: CUSTOMERTYPE;
        I,J: INTEGER;
    BEGIN
        FOR I:=1 TO NUMBEROFRECORDS-1 DO
            FOR J:=1 TO NUMBEROFRECORDS-I DO
                IF CUSTOMER[J].PHONENUMBER > CUSTOMER[J+1].PHONENUMBER
                THEN
                    BEGIN  (* SWAP CUSTOMER[J] AND CUSTOMER[J+1] *)
                        WORKSPACE:=CUSTOMER[J];
                        CUSTOMER[J]:=CUSTOMER[J+1];
                        CUSTOMER[J+1]:=WORKSPACE
                    END
    END;
```

In this example we have an array that contains records. The records in this example contain arrays: the arrays of characters for names, addresses and phone numbers. In general a record can contain any type, including other records.

INPUT AND OUTPUT OF RECORDS

The record is a convenient form for moving the groups of fields around in the main memory of the computer. But we have not yet said how such structures may be read into or written out from the main memory. The input-output statements that we have had so far, the READ and WRITE, can be used to read or print individual fields of a record in exactly the same way as the values of individual variables are read or printed. The next section will show how READ and WRITE can transfer the record as a unit when the program has explicit declarations for files. If you input records from cards, each field is read independently. Here is a program that reads a set of at most 25 customer records, sorts them and prints them:

```
$JOB 'STEPHEN ALEXANDER'
 (* READ, SORT BY NUMBER, AND PRINT CUSTOMER RECORDS *)
 PROGRAM NUMBERS (INPUT,OUTPUT);
    TYPE CUSTOMERTYPE=
       RECORD
          NAME: PACKED ARRAY[1..20] OF CHAR;
          ADDRESS: PACKED ARRAY[1..30] OF CHAR;
          PHONENUMBER: PACKED ARRAY[1..8] OF CHAR
       END;
    VAR WORKSPACE: CUSTOMERTYPE;
       CUSTOMER: ARRAY[1..25] OF CUSTOMERTYPE;
       I,J,NUMBEROFRECORDS: INTEGER;
    (copy procedure SORT here)
    BEGIN
       READLN(NUMBEROFRECORDS);
       (* READ RECORDS INTO ARRAY *)
       FOR I:=1 TO NUMBEROFRECORDS DO
          BEGIN
             FOR J:=1 TO 20 DO
                READ(WORKSPACE.NAME[J]);
             FOR J:=1 TO 30 DO
                READ(WORKSPACE.ADDRESS[J]);
             FOR J:=1 TO 8 DO
                READ(WORKSPACE.PHONENUMBER[J]);
             CUSTOMER[I]:=WORKSPACE;
             READLN
          END;
       (* SORT RECORDS BY PHONENUMBER *)
       SORT(NUMBEROFRECORDS);
       (* PRINT SORTED ARRAY OF RECORDS *)
       FOR I:=1 TO NUMBEROFRECORDS DO
          WRITELN(CUSTOMER[I].PHONENUMBER,
             ' ',CUSTOMER[I].NAME,CUSTOMER[I].ADDRESS)
    END.
$DATA
 5
JOHNSTON,R.L.      53 JONSTON CRES.          491-6405
KEAST,P.           77 KREDLE HAVEN DR.       439-7216
LIPSON,J.D.        15 WEEDWOOD ROAD          787-8515
MATHON,R.A.        666 REGINA AVE.           962-8885
CRAWFORD,C.R.      39 TREATHERSON AVE.       922-7999
```

The output for this program will be

```
439-7216  KEAST,P.        77 KREDLE HAVEN DR.
491-6405  JOHNSTON,R.L.   53 JONSTON CRES.
787-8515  LIPSON,J.D.     15 WEEDWOOD ROAD
922-7999  CRAWFORD,C.R.   39 TREATHERSON AVE.
962-8885  MATHON,R.A.     666 REGINA AVE.
```

In this example we are referring to characters in the three fields of the record named WORKSPACE using the variable names WORKSPACE.NAME[J], WORKSPACE.ADDRESS[J], and WORKSPACE.PHONENUMBER[J]. In Pascal there is a way to avoid repetition of the record name by using the WITH statement. It has the form

```
WITH record name DO
    BEGIN
        statements referencing field name only
    END
```

In our program we could have used this set of statements instead of what we had

```
WITH WORKSPACE DO
    BEGIN
        FOR J:=1 TO 20 DO
            READ(NAME[J]);
        FOR J:=1 TO 30 DO;
            READ(ADDRESS[J]);
        FOR J:=1 TO 8 DO
            READ(PHONENUMBER[J])
    END;
```

FILES IN SECONDARY MEMORY

In our discussion of files so far, we have had the files stored in the main memory. In most real file applications, the files are too large to be contained in main memory. The part of the file being processed must be brought into main memory, but the complete file is stored in secondary memory. The secondary memory may be magnetic tape or magnetic disk.

A file in secondary storage is a collection of values all of the same type. The collection is sometimes called a dataset. One item at a time may be transferred from the dataset to a structure in main memory, or from a structure in main memory to the dataset. The item that is transferred must be the next item in the sequence of records in the dataset. We say that the file can be read sequentially from the secondary memory to the main memory or written sequentially from the main memory to secondary memory. This kind of file is called a sequential file. It is not possible at any moment to get access to an arbitrary item in the file; the next item in sequence is the only one that is available.

Since files in secondary storage are to be accessed sequentially, there must be a statement in the program that will position the file reader at the first item of the dataset. Before a file in secondary storage can be read, we must have a statement of the form

```
RESET(file name);
```

The file name is that of the whole dataset or file. It may, for example, be named OLDFILE. This identifier is declared at the beginning of the procedure by

        VAR OLDFILE: FILE OF CUSTOMERTYPE;

In general, a file may be declared as a FILE OF any type, such as FILE OF INTEGER or FILE OF PACKED ARRAY[1..10] OF CHAR.

    To read the next item from the file in secondary storage, we write a statement of the form

        READ (file identifier,variable);

We can read records from OLDFILE into variables such as CUSTOMER whose type is CUSTOMERTYPE using this statement.

        READ (OLDFILE,CUSTOMER);

    If a file is to be written, it must first be prepared for writing using the statement

        REWRITE(file identifier);

To write a record into such a file, we use a statement of this form

        WRITE (file identifier,expression);

As with input files, an output file must be declared as a FILE and can receive only values (expressions) of the type given following FILE OF.

    Following RESET the file can be read but not written. Following REWRITE the file can be written but not read. Once a file has been written, the program can RESET the file and then read it.

    The names of files used by a program must appear in the program heading statement. In all programs we have shown so far the input came from the card reader (or keyboard input device) and the output went to the printer. These "files" have the standard names INPUT and OUTPUT. That is why we always preface our programs with the line

        PROGRAM identifier(INPUT,OUTPUT);

If in addition to these two files we intend to use files named OLDFILE and NEWFILE our program heading would be

        PROGRAM identifier(INPUT,OUTPUT,OLDFILE,NEWFILE);

If a file is (local), meaning it is created by the program and not saved afterwards, then its name does not need to appear in the program heading.

FILE MAINTENANCE

As an example of reading and writing files we will program a simple file-maintenance operation. We will assume that there exists a file of CUSTOMER records called OLDFILE, and we want to update this file by adding new customers. The information about the new customers is punched on cards. Each card corresponds to a transaction that must be posted in the file to produce an up-to-date customer file, which we will call NEWFILE. This is an example of file maintenance. The file OLDFILE is ordered alphabetically by CUSTOMER.NAME and the transactions are arranged alphabetically. This program will be very similar to the merge-sort program of Chapter 13, except that the records of the two files being merged are not in an array.

```
$JOB 'HARRIET LOGAN'
 PROGRAM UPDATE (INPUT,OUTPUT,OLDFILE,NEWFILE);
    (* ADD NEW CUSTOMERS TO CUSTOMER FILE *)
    CONST DUMMY='ZZZZZZZZZZZZZZZZZZZZ';
    TYPE CUSTOMERTYPE=
         RECORD
            NAME: PACKED ARRAY[1..20] OF CHAR;
            ADDRESS: PACKED ARRAY[1..30] OF CHAR;
            PHONENUMBER: PACKED ARRAY[1..8] OF CHAR
         END;
    VAR OLDFILE,NEWFILE: FILE OF CUSTOMERTYPE;
        CUSTOMER,TRANSACTION: CUSTOMERTYPE;
        J: INTEGER;
    BEGIN
       REWRITE(NEWFILE);
       RESET(OLDFILE);
       (* READ FIRST CUSTOMER RECORD FROM FILE *)
       READ(OLDFILE,CUSTOMER);
       (* READ FIRST TRANSACTION FROM CARD *)
       WITH TRANSACTION DO
          BEGIN
             FOR J:=1 TO 20 DO
                READ(NAME[J]);
             FOR J:=1 TO 30 DO
                READ(ADDRESS[J]);
             FOR J:=1 TO 8 DO
                READ(PHONENUMBER[J])
          END;
       READLN;
       (* POST TRANSACTIONS TO CUSTOMER FILE *)
       WHILE(TRANSACTION.NAME<>DUMMY) OR (CUSTOMER.NAME<>DUMMY) DO
          IF CUSTOMER.NAME>TRANSACTION.NAME THEN
             BEGIN
                WRITE(NEWFILE,TRANSACTION);
                WITH TRANSACTION DO
                   BEGIN
                      FOR J:=1 TO 20 DO
                         READ(NAME[J]);
                      FOR J:=1 TO 30 DO
                         READ(ADDRESS[J]);
                      FOR J:=1 TO 8 DO
                         READ(PHONENUMBER[J])
                   END;
                READLN
             END
          ELSE
             BEGIN
                WRITE(NEWFILE,CUSTOMER);
                READ(OLDFILE,CUSTOMER)
             END;
       (* ADD DUMMY RECORD TO END OF FILE *)
       WRITE(NEWFILE,CUSTOMER)
    END.
$DATA
(transactions one to a card)
ZZZZZZZZZZZZZZZZZZZZ                 NULL                   NULL
```

The DUMMY value of ZZ...Z alphabetically follows any legal names
in the file. This value is used because in the merging loop,
comparisons with DUMMY will force all legal names to be merged
before the DUMMY value.

We can use the function EOF(OLDFILE) to determine when no
more records can be read. The WHILE...DO test can be replaced by
this:

WHILE (NOT EOF) AND (NOT EOF(OLDFILE)) DO

⁎Notice that when EOF has no parameter it applies to the standard
input file.

PASCAL TEXT FILES

The two standard files INPUT and OUTPUT are implicitly
declared as

VAR INPUT,OUTPUT: FILE OF CHAR;

RESET(INPUT) and REWRITE(OUTPUT) are implicitly performed as the
program begins execution.   The program should not explicitly
perform RESET or REWRITE for INPUT or OUTPUT.

A file which is declared as FILE OF CHAR is called a text
file, and can equivalently be declared using the predeclared type
TEXT.   Text files, such as INPUT and OUTPUT are special in that
READ, READLN, WRITE and WRITELN can transfer values other than
the file's type which is CHAR. In particular, INTEGER and REAL
values can be read and INTEGER, REAL and string values can be
written, and formatting can be specified. If F is declared as

VAR F: TEXT

then WRITE(F,'X IS',12:3) is a legal statement.   The first
parameter to WRITE or WRITELN is a TEXT file variable; if the
parameter is omitted, the OUTPUT file is used. Similarly READ
and READLN have as their first parameter a TEXT file variable,
which is taken to be INPUT if omitted. Text files other then
INPUT and OUTPUT must have explicit RESET and REWRITE operations.

CHAPTER 15 SUMMARY

In this chapter we introduced programming language constructs
for manipulating records and using files in secondary memory.
The following important terms were discussed in this chapter:

Record - a collection of fields of information. For example,
    a record might be composed of a name field, an address
    field and a telephone number field.

RECORD type - the Pascal construct for records. For example, this declaration establishes a record type called DIRECTORYENTRY with name, address and telephone-number fields.

```
TYPE DIRECTORYENTRY=
   RECORD
      NAME: PACKED ARRAY[1..20] OF CHAR;
      ADDRESS: PACKED ARRAY[1..30] OF CHAR;
      PHONENUMBER: PACKED ARRAY[1..8] OF CHAR
   END;
VAR CLIENT: DIRECTORYENTRY;
```

CLIENT is a variable whose type is a record.

Array of records - to declare an array of records of the record type DIRECTORYENTRY we use the declaration:

```
VAR PHONEBOOK: ARRAY[1..50] OF DIRECTORYENTRY;
```

This creates an array of 50 records where each record has the same fields as CLIENT. PHONEBOOK[5].NAME refers to the name field of the fifth record in the array.

Assigning records - if two record variables are of the same type as each other, one can be assigned to the other by a single assignment statement. For example, we can write

```
PHONEBOOK[5]:=CLIENT;
```

to assign the three fields of CLIENT to the corresponding three fields of PHONEBOOK[5].

Dataset - a file of information residing on secondary storage, typically on a disk or tape.

Sequential files - files that are always accessed (read or written) in order, from first item to second item to third item and so on.

RESET a file - means to prepare a file for reading by a program. A file in Pascal can be opened for input using:

```
RESET(file name);
```

The file is positioned to its first item (if any). The file can be read but not written.

REWRITE a file - means to prepare a file for writing by a program. A file in Pascal can be opened for output using:

```
REWRITE(file name);
```

The file is positioned to write the first item and
previous contents of the file are lost. The file can be
written but not read.

READ – access the next (or first) value in a file. The READ
statement has the form

        READ (file name, variable);

WRITE – add a record to a file. The WRITE statement has the
        form:

        WRITE (file name, expression);

File declaration – a file that is used in a program can be
        declared using the form

        VAR file name: FILE OF type;

Program heading – programs that use permanent files in
        secondary storage must have the file names listed,
        separated by commas, in the program heading. For
        example, if files named OLDFILE and NEWFILE are to be
        used the heading would be

        PROGRAM name(INPUT,OUTPUT,OLDFILE,NEWFILE);

File maintenance – means to keep a file up to date. This
        involves reading transactions and adding, deleting or
        modifying file records.

WITH statement – when a series of references is made to the
        fields of a single record, rather than referencing each
        field by its full name, namely

        record name . field name

        We can use a WITH statement whose form is

        WITH record name DO
          BEGIN
             statements using field name only
          END

        This cuts down on the length of names and simplifies the
        program.

TEXT file – a file variable declared as TEXT or FILE OF CHAR
        can use the READ, READLN, WRITE and WRITELN operations
        usually associated with the standard input and output
        files.

CHAPTER 15 EXERCISES

The exercises for this chapter are based on a data processing system to be used by Apex Plumbing Supplies. For each of its customers, Apex has a card with the fields:

    Name   (card column 1-20)
    Address   (card column 21-40)
    Balance   (card column 41-50)
    Credit limit   (card column 51-60)

These records are presently on punch cards. However, they are to be transferred to a disk file. A sample of the data is shown:

```
ABBOT PLUMBING      94 N.ELM            3116     50000
DURABLE FIXIT       247 FOREST HILL        0     10000
ERICO PLUMBING      54 GORMLEY          9614      5000
  ...
```

The exercises for this chapter require you to write programs for various parts of the data processing system for Apex.

1. Write a program to read cards and create a master file for Apex Plumbing Supplies.

2. Write a program to read an old version of the master file for Apex, sort the file, creating a new master file that is guaranteed to be in alphabetic order according to the name field.

3. Write a program that takes an existing master file for Apex and creates a new master file by deleting or adding new customer records. For example, the transaction data cards for your program might be

```
DAVIS REPAIR        4361 MAIN           2511     10000
ERICO PLUMBING      DELETE                 0         0
  ...
```

You can assume that these cards are in alphabetic order. If the address field on the account card specifies DELETE, the account is to be deleted from the file.

4. Write a program that reads the Apex master file and prints the list of customers whose balances exceed their credit limits.

5. Write a program that reads the Apex master file and prints a bill for each customer whose balance is greater than zero. For example, for the file record

```
    DAVIS REPAIR        4361 MAIN          2511      10000
```

your program should print

```
TO: DAVIS REPAIR
    4361 MAIN

DEAR SIR OR MADAM:
    PLEASE REMIT $25.11 FOR PLUMBING SUPPLIES.
                 THANK YOU,

                 JOHN APEX, PRES.
                 APEX PLUMBING SUPPLIES
                 416 COLLEGE ST.
```

6. Write a program that updates the master file using billing and payment transactions. A billing transaction is a card of the form

```
name        (columns 1-20)
amount      (columns 41-50)
            (columns 51-80 are blank)
```

For each billing transaction, the balance of the account is to be increased by the specified amount. A payment transaction is a card of the form

```
name        (columns 1-20)
amount      (columns 41-50)
CR          (columns 51-52)
```

For each payment transaction, the balance of the account is to be decreased by the specified amount. The billing and payment cards are not in order, so they should be sorted before creating the new master file.

Chapter 16
DATA STRUCTURES

In the last chapter we introduced the idea of records. By using these data structures we could move a group of items of data around in the computer as a unit. Also, we can have arrays of records.

All of the classifications, variables, arrays of single variables, records, and arrays of records are examples of what we generally call data structures. Just as we systematize our programs by attempting to write well-structured programs, we systematize the way in which data is stored. We structure data.

In this chapter we will describe other structural forms for data and give examples of how these structures are useful to us. We will describe data structures called linked lists and tree structures. There are many kinds of lists, for example stacks, queues, doubly-linked lists, and so on. Tree structures can be limited to binary trees, or may be more general.

Pascal contains a feature called pointers that can be used to implement linked lists but it is possible to implement all of these data structures without pointers using arrays instead. We will do this first and then show how Pascal pointers can be used.

LINKED LISTS

Suppose that we had a file of records stored in an array called DATA. The records are arranged in sequence on some key. For simplicity, we will consider that each record consists only of a single field which is the key to the ordering. We know that if the order is ascending and no two keys are identical, then

DATA[I+1] > DATA[I]

The difficulty with this kind of data structure for a file comes
when a new item is to be added to the file; it must be inserted
between two items.   This means we would have to move all the
items with a key higher than the one to be inserted, one location
on in the array.   For example, you can see what happens when we
insert the word DOG in this list:

	before	after inserting DOG
DATA[1]	CAT	CAT
DATA[2]	DUCK	DOG
DATA[3]	FOX	DUCK
DATA[4]	GOOSE	FOX
DATA[5]	PIG	GOOSE
DATA[6]	-	PIG

Any list that is changing with time will have additions and
deletions made to it. A deletion will create a hole unless
entries are moved to fill the hole.

    When the list changes with time we can use the data structure
called the linked list. In the linked list each item has two
components, the data component and the linking component or link.
(We will be using Pascal pointers to implement links later.) We
associate with each entry in the DATA array an entry in a second
array of integers called LINK. The number stored in LINK[I] is
the index of the next entry in the sequence of the DATA array.
This means that the actual or physical sequence in the DATA array
is different from the logical sequence in the list. Here is an
example showing our previous list as a linked list. The start of
the list is stored in the INTEGER variable FIRST.

	FIRST	3		
DATA[1]	PIG	LINK[1]	0
DATA[2]	FOX	LINK[2]	4
DATA[3]	CAT	LINK[3]	5
DATA[4]	GOOSE	LINK[4]	1
DATA[5]	DUCK	LINK[5]	2
DATA[6]	-	LINK[6]	-

data array   *link array*

Here is a diagram of this:

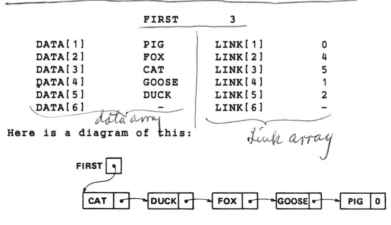

You can follow the list by beginning with the value of FIRST,
which is 3. The first entry will be in DATA[3]; it is CAT.   By
looking then at LINK[3] you find a 5 which is the index of the
next list item, DATA[5], which is DUCK. You follow the list down
until you reach a LINK whose value is 0; this is the signal that
you have reached the end of the list. Other signals can be used,
such as having a negative number.

INSERTING INTO A LINKED LIST

To see the merit of a linked list we must see how to insert new entries. We will add DOG in its proper list position. We will do this first by hand; afterwards we will have to program it for the computer. We will place DOG in DATA[6] since it is an available or free location. We must now change the values of certain of the links so that the new entry will be inserted. We must put a value into LINK[6] and change the value of the LINK of the entry before DOG, which is CAT, to point to DATA[6]. This means that LINK[3] must be changed to 6 and LINK[6] must be set to 5 so that the entry after DOG is DUCK, which is DATA[5].

The linked list then becomes

	FIRST	3		
DATA[1]	PIG		LINK[1]	0
DATA[2]	FOX		LINK[2]	4
DATA[3]	CAT		LINK[3]──→	6
DATA[4]	GOOSE		LINK[4]	1
DATA[5]	DUCK		LINK[5]	2
DATA[6]	DOG		LINK[6]──→	5

changes!

Here is a diagram:

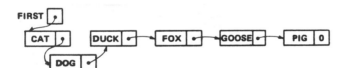

To add DOG, one LINK must be changed and one set. No movement of the existing items in DATA is necessary. This is surely an improvement over moving half the list, on the average, to insert a new entry. The cost of this improved efficiency of operation comes in having to reserve memory space for the LINK array. This array gives the structure of the list and is stored explicitly for a linked list. In an array, the sequence or structure is implicit; each entry follows its neighbor. We will see several other kinds of structures that require us to store the structure information explicitly.

MEMORY MANAGEMENT WITH LISTS

With linked lists, some of the memory is used for structure information and some for data. For any list, as the list grows, we use more memory; as it shrinks, we use less. This means we must reserve enough memory to hold the longest list that we ever expect to have. But we should not waste memory. As we stop using certain elements of the array by deleting entries, we must keep track of where they are, so when additions occur we can

reuse these same elements. To keep track of the available array
elements we keep them together in a second linked list. The list
of available array elements does not have any useful information
in the DATA part, but it is structured as a list using values in
the LINK part. We must keep track of the beginning of this list
so we keep the index of its beginning in a INTEGER variable
AVAILABLE.

   Here is an array of 10 elements that stores our previous data
items in a different set of locations and has the available space
linked up:

	FIRST	10		AVAILABLE	7
DATA[1]	GOOSE		LINK[1]	9	
DATA[2]	FOX		LINK[2]	1	
DATA[3]	–		LINK[3]	6	
DATA[4]	DUCK		LINK[4]	2	
DATA[5]	–		LINK[5]	0	
DATA[6]	–		LINK[6]	5	
DATA[7]	–		LINK[7]	3	
DATA[8]	DOG		LINK[8]	4	
DATA[9]	PIG		LINK[9]	0 ← End	
DATA[10]	CAT		LINK[10]	8	

In these arrays there are two linked lists, one containing the
actual data, the other containing elements available for use.
Each list has a pointer to its start; each has a last element
with a link of 0. Every element of the array is in one list or
the other.

   The next problem is to write a procedure for adding a new
item to the list. We will develop the algorithm for this using
step-by-step refinement.

PROCEDURE FOR INSERTING INTO A LINKED LIST

   The first step is to construct a solution tree. We will
presume the value to be added is in the variable NEWDATA:

```
                        Insert NEWDATA
                        into linked list
                               |
        _____
       |                        |                          |
Obtain storage          Place NEWDATA            Insert storage
element with            in storage element       element with
index NEW from          NEW                      index NEW into
available list                                   the linked list
```

The expansion of the left branch of the solution tree requires us
to find the index NEW of the first element of the list of

available elements and remove the element from the list. Here is the program segment that does this:

```
NEW:=AVAILABLE;
AVAILABLE:=LINK[AVAILABLE];
```

The middle branch is also simple. It is

```
DATA[NEW]:=NEWDATA;
```

We must expand the right branch still further:

```
                    Insert storage
                    element with
                    index NEW into
                    the linked list
                         |
         IF NEWDATA goes first in list THEN
             place element at beginning of list
         ELSE find place to insert NEWDATA
             and adjust links to make insertion
```

NEWDATA will go first in the list if either the list is empty or NEWDATA is less than the first element of the list. So we can write, "IF NEWDATA goes first in list," in this way:

```
IF (FIRST=NULL) OR (NEWDATA<DATA[FIRST]) THEN
```

We have assumed that NULL is a named constant whose value is zero. We can write, "Place element at beginning of list," in this way:

```
BEGIN
    LINK[NEW]:=FIRST;
    FIRST:=NEW
END
```

For the part of the program after the ELSE we need to examine the entries in the list and compare them with NEWDATA. The index of the element being compared we will call NEXT. The index of the previously compared element we will call PREVIOUS. We need to keep track of this previous element, because if

```
NEWDATA < DATA[NEXT]
```

we must insert our element with index NEW between PREVIOUS and NEXT. Here is the program segment for this:

```
      BEGIN
         (* FIND PLACE TO INSERT NEWDATA *)
         PREVIOUS:=FIRST;
         NEXT:=LINK[FIRST];
         WHILE (NEXT<>NULL) AND (NEWDATA>=DATA[NEXT])DO
            BEGIN
               PREVIOUS:=NEXT;
               NEXT:=LINK[NEXT]
            END;
         (* ADJUST LINKS TO MAKE INSERTION *)
         LINK[PREVIOUS]:=NEW;
         LINK[NEW]:=NEXT
      END
```

The whole procedure can now be written out. We are presuming that DATA, LINK, FIRST, and AVAILABLE are global to this procedure. The type of entries in the list is ENTRYTYPE, which could be PACKED ARRAY[1..5] OF CHAR for our example, but the procedure would also be correct for other types such as INTEGER.

```
 (* INSERT NEW DATA INTO LINKED LIST *)
 PROCEDURE INSERT(NEWDATA:ENTRYTYPE);
    VAR NEW,PREVIOUS,NEXT: INTEGER;
    BEGIN
       (* OBTAIN STORAGE ELEMENT FOR NEW DATA *)
       NEW:=AVAILABLE;
       AVAILABLE:=LINK[AVAILABLE];
       (* PLACE NEWDATA IN STORAGE ELEMENT *)
       DATA[NEW]:=NEWDATA;
       (* SEE IF NEWDATA GOES FIRST IN LIST *)
       IF (FIRST=NULL) OR (NEWDATA<DATA[FIRST]) THEN
          BEGIN
             LINK[NEW]:=FIRST;
             FIRST:=NEW
          END
       ELSE
          BEGIN
             (* FIND PLACE TO INSERT NEW DATA *)
             PREVIOUS:=FIRST;
             NEXT:=LINK[FIRST];
             WHILE (NEXT<>NULL) AND (NEWDATA>=DATA[NEXT])DO
                BEGIN
                   PREVIOUS:=NEXT;
                   NEXT:=LINK[NEXT]
                END;
             (* ADJUST LINKS TO MAKE INSERTION *)
             LINK[PREVIOUS]:=NEW;
             LINK[NEW]:=NEXT
          END
    END;
```

So far we have ignored a problem in our INSERT procedure. The conditions for both the IF statement and the WHILE loop use an element of the DATA array which may have the index NULL (0). To avoid an out-of-bounds index, the DATA array should be declared with a lower bound of zero. DATA[0] should be given a value, although the value is not actually part of the list.

DELETING FROM A LINKED LIST

The process of deletion is very similar. We will just record the complete procedure.

```
(* DELETE SPECIFIED DATA FROM LINKED LIST *)
PROCEDURE DELETE(OLDDATA:ENTRYTYPE);
    VAR PREVIOUS,OLD: INTEGER;
    (* FIND THE ITEM TO BE DELETED *)
    BEGIN
        OLD:=FIRST;
        WHILE DATA[OLD]<>OLDDATA DO
            BEGIN
                PREVIOUS:=OLD;
                OLD:=LINK[OLD]
            END;
        (* REMOVE ITEM FROM LIST *)
        IF FIRST=OLD THEN
            FIRST:=LINK[OLD]
        ELSE
            LINK[PREVIOUS]:=LINK[OLD];
        (* ADD STORAGE ELEMENT TO FREE LIST *)
        LINK[OLD]:=AVAILABLE;
        AVAILABLE:=OLD
    END;
```

✷ Before using these two procedures we must set FIRST to NULL, set AVAILABLE to 1, and LINK[I] to I+1, with the exception of the last element which should have a NULL link.

RECORDS AND NODES

We have used links that are in separate arrays from the arrays that hold the actual data values. Sometimes we collect the data and the link to form a record. For example, we could use these declarations

```
TYPE NODE=
    RECORD
        DATA: ENTRYTYPE;
        LINK: INTEGER
    END;
VAR LIST: ARRAY[1..MAXQUEUE] OF NODE;
```

Each item in a list is called a node. With these declarations, we refer to the data in node I as LIST[I].DATA and the link as LIST[I].LINK.

STACKS

In the preceding sections we showed how to insert and delete items for a linked list. The insertions and deletions could be anywhere in the list. In each case, as the list of data items was changed, a second linked list of available storage elements was maintained. A deletion from the list of data items resulted in an addition to the list of available elements; an addition in the data list produced a deletion in the available list. The actions involving the available storage list were much simpler. This is because the additions and deletions for it always were to the beginning of that list. A list that is restricted to having entries to or removals from the beginning only is called a stack. The situation is similar to a stack of trays in a cafeteria. When you want a tray you take it off the top of the stack; when you are through with a tray you put it back on the top. When a list is used as a stack, we often call the pointer to the beginning of the list TOP. When an entry is removed from the top we say we have popped an entry off. TOP must then be adjusted to point at the next entry. When we add an entry we say we have pushed it onto the stack.

Because a stack change only occurs at one end, it is convenient to implement a stack without using a linked list; an ordinary array will do. In our examples, a linked list is necessary for our stack of available storage elements because they are scattered all over. Stacks have other uses so we will show how a stack can be implemented using an array. We will call the array STACK. The bottom of the stack will be in STACK(1), the next entry in STACK(2), and so on. Sorry if our stack seems to be upside down! Here is a stack of symbols:

```
TOP             4

STACK(1)        +
STACK(2)        -
STACK(3)        +
STACK(4)        /
```

This sort of stack is often used in compilers for translating arithmetic expressions into machine language.

Before using the stack we initialize it to be empty by setting TOP to zero:

```
TOP:=0;
```

To add an item to the stack we can call the procedure PUSH:

```
PROCEDURE PUSH(SYMBOL:ENTRYTYPE);
   BEGIN
      TOP:=TOP+1;
      STACK[TOP]:=SYMBOL
   END;
```

To remove the top item from the stack we can call the <u>procedure</u> <u>POP</u>:

```
PROCEDURE POP(VAR SYMBOL:ENTRYTYPE);
    BEGIN
        SYMBOL:=STACK[TOP];
        TOP:=TOP-1
    END;
```

The variable TOP and the array STACK must be global to the PUSH and POP procedures. Stacks may be implemented in other ways than shown here.

RECURSIVE PROCEDURES

If we want to read a list of integers and print it in reverse order then we can program it this way using a stack.

```
(* Print numbers in reverse order *)
WHILE there are more numbers to read DO
    BEGIN
        Read number N;
        Push number N onto the stack
    END;
WHILE the stack is not empty DO
    BEGIN
        Pop number N from the stack;
        Write number N
    END
```

Another way of programming this is by using a recursive procedure, which is a procedure that calls itself. In the execution of a recursive procedure there is an implicit stack.

```
$JOB 'LEN VANEK'
 PROGRAM REVERSE(INPUT,OUTPUT);
    PROCEDURE PRINTINREVERSE;
        VAR N: INTEGER;
        BEGIN
            IF NOT EOF THEN
                BEGIN
                    READLN(N);
                    PRINTINREVERSE;   (* PRINT ANY OTHER NUMBERS *)
                    WRITELN(N)
                END
        END;
    BEGIN
        PRINTINREVERSE
    END.
$DATA
5
10
```

The main program calls PRINTINREVERSE. This causes local variable N to be created and 5 is read into it. Next, PRINTINREVERSE calls itself, which creates a new new local variable called N, which has 10 read into it. These two local variables are quite separate from each other even though they have the same name. Next, PRINTINREVERSE calls itself again, but finding that EOF is now true, it returns without reading. This return is to the activation of PRINTINREVERSE where N is 10. After 10 is printed, the return goes back to the activation in which N is 5 and 5 is printed. Then a return is made to the main program and execution is complete.

Each new recursive call to PRINTINREVERSE creates a new copy of local variable N. These variables are stacked in a LIFO manner (last in first out), so that each return finds the previous value of N. Because of this implicit creation of a stack of variables, we do not have to use an array to implement a stack.

QUEUES

Another specialized type of list is a <u>queue</u>. For it, entries are made at the end of the list, deletions are made from the beginning. Rather than search for the end of the list each time an entry is made, it is usual to have a pointer indicating the last entry. Queues involve using things in a manner referred to as, "First in first out" (FIFO) or, "First come first served" (FCFS). This is the usual way for a queue waiting for tickets at a box office to operate.

A queue is not so easy as a stack to implement using an array. It is always growing at one end and shrinking at the other. If an array is used, when the growth reaches the maximum limit of the array, we start it at the beginning again. Here is a queue of users of a computer waiting for service. We have a maximum of 8 elements. Five people are in the queue. The next person to be served is named GREEN.

FIRST 6	LAST 2
QUEUE[1]	GEORGE
QUEUE[2]	JOHNSTON
QUEUE[3]	-
QUEUE[4]	-
QUEUE[5]	-
QUEUE[6]	GREEN
QUEUE[7]	LINNEMANN
QUEUE[8]	JACOBS

Here are procedures used to ENTER or LEAVE this queue. We will use a constant named MAXQUEUE whose value is 8 so we can easily change the maximum size of the queue. Before using these procedures the queue can be initialized to be empty by setting FIRST to 1 and LAST to MAXQUEUE.

```
CONST MAXQUEUE=8;
PROCEDURE ENTER(NAME:ENTRYTYPE);
    BEGIN
        LAST:=LAST+1;
        IF LAST > MAXQUEUE THEN
            LAST:=1;
        QUEUE[LAST]:=NAME
    END;

PROCEDURE LEAVE(VAR NAME:ENTRYTYPE);
    BEGIN
        NAME:=QUEUE[FIRST];
        FIRST:=FIRST+1;
        IF FIRST > MAXQUEUE THEN
            FIRST:=1
    END;
```

We have used wrap-around or modulo arithmetic in that we wanted FIRST and LAST to keep increasing until they reach MAXQUEUE and then to wrap back to 1. The IF statements in the ENTER and LEAVE procedures make sure that wrap around occurs. There is a MOD operator that accomplishes wrap-around by returning the remainder of dividing one integer by another. We can write

```
FIRST:=(FIRST MOD MAXQUEUE)+1;
```

This means to set FIRST to one more than the remainder of FIRST divided by MAXQUEUE. As long as FIRST has a value of 1, 2 up to one less than QUEUESIZE, then this just adds one to FIRST. But if FIRST equals MAXQUEUE then MOD returns a value of zero which added to one causes FIRST to be assigned the value one. So we can shorten the ENTER and LEAVE procedures by using MOD.

Queues can be implemented by linked lists as well as by simple arrays. Queues are used in the programs called operating systems that operate computer systems. Different jobs requiring service are placed in different queues, depending on the demands they are making on the system's resources and the priority that they possess to be given service. Also, in programs that simulate other systems such as factories, queues are maintained to determine the length of time jobs are required to wait to be served when other jobs are competing for the same production facilities.

TREES

A linked list is an efficient way of storing a list that is changing with time, but it introduces an inefficiency in retrieval of information from the list. In Chapter 14 we saw that a binary search for an item in a list is much more efficient for long lists than a linear search. Unfortunately, there is no possibility of doing a binary search in a linked list; we must start at the beginning and trace our way through. There is no direct access to the middle of a linked list. It is for this reason that a more complicated data structure called a <u>tree</u> is used. We can get the efficiency of a binary search by having the elements linked into a <u>binary tree structure</u>.

To show how a binary tree is formed, we will look at the example of our list of names of animals:

```
        3--> CAT
      2------> DOG
              DUCK
    1----------> FOX
              GOOSE
              PIG
              SNAKE
```

To do a binary search we should begin in the middle. We have added SNAKE to the list so the list has a middle entry. If we are looking for the name CAT we find that CAT < FOX, so we then discard the middle entry and the last half of the list. The next comparison is with the middle entry of the remaining list, namely with DOG. Since CAT < DOG we eliminate the last half of the smaller list. By this time, we are down to one entry, which is the one we are looking for. It took three comparisons to get there. A linear search for CAT would, as it happens, have taken only 1 comparison. On the <u>average</u>, the binary search takes fewer comparisons than a linear search. A short list is not a good example for showing off the efficiency of binary searching, but it is much easier to write out all the possibilities.

We will now look at the binary tree that would be used to give the same searching technique. Here it is:

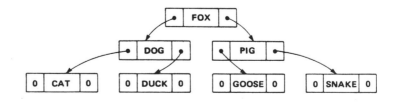

Each data element in the tree structure consists of three parts, the DATA itself and two links that we designate as LEFTLINK and RIGHTLINK. The word FOX is in a special position in the tree, called the root. From FOX we have branches going to the left to DOG and to the right to PIG. In a sense, DOG is in the root position of a smaller tree, what we call the left subtree of the main tree. PIG is at the root of the right subtree. The words CAT, DUCK, GOOSE, and SNAKE are at the end of branches and are called leaves of the tree. All the data elements are in nodes of the tree; FOX is the root node and CAT is a leaf node. To search for an entry in a binary tree, we compare the element in the root node with the one we are seeking. If the root is the same, we have found it. If the root is larger we follow the LEFTLINK to the next entry; if smaller, we follow the RIGHTLINK. We are then at the root of a smaller tree, a tree with half as many entries as the original. The process is then repeated until the looked-for data is found.

Here is our tree structure as it might be stored in three arrays called DATA, LEFTLINK, and RIGHTLINK. The variable ROOT holds the link to the root element. We have jumbled up the sequence to show that the actual order in the DATA array makes no difference. A zero link is used to indicate the end of a branch.

ROOT 4

DATA	LEFTLINK	RIGHTLINK
[1] GOOSE	0	0
[2] SNAKE	0	0
[3] DOG	6	7
[4] FOX	3	5
[5] PIG	1	2
[6] CAT	0	0
[7] DUCK	0	0

Starting at ROOT, we find the root is in DATA[4]. LEFTLINK[4] leads us to DATA[3] which is DOG. RIGHTLINK[3] leads us to DATA[7] which is DUCK. You can see how it works.

A tree structure is a hierarchical structure for data; each comparison takes us one level down in the tree.

ADDING TO A TREE

To add a data item to a tree structure we simply look for the element in the tree in the usual manner, starting at the root. If the element is not already in the tree, we will come in the search to a link that is null (zero). This is where the element belongs. In our example, if we want to add COW, we would start at FOX, then go to DOG, then to CAT. At this point we would want to follow the right link of CAT, but we find a zero. If we stored the new entry in DATA[8], we would change RIGHTLINK[6] to 8 and set

```
DATA[8]    LEFTLINK[8]    RIGHTLINK[8]

COW            0              0
```

As we add items to a tree, the tree becomes lopsided; it is not well balanced. Searching efficiency depends on trees being well balanced, so that in an information retrieval data bank using a tree structure, an effort should be made to keep the tree balanced. We started with a balanced tree and it became unbalanced by adding a new item. If a tree is grown from scratch using the method we have described for adding a new entry, it is unlikely to be well balanced.

DELETING FROM A TREE

Removing an entry from a tree is a more difficult operation than adding an entry. The same method is used to find the element to be deleted, but then the problem comes. It is not difficult if both links of the element to be deleted are zero, that is, if it is a leaf. We just chop it off and make the link pointing to it zero. If only one link is zero it is similar to an ordinary linked list and deletion is similar to that. We just bypass it:

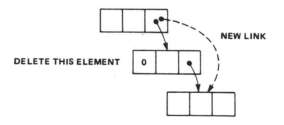

If neither link is zero in the element to be deleted, we must move another element into its position in the tree. In our original tree, if FOX is to be deleted, it must be replaced by an element that is larger then all other elements in the left subtree or smaller than all the elements in the right subtree. This means that either DUCK or GOOSE is the only possible choice. The one to be moved must be deleted in its present position before being placed in its new position.

Remember, in a linked structure, we never move a data item from its physical location in the data array; we only change the links to alter its logical position.

PRINTING A TREE IN ORDER

Trees are used where searching and updating are the main
activities. Sometimes we must print out the contents of a tree.
We must be systematic about it and be sure to print every node.
We will show how to print it alphabetically.

An algorithm for printing a tree alphabetically can be
written in this way:

Print a tree
alphabetically

Print the left subtree	Print the root	Print the right subtree

We see that we have described our algorithm in terms of three
parts. The middle part, "Print the root," is easy, but the other
two require us to, "Print a tree." This is exactly what our
problem is, to "Print a tree." We have defined the solution to a
problem in terms of the original problem. This kind of
definition is called a <u>recursive</u> definition of a solution. It
seems rather pointless, as if we were just going in a circle, but
it really is not. The reason it is not pointless is that the
tree we are attempting to print when we say, "Print the left
subtree," is a smaller tree than the original tree when we said
"Print a tree." When we try to print the left subtree we get
this solution:

Print the left
subtree

Print the left subtree of the left subtree	Print the root of the left subtree	Print the right subtree of the left subtree

This time the left subtree of the left subtree has to be printed.
It is smaller still. The algorithm is again repeated. Each
application of the algorithm is on a smaller tree, until you
reach a point where there is a zero link and there is <u>no</u> left
subtree at all. Then the action of printing it is to do nothing:
no tree, no printing. That is how recursive algorithms work. In
programming terms, the algorithm calls itself over and over, each
time to do a reduced task, until the task is easy to do.

In Pascal a procedure may indeed call itself as we saw in the
example of printing a list of numbers in reverse order. Here is
a Pascal procedure for printing a tree in alphabetic order, given

that its root is ROOT and its data and links DATA,   LEFTLINK   and
RIGHTLINK are global variables.

```
PROCEDURE PRINTTREE(ROOT:INTEGER);
   BEGIN
      IF LEFTLINK[ROOT]<>NULL THEN
         PRINTTREE(LEFTLINK[ROOT]);
      WRITELN(DATA[ROOT]);
      IF RIGHTLINK[ROOT]<>NULL THEN
         PRINTTREE(RIGHTLINK[ROOT])
   END;
```

Each time the procedure is entered for a new subtree, a
different node is referred to by ROOT. For this job, a recursive
procedure is very easy to program. It is much more difficult to
program this job non-recursively. In a recursive algorithm, each
time   a   program calls itself, a record must be kept of the point
in the program where the procedure was called,   so   that   control
can   return   properly. Each new activation of the procedure gets
new parameters and local variables; in this example there are no
local variables but each activation of PRINTTREE gets a different
value of ROOT. As the procedure recursively calls itself, a list
is   built of the points of return. Each point of return is added
on top of the stack of other points of return. Finding   the   way
back involves taking return points, one after the other, off this
stack. This is all set up automatically by the compiler.

CHAPTER 16 SUMMARY

In   previous   chapters   we have presented arrays and records,
which are data structures provided by PS/k. In this   chapter   we
showed how to build up new data structures using arrays. Some of
these new data structures use links to give the ordering of data
items.   The   link   (or   links)   for a given item gives the array
index of the next   item.   The   following   important   terms   were
discussed:

   Linked list - a linked sequence of data items. The next item
      in the list is found   by   following   a   link   from   the
      present   item.   The   physical   order   of a collection of
      items, as given by   their   positions   in   an   array,   is
      different   from   their   logical   order,   as given by the
      links.

   Inserting   into   a   linked   list   -   a   new   data item can be
      inserted by changing links, without actually moving data
      items.

   Deleting   from   a linked list - a data item can be deleted by
      changing links, without moving data items.

   Available   list   -   the collection of data elements currently
      not in use.

Stack - a data structure that allows data items to be added, or <u>pushed</u>, on to one end and removed, or <u>popped</u>, from the same end. A stack does not require the use of links. A stack handles data items in a last-in-first-out (LIFO) manner.

Queue - a data structure that allows data items to be added at one end and removed from the other. A queue handles data items in a first-in-first-out (FIFO) manner.

Binary tree - a data structure in which each item or <u>node</u> has two links, a left link and a right link. The left link of a node locates another node and with it a subtree. Similarly, the right link locates a subtree. There is a unique beginning node called the <u>root</u>. If both links of a particular node are null, meaning they do not currently locate other nodes, then the node is called a <u>leaf</u>.

Recursive procedure - a procedure that calls itself. Each time the procedure is called, it is allocated new formal parameters and local variables.

CHAPTER 16 EXERCISES

1. The FLY-BY-NITE Airline company is computerizing its reservations system. There are four FLY-BY-NITE flights with the following capacities:

```
FLIGHT #1     5 seats
FLIGHT #2     5 seats
FLIGHT #3     8 seats
FLIGHT #4     4 seats
```

The information for passenger reservations is to be stored in a linked list. At some point during the booking period, the following diagram might represent the current passenger bookings.

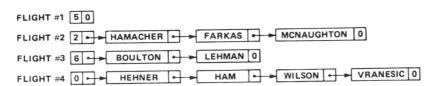

The above diagram shows the first element in each list holding the number of seats remaining. Each succeeding element holds the name of a passenger and either points to the next element or holds a 0 to indicate the end of the linked list.

In order to set up such a linked list system you will need two arrays. The first, called FLIGHT, will contain the four

"first" elements.   Each   of   these elements holds two pieces of
information, the number of seats remaining and the   location   of
the first passenger.

The   second   array called PASSENGER holds all the passengers.
If all seats on all flights are taken, there will be CAPACITY=22
passengers.   Hence PASSENGER will   need   a maximum of CAPACITY
locations.   Each element of the PASSENGER array contains two
pieces   of   information, the passenger's name and the location of
the next passenger, if any.

The   PASSENGER   array must be declared as an array of records
in order to contain two different data types:

```
    TYPE ENTRY=
       RECORD
          NAME: PACKED ARRAY[1..20] OF CHAR;
          LINK: INTEGER
       END;
    VAR PASSENGER: ARRAY[1..CAPACITY] OF ENTRY;
```

This   will   designate each element of PASSENGER[J] to contain two
parts:

    PASSENGER[J].NAME and PASSENGER[J].LINK

Before   any   events   happen,   the   free   locations must be linked
together.   Arrange that each PASSENGER[J].LINK contains   a   value
J+1, except PASSENGER[CAPACITY].LINK which contains a 0 as end of
the list.

A   variable AVAILABLE contains the location of the head of
this chain of available locations.   For the example given   above,
AVAILABLE contains 10 and PASSENGER could have these values:

PASSENGER[1]	PASSENGER[5]	PASSENGER[9]
NAME HAMACHER	NAME LEHMAN	NAME VRANESIC
LINK 6	LINK 0	LINK 0
PASSENGER[2]	PASSENGER[6]	PASSENGER[10]
NAME BOULTON	NAME FARKAS	NAME
LINK 5	LINK 7	LINK 11
PASSENGER[3]	PASSENGER[7]	.
NAME HAM	NAME MCNAUGHTON	.
LINK 8	LINK 0	.
PASSENGER[4]	PASSENGER[8]	PASSENGER[22]
NAME HEHNER	NAME WILSON	NAME
LINK 3	LINK 9	LINK 0

The reservation system is to accept four types of transactions:

Type 1 is a request for a reservation. The data card contains the
    code word RES, name of the passenger, and the flight   number.

Type 2 is a request to cancel a reservation. The data card contains the code word CAN, name of passenger, and the flight number.

Type 3 is a request to print out the number of seats remaining on a specified flight. The data card contains the code word SEATS and a flight number.

Type 4 is a request to print out a passenger list for the flight indicated. The data card contains the code word LIST and a flight number.

Each type of transaction is to be handled by a procedure. PASSENGER, FLIGHT and AVAILABLE are global variables; all other variables are local to the procedure in which they are used. Here are descriptions of the procedures:

ADD(WHO,NUMBER). Adds passenger WHO to flight NUMBER. If that flight is filled, a message is printed to that effect. ADD uses a location in PASSENGER and must update AVAILABLE.

CANCEL(WHO,NUMBER). Cancels the reservation made in the name of WHO on flight NUMBER. The location in PASSENGER is returned to the free storage pool. AVAILABLE must be updated.

INFO(NUMBER). Prints out number of seats remaining on flight NUMBER.

PRINT(NUMBER). Prints a passenger list for flight NUMBER.

The data should simulate a real reservation system in that input of type 1, 2, 3, 4 should be intermixed. It would seem reasonable to assume that most cancellations would be made by persons holding reservations. However, people being what they are, you should not assume too much. In order to get your system off the ground, several reservation cards should be first.

Write and test each procedure as a main procedure before putting the procedures together. Write PRINT first and call it from ADD or CANCEL to help in debugging. If you work in pairs - and this is strongly recommended for this exercise - one person should program ADD and PRINT, the other CANCEL and INFO. Turn in several runs which show the capabilities of your system. Be sure to test "odd" situations as well as the obvious ones.

2. The INSERT and DELETE routines in this chapter use zero as the value of NULL. Lines such as

IF(FIRST=NULL) OR (NEWDATA<DATA[FIRST]) THEN

cause an out-of-bounds array index when FIRST=NULL unless the DATA array allows a zero subscript. Rewrite INSERT and DELETE so NULL can be any negative value.

3. The INSERT procedure in this chapter assumes that there are always enough elements to hold all items. Modify it to print an

error   message when there is not enough room for a new item.   The
DELETE procedure assumes that the item to be deleted is actually
in the list. Modify it to print an error message when the item
to be deleted is not in the list.

Chapter 17
PS/8: POINTERS AND
FILE BUFFERS

In this chapter we introduce PS/8, which has features of Pascal that are helpful in organizing data structures and managing the reading and writing of files. These are pointers and file buffers.

POINTERS

We have been looking at linked lists and have shown how this kind of data structure could be implemented in Pascal using the array structure. The Pascal language provides a data structure that is designed to suit the processing of linked lists. Each element of the linked list is defined as a record and, within the record, one of the fields is a pointer to the next element in the linked list. Suppose that our list element consisted of a single data item and a link, and that the link to the first item in the list was stored in the variable FIRST. FIRST would be of a pointer type as would the LINK of each list item. The LINK of the last item in a list has the value NIL. NIL is a reserved word in Pascal and is the special pointer value that refers to no value at all.

In a program which uses these Pascal facilities for handing linked lists we would have to have definitions and declarations of this kind:

```
TYPE ENTRYTYPE= PACKED ARRAY[1..5] OF CHAR;
     DATALINK= ↑LISTRECORD;           ← note arrow
     LISTRECORD=
        RECORD
           DATA: ENTRYTYPE;
           LINK: DATALINK
        END;
VAR FIRST: DATALINK;
    ITEM: ENTRYTYPE;
```

The definitions of the DATALINK and LISTRECORD types are
interlocking (a characteristic of linked lists). We say that the
data structures are recursive because in their definitions they
refer to each other. The <u>vertical arrow</u> (↑) in the definition of
the DATALINK type indicates that it is a pointer type pointing to
values of the type LISTRECORD. Then with the definition of the
type LISTRECORD we see that the LINK field of the RECORD type has
type DATALINK. The data part of the list element is of type
ENTRYTYPE which has been defined here. We can store values such
as the strings DOG, CAT, FOX, etc. in the data part.

In addition we need to define FIRST as a pointer type of the
same type, DATALINK, as each of the LINK parts of the list
elements. The variable ITEM will contain a data item of the same
type as those in the linked list.

We will now give a procedure for searching the list to find
if the data in ITEM is in the list. If it is we will set the
place where it can be found in the pointer type variable PLACE.
If it is not in the list PLACE will be set to NIL.

In the procedure we will use the notation

        LOCATION↑

which means the list element which is pointed to by the pointer
in LOCATION. The DATA field for this element is LOCATION↑.DATA.
Here is the procedure:

```
PROCEDURE LOCATE(ITEM:ENTRYTYPE; FIRST:DATALINK;
                 VAR PLACE:DATALINK);
   VAR LOCATION:DATALINK;
   BEGIN
      LOCATION:=FIRST;
      PLACE:=NIL; (* VALUE IF ITEM NOT FOUND *)
      WHILE(PLACE=NIL) AND (LOCATION<>NIL) DO
         IF LOCATION↑.DATA=ITEM THEN
            PLACE:=LOCATION
         ELSE
            LOCATION:=LOCATION↑.LINK
   END;
```

If the ITEM is not in the list then LOCATION ends with the value
NIL. Once LOCATION becomes NIL, then LOCATION↑.DATA is
meaningless because LOCATION does not point to a list element.

It is tempting to rearrange the statements and write the WHILE condition as

    WHILE(LOCATION↑.DATA◇ITEM) AND (LOCATION◇NIL) DO

But this would cause an error when the ITEM is not in the list, because LOCATION would become NIL.

MEMORY MANAGEMENT WITH POINTERS

Our example procedure LOCATE shows how pointers can be used in representing lists. We follow the FIRST pointer to the first item and then we locate successive items by pointers within previous items. This means, as in the previous chapter, that the items can be scattered about, not necessarily in the same place. But pointers provide still more flexibility than we had in the last chapter, where we used arrays to hold the list items. All the items for the list had to be in one array and we had to know the maximum number of items so we could declare the bounds of the arrays.

With pointers we do not need to know when we are writing the program how many items might be in a list, because the items are allocated by a predeclared procedure NEW in this way:

    NEW(pointer);

The NEW procedure finds space for the item and sets the value of the pointer to point to this space.

Suppose that we wanted a procedure to insert a data item NEWDATA into our linked list, assuming that the data items in our list are ordered alphabetically. As before the main program must have the type definition and variable declarations that we have shown. Here is the procedure

```
PROCEDURE INSERT(NEWDATA:ENTRYTYPE);
   VAR PLACE,PREVIOUS,NEXT: DATALINK;
      FOUND: BOOLEAN;
   BEGIN
      NEW(PLACE); (* OBTAIN STORAGE ELEMENT FOR NEWDATA *)
      PLACE↑.DATA:=NEWDATA;
      NEXT:=FIRST;
      FOUND:=FALSE;
      WHILE(NOT FOUND) AND (NEXT<>NIL)DO
         IF NEWDATA<NEXT↑.DATA THEN
            FOUND:=TRUE
         ELSE
            BEGIN
               PREVIOUS:=NEXT;
               NEXT:=NEXT↑.LINK
            END;
      (* STORE LINK FOR NEWDATA *)
      PLACE↑.LINK:=NEXT;
      (* ADJUST LINKS TO MAKE INSERTION *)
      IF NEXT=FIRST THEN
         FIRST:=PLACE
      ELSE
         PREVIOUS↑.LINK:=PLACE
   END;
```

You can see that memory management is done for you automatically by the NEW procedure. There is no need to keep a linked list of available locations as we did when we used arrays to store linked lists. This kind of memory allocation is said to be _dynamic_ _allocation_. Only as much memory as is needed at any time has to be reserved for the storage of a linked list. When you use arrays their size must be declared at the time the program is compiled. But with pointers the memory, as needed, is requested at execution time.

You can return any unused memory locations to the system so that they can be used again. This is done by calling the predeclared procedure DISPOSE by

```
DISPOSE(pointer to element no longer needed);
```

The procedure would be used whenever a data item is deleted from a linked list and its memory location no longer needed.

DANGLING POINTERS

When DISPOSE is used, there is a danger that the programmer must avoid. Suppose a program has this sequence of statements involving pointers P and Q.

```
NEW(P);
Q:=P;    (* Q LOCATES SAME ITEM AS DOES P *)
...
DISPOSE(P); (* STORAGE FOR P'S ITEM IS FREED *)
```

...(Now what does Q point to?)

Pointer Q is made to locate an item, and then that item is
disposed of. We say Q is a dangling pointer because it is left
pointing at a discarded object. After the DISPOSE we must not
use Q↑, because Q↑ is now meaningless. The analogous problem
with arrays is A[I] when I is not within the declared bounds of
A; this too is meaningless and must be avoided. Many Pascal
systems do not check for dangling pointers and a program may
cause disastrous damage to itself or other programs if it changes
a discarded item as in the statement Q↑:=VALUE. The problem is
that the space used for the old item may have been re-used for a
new item and the new item may be damaged.

USING POINTERS

In principle we never need to use pointers; we could use
arrays instead as we did in the last chapter. However, pointers
provide two main advantages. First, they are somewhat more
efficient than arrays, for example

    A[I].DATA:=VALUE

is slower to execute than

    P↑.DATA:=VALUE

Second, they allow memory to be traded off from one kind of item
to another. For example, suppose a program first needs to store
many items of type T and then successively needs to store fewer
of these items but more items of type U. This is easy to
accomplish using pointers by creating items of types T and U as
needed using NEW and then deleting them with DISPOSE when they
are no longer needed. But with arrays, this would be quite
difficult.

Just as arrays can contain various types (including records
and other arrays), pointers can point to various types.
Elaborate data structures, including trees, can be built up using
pointers, records and arrays.

Sometimes a WITH statement can simplify a program that uses
pointers. For example, instead of

    LOCATION↑.LINK:=NEXT;
    LOCATION↑.DATA:=NEWDATA

we could write

    WITH LOCATION↑ DO
       BEGIN
          LINK:=NEXT;
          DATA:=NEWDATA
       END

Within the WITH statement, the value of LOCATION should not be changed. For example, the BEGIN...END should not include the statement LOCATION:=PREVIOUS.

FILE BUFFERS

As a file is read into memory, data items pass from the file to intermediate storage called the <u>file buffer</u>. File buffers are similar to items located by pointers, for example, the file buffer for file F is F↑. Suppose that an input file is declared by

```
TYPE FILEITEM=
   RECORD
      (field declarations)
   END;
VAR F: FILE OF FILEITEM;
    V: FILEITEM;
```

In this case the data items in the file are records. So far in order to read this file, assuming that it has been RESET, we would use the statement

```
READ(F,V);
```

The READ is a predeclared procedure in Pascal which really consists of two more basic Pascal statements. These are

```
V:=F↑;
GET(F)
```

In these F↑ means "the buffer associated with file F". The first statement assigns the current contents of the file buffer to variable location V. Note that V has been declared to be of the same data type as the data items in the file. The statement GET(F) is an invocation of the procedure GET which places the next data item on file F, if any, in the buffer associated with file F, namely F↑. If there are no more items in the file then F↑ becomes undefined, in a way that depends on the particular Pascal implementation, and EOF(F) becomes true. Attempting to execute GET(F) when EOF(F) is true is an undefined operation.

The RESET operation, which must be performed on a file F before any READ(F,V) statement is executed, resets the file to the first position. The file buffer F↑ is assigned the first value in the file, if any; if none exists, F↑ is undefined. EOF(F) becomes false unless the file is empty in which case EOF(F) becomes true.

When a file F is opened for output by a REWRITE(F) statement the present contents of the file are discarded and EOF(F) becomes true. When a call to the predeclared procedure

```
WRITE(F,expression)
```

is given it is equivalent to these two more basic Pascal statements

```
F↑:=expression;
PUT(F)
```

Here the value of the expression is assigned to the buffer associated with file F and then by the PUT procedure the contents of the buffer are appended to the end of the file. EOF(F) must be true before the PUT and remains true after. When writing has taken place the value of F↑ becomes undefined.

In previous chapters, all file accessing was done using READ and WRITE and not GET and PUT, so we did not directly refer to the file buffer. But we can use it directly as the next example shows.

FILE MERGE USING BUFFERS

In Chapters 13 and 15 we showed how to merge two sorted files to make a third sorted file. The following program merges the files MASTER and TRANSACTION to form the new MASTERFILE. The items in these files are of a record type that is ordered by a field called KEY.

```
PROGRAM MERGE(OUTPUT,MASTER,TRANSACTION,NEWMASTER);
(* MERGE MASTER AND TRANSACTION FILES TO MAKE NEWMASTER *)
    TYPE ITEM=
        RECORD
            KEY: type of key;
            other fields
        END;
    VAR MASTER,TRANSACTION,NEWMASTER: FILE OF ITEM;
        BEGIN
            RESET(MASTER);
            RESET(TRANSACTION);
            REWRITE(NEWMASTER);
            WHILE(NOT EOF(MASTER)) AND (NOT EOF(TRANSACTION)) DO
                IF MASTER↑.KEY < TRANSACTION↑.KEY THEN
                    BEGIN
                        NEWMASTER↑:=MASTER↑; (* COPY MASTER ITEM *)
                        GET(MASTER);
                        PUT(NEWMASTER)
                    END
                ELSE
                    BEGIN
                        NEWMASTER↑:=TRANSACTION↑; (* COPY TRANSACTION *)
                        GET(TRANSACTION);
                        PUT(NEWMASTER)
                    END;
            (* COPY REST OF MASTER OR TRANSACTION FILE *)
            WHILE NOT EOF(MASTER) DO
                BEGIN
                    NEWMASTER↑:=MASTER↑;
                    GET(MASTER);
                    PUT(NEWMASTER)
                END;
            WHILE NOT EOF(TRANSACTION) DO
                BEGIN
                    NEWMASTER↑:=TRANSACTION↑;
                    GET(TRANSACTION);
                    PUT(NEWMASTER)
                END
        END.
```

This procedure uses MASTER.KEY to access the KEY field in the
master file's buffer. The statement

```
    NEWMASTER↑:=MASTER↑;
```

copies the entire record in the master file's buffer to the new
master file's buffer. This method of merging using GET and PUT
and file buffers directly is somewhat more efficient than using
READ and WRITE because READ and WRITE involve extra copying of
the file items.

CHAPTER 17 SUMMARY

In this chapter we introduced programming language features
called pointers and file buffers. Pointers are particularly
suited for constructing efficient linked lists and they allow
dynamic allocation of variables. A file buffer is the
intermediate storage that items on a file are read into or
written from. The following important terms were discussed in
this chapter:

Pointer - In Pascal each pointer can point to an item of only
  one type, for example pointer P can locate only values
  of type T:

      VAR P: ↑T;

  This declaration of P creates a pointer but P does not
  yet point to a value. Pointers to the same type can be
  compared for equality and assigned. For example if Q is
  also a pointer to T then P=Q determines if P and Q
  locate the same item or are both NIL. After Q:=P, Q
  locates the same item as P (or is also NIL). After
  Q↑:=P↑, the item pointed to by Q has the same value as
  the item pointed to by P.

NIL - any pointer can be assigned or compared to the special
  pointer value NIL.

NEW - a predeclared procedure that creates an item.

      NEW(P)

  creates an item of type T, where P is of type ↑T
  (pointer to T). P points to the new item.

DISPOSE - a predeclared procedure that frees storage located
  by a pointer. Given that P locates an item,

      DISPOSE(P)

  frees the storage used by the item.

Dangling pointer - a pointer Q is dangling if it is left
  pointing at an item that was disposed of using another
  pointer. Dangling pointers are meaningless and the
  "ghost items" they locate must not be used.

File buffer - given file F declared as FILE OF T, then F↑ is
  the intermediate storage for the file.

PUT - The statement PUT(F) causes the buffer value F↑ to be
  appended to file. EOF(F) must be true before PUT(F) is
  executed and remains true afterwards.

GET - The statement GET(F) causes the buffer value F↑ to receive the next value in the file if any. EOF(F) must be false before GET(F) is executed. EOF(F) becomes true if the file contains no more values, in which case F↑ becomes undefined.

CHAPTER 17 EXERCISES

1. Rewrite the DELETE procedure of Chapter 16 using pointers.

2. Using the description of binary trees from Chapter 16, write procedures that insert an item into an alphabetically ordered tree and that print the tree in order. Use pointers to represent the tree.

3. Using pointers computerize the FLY-BY-NITE airline company described in exercise 1 of Chapter 16.

4. Define a record called PERSON that has fields for the person's name, sex, father, spouse, first-born, and younger sibling. These last four fields will be pointers to this same record type. Assuming that a collection of such records has been appropriately interconnected using these pointers, write four procedures which accept a pointer to such a record and (a) print the person's children, (b) print the person's ancestors, (c) print the person's descendants and (d) print the person's patriarchal descendant family tree.

5. Do exercise 3 of Chapter 15 using file buffers.

6. Do exercise 6 of Chapter 15 using file buffers.

Chapter 18
SCIENTIFIC CALCULATIONS

Most of the applications that we have discussed so far in this book are connected with the use of computers in business or in the humanities. We do business applications on computers because of the large numbers of each calculation that must be done. A single payroll calculation is simple, but if a company has thousands of employees, computer processing of payroll is warranted. Computers were originally developed with scientific and engineering calculations in mind. This is because many scientific and engineering calculations are so long that it is not practical to do them by hand, even with the help of a pocket calculator.

Often the scientific laws describing a physical situation are known in the form of equations, but these equations must be solved for the situation of interest. We may be designing a bridge or aircraft or an air-conditioning system for a building. A computer can be used to calculate the details of the particular situation.

Another important use of computers in science is to find equations that fit the data produced in experiments. These equations then serve to reduce the amount of data that must be preserved. Science as a word means knowledge. The object of scientific work is to gather information about the world and to systematize it so that it can be retrieved and used in the future. There is such a large amount of research activity now in science that we are facing an information explosion. We have talked about retrieving information from a data bank and computers will undoubtedly help us in this increasingly difficult and tedious job. But the problem of data reduction is of equal importance.

In this chapter we will try to give some of the flavor of scientific calculations, but we will not be including enough detail for those people who will need to work with them. We will give only an overview of this important use of computers. In the next chapter we will present more details and applications of scientific calculations.

EVALUATING FORMULAS

To solve certain scientific problems we must substitute values into formulas and calculate results. For example, we could be asked to calculate the distance traveled by a falling object after it is dropped from an airplane. A formula that gives the distance in meters traveled in time t seconds, neglecting air resistance, is

$$d = 4.9t^2$$

Here the constant 4.9 is one-half the acceleration due to gravity. Here is a program to compute the distance at the end of each second of the first 10 seconds after the drop:

```
PROGRAM FALL (INPUT,OUTPUT);
   (* PRINT TABLE OF DISTANCE FALLEN VERSUS TIME *)
   VAR DISTANCE,TIME: REAL;
      I: INTEGER;
   BEGIN
      TIME:=0;
      (* LABEL TIME-DISTANCE TABLE *)
      WRITELN(' TIME           ','DISTANCE');
      FOR I:=1 to 10 DO
         BEGIN
            TIME:=TIME+1;
            DISTANCE:=4.9*TIME*TIME;
            WRITELN(TIME,DISTANCE)
         END
   END.
```

The output for this program is

TIME	DISTANCE
1.00000E+00	4.90000E+00
2.00000E+00	1.96000E+01
3.00000E+00	4.41000E+01
4.00000E+00	7.84000E+01
5.00000E+00	1.22500E+02
6.00000E+00	1.76400E+02
7.00000E+00	2.40100E+02
8.00000E+00	3.13600E+02
9.00000E+00	3.96900E+02
1.00000E+01	4.90000E+02

This example prints a table of values of DISTANCE for different times. Printing of tables is an interesting and historic scientific use of computers. Scientific calculations are usually done using REAL variables. In the output the distances and times are printed with six digits in the fraction part, one digit to the left and five to the right of the decimal point. Not all these digits are <u>significant</u>; the constant 4.9 in the formula is only expressed with two digits. We must realize then that only about two digits of the distance traveled are significant.

The calculations are carried out in the computer keeping 6 digits, but this does not imply that they are meaningful. Even if the constant in the formula were entered to 6-digit precision, we would not necessarily have 6 significant digits in the answer. Because computers represent REAL numbers only to a limited precision, there are always what are called numerical errors. These are not mistakes you make but are inherent in the way that REAL numbers are represented in the computer. When two REAL numbers are multiplied, the product is rounded off to the same precision as the original numbers; no more digits in the product would be significant. As calculations proceed, the rounding process can erode the significance even of some of the digits that are maintained. We usually quote numerical errors by saying that a value is, for example,

19.25 ± 0.05

This means that the value could be as high as 19.30 or as low as 19.20. If the error were higher, say 0.5 instead of 0.05, then the values could range between 19.75 and 18.75. In this case the fourth digit in the value is certainly not significant, and you would say instead that the value was

19.2 ± 0.5

Or we might round it off instead of truncating the insignificant digit, and write

19.3 ± 0.5

The estimation of errors is an important job that is done by <u>numerical analysts</u>. If you are doing numerical calculations, you should be aware of the fact that answers are not exact but have errors.

PREDECLARED FUNCTIONS

Scientific calculations require mathematical functions that are not commonly used in business calculations. For many of these functions, procedures have already been written for Pascal; they are predeclared in the compiler. For example, suppose for our falling-body calculation we wanted to compute the times when the body reached different distances. To calculate the time, given the distance, we use this form of the same formula:

       t =   d/4.9

Now we need to be able to calculate a square root. This can be
done by using the built-in function for square root, which is
called SQRT. We would write in the program:

    TIME := SQRT(DISTANCE/4.9);

Other predeclared functions available to Pascal for scientific
calculations are connected with trigonometry. They include SIN
and COS. These give the values of the sine and cosine, when the
argument of the function is in radians. ARCTAN(X) gives the
angle in radians whose tangent is X. The natural logarithm is
obtained by using LN, the exponential by using EXP.

                      GRAPHING A FUNCTION

    Frequently a better understanding of a scientific formula can
be had if you draw a graph of the function. In the first example
of this chapter we evaluated a function at regular intervals. It
is possible to use these values to plot a graph on the printer.
We could, for instance, plot a distance-time graph for the
falling object. We will show one way to plot a graph on the
printer, but there are lots of other ways.

    When you draw a graph of X versus Y you usually make the X-
axis horizontal and have the Y-axis vertical. The values of X,
which is the independent variable, increase uniformly; the
corresponding values of Y are obtained by substituting X into the
function Y=f(X). When we plot a graph on the printer the lines
of printing are uniformly spaced, so we will use the distance
between lines to represent the uniform interval between the Xs.
This means that the X-axis will be vertical and the Y-axis
horizontal. To see the graph in the normal orientation, just
rotate the page 90 degrees counterclockwise. Here is a graph
for $Y=X^2-X-2$ plotted between X=-2 and X=3:

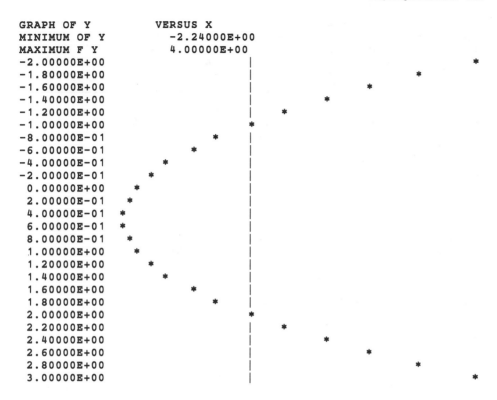

```
GRAPH OF Y           VERSUS X
MINIMUM OF Y          -2.24000E+00
MAXIMUM F Y           4.00000E+00
-2.00000E+00                   |                              *
-1.80000E+00                   |                         *
-1.60000E+00                   |                      *
-1.40000E+00                   |                  *
-1.20000E+00                   |             *
-1.00000E+00                   |          *
-8.00000E-01              *     |
-6.00000E-01            *       |
-4.00000E-01         *          |
-2.00000E-01        *           |
 0.00000E+00      *             |
 2.00000E-01      *             |
 4.00000E-01    *               |
 6.00000E-01    *               |
 8.00000E-01     *              |
 1.00000E+00      *             |
 1.20000E+00       *            |
 1.40000E+00        *           |
 1.60000E+00          *         |
 1.80000E+00            *       |
 2.00000E+00                 *  |
 2.20000E+00                   |    *
 2.40000E+00                   |         *
 2.60000E+00                   |              *
 2.80000E+00                   |                   *
 3.00000E+00                   |                         *
```

We represent the Y-value corresponding to the X of a particular printed line by printing an asterisk in the print position that approximates its value. We use 51 columns to print the range of Ys. If the lowest Y-value that we must represent is YMINIMUM and the highest is YMAXIMUM, then the 51 print positions must represent a range of

    YRANGE = YMAXIMUM - YMINIMUM

To find the print position for a value Y we compute an INTEGER variable YPRINT from

    YPRINT:=ROUND(50*(Y-YMINIMUM)/YRANGE)+1;

The value 1 is added to put YMINIMUM in the first position. We are assuming YRANGE is not zero so that we can divide by it. To form a string of characters for printing, we replace the blank in the YPRINT position of a string of blanks by an asterisk. We create a string variable called BLANKS that holds a string of blanks. The line of characters to be printed, which is a packed array of characters, we call YLINE. We put an X-axis on our graph if it is in the proper range. To do this we place a vertical bar in the line of blanks and call the new variable BASICLINE. The axis is placed in the position where a zero value of Y would be placed. The axis does not appear at all if 0 is less than YMINIMUM or greater than YMAXIMUM. Here is the program segment for forming the BASICLINE.

```
BASICLINE:=BLANKS;
ZEROPRINT:=ROUND(50*(0-YMINIMUM)/YRANGE)+1;
IF(ZEROPRINT>=1) AND (ZEROPRINT<=51) THEN
    BASICLINE[ZEROPRINT]:='|';
```

For each line we set YLINE to BASICLINE and then place an asterisk in the proper position. This is done by

```
YLINE:=BASICLINE;
YLINE[YPRINT]:='*';
```

We do not print a Y-axis, but we list the X-values corresponding to each line opposite the line.

A PROCEDURE FOR PLOTTING GRAPHS

Here is the complete procedure for plotting a graph from N pairs of REAL values of X and Y stored in arrays of those names. The values of X are uniformly spaced. The actual names of the variables to be plotted will be given as arguments XNAME and YNAME, which are of type NAME. The calling statement would be of the form

```
GRAPH(X,Y,N,XNAME,YNAME);
```

We will call a procedure to find YMAXIMUM and YMINIMUM. It will be called MINMAX. We are using the named constant WIDTH=51 so the graph width can be easily changed.

```
(* PROCEDURE TO PLOT A GRAPH *)
PROCEDURE GRAPH(X,Y:TABLE; N:INTEGER ;XNAME,YNAME:NAME);
    CONST WIDTH=51;
    TYPE LINE=PACKED ARRAY[1..WIDTH] OF CHAR;
    VAR BLANKS,BASICLINE,YLINE: LINE;
        YMINIMUM,YMAXIMUM,YRANGE: REAL;
        ZEROPRINT,YPRINT,I: INTEGER;

    (* FIND SMALLEST AND LARGEST VALUES IN TABLE ARRAY *)
    PROCEDURE MINMAX(VALUE:TABLE;N:INTEGER;VAR MINIMUM,MAXIMUM:REAL);
        BEGIN
            MINIMUM:=VALUE[1];
            MAXIMUM:=VALUE[1];
            FOR I:=2 TO N DO
                BEGIN
                    IF VALUE[I]<MINIMUM THEN
                        MINIMUM:=VALUE[I];
                    IF VALUE[I]>MAXIMUM THEN
                        MAXIMUM:=VALUE[I]
                END
        END;

    BEGIN
        (* FIND RANGE OF Y TO BE PLOTTED *)
        MINMAX(Y,N,YMINIMUM,YMAXIMUM);
        YRANGE:=YMAXIMUM-YMINIMUM;
        (* FORM STRING OF WIDTH BLANKS *)
        FOR I:=1 TO WIDTH DO
            BLANKS[I]:=' ';
        (* PLACE X-AXIS MARK IN BASICLINE *)
        BASICLINE:=BLANKS;
        ZEROPRINT:=ROUND((WIDTH-1)*(0-YMINIMUM)/YRANGE)+1;
        IF(ZEROPRINT>=1) AND (ZEROPRINT<=WIDTH) THEN
            BASICLINE[ZEROPRINT]:='|';
        (* LABEL GRAPH *)
        WRITELN(' GRAPH OF ',YNAME,' VERSUS ',XNAME);
        WRITELN(' MINIMUM OF ',YNAME,YMINIMUM);
        WRITELN(' MAXIMUM OF ',YNAME,YMAXIMUM);
        (* PREPARE AND PRINT LINES OF GRAPH *)
        FOR I:=1 TO N DO
            BEGIN
                YPRINT:=ROUND((WIDTH-1)*(Y[I]-YMINIMUM)/YRANGE)+1;
                YLINE:=BASICLINE;
                YLINE[YPRINT]:='*';
                WRITELN(X[I],'   ',YLINE)
            END
    END;
```

USING THE GRAPH PROCEDURE

We will now give the program that was used to plot the function of x,

$$y = x^2 - x - 2$$

between the values x=-2 and x=3. We plot it at intervals of x that are 0.2 wide. There are 26 points in all. Here is the program:

```
$JOB 'MARK NAIRN'
 (* PLOT THE FUNCTION Y=X*X-X-2 *)
 PROGRAM CURVE (INPUT,OUTPUT);
    CONST TABLESIZE=50;
        INTERVAL=0.2;
        POINTS=26;
    TYPE TABLE=ARRAY[1..TABLESIZE] OF REAL;
        NAME=PACKED ARRAY[1..10] OF CHAR;
    VAR X,Y: TABLE;
        I: INTEGER;
        XNAME,YNAME: NAME;
    (copy GRAPH procedure here)
    (* COMPUTE VALUES FOR X AND Y ARRAYS *)
    BEGIN
        FOR I:=1 TO POINTS DO
            BEGIN
                X[I]:=-2+(I-1)*INTERVAL;
                Y[I]:=X[I]*X[I]-X[I]-2
            END;
        XNAME:='X        ';
        YNAME:='Y        ';
        GRAPH(X,Y,POINTS,XNAME,YNAME)
    END.
```

The output for this program was shown earlier in this chapter. You will notice that as the graph crosses the X-axis the vertical bar is replaced by an asterisk. It crosses twice, at

```
x = -1.00000E+00    and at
x = +2.00000E+00
```

We say that x=-1 and x=2 are the roots of the equation

$$x^2 - x - 2 = 0$$

The function (x^2-x-2) becomes zero at these values of x. This graphical method is one way of finding the roots of an equation. We will look later in this chapter at another way of finding roots that is numerical rather than graphical.

FITTING A CURVE TO A SET OF POINTS

In the last sections we have seen how to compute a set of points of corresponding X and Y values from a formula and then to plot a graph of these points. In some scientific experiments we measure the value of a variable Y as we change some other variable X in a systematic way. The results are displayed by plotting X and Y. If there is a theory that relates the values of X to Y in a formula or equation, then we can see how well the results fit the theoretical formula.

One way would be to compute the values of Y for each X from the formula. The measured values could be called Y(experimental) and the calculated ones Y(theoretical). The differences between corresponding values

Y(experimental) - Y(theoretical)

are called <u>deviations</u> of experimental from theoretical values.

We have spoken so far as if it were possible to compute the proper theoretical value that corresponds to each experimental value. This is the case if the formula has no other variable in it. Frequently there are other variables in the formula that can change. For example, here is the formula for V, the velocity of an object at time T, given that its initial velocity is VINITIAL and its acceleration is A.

V := VINITIAL + A*T

If we measured the velocity of an object that has a uniform acceleration we could plot a graph between V and T:

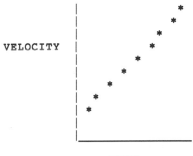

VELOCITY

TIME

Theoretically, the graph should be a straight line, but the experimental points are scattered. It is possible to draw a line by eye that is placed so that the deviations of points from the line are small. Since some deviations, V(experimental)-V(theoretical), are positive and some negative their sum might be small even though individual deviations were large. To get a good fit we minimize the sum of the squares of the deviations rather than the sum of the deviations. The squares of the deviations are always positive. We choose as the best straight line the one that makes the sum of the squares of the deviations the least. This is called <u>least-squares</u> <u>fitting</u> of a curve (here a straight line) to experimental points. This process can be done very efficiently by a computer. Most computer installations provide standard procedures for least-squares fitting, so that scientists do not have to write their own.

Sometimes no theoretical curve is known. We can still fit our data to an equation. We choose an equation that has a form resembling our data. If there is no theory we say it is an <u>empirical</u> fit, meaning that it is an equation based on the observations.

SOLVING POLYNOMIAL EQUATIONS

The graph that we plotted as an example was of the function

$$y = x^2 - x - 2$$

This is a <u>polynomial</u> function of x. The places where the graph crosses the x-axis are the <u>roots</u> of the equation

$$x^2 - x - 2 = 0$$

This is a second-degree equation since the highest power of the unknown x is the second power. It is a <u>quadratic</u> <u>equation</u>. There are general formulas for the roots of a quadratic equation. For the equation

$$ax^2 + bx + c = 0$$

the two roots x1 and x2 are given by the formulas

$$x1 = (-b + \sqrt{b^2 - 4ac})/(2a) \qquad \text{and}$$

$$x2 = (-b - \sqrt{b^2 - 4ac})/(2a)$$

Most students of mathematics know these formulas. If the quantity $(b^2 - 4ac)$ inside the square root sign is positive, all is straightforward. If it is negative, then the formula requires us to find the square root of a negative number, and we say the roots are <u>complex</u>. This means, in graphical terms, that the curve does not cross, or touch, the X-axis anywhere. It is either completely above or completely below the X-axis. There is no use looking for values of x where the function is zero.

Here is a procedure for finding the roots of a quadratic equation.

```
(* FIND ROOTS OF A*X*X+B*X+C=0 *)
PROCEDURE ROOTS(A,B,C: REAL);
    VAR TEST,ROOT1,ROOT2,SQROOT: REAL;
    BEGIN
        TEST:=B*B-4*A*C;
        IF TEST >= 0 THEN
            BEGIN
                SQROOT:=SQRT(TEST);
                ROOT1:=(-B+SQROOT)/(2*A);
                ROOT2:=(-B-SQROOT)/(2*A);
                WRITELN(' ROOTS ARE',ROOT1,ROOT2)
            END
        ELSE
            WRITELN(' ROOTS ARE COMPLEX')
    END;
```

In this procedure the formulas for finding the roots do not provide values that are accurate under various circumstances. For example, if ROOT1 is nearly zero because B and SQROOT are very close in value, a better approximation to it can be obtained by working out ROOT2 and using the assignment:

```
ROOT1:=C/(A*ROOT2);
```

to compute ROOT1. This relationship holds in general so it can always be used. Can you see why it is true?

For equations that are polynomial in x of degrees higher than two, the method for finding the roots is not as easy. For an equation of degree three or four, there is a complicated formula for the roots. For larger degrees there are no formulas and we must look for the roots by a numerical method.

The secret of any search is first to be sure that what you are looking for is in the right area, then to keep narrowing down the search area. One method of searching for roots corresponds to the binary search we discussed in Chapter 14. First we find two values of x for which the function has different signs. Then we can be sure that, if it is continuous, the graph will cross the x-axis at least once in the interval between these points. The next step is to halve the interval and look at the middle. If there is only one root in the interval, then in the middle the function will either be zero, in which case it is the root, or it will have the same sign as one of the two end points. Remember they have opposite signs. We discard the half of the interval that is bounded by the middle point and the end with the same sign and repeat the process. After several steps we will have a good approximation to the location of the root. We can continue the process until we are satisfied that the error, or uncertainty, in our root location is small enough. There is no point in trying to locate it more accurately than the precision with which the numbers are stored in the computer. A numerical analyst could determine the accuracy of the calculated answer.

SOLVING LINEAR EQUATIONS

Computers are used to solve sets of linear equations. If we have two unknowns, we must have two equations to get a solution. We can solve the set of equations

    x-y=10
    x+y=6

to get the result x=8, y=-2. To solve the equations we first eliminate one of the unknowns. From the first equation we get

    x=y+10

Substituting into the second eliminates x. It gives

    (y+10)+y=6   or 2y=-4   or y=-2

Then substituting back gives

    x=-2+10 or .x=8

This process of elimination can be carried out a step at a time for more equations in more unknowns. Each step lowers the number of unknowns by one and the number of equations by one. A computer program can be written to perform this job, and can be used to solve a set of linear equations. What we must provide is the coefficients of the unknowns and the right-hand sides of the set of equations. A common method is called the Gauss elimination method.

COMPUTING AREAS

Another numerical method that is relatively easy to understand is the calculation of areas by the trapezoidal method. Suppose we have a curve of y=f(x) and we want to find the area between the curve and the X-axis and between lines at x=X1 and x=Xn.

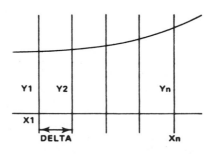

We will divide the distance between X1 and Xn into intervals of size DELTA. In the drawing we have shown four intervals. The area of the first section, thinking of it as a trapezoid, is

    (Y1+Y2)*DELTA/2

The total area under the curve is approximated by the sum of all the trapezoids. The total area of the trapezoids is

    (Y1+Y2)*DELTA/2+(Y2+Y3)*DELTA/2+...(Y[n-1]+Yn)*DELTA/2

If we factor out DELTA the formula becomes

    ((Y1+Yn)/2+Y2+Y3+... +Y[n-1])*DELTA

This is half the sum of Y1 and Yn plus the sum of the other Ys multiplied by the width of the trapezoids. As DELTA is made smaller, the sum of the areas of the trapezoids comes closer and closer to the area under the curve. It is a better and better approximation. There is, however, a limit to the accuracy that can be obtained, due to the precision of the REAL numbers. Here is a program segment to compute the area if the Ys are stored in an array:

    SUM:=(Y[1]+Y[N])/2;
    FOR I:=2 TO N-1 DO
       SUM:=SUM+Y[I];
    AREA:=SUM*DELTA;

CHAPTER 18 SUMMARY

This chapter has given an introduction to the use of computers in scientific calculations. Generally, these calculations are done using REAL numbers. The scientist needs to know the accuracy of the final answers. The answers may be inaccurate because of:

   Measurement errors - the original data was collected by measuring physical quantities, such as length or speed. These measurements can never be perfect and an estimate of the measurement error should be made.

   Round-off errors by the computer - a given computer stores REAL numbers with a particular precision, typically 6 decimal digits of accuracy. Calculations using REAL numbers will be no more accurate than the number of digits of precision provided by the computer. They could even be less accurate due to the cumulative effect of round-off. (Note: sometimes the programmer can choose between "single-precision" REAL, giving typically 6 digits of accuracy and "double-precision" REAL, giving typically 14 digits accuracy.)

Truncation errors in repeated calculations – some calculations, such as searching for the roots of a polynomial equation, produce approximations that are successively closer to the exact answer. When the repeated calculation stops, we have a truncation error, which is the difference between the final approximation and the exact answer (ignoring errors due to measurement and round-off).

The number of digits of accuracy in a particular answer is called its number of <u>significant figures</u>. The scientist needs to know that the computer produces a particular answer with enough significant figures for his purposes.

Pascal provides predeclared functions that are useful in solving scientific or mathematical problems. The function SQRT takes the square root of a non-negative number. The functions SIN, COS and ARCTAN operate on or return angles in radians. LN takes the natural logarithm of a number, and EXP raises e to a specified power.

This chapter presented the following typical scientific and mathematical uses of computers.

Evaluating formulas – a computer can produce tables of numbers, for example tables of navigational figures used on sailing boats.

Graphing functions – a computer can plot a particular function; sometimes a special <u>plotter</u> machine is attached to the computer so it can draw continuous lines as well as printing characters.

Fitting a curve to a set of points – data points from an experiment can be read by a program and used to determine an equation (a curve) that describes the data.

Solving polynomial equations – a polynomial equation such as

$$X^3+9X^2+6X-23=0$$

can be solved by a program that reads the coefficients (1, 9, 6 and -23).

Solving linear equations – a set of equations such as

$$2X + 9y = 7$$
$$10X - 4y = 2$$

can be solved by a program that reads the coefficients of the unknowns (2, 9, 10 and -4) and the right sides of the equations (7 and 2).

Areas under curves – a program can find the area under a given curve by using the heights of the curve at many points. Essentially, the program slices the area into narrow strips and adds up the areas of the strips. This process is sometimes called numerical integration or quadrature.

CHAPTER 18 EXERCISES

1. One jet plane is flying 1083.7 kilometers per hour; another jet plane, chasing it from behind, is flying 1297.9 kilometers per hour. What is the relative speed of the second plane, that is, how fast is it catching up to the first plane? The speed of the first plane is known to an accuracy of ±5 km/hr and the speed of the second is known to an accuracy of ±0.5 km/hr. How accurately can we calculate the relative speed? How many significant figures are there in the first plane's speed, the second plane's speed and the relative speed?

2. Use the graphing procedure given in this chapter to plot the function SIN(X) for X varying from zero to three in steps of one tenth.

3. Use the graphing procedure given in this chapter to plot the function X*SIN(X) for X varying from 0 to 12 in steps of 0.25.

4. A moon rocket has an instrument that measures the rocket's acceleration every second and transmits the measurement to an on-board minicomputer. A program in the minicomputer estimates the speed of the rocket, assuming a speed of zero at launch time. Essentially, this program determines the area under the curve of acceleration plotted against time. Using the trapezoidal method described in this chapter, the speed at time Tn will be approximately

    ((A1+An)/2+A2+A3+ .. + A[n-1])* DELTAT

In this case, DELTAT is 1 second and each acceleration is measured in kilometers per second per second. The formula to give the speed in kilometers per second n seconds after blast-off is simply

    [A1+An)/2+A2+A3+...+A[n-1]

Write a program that reads in the accelerations and prints out the speeds after each second. If you are clever you can avoid recalculating the entire series for each acceleration reading, and you can avoid using an array.

Chapter 19
NUMERICAL METHODS

In the last chapter we outlined some of the important types of calculations used in scientific and engineering computing. In any calculations, for example those for evaluating functions such as the trigonometric functions sin and cos or finding the area under a curve, the calculation can be carried out to varying degrees of accuracy. Usually the more calculating you do, the more accurate the answer you get. But some methods are better than others; for the same amount of work you get greater accuracy. We will, for instance, be looking at a way of finding areas under curves that is usually superior to the trapeziodal rule described in the last chapter. As well we will show a general method of solving linear equations and a method for least-squares fitting of a straight line to a set of experimental points. But first we will look at an efficient way of evaluating a polynomial.

EVALUATION OF A POLYNOMIAL

In doing numerical calculations we should be concerned with getting the best calculation we can for the least cost in terms of computer time. This is one of the concerns of people who design what are called numerical methods. They are not just concerned about getting an answer but about whether the cost of getting the answer can be decreased.

As an example of how different methods giving apparently the same result can have different costs, we will look at the calculation of the value of a polynomial. We will look at a third-degree polynomial and then generalize the result later for a polynomial of degree N. A third-degree polynomial has the form

$$Y(X) = A3 \ X^3 + A2 \ X^2 + A1 \ X + A0$$

One way of evaluating this is

    Y = A3*X*X*X + A2*X*X + A1*X + A0

In this evaluation there are 6 multiplications (count the asterisks) and 3 additions. For a fourth-degree polynomial there would be 10 multiplications and 4 additions. For an Nth-degree polynomial there would be $N+(N-1)+(N-2)+...+1=N(N+1)/2$ multiplications and N additions.

Now we will look at a different method of evaluating the third-degree polynomial. It is

    Y = (((A3)*X+A2)*X+A1)*X+A0)

Here there are 3 multiplications and 3 additions. (Just count the asterisks.) For an Nth-degree polynomial there would be N multiplications and N additions. This method is called Horner's rule and is certainly much more efficient, particularly for polynomials of higher degree.

We will now write a function subprogram that will evaluate a polynomial of degree N by this method given that the coefficients of the powers of X namely the As are stored in a one-dimensional array. Here is a program segment that would work for the third-degree polynomial of our example.

```
SUM:=A[3];
FOR I:=2 DOWNTO 0 DO
   SUM:=SUM*X+A[I];
```

If we extend this now to work for an Nth degree polynomial we would write

```
SUM:=A[N];
FOR I:=N-1 DOWNTO 0 DO
   SUM:=SUM*X+A[I];
```

The complete function subprogram would be

```
(* FUNCTION TO EVALUATE POLYNOMIAL OF DEGREE N *)
FUNCTION POLY(A:ARRAYTYPE; X:REAL; N:INTEGER): REAL;
   VAR I: INTEGER;
      SUM:=REAL;
   BEGIN
      SUM:=A[N];
      FOR I:=N-1 DOWNTO 0 DO
         SUM:=SUM*X+A[I];
      POLY:=SUM
   END;
```

In the main program the type ARRAYTYPE could be defined as

    TYPE ARRAYTYPE=ARRAY[0..10] OF REAL;

The value of N could not be larger than 10 but could be any value up to and including 10.

ROUND-OFF ERRORS

Since a real number is represented in a computer by a finite string of bits an error is usually introduced. This error is called a round-off error. The last bit in the string may be inexact. In decimal notation if the fraction 0.132762 is to be represented by a string of decimal digits of length 4 then the four digits will be either .1327 or .1328. The string may simply be chopped off after the 4th digit, which is called rounding by chopping, or 5 may be added to the 5th digit and the sum then chopped to 4 digits. This latter form of round off is probably somewhat better and is the method that you usually are thinking of if you ask that a number be rounded off.

As numbers are combined in the arithmetic operations of addition, subtraction, multiplication and division, the round-off error may increase. We say that a further error is generated. As operations continue, the generated error may grow and is said to be a propagated error.

In adding or subtracting two numbers the error in the sum, or difference is equal to the sum of the errors in the two numbers. Suppose for instance that the number 0.132762 is represented as the 4-digit string 0.1328. The error in this representation due to rounding off is 0.000038. If the number 0.521689 is represented as 0.5217 the error is 0.000011. The sum of the numbers will be 0.6545 as compared with the result of adding the two 6-digit representations which gives 0.654451. The error in the sum is 0.000049 which is the sum of 0.000038 and 0.000011.

In multiplication the relative (or percentage) error introduced in the product is equal to the sum of the relative (or percentage) errors of the two factors. In division the relative error of the quotient is the difference between the relative errors of the dividend and divisor. In any event all arithmetic operations serve to propagate errors due to rounding.

We found that Horner's rule was more efficient for evaluating polynomials than the straightforward method because there were fewer multiplications. Now we can see that it is also more accurate since the propagation of round-off error is less when there are fewer arithmetic operations. This is why we can say that it is a better method; it is more accurate and costs less.

LOSS OF SIGNIFICANT FIGURES

We have seen that arithmetic operations result in errors and these cause the rounding due to the finite representations of real numbers in a computer to grow larger. The number of digits in our final result that are significant gradually decreases as errors are propagated.

There are more drastic ways of losing significant figures. One place where this occurs is in the situation where two nearly equal numbers are subtracted. When 0.3572 is subtracted from 0.3581 the answer is 0.0009 which is normalized to 0.9???E-03. The digits that are written as question marks could be anything; only the 9 is significant. We had 4 significant figures in each of the original numbers and now we have only 1 significant figure in the difference. One way to cope with this loss of precision is to avoid calculations of this sort. Often by regrouping or resequencing operations the offending subtraction can be eliminated. If it is not possible then it may be necessary to work to greater precision, say double precision, during the part of a calculation where this can occur. Loss of significant figures can also occur when divisors are small or multipliers large.

EVALUATION OF INFINITE SERIES

Many mathematical functions can be represented by an infinite series of terms to be added. For example,

$$\exp(x) = 1+(x/1!)+(x^2/2!)+(x^3/3!)+...$$

$$\sin(x) = (x/1!)-(x^3/3!)+(x^5/5!)-...$$

$$\cos(x) = 1-(x^2/2!)+(x^4/4!)-...$$

$$\log(1+x) = (x/1)-(x^2/2)+(x^3/3)-...$$

The series for sin and cos are for angles x in radians. The series for log(1+x) is valid only for values of x whose magnitudes are less than 1.

If we evaluate the infinite series for say sin(x) for a value of x=PI/4 we would get terms that alternately are positive and negative and decrease in magnitude as successive terms are calculated. Here is a program that prints the value of the sum of the sine series up to a given term as well as the value of the latest term added for eight terms.

```
$JOB 'MARIA KLAWE'
 (* COMPUTE SERIES FOR SIN(X) TERM BY TERM *)
 PROGRAM SINSERIES(INPUT,OUTPUT);
    CONST PI=3.141593;
    VAR X,SQRX,SINE,TERM: REAL;
       I: INTEGER;
    BEGIN
       X:=PI/4;
       SQRX:=X*X;
       WRITELN(' SIN(X)          TERM');
       TERM:=X;
       SINE:=TERM;
       FOR I:=1 TO 8 DO
          BEGIN
             WRITELN(SINE,TERM);
             TERM:=-1*(TERM*SQRX)/(2*I*(2*I+1));
             SINE:=SINE+TERM
          END;
       WRITELN(' VALUE OF SINE USING PREDECLARED FUNCTION SIN IS',
               SIN(PI/4))
    END.
```

The output for this program is

```
SIN(X)                  TERM
  7.853980E-01            7.853980E-01
  7.046525E-01           -8.074544E-02
  7.071429E-01            2.490392E-03
  7.071063E-01           -3.657614E-05
  7.071066E-01            3.133609E-07
  7.071066E-01           -1.757242E-09
  7.072066E-01            6.948429E-12
  7.071066E-01           -2.041018E-14
VALUE OF SINE USING PREDECLARED FUNCTION SIN IS  7.072069E-01
```

You can see that the terms become progressively smaller right
from the start. This is because x is less than 1. The ratio of
the one term to the next term is $x^2/(2i(2i+1))$. This ratio
becomes smaller as i becomes larger. The terms are decreasing
faster and faster. Terms after the 5th do not make any
difference. This series for sin(x) can be used even when x is
greater than 1. Here is the output if we run the previous
program again with the statement X:=PI/2 instead of X:=PI/4 and
print the value of sin(PI/2) which is 1.

```
SIN(X)                  TERM
  1.570796E+01            1.570796E+00
  9.248325E+00           -6.459635E+01
  0.1004524E+01           7.969242E-02
  9.998425E+00           -4.681736E-03
  1.000003E+01            1.604404E-04
  9.999993E+00           -3.598822E-06
  9.999993E+00            5.692136E-08
  9.999993E+00           -6.687983E-10
VALUE OF SINE USING PREDECLARED FUNCTIONS SIN IS  1.000000E+00
```

This time the terms do not decrease as rapidly; but they are not affecting the result after the 6th term. The accuracy obtained from the evaluation of a fixed number of terms depends on the value of the parameter x.

If the series is stopped after 3 terms the value of sine differs from the true value of sin(PI/2) which is 0.100000E01 by 0.0004524E01 which is 4/10 of 1 percent. We say that this error is partly due to truncating the series. If truncation occurs after 4 terms the error is 0.0001575E01 which is 1/10 of 1 percent. The more terms we calculate, the smaller is the truncation error. By taking sufficient terms we can make the truncation error as small as we want.

One way of deciding how many terms of a series are enough is to stop when the absolute value of the most recent term is less than a certain amount. The amount we usually choose is such that it will not change the value of the sum in a noticeable way. It is useless to evaluate more terms because they do not matter.

Even when we have evaluated enough terms so that the contribution of the last term is insignificant, there still remain errors due to round off. In our example, the round-off error would be present even in the first term of the series; as each term is added another round off occurs. These errors may tend to cancel each other; sometimes the number is rounded up, sometimes down. It is possible that all errors are in the same direction so that the total possible error introduced in this way grows larger with the number of terms. We must expect the worst. The round-off error in the sine of PI/4 seems to be 0.0000003, that in sine of PI/2 seems to be 0.0000007. In each case the last figure printed is dubious.

One way of avoiding the accumulation of round-off errors is to work in double precision. In double precision each number is represented by a string of bits that is twice as long as in single precision. The round-off error will then accumulate in the least significant bits of the double precision number. When the result is finally reduced to single precision, a single round off occurs.

A relationship between the functions sine and cosine may be used to improve the accuracy of the result for a given number of terms in the series. This relationship is

SIN(X)=COS((PI/2)-X)

This means that for angles greater than PI/4 but less than PI/2 we can compute the sine by using the series for cosine with the argument ((PI/2)-X). This will be equal to or less than PI/4 and comparable accuracy can be obtained using the same number of terms in the series.

When a fixed number of terms has been decided on, say six, the evaluation of the series becomes the evaluation of a polynomial. We can take advantage of the efficiencies of

Horner's method. In the series for sine and cosine not every power of X is present so the polynomial is really like one in X^2 rather than X. For example, the series for sine to 5 terms can be written as

$$\sin(X) = ((((X^2/9!)-(1/7!))X^2+(1/5!))X^2+1)X$$

The coefficients (1/9!), (1/7!), and (1/5!) can all be evaluated once and for all and stored as constants in the program.

All values of angles greater than PI/2 must be reduced to be related to either the sin or cos series for X less than or equal to PI/4.

ROOT FINDING

In the last chapter we looked at one method for finding the value of X where a polynomial in X has a zero value. This same method applies to any function of one variable, say f(X). If there are two values, say X1 and X2, of X at which f(X) has opposite signs then, provided the function is continuous, there must be at least one point in between these values where the function has a zero value. We described a search technique that halved the interval between the given values of X and determined in which half the zero of the function lay. This process can then be repeated in a manner similar to a binary search.

This interval-halving method can be improved upon and numerous other methods for finding zeros, or roots, of a function of one variable have been devised. The purpose of these methods is to provide a faster way of homing in on a root once it has been located between two values of X.

A technique called the secant method uses, instead of the mid-point, the point at which a line drawn between the point (X1,f(X1)) and (X2,f(X2)) cuts the X-axis. This will be at a point X given by solving the equation

$$f(X2)/(X2-X) = f(X1)/(X-X1)$$

or X = (f(X1)X2+f(X2)X1)/(f(X2)+f(X1))

If you have studied analytical geometry you can see this from the diagram.

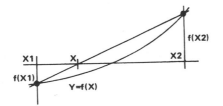

This process is repeated using the point X as a replacement for either X1 or X2. The choice depends on which gives a value to the function opposite to the value at X. As the iteration proceeds the interval is always being narrowed down.

Both the interval-halving method and the secant method will converge on the root. The rate of the convergence depends on the particular function whose zero is being sought. The rate of convergence can sometimes be improved at the cost of the guarantee of convergence. In the secant method, instead of using one of the end points all the time, two intermediate points can be used. Of course, there may not be a zero between these points but the search interval is much smaller.

A method called the Newton-Raphson method is useful for simple functions, like polynomials, whose slopes can be computed using calculus. The iteration formula for approximating the root is

$$X(N+1) = XN-f(XN)/S(XN)$$

where X(N+1) is the approximation to the root at the (N+1)th iteration, XN is the Nth approximation, f(XN) is the value of the function at XN, and S(XN) is the value of the slope of the function at XN.

For those who have studied calculus, if, for example,

$$f(X) = 3X^2+2X+1 \text{ then}$$

$$S(X) = 6X+2$$

S(X) is the derivative of f(X).

The Newton-Raphson method has very rapid convergence, but convergence is not always guaranteed.

PROCEDURE FOR ROOT FINDING

We will give a program for a procedure which uses the interval-halving method. It is perhaps slow, but safe. For the function evaluations it will call on a function FUNC. The parameter EPSILON stands for the Greek letter epsilon. In mathematics, we use epsilon to stand for the small difference between an approximation and a true value. We will use as a stopping condition the fact that two successive approximations to the root differ from each other by less than EPSILON. When you use the procedure SOLVE you must decide what accuracy you want. Of course there is no use asking for greater accuracy than is permitted by the finite representation of the numbers.

```
(* FIND ROOTS OF FUNC(X)=0 BY INTERVAL HALVING *)
PROCEDURE SOLVE(LEFT,RIGHT,EPSILON:REAL;VAR ROOT:REAL);
    VAR X1,X2:REAL;
    BEGIN
        X1:=LEFT;
        X2:=RIGHT;
        WHILE (X2-X1)>EPSILON DO
            BEGIN
                ROOT:=(X1+X2)/2;
                IF FUNC(X1)*FUNC(ROOT)>0 THEN
                    X1:=ROOT
                ELSE
                    X2:=ROOT
            END
    END;
```

We will now use this procedure to find the zero of

$$f(x) = x^2 - x - 2$$

that is between x=0 and x=3 to an accuracy of 0.00005E00.

```
$JOB 'DORON COHEN'
 (* FIND ONE ROOT OF F(X)=X*X-X-2 *)
 PROGRAM ZERO(INPUT,OUTPUT);
    VAR RESULT:REAL;
    FUNCTION FUNC(X:REAL):REAL;
        BEGIN
            FUNC:=(X-1)*X-2;
        END;
    (include declaration of SOLVE here)
    BEGIN
        SOLVE(0,3,5E-5,RESULT);
        WRITELN(' ZERO OF QUADRATIC IS',RESULT)
    END.
```

The output for this program is

ZERO OF QUADRATIC IS   2.000015E+00.

Notice that the polynomial is being evaluated by Horner's method. We do not need to use this kind of method of root finding for a quadratic but it illustrates the method in a case where we can compute the correct answer which is

   2.000000E00

NUMERICAL INTEGRATION

    In calculus, we find that the area under a curve can be calculated by evaluating the definite integral of the function that represents the curve between the two limiting values of the independent variable. Not every function can be integrated analytically but a numerical approximation can be obtained for

any continuous function. In the last chapter we presented the
trapezoidal rule for calculating areas under curves; the function
is evaluated at uniformly spaced intervals between the limiting
values and the function values are used to find the area. The
accuracy of the result improves as smaller intervals are chosen
and more function evaluations made.

For the same number of function evaluations it is possible to
have an integration formula that combines the values to give a
better approximation to the area.

One formula which is usually better than the trapezoidal
formula is called Simpson's rule. The trapezoidal formula
assumes that each little slice of the area has the shape of a
trapezoid; Simpson's rule assumes that the curved boundary of two
adjacent slices has the shape of a parabola (a second-degree
polynomial). It uses the area under such a parabola that can be
found using calculus to give a way of finding the area under the
curve. The area must be divided into an even number of slices.
The area of any pair of slices is the slice width DELTA,
multiplied by one-third of the sum of the values of the function
at the outside together with four times the value in the middle.
If the complete area is divided into 2 pairs of slices then the
area is

DELTA*(f(X1)+4*f(x2)+2*f(X3)+4*f(X4)+f(X5))/3

You can see how to extend this for more pairs of slices.

We will write a program to compare the accuracy of the result
obtained with the same number of function evaluations (slices)
using the trapezoidal rule and Simpson's rule. We will calculate
the area for a simple curve so that a calculus result can give
the exact area for comparison. We will compute the area under
the curve

f(X)=sin(X)

between the values of X=0 and PI. From calculus we know the
answer should be 2.0000000. We will use 6 slices so that DELTA
will be PI/6.

```
$JOB    'COROT REASON'
 (* COMPARE SIMPSON'S AND TRAPEZOIDAL RULE *)
 PROGRAM INTEGRATE(INPUT,OUTPUT);
    CONST PI=3.141592;
    VAR DELTA,TRAP,SIMP,ODD,EVEN,MIDDLE: REAL;
        I: INTEGER;
        F: ARRAY[1..7] OF REAL;
    BEGIN
        DELTA:=PI/6;
        (* EVALUATE SIN(X)AT 7 VALUES OF X *)
        FOR I:=0 TO 6 DO
            F[I+1]:=SIN(I*DELTA);
        (* COMPUTE AREA BY TRAPEZOIDAL RULE *)
        MIDDLE:=F[2]+F[3]+F[4]+F[5]+F[6];
        TRAP:=DELTA*(F[1]+2*MIDDLE+F[7])/2;
        (* COMPUTE AREA BY SIMPSON'S RULE *)
        EVEN:=F[2]+F[4]+F[6];
        ODD:=F[3]+F[5];
        SIMP:=DELTA*(F[1]+4*EVEN+2*ODD+F[7])/3;
        WRITELN(' TRAPEZOIDAL METHOD GIVES',TRAP);
        WRITELN('  SIMPSONS  METHOD GIVES',SIMP)
    END.
```

Here is the output

```
TRAPEZOIDAL METHOD GIVES   1.954096E+00
  SIMPSONS  METHOD GIVES   2.000861E+00
```

You can see that the error in the trapezoidal method is 0.04590, that in Simpson's rule is 0.00086. This shows that Simpson's rule is a superior one here, the error is smaller.

LINEAR EQUATIONS USING ARRAYS

We have looked at the problem of solving two linear equations in two unknowns. We do not use computers to solve such simple systems. But computers are useful when we have many equations in many unknowns. In handling these problems we store the coefficients of the unknowns in an array. If we had four equations in four unknowns the equations might be written as

$$A[1,1]X1+A[1,2]X2+A[1,3]X3+A[1,4]X4=B1$$

$$A[2,1]X1+A[2,2]X2+A[2,3]X3+A[2,4]X4=B2$$

$$A[3,1]X1+A[3,2]X2+A[3,3]X3+A[3,4]X4=B3$$

$$A[4,1]X1+A[4,2]X2+A[4,3]X3+A[4,4]X4=B4$$

where A is a two-dimensional array of the coefficients. We can write the Bs, the right-hand sides of these equations, as part of the A array by letting B1=A[1,5], B2=A[2,5] and so on. To solve the equations, we must reduce these equations in turn to three equations in three unknowns, two equations in two unknowns, and then one equation in one unknown. This method eliminates all the unknowns except one. Then by substituting back you can find the value of all unknowns. If the array of coefficients was of the form

```
A[1,1] A[1,2] A[1,3] A[1,4] A[1,5]
  0    A[2,2] A[2,3] A[2,4] A[2,5]
  0      0    A[3,3] A[3,4] A[3,5]
  0      0      0    A[4,4] A[4,5]
```

then we could see from the last line that X4=A[4,5]/A[4,4]. Then using this we could substitute back into the equation represented by the second last line namely

A[3,3]X3+A[3,4]X4=A[3,5]

and solve for X3, and so on to get X2 and X1.

What we have to do is move from the original array of coefficients to the one with all the zeros in the lower left corner. We do this by dividing each element of the first row by A[1,1] and storing it back in the same location. This makes the new value of A[1,1] a 1. Next multiply this row by A[2,1] and subtract it from each element of row two, storing the result back in the same location. The new value of A[2,1] will be zero. The process will eventually result in an array with zeros in the lower left.

Certain problems of loss of precision can arise if the element that is currently to be reduced to 1 is small. This element, referred to as the pivot element, should be as large as possible. Various ways of rearranging the array can help prevent difficulties but trouble is always possible. This sort of problem provides great interest to numerical analysts.

LEAST SQUARES APPROXIMATION

Very often in scientific experiments, measurements of a quantity Y are made at various values of an independent variable X. It may be known from theory that the relationship between Y and X is a linear one, for example

Y=AX+B

The various corresponding values of X and Y can be plotted on a graph; there would be a number of points, say N. A straight line drawn through any two of these points would not pass exactly through the others. We want to choose the values of the constants A and B so that they define a straight line in such a way that the sum of the squares of deviations of the actual points from the straight line is a minimum, that is, the sum of squares is least. For the Ith point, say at (XI,YI), the deviation squared is

$$(YI-(A*XI+B))^2$$

We want the minimum so we use calculus and set the derivatives with respect to the variables equal to zero. We can differentiate a sum of squares of this type partially with respect to A and B, the values that can be varied, and set the derivatives equal to zero. This gives two equations. One is the sum of N terms of the form

$$YI-(A*XI+B)$$

set equal to zero. The value of I goes from 1 to N. The other is the sum of N terms of the form

$$(YI-(A*XI+B))*XI$$

set equal to zero. These two equations can be written as two equations in two unknowns, A and B. These are

$$C1*A + C2*B = C3$$

$$C4*A + C5*B = C6$$

where C1 is the sum of values XI with I going from 1 to N. C2 is N and C3 is the sum of values YI with I going from 1 to N. C4 is the sum of XI*XI from 1 to N, C5 the sum of XI from 1 to N, and C6 the sum of XI*YI from 1 to N. The solution to the two equations can easily be found once they are formed.

This same technique can be used for points that in theory lie on a higher degree curve than a straight line but the calculation is more complex.

MATHEMATICAL SOFTWARE

We have been describing a few of the simpler numerical methods used in scientific calculations. Over the years these methods have been changed and made more reliable, more efficient and more accurate. Nowadays we usually rely on a packaged program for carrying out this type of calculation. We call the program packages mathematical software, to distinguish them from the programs that operate the system or compile programs. These latter are called systems software and compilers respectively.

Mathematical software packages exist for almost every standard numerical calculation. All that you must do is to find out how to call them in your program, and what their limitations are. Every piece of software should be documented so that you do not need to read it to be able to use it. You must know what each input parameter of the subprogram is and what range of values is permitted. You must know also how the output is stored so that you can use it.

Frequently software packages are stored in the secondary memory of the computer and may be included in your program by using special control cards. In any event if a deck of cards for a package exists this can be included with your own deck in a position appropriate to a subprogram.

One of the great things about science is that we build on the work of others and using subprograms prepared by others is good scientific practice. Of course these subprograms must meet the highest standards.

CHAPTER 19 SUMMARY

In this chapter we have been examining numerical methods for evaluating polynomials and infinite series, calculating areas under curves, solving systems of linear equations and obtaining least squares approximations. We were concerned particularly with certain properties of the methods.

Efficiency of a method - the amount of work, as measured in number of basic arithmetic operations required to obtain a certain numerical result. Horner's rule for polynomial evaluation is more efficient than the straightforward method. It is more efficient because it requires fewer multiplications.

Horner's rule - a method for computing the value of a polynomial that is efficient. The polynomial

$$Y = 5X^2 + 2X + 3$$

is evaluated by the Pascal statement which represents Horner's rule

        Y := (5*X+2)*X+3

rather than

        Y := 5*X*X+2*X+3

Round-off error - error in real numbers introduced because a computer represents the number by a finite string of bits. When real numbers are added or subtracted the round-off error of the sum or difference is the sum of the round-off errors of the two individual numbers. In multiplications the relative errors add.

Generated error - round-off errors produced due to arithmetic operations. The fewer the arithmetic operations the smaller the round-off error generated.

Propagated error - generated round-off errors that grow as calculations proceed.

Significant digits - digits in the representation of a real
number that are not in error. Numbers are often quoted with
a final decimal digit that may be in error by as much as
unity. Digits that are not significant should not be quoted
in an answer.

Loss of significant digits - this may occur as the result of
subtraction of nearly equal numbers, or division by very
small numbers, or multiplication by very large numbers.

Infinite series - many mathematical functions such as sin, cos,
exp and log can be written as a sum of an infinite series of
terms. These series may be used to evaluate the functions.
Because the terms in the series eventually decrease in
magnitude a good approximation can be obtained by stopping
the addition after a certain number of terms.

Convergence of series - the way in which the terms of an infinite
series become smaller and smaller.

Rate of convergence - the ratio of the magnitude of two adjacent
terms of an infinite series. For sin(X) the ratio is
$X^2/(2i(2i+1))$. If X is less than 1 then this ratio is always
less than one. If X is greater than 1 the terms might
initially get larger but eventually get smaller. A series
cannot converge if the term ratio never becomes less than 1.

Double precision - keeping twice the normal number of bits to
represent a number in the computer. Calculations carried out
to double precision maintain a larger number of significant
figures.

Interval-halving method - for finding a root of an equation
f(X)=0 by a method similar to binary search. The method is
guaranteed to converge on a root since the root is always
kept between the end points of the interval and the interval
is constantly decreasing in size.

Secant method - a method that sometimes has better convergence
properties than interval halving for finding a root of an
equation.

Newton-Raphson - a method for finding a zero of a function whose
derivative can be computed. Convergence is rapid but not
guaranteed.

Stopping criterion - the size of error that is to be tolerated in
a result due to truncating such as in evaluating an infinite
series term by term or iterating to find a root.

Numerical integration - approximation of the value of the
definite integral which represents the area under a curve
between two limits.

Simpson's rule - for numerical integration, assumes each pair of
slices of area under a curve is bounded by a parabola. The

trapezoidal method assumes each slice is bounded by a straight line. Simpson's rule often gives greater accuracy for the same number of slices (function evaluations).

Array of coefficients - for linear equations. This is manipulated so as to be transformed into an array that is triangular, that is, has zero elements on the lower left of the diagonal. This is accomplished by operations such as multiplying a row by a constant and subtracting one row from another. Neither of these operations alters the values of the unknowns.

Back substitution - evaluating the unknown once the transformed set of linear equations can be represented by a triangular array.

Least squares approximation - finding an equation to represent experimental information so that the sum of the squares of the deviations is a minimum. We investigated the case of fitting a straight line to a set of experimental points.

Mathematical software - prefabricated subprograms embodying good numerical methods for getting standard results. The software should be documented to alert the user to the accuracy to be expected, the cost of the result, and any limitations that must be respected.

CHAPTER 19 EXERCISES

1. Write a function subprogram that will give the sine of an angle whose value in radians is between 0 and PI/2. Use the series for sine for angles between 0 and PI/4 and for cosine between PI/4 and PI/2. Use the same number of terms in each series. Test your program and compare the results with those obtained by using the predeclared function SIN. Try varying the number of terms in the series.

2. Compute the value of exp(1) using the series. Find the values as each term is added up to a maximum of 8 terms.

3. Use the predeclared function for exp(X) to tabulate values of this function for X going from -10. to +10. Sketch the graph of the function for this range. You might think of using the program for graph plotting on the printer.

4. Use the interval-halving subroutine to find a root of the equation

$$2X-\tan(X)=0$$

given that there is at least one between 0 and PI radians.

5. Use Newton's method of finding roots to find a root of the polynomial

$$X^4 + 6X^2 - 1 = 0$$

6. Use Simpson's rule to find the area under the curve

$$Y = X^2 - 2X - 1$$

from X=0 to 3. Does it matter how many slices you have? Test this.

7. Write a procedure that keeps doubling the number of slices in an area calculation using Simpson's rule until two successive results for the area under a curve agree to within an accuracy EPSILON. Make sure you do not have to reevaluate the function at places already computed.

8. Compare Simpson's rule and the trapezoidal rule for finding areas under a curve for Y=exp(X) between X=0 and X=1.   Do you know the answer from calculus?

9. Write a procedure that will solve a set of N equations in N unknowns. Do not include any form of pivoting. Would you expect this to be a good piece of mathematical software?

10. Write a procedure that will solve two linear equations in two unknowns. Do you encounter any problems about loss of accuracy with such a small system of equations? What happens when there is no solution, for example, if the two equations represent parallel lines?

11. Write a procedure that accepts two arrays X and Y of N values that represent N points and prints out the equation of the straight line that gives a minimum value to the sum of the square of the deviations of the points from the straight line.

Chapter 20
PROGRAMMING IN OTHER LANGUAGES

In this book we have been presenting structured programming in the high-level language Pascal. Pascal was introduced in 1971 by Niklaus Wirth. It has influenced the design of a number of other high-level languages such as Euclid. It grew out of the development of Algol-W which was an extension of Algol 60. Algol 60 was a language designed with the hope that it might be a universal language for scientific computing. Cobol was a language designed for business data processing. Cobol stands for COmmon Business Oriented Language; it is used very widely in business applications of computers. As it stated in the official Cobol report "Cobol is an industry language and is not the property of any company or group of companies; or of any organization or group of organizations".

PL/1, or Programming Language One, was designed in an attempt to combine the capabilities of Algol, Fortran and Cobol.

Fortran, perhaps the earliest of the common high-level languages, has had many improvements made in it since it was presented in 1956. Some of these improvements were incorporated in Standard Fortran, or Fortran 66, by the American National Standards Institute. And now further improvements are contained in Fortran 77.

In this chapter we will be looking at these different languages so you can see that, once you have learned to program in one, it would not be difficult to program in another. You will have learned the fundamentals of programming and can quickly adapt to a new language.

PL/1 AND FORTRAN 77

We cannot present very much of the syntax of the PL/1 or Fortran 77 languages in this book but we will compare them with Pascal by way of a single example program. This will give you an idea of the similarities between the three languages. The example has been chosen to demonstrate the two kinds of loops: the counted loop and the conditional loop. A series of data cards is to be read, each containing, in the first 8 columns right-justified, the cost in cents of a certain item, then a blank column and, in the next two columns, the expected lifetime in years of the item. The program reads these cards, until the end-of-file card with a lifetime of 99 years is reached. For each card it calculates and prints a table, with an appropriate label, giving the balance at the end of each year for the item after the depreciation has been subtracted. This is done for the lifetime of the item. The balance in the last year will be close to zero, if it is not precisely zero.

Thus for input data

500.00 5

the computer should print

```
COST=   500.00 LIFE=   5
   1   400.00
   2   300.00
   3   200.00
   4   100.00
   5     0.00
```

The three programs have their lines numbered so we can make reference to them. Some lines are left blank so that corresponding parts of the program are on the same line number.

FORTRAN 77

```
 1 $JOB    FORTRAN 77
 2
 3 C THIS IS A COMMENT
 4         INTEGER LIFE,YEAR
 5         REAL COST,DEPREC,BALNCE
 6         READ 50,COST,LIFE
 7 50      FORMAT(F8.2,1X,I2)
 8 80      IF(LIFE.EQ.99)GO TO 250
 9         PRINT 90,'COST= ',COST,' LIFE= ',LIFE
10 90      FORMAT(' ',A6,F8.2,A7,I2)
11         DEPREC=COST/LIFE
12         BALNCE=COST
13         DO 150 YEAR=1,LIFE
14         BALNCE=BALNCE-DEPREC
15         PRINT 100,YEAR,BALNCE
16 100     FORMAT(' ',I2,F8.2)
17 150     CONTINUE
18         READ 200,COST,LIFE
19 200     FORMAT(F8.2,1X,I2)
20         GO TO 80
21 250     CONTINUE
22      STOP
23      END
24 $ENTRY
        500.00   5
        480.00   3
          0.00  99
```

We will compare the three programs line by line. Line 1 is the job control card which is different in the way the job identification is given. As well there may be a different character used immediately after the $JOB to indicate different compilers. In line 2 we have the heading that is necessary for all PL/1 and Pascal programs. EXAMPLE is a name the programmer has chosen, but the rest is all standard. A Fortran program requires no such introductory line. Line 3 shows how comments are handled. Lines 4 and 5 give the declarations of variables. Fortran uses the keywords INTEGER and REAL, just like Pascal for what PL/1 calls FIXED and FLOAT. By this time you will have noticed that PL/1 statements are <u>terminated</u> by a semicolon. This is so they could all be run together on the same card. Pascal statements are <u>separated</u> by a semicolon. Fortran must be placed properly on cards or the compiler would be very confused since it has no punctuation to end statements.

Both PL/1 and Fortran 77 have more formatting control for the input statement than does Pascal. The formatted input statement in PL/1 is GET EDIT. In PL/1 the list of format items is in parentheses after the list of output items and is in the same statement. In Fortran, a separate FORMAT line gives the format items. We have split the single PL/1 statement into two lines to show the parallelism. In Pascal we have simply READLN.

Here is the program written in Pascal.

PASCAL

```
 1    $JOB   'PASCAL'
 2    PROGRAM EXAMPLE(INPUT,OUTPUT);
 3       (* THIS IS A COMMENT *)
 4       VAR LIFE,YEAR:INTEGER;
 5           COST,DEPREC,BALNCE:REAL;
 6       BEGIN
 7          READLN(COST,LIFE);
 8          WHILE LIFE<>99 DO
 9             BEGIN
10                WRITELN(' COST= ',COST:8:2,' LIFE= ',LIFE:2);
11                DEPREC:=COST/LIFE;
12                BALNCE:=COST;
13                FOR YEAR:=1 TO LIFE DO
                      BEGIN
14                       BALNCE:=BALNCE-DEPREC;
15                       WRITELN(YEAR,BALNCE:8:2)
16
17                    END;
18                READLN(COST,LIFE)
19
20             END
21
22    END.
```

```
$DATA
    500.00   5
    480.00   3
      0.00  99
```

PL/1

```
1    $JOB ID='PL/1'
2     EXAMPLE:PROCEDURE OPTIONS(MAIN);
3        /* THIS IS A COMMENT */
4        DECLARE(LIFE,YEAR)FIXED;
5        DECLARE(COST,DEPREC,BALNCE)FLOAT;
6        GET EDIT(COST,LIFE)
7            (F(8,2),X(1),F(2));
8        DO WHILE(LIFE¬=99);
9            PUT SKIP EDIT('COST= ',COST,' LIFE= ',LIFE)
10               (A(6),F(8,2),A(7),F(2));
11           DEPREC=COST/LIFE;
12           BALNCE=COST;
13           DO YEAR=1 TO LIFE;
14               BALNCE=BALNCE-DEPREC;
15               PUT SKIP EDIT(YEAR,BALNCE)
16                   (F(2),F(8,2));
17               END;
18           GET EDIT(COST,LIFE)
19               (F(8,2),X(1),F(2));
20           END;
21
22       END;
23
24   $DATA
         (same data as before)
```

In line 8 we have the beginning of the conditional loop. In Fortran the <u>termination condition</u> is given after the IF. In PL/1 the <u>continuation condition</u> is given after the DO WHILE. The one condition is the opposite of the other. The relational operator that we would write in Fortran as .NE., we write in PL/1 as ¬= and in Pascal we use the predeclared Boolean function EOF and write NOT EOF.

In the output labelling in lines 9 and 10, the SKIP in PL/1 does the same thing as the ' ' in the FORMAT of Fortran, namely starts the printing on a new line. In Pascal using WRITELN instead of WRITE does this.

In line 13 a counted loop begins. Notice that in PL/1 as in Pascal there is no need to say where the loop ends. The compiler is perfectly capable of deciding which END goes with which DO. In line 20 the end of the conditional loop is signified; control is automatically returned to line 8 in PL/1 or Pascal and explicitly returned in Fortran by the GO TO 80. In PL/1, END is all that is necessary to terminate the program. Note that it has a semicolon following it and not, as in Pascal, a period. Fortran has STOP before END.

ALGOL 60

We will now show a program written in Algol to produce the same result as we showed in Pascal, Fortran 77 and PL/1. The actual dialect is that of Algol-W.

ALGOL-W

```
1   $JOB    ALGOL-W
2      BEGIN
3         COMMENT THIS IS A COMMENT;
4         INTEGER LIFE,YEAR;
5         REAL COST,DEPREC,BALNCE;
6         READ(COST,LIFE);
7
8         WHILE(LIFE¬=99)DO
9            BEGIN WRITE('COST= ',COST,' LIFE= ',LIFE);
10
11           DEPREC:=COST/LIFE;
12           BALNCE:=COST;
13           FOR YEAR:=1 UNTIL LIFE DO
14              BEGIN
15                 BALNCE:=BALNCE-DEPREC;
15                 WRITE(YEAR,BALNCE)
16
17              END;
18           READ(COST,LIFE)
19
20           END
21
22      END.
23
24   $DATA
```

This program is closer to Pascal than to the PL/1 and Fortran programs already given. It has the keyword BEGIN as a header and this is also used to begin the body of the conditional loop in line 9 and the indexed loop in line 14. Each BEGIN has its corresponding END. There is no input or output formatting at all in Algol-W, so we use the unformatted READ and WRITE. You probably can see that these four languages have many similarities. The assignment statement of Pascal and Algol uses ":=" instead of "=" as do PL/1 and Fortran.

For a while Algol-60 enjoyed considerable popularity partly because it was hoped that it might become an international standard language, not linked to any specific machine manufacturer. (Fortran had originated with IBM). Two other virtues that it enjoyed were that it supplied control structures that permitted well-structured programs and, perhaps less important, that its syntax had been defined in a formal way.

Fortran has maintained its prominence over the years and, since Fortran 66, is no longer connected with just one manufacturer. Its syntax is formally described by the American

National Standards Institute (X3.9-1978). The fact that Fortran 77 now has an IF...THEN...ELSE helps structured programming. Its new character handling ability (which Algol-W had) enlarges its usefulness. And format-free input and output (which Algol-W had) makes it easier for the beginner. Ultimately most programs require formatted input and output so that the format-free statements are not often used by experienced programmers.

COBOL

A complete Cobol program consists of a number of different divisions which permit great flexibility in the use of the various input-output components of a computer system. These are called the IDENTIFICATION, ENVIRONMENT, and DATA divisions. Some compilers, such as Watbol from the University of Waterloo allow a beginning Cobol programmer to by-pass these divisions by using a standard assignment for files, card reader, and printer. We will just show the remaining part of a Cobol program which consists of the WORKING STORAGE SECTION and the PROCEDURE DIVISION. These are the parts that correspond to our other programs. The WORKING STORAGE SECTION contains the parts that are in declarations and format specifications. Variables and formats are described in terms of pictures (PIC). In the PIC description a 9 indicates a digit, an X any character, and a V a decimal point. A picture described as

    PIC 9(6)V9(2)

is of a number with 6 digits to the left of the decimal point and 2 digits to the right. The name FILLER is used for blanks in a record or print line. Like Pascal, Cobol has records. PL/1 also has records but Fortran does not. The record name is defined at level 01, the fields at level 02. Although our example does not show it, a record may be moved from one place to another as a unit. This is a feature that PL/1 also has. Individual variables not used for input or output have level 77.

Cobol was intended to provide business people with very readable programs, a goal that we applaud, but sometimes as a programmer it gets monotonous writing out all the keywords in a Cobol sentence. There are alternatives; for instance, the sentence

    SUBTRACT DEPREC FROM BALNCE.

could be written as

    COMPUTE BALNCE=BALNCE-DEPREC.

and then it would look like our other languages.

Each Cobol sentence ends with a period. The corresponding line numbers of the other programs are given along the left margin. The Cobol program itself is punched on cards starting in

column 8 (called margin A), and most of the program is intended
to start in column 12 (called margin B).

COBOL Program

```
        WORKING STORAGE SECTION.
4       77  YEAR        PIC 9(2).
5       77  DEPREC      PIC 9(6)V9(2).
5       77  BALNCE      PIC 9(6)V9(2).


        01  INPUT-RECORD
5           02  IN-COST  PIC 9(6)V9(2).
            02  FILLER   PIC X(1) VALUE IS SPACE.
4           02  IN-LIFE  PIC 9(2).
            02  FILLER   PIC X(69).


        01  OUTPUT-LABEL
9-10        02  FILLER   PIC X(6) VALUE IS 'COST= '.
9-10        02  OUT-COST PIC 9(6)V9(2).
9-10        02  FILLER   PIC X(7) VALUE IS ' LIFE= '.
9-10        02  OUT-LIFE PIC 9(2)


        01  OUTPUT-RECORD
            02  FILLER   PIC X(1) VALUE IS SPACE.
15-16       02  OUT-YEAR PIC 9(2).
15-16       02  OUT-BALNCE PIC 9(6)V9(2).


2       PROCEDURE DIVISION.
            OPEN INPUT INPUT-FILE
                OUTPUT PRINTER.
6-7         READ INPUT-FILE INTO INPUT-RECORD
                AT END MOVE HIGH-VALUES TO IN-LIFE.
8           PERFORM OUTER-LOOP
8               UNTIL IN-LIFE EQUALS HIGH-VALUES.
            CLOSE INPUT-FILE
                PRINTER.
22          STOP RUN.
        OUTER-LOOP.
9-10        MOVE IN-COST TO OUT-COST.
9-10        MOVE IN-LIFE TO OUT-LIFE.
9-10        WRITE PRINT-LINE FROM OUTPUT-LABEL
9-10            AFTER ADVANCING 1 LINE.
11          DIVIDE IN-LIFE INTO IN-COST
11              GIVING DEPREC ROUNDED.
12          MOVE IN-COST TO BALNCE.
13          PERFORM INNER-LOOP
13              VARYING YEAR FROM  1 BY 1
13              UNTIL YEAR IS GREATER THAN IN-LIFE.
18-19       READ INPUT-FILE INTO INPUT-RECORD
                AT END MOVE HIGH-VALUES TO IN-LIFE.
        INNER-LOOP.
14          SUBTRACT DEPREC FROM BALNCE.
15-16       MOVE YEAR TO OUT-YEAR.
15-16       MOVE BALNCE TO OUT-BALNCE.
15-16       WRITE PRINT-LINE FROM OUTPUT-RECORD
15-16           AFTER ADVANCING 1 LINE.
```

In the PROCEDURE DIVISION it is necessary to OPEN the input and output devices and at the end to CLOSE them before STOP RUN. HIGH-VALUES is a keyword meaning a value beyond the normal range of a variable similar to putting 99 for LIFE in the Fortran or PL/1 programs to indicate the end-of-file. A loop body is listed separately under a paragraph name. For example, the outer conditional loop, called OUTER-LOOP, is invoked by the sentence

```
PERFORM OUTER-LOOP
    UNTIL IN-LIFE EQUALS HIGH-VALUES.
```

The body of this loop is listed after the paragraph heading.

```
OUTER-LOOP.
```

In the outer loop the counted inner loop is invoked by

```
PERFORM INNER-LOOP
    VARYING YEAR FROM 1 BY 1
    UNTIL YEAR IS GREATER THAN IN-LIFE.
```

and the inner loop body is listed after the paragraph name

```
INNER-LOOP.
```

There is no doubt that the Cobol program is longer and wordier, but Cobol is still the most commonly used language for business data processing.

CHAPTER 20 SUMMARY

In this chapter we have been comparing Pascal with some other high-level programming languages. These were PL/1, Fortran (both 66 and 77), Algol 60 and Cobol. It is clear that the fundamentals of programming learned in Pascal make it relatively easy to learn other languages.

The following important terms were introduced in this chapter.

Incompatible - dialects of the same basic programming language are incompatible if programs that are correct in one dialect are incorrect in another. Fortran was standardized to minimize incompatibilities among the various Fortran compilers. Pascal is well standardized because it was carefully defined.

Compatible subset - a portion of a more extensive language that does not contain all the constructs present in the larger language but may contain some restrictions on the use of the language not enforced in the main language. PS/k is a compatible subset of Pascal.

Extensions - constructs that are added to a language thus making the extended language incompatible with the original language. Fortran 77 added a number of extensions to Fortran 66. Fortran 66 programs are compatible with Fortran 77 but not vice versa.

Portable - a program is portable if it can be run on different computers. One way of making programs portable is to write them in a high-level language that is an accepted standard such as Pascal or Fortran 77. Programs written in PS/k will run on any machine that has a Pascal compiler.

PL/1 - short for Programming Language One, a programming language developed to contain the constructs necessary for both scientific applications and business data processing.

Algol-60 - a programming language that many hoped would become an international standard language for scientific computing. In its dialect Algol-W, the ability to handle characters and have format-free input-output was added. Pascal evolved from this language.

CHAPTER 20 EXERCISES

1. Translate the following PS/k program segment to Algol, PL/1, and Fortran 77

```
IF A >= B THEN
    BEGIN
        A:=5;
        WRITELN(B)
    END
```

2. Find any three complete programs or subprograms in other chapters of this book, each at least 15 lines long, and try to translate them to Algol 60, PL/1, and Fortran 77. List any questions about these three languages that arise in trying to make the translations. If you have any of these compilers available try running the program.

3. Why are statement labels not needed in the Pascal, Algol and PL/1, programs that we have shown.

4. Find a text giving Cobol programs and see if you can read and understand some of them.

5. Various compilers respond to program syntax errors in different ways. Try purposely making a few errors in programs for PL/1 or Fortran 77 to see what response you get from the compiler. How does it compare with your Pascal compiler?

6. Consult a textbook on PL/1 and list three features of the language that you did not know about after reading this chapter.

Chapter 21
ASSEMBLY LANGUAGES
AND MACHINE LANGUAGE

In this book we have presented programming in terms of the Pascal language. Pascal is a <u>high-level language</u>; it provides us with a convenient means for directing a computer to do work. The computer cannot execute Pascal programs directly; it can only execute programs in machine language, a <u>low-level language</u>. Before a Pascal program can be executed by a computer, the program must be <u>translated</u> or <u>compiled</u> to machine language. In this chapter we will explain how a computer carries out instructions. We will present features of machine languages and their associated assembly languages.

MACHINE INSTRUCTIONS

In Chapter 2 we gave a brief introduction of machine language. We explained that the instructions a computer can execute are much more basic than Pascal statements. These <u>machine instructions</u> use a special location, called the <u>accumulator</u>, when doing arithmetic or making assignments. For example, the assignment of J to I, written as the Pascal statement

    I:=J;

could be translated to the instructions

    LOAD J   (copy J into the accumulator)
    STORE I   (copy the accumulator into I)

As another example, the Pascal statement

    I:=J+K;

could be translated into the three instructions

```
LOAD   J    (copy J into the accumulator)
ADD    K    (add K to the accumulator)
STORE  I    (copy the accumulator into I)
```

Different kinds of computers have different machine languages. Some computers have many accumulators and some have few. Some computers have many instructions and some have few. We will introduce common features of machine languages by inventing a very simple computer. We will call our computer VS, for <u>very</u> <u>simple</u> computer.

The machine instructions for the VS computer are designed to be convenient for representing programs written in a subset of Pascal. The VS computer has never been built; it is just a hypothetical machine that we will use to illustrate points about computer languages.

The instructions for the VS computer have the form

```
operator operand
```

for example,

```
STORE I
```

The <u>operator</u> of an instruction tells the computer what to do; the <u>operand</u> tells the computer what to do it to.

After the computer executes one instruction, it continues to the next, unless the executed instruction directs the computer to jump to another instruction or to skip an instruction. We can translate the Pascal statements

```
IF I<=K THEN
   K:=I+J;
I:=J;
```

into the VS computer instructions

```
    LOAD    K    (copy K into the accumulator)
    SKIPLE  I    (if I<=accumulator, skip next instruction)
    JUMP    L    (jump to instruction labeled L)
    LOAD    I    (copy I into the accumulator)
    ADD     J    (add J to the accumulator)
    STORE   K    (copy the accumulator into K)
L:  LOAD    J    (copy J into the accumulator)
    STORE   I    (copy the accumulator into I)
```

In this example, L is the <u>label</u> of an instruction; instructions are labeled so they can be jumped to. In full Pascal, but not in PS/k, there are statement labels and there is a GOTO statement that is analogous to the JUMP machine instruction. In full Pascal, the following statements are equivalent to the example we just gave:

```
    IF I>K THEN
        GOTO 23;
    K:=I+J;
 23:I:=J;
```

GOTO statements were purposely left out of PS/k because careless use of them leads to unreadable programs. One of the reasons that low-level languages are inconvenient to use is that they do not directly provide looping constructs, such as WHILE...DO, and selection constructs, such as IF...THEN...ELSE. The programmer must build up these constructs using instructions like jumps and skips. When an PS/k program is translated into a low-level language, the loop and selection constructs appear as jumps and skips.

INSTRUCTIONS FOR A VERY SIMPLE COMPUTER

The VS computer has an instruction to print the value in the accumulator:

PUTINTEGER

This instruction needs no operand because the accumulator's value is always printed. There is an instruction to print messages:

PUTSTRING   operand

The operand represents a string to be printed. There is an instruction that directs the machine to stop executing a program:

HALT

The HALT instruction has no operand.

Altogether the VS computer has nine instructions; most real computers have many more instructions, typically around 100. This table lists the VS instructions.

	Operator	Operand	Action by Computer
1	LOAD	variable	Assign variable to accumulator.
2	STORE	variable	Assign accumulator to variable.
3	ADD	variable	Add variable to accumulator.
4	SUBTRACT	variable	Subtract variable from accumulator.
5	JUMP	label	Jump to labeled instruction.
6	SKIPLE	variable	If variable<=accumulator then skip next instruction.
7	PUTINTEGER	(none)	Print the integer in the accumulator.
8	PUTSTRING	string	Print the string.
9	HALT	(none)	Halt, the program is finished.

We have purposely kept the VS computer simple by leaving out instructions that might normally be part of the instruction set

of a computer. We have left out a whole set of skip
instructions, such as SKIPGT (skip when greater than). We left
out instructions for doing REAL arithmetic and for reading from
data cards. We left out instructions for manipulating character
strings, indexing arrays, and calling and returning from
procedures. These additional instructions are important in a
real computer; if you like, you can design a "super" VS computer
that includes them.

TRANSLATION OF A PASCAL PROGRAM

If we use some care in picking our example, we can translate
an entire Pascal program into VS instructions. This example
Pascal program requires only the types of instructions available
on the VS computer:

High-Level Language   Low-Level Language

```
PROGRAM T (INPUT,OUTPUT);
   VAR I: INTEGER;
   BEGIN
      WRITELN(' POWERS OF 2');       PUTSTRING TITLE
      I:=1;                          LOAD      ONE
                                     STORE     I
      WHILE I<=8 DO              L1:LOAD        EIGHT
         BEGIN                       SKIPLE    I
                                     JUMP      L2
            WRITELN(I);              LOAD      I
                                     PUTINTEGER
            I:=I+I                   LOAD      I
                                     ADD       I
                                     STORE     I
         END                        JUMP      L1
   END.                         L2:HALT
```

The first VS instruction in this example has as its operand
TITLE; TITLE gives the location of the string ' POWERS OF 2'.
Similarly, ONE and EIGHT give the locations of the values 1 and
8.

MNEMONIC NAMES AND MACHINE LANGUAGE

Up to this point we have written VS instructions using names
such as LOAD, STORE, I and J. These names are not present in the
machine language that a computer executes; they are replaced by
numbers. We will now show how these names can be translated into
appropriate numbers.

As you may recall from Chapter 2, the main memory of the
computer consists of a sequence of words. The words of memory
are numbered; the number that corresponds to a particular word is
called the location or address of the word. Words can be used to

represent variables. For example, the variables I, J and K could be represented by the words with locations 59, 60 and 61. Here we show these three words after I, J and K have been assigned the values 9, 0 and 14.

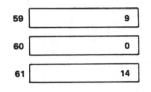

There is no special significance to 59, 60 and 61. We could just as well represent I, J and K by locations 42, 3 and 87; the important thing is to remember which location corresponds to which variable.

If I, J and K correspond to location 59, 60 and 61, we can write the instructions

```
LOAD   J
ADD    K
STORE  I
```

as

```
LOAD  60       (copy contents of word 60 into accumulator)
ADD   61       (add contents of word 61 to accumulator)
STORE 59       (copy accumulator into word 59)
```

The VS instruction operators, LOAD, STORE and so on, are numbered. LOAD is operator number 1, STORE is 2, ADD is 3 and so on. The names LOAD, STORE and ADD as used in the VS instructions are <u>mnemonic</u> <u>names</u>; a mnemonic name is an "easy-to-remember" name. We can choose the names of the operands so that they too are easy to remember.

Using the numbers of the operators we can write

```
LOAD  60
ADD   61
STORE 59
```

as

```
1    60
3    61
2    59
```

Instructions that consist only of numbers are in <u>machine</u> <u>language</u>. Instructions that contain mnemonic names, such as LOAD and I, are in <u>assembly</u> <u>language</u>.

```
Assembly Language          Machine Language

    LOAD  J                      1   60
    ADD   K                      3   61
    STORE I                      2   59
```

As you can see, there is a simple translation from assembly language to machine language. Writing programs in machine language is even more inconvenient than writing programs in assembly language. People almost always prefer assembly language over machine language; they use a program called an <u>assembler</u> to translate mnemonic names in assembly language programs to corresponding numeric operators and operands. Although we do not show it here, assemblers allow the programmer to reserve and initialize memory for variables and constants. For example, location 59 would be reserved for I, and location 98 could be reserved for EIGHT and initialized to 8.

STORING MACHINE INSTRUCTIONS IN WORDS

The values of variables of a program are stored in words of the computer's memory. In a similar manner, the instructions of the program are stored in words of memory. We can use two words to hold each VS instruction; one word for the operator and one word for the operand. Here we show three instructions stored in locations 18 through 23:

```
LOAD J    18 [            1 ]   19 [          60 ]

ADD K     20 [            3 ]   21 [          61 ]

STORE I   22 [            2 ]   23 [          59 ]
```

We could have saved space if the VS computer allowed us to pack the operator and operand into a single word. For example, the instruction

    1   59

could be packed into a single word as

    1059

with the convention that the rightmost three digits are the operand and the other digits are the operator. Instructions for real computers are packed into words to save space, but to keep things simple, the VS computer uses two words for its instructions.

A JUMP instruction has as its operand the label of an instruction. When a JUMP instruction is written in machine language, the label must be a number. The number used is the

location of the instruction being jumped to. Here is a
translation of assembly language into machine language; the label
L becomes 48:

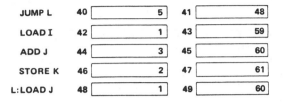

JUMP L	40	5	41	48
LOAD I	42	1	43	59
ADD J	44	3	45	60
STORE K	46	2	47	61
L:LOAD J	48	1	49	60

   Just as the variables and instructions are stored in words in
memory, strings such as ' POWERS OF 2' are stored in memory. In
real computers this is done by packing several characters into
each word. Since mixing characters and numbers is confusing, we
will assume that the VS computer has a separate part of its
memory used only for strings. Each string is saved in a
different location in the special string memory. If the string
' POWERS OF 2' is in location number 1 in the special string
memory, then we translate the Pascal statement

   WRITELN(' POWERS OF 2');

to the machine instruction

   8   1   (PUTSTRING TITLE)

We have now shown how to translate all VS instructions into
numbers and thus into machine language. We will return to our
program that prints powers of 2 and will translate it to machine
language.

A COMPLETE MACHINE LANGUAGE PROGRAM

   We will assume that a VS computer starts by executing the
instruction in words 0 and 1. So we will place our machine
language instructions in words 0, 1, 2, 3, ... We will continue
assuming that variable I corresponds to memory location 59. The
integer constants 1 and 8 will be represented by memory locations
91 and 98; these locations are initialized to hold the values 1
and 8 before the program is executed. We show the program as it
would appear in memory after having executed instructions in
locations 0 through 14. Up to this point the program has printed

   POWERS OF 2
            1

The VS computer has an <u>instruction pointer</u>, presently set to 16,
that locates the next instruction to be executed. When an
instruction has no operand, we give it a dummy operand of zero;
for example, HALT becomes 9 0.

STORAGE OF PROGRAM IN COMPUTER

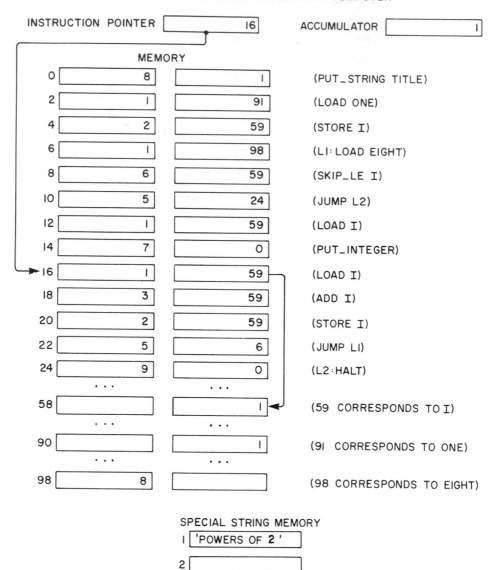

INSTRUCTION POINTER [16] ACCUMULATOR [1]

MEMORY

0	8	1	(PUT_STRING TITLE)
2	1	91	(LOAD ONE)
4	2	59	(STORE I)
6	1	98	(LI: LOAD EIGHT)
8	6	59	(SKIP_LE I)
10	5	24	(JUMP L2)
12	1	59	(LOAD I)
14	7	0	(PUT_INTEGER)
16	1	59	(LOAD I)
18	3	59	(ADD I)
20	2	59	(STORE I)
22	5	6	(JUMP LI)
24	9	0	(L2: HALT)
...		...	
58		1	(59 CORRESPONDS TO I)
...		...	
90		1	(91 CORRESPONDS TO ONE)
...		...	
98	8		(98 CORRESPONDS TO EIGHT)

SPECIAL STRING MEMORY

1	'POWERS OF 2 '
2	
...	

SIMULATING A COMPUTER

A VS computer has never been built and undoubtedly never will be built. It might seem that we can never have a VS machine language program executed. But we can, by making an existing computer <u>simulate</u> a VS computer. This is done by writing a program, called a <u>simulator</u>, that acts as if it is a VS computer. We will discuss later in more detail the importance of simulators in computing, but first we will develop a Pascal procedure that is a simulator for the VS computer.

The VS computer has an accumulator, which can be simulated by a variable declared by

    VAR ACCUMULATOR: INTEGER;

It also has a memory containing 100 words, whose addresses are 0 to 99. This can be simulated by an array:

    CONST MEMORYSIZE=99;
    VAR MEMORY: ARRAY[0..MEMORYSIZE] OF INTEGER;

There is a special string memory. Assuming that the VS computer can hold, at most, 10 strings of length at most 80, we can simulate the string memory by another array:

    CONST STRINGSIZE=80;
       NUMBEROFSTRINGS=10;
    VAR STRING: ARRAY[1..NUMBEROFSTRINGS] OF
       PACKED ARRAY[1..STRINGSIZE] OF CHAR;

We need an instruction pointer to keep track of which instruction is to be executed next.

    VAR INSTRUCTIONPOINTER: INTEGER;

When the VS computer is executing, the instruction pointer has a particular value, say 10, indicating that word 10 contains the operator of the next instruction to be executed. Word 11 contains the operand. If OPERATOR and OPERAND are declared as INTEGER variables in the simulator, then they should be given values by:

    OPERATOR:=MEMORY[INSTRUCTIONPOINTER];
    OPERAND:=MEMORY[INSTRUCTIONPOINTER+1];

If the OPERATOR is 1, meaning LOAD, the simulator carries out the LOAD machine instruction by executing:

    ACCUMULATOR:=MEMORY[OPERAND];

If the OPERATOR is 2, meaning STORE, the simulator carries out the STORE instruction by executing:

    MEMORY[OPERAND]:=ACCUMULATOR;

Similarly, the simulator can carry out the other VS instructions. After each instruction is carried out, the INSTRUCTIONPOINTER is incremented by 2 and OPERATOR and OPERAND are set for the next instruction. When the instruction is a JUMP or SKIP, then INSTRUCTIONPOINTER can be modified so an instruction other than the next sequential instruction will be selected. For example, if the OPERATOR is 6, for SKIPLE, the simulator executes this:

```
IF MEMORY[OPERAND]<=ACCUMULATOR THEN
    INSTRUCTIONPOINTER:=INSTRUCTIONPOINTER+2;
```

We will use named constants for each of the VS instructions:

```
CONST LOAD=1;
    STORE=2;
    ...
    HALT=9;
```

These declarations should be global to the simulator procedure. and we will use

```
CONST FIRSTINSTRUCTION=0;
```

to specify that execution begins with the instruction in words zero and one.

Now we give the complete simulator as a Pascal procedure. This procedure assumes that the MEMORY and STRING arrays have been declared and initialized.

```
(* THIS PROCEDURE SIMULATES A VERY SIMPLE COMPUTER *)
PROCEDURE SIMULATOR;
    VAR ACCUMULATOR,INSTRUCTIONPOINTER,
        OPERATOR,OPERAND: INTEGER;
    BEGIN
        INSTRUCTIONPOINTER:=FIRSTINSTRUCTION;
        OPERATOR:=MEMORY[INSTRUCTIONPOINTER];
        OPERAND:=MEMORY[INSTRUCTIONPOINTER+1];
        WHILE OPERATOR<>HALT DO
            BEGIN
                CASE OPERATOR OF
                    LOAD:
                        ACCUMULATOR:=MEMORY[OPERAND];
                    STORE:
                        MEMORY[OPERAND]:=ACCUMULATOR;
                    ADD:
                        ACCUMULATOR:=ACCUMULATOR+MEMORY[OPERAND];
                    SUBTRACT:
                        ACCUMULATOR:=ACCUMULATOR-MEMORY[OPERAND];
                    JUMP:
                        INSTRUCTIONPOINTER:=OPERAND-2; (* 2 ADDED BELOW *)
                    SKIPLE:
                        IF MEMORY[OPERAND]<=ACCUMULATOR THEN
                            INSTRUCTIONPOINTER:=INSTRUCTIONPOINTER+2;
                    PUTINTEGER:
                        WRITELN(ACCUMULATOR);
                    PUTSTRING:
                        WRITELN(STRING[OPERAND])
                END;
                INSTRUCTIONPOINTER:=INSTRUCTIONPOINTER+2;
                OPERATOR:=MEMORY[INSTRUCTIONPOINTER];
                OPERAND:=MEMORY[INSTRUCTIONPOINTER+1]
            END
    END;
```

If you want to run a VS machine language program, you can write a main procedure to put the numbers representing the program and constants into the MEMORY array, initialize the STRING array and then call the SIMULATOR procedure.

USES OF SIMULATORS

We will now discuss some of the uses of simulators. Our simulator for the VS computer can be used to execute VS machine language programs. But it can serve another purpose, too. By reading the SIMULATOR procedure, you can determine the actions carried out for each VS instruction; if you did not know how a VS computer worked, you could find out by studying its simulator. So not only can the simulator direct one computer to act like another, it can also show how a computer works.

Computer simulators are often used to allow programs written for one machine to execute on another machine. For example, a business may buy a new computer to replace an old computer. After the old computer is removed, programs written for the old computer can be executed by a simulator running on the new machine.

Sometimes a hypothetical computer is designed to help solve some particular problem. This is the case with several Pascal compilers especially those that run on microcomputers and minicomputers. A hypothetical computer is designed to allow easy translation from Pascal programs to the hypothetical computer's machine language. The translated Pascal programs are executed using a simulator for the hypothetical machine. Other compilers, such as the Pascal 6000 compiler, translate programs into the real computer's machine language; then a simulator is not required because the translated program is executed directly by the computer.

CHAPTER 21 SUMMARY

In this chapter we have presented features of machine language in terms of a very simple hypothetical computer called VS. The VS computer has an accumulator that is used for doing calculations. There are VS machine instructions for loading, storing, adding to, subtracting from, and printing the accumulator. There is a machine instruction for printing strings. There are instructions for jumping to instructions, skipping instructions and for halting. The nine VS machine instructions were sufficient for the translation of the example Pascal program given in this chapter. Real computers typically have many more instructions. The following important terms were discussed in this chapter:

Word - the computer's main memory is divided into words. Each word can contain a number. In real computers, a word can contain several characters, for example, 4 characters.

Location (or address) - the number that locates a particular word in the computer's main memory.

Operators and operands - most VS machine instructions, such as,

    LOAD I

consist of an operator and an operand; these are LOAD and I in this example. Some instructions have an operator but no operand.

Mnemonic name - a name that helps programmers remember something. For example, STORE is the mnemonic name for VS machine instruction number 2.

Machine language - the purely numeric language that is directly executed by a particular type of computer. Some computer manufacturers sell families of computers, of various sizes and speeds, that all use the same machine language.

Assembly language - programs in assembly language use mnemonic names corresponding to the numeric operators of machine language. They also permit programmers to choose mnemonic names for the operands and labels.

Assembler - a program that translates programs written in assembly language to machine language.

Label - a name that gives the location of a machine instruction or a statement. The JUMP machine instruction, as written in assembly language, transfers control to a labeled instruction. The GOTO statement, as written in full Pascal, but not in PS/k, transfers control to a labeled statement.

Simulator - a program that simulates some system such as a computer. A simulator treats a sequence of numbers as a machine language program and carries out the specified operations.

CHAPTER 21 EXERCISES

1. The VS computer described in this chapter does not have an instruction for reading data. Invent an instruction named GETINTEGER that reads the next integer in the data into the accumulator. Show how to translate a statement such as

    READ(K);

into VS machine language, as augmented by GETINTEGER. Show how the SIMULATOR procedure given in this chapter can be modified to execute GETINTEGER instructions.

2. Translate the following Pascal program into VS assembly language and then into VS machine language.

```
PROGRAM T (INPUT,OUTPUT);
   VAR I,J: INTEGER;
   BEGIN
      I:=1;
      J:=5;
      IF I<=J THEN
         WRITELN(' I IS SMALLER')
      ELSE
         WRITELN(' J IS SMALLER')
   END.
```

3. What will the following VS assembly language program print? Translate the program to both machine language and Pascal.

```
        LOAD    ZERO
        STORE   PREVIOUS
        LOAD    ONE
        STORE   CURRENT
    L1:LOAD     FIFTY
        SKIPLE  CURRENT
        JUMP    L2
        LOAD    CURRENT
        ADD     PREVIOUS
        STORE   NEXT
        LOAD    CURRENT
        STORE   PREVIOUS
        LOAD    NEXT
        STORE   CURRENT
        PUTINTEGER
        JUMP    L1
    L2:HALT
```

4. In this chapter an example program was given that prints powers of 2. Have this program executed by the VS simulator given in this chapter. This can be done by writing a main procedure that declares MEMORY and STRING arrays, initializes these arrays to hold the machine language version of the example program, and then calls the SIMULATOR procedure.

5. Invent new instructions for the VS computer that allow array indexing and procedure call and return.

Chapter 22
PROGRAMMING LANGUAGE COMPILERS

High-level languages such as Pascal provide a convenient tool to help us use computers. We use a <u>translator</u> or <u>compiler</u> to translate our Pascal programs to machine language.

In this chapter we will show how compilers bridge the gap between high-level languages, which are convenient for people, and machine languages, which can be directly executed by a computer. We will define a simple programming language called PPS/3, and then we will show how programs written in that language can be translated to the machine language for the very simple (VS) computer described in the last chapter.

We will give a compiler that reads cards containing a PPS/3 program and translates the program to VS machine language. Our compiler will be written as a Pascal procedure that is about 200 lines long. Since our compiler is longer than any program we have given before, it provides better examples of step-by-step refinement and modular programming. Compilers are usually very large programs.

A SIMPLE HIGH-LEVEL LANGUAGE

We will invent a simple high-level language to illustrate points about compilers and computer languages. We will call our language PPS/3, because it contains <u>part</u> of the features of PS/3.

PPS/3 does not have any of the features of PS/4 through PS/8: no character variables, no arrays, no procedures, and no files. PPS/3 allows:

-INTEGER variables named A or B or C ... or Z, but no REAL variables. All INTEGER variables used in a program must be declared via

VAR list of variables separated by commas: INTEGER;

- Addition and subtraction, but no multiplication or division, and no parentheses in expressions.

- INTEGER constants 0, 1, 2,..., 9, but no multiple-digit constants such as 21, no signed constants and no REAL constants.

- WRITELN statement. Exactly one output item must be given. The output item can be a literal such as ' HI THERE' or an integer expression. Literals may not contain an embedded quote, so ' DON''T' is not allowed.

- Assignment statements.

- WHILE loops. The only allowed comparison is <= (the following are not allowed >=, =, <, >, <>). No logical operators (AND , OR, NOT) are allowed. We will also assume that there is a compound statement after the WHILE so that there would always be a BEGIN..END. Counted FOR loops and IF statements are disallowed.

- Every PPS/3 program is named T, so each program begins

PROGRAM T (INPUT,OUTPUT);

This list of restrictions applied to PS/3 defines the PPS/3 language.

Since PPS/3 is a subset of PS/k, a PPS/3 program can be translated by a Pascal compiler. PPS/3 is so limited that it is not particularly useful for solving problems; we impose these limitations so we can develop a complete PPS/3 compiler in this chapter.

Things have been arranged so that it is relatively easy to translate PPS/3 programs to machine language for the very simple (VS) computer described in the last chapter. The program from the last chapter that prints powers of 2 is an example of a PPS/3 program.

SYNTAX RULES

Each programming language has rules that a programmer must follow when writing a program. For example, in Pascal, statements must be separated by a semicolon and each BEGIN must be matched by a following END. Rules such as these give the grammar or syntax of the language. By now you should know the syntax for the PS/k subsets of Pascal by heart; this means you should be able to tell whether a PS/k statement is correctly formed.

We have described the PPS/3 language by explaining how it differs from PS/3. We will now describe PPS/3 more directly by giving its syntax. The syntax for PPS/3 consists of nine rules. In the syntax rules, the wiggly brackets ⎨⎬ mean that the enclosed item is optional or can be repeated any number of times. Thus, the notation

        variable ⎨,variable⎬

means a list of variables separated by commas.

1. A <u>program</u> is:
                PROGRAM T (INPUT,OUTPUT);
                    VAR variable⎨,variable⎬: INTEGER;
                    BEGIN
                        statement⎨;statement⎬
                    END.

2. A <u>statement</u> is one of the following:
                    a. WRITELN(output item)
                    b. variable := expression
                    c. WHILE expression <= expression DO
                        BEGIN
                            statement⎨;statement⎬
                        END

3. An <u>output item</u> is one of the following:
                    a. expression
                    b. literal

4. An <u>expression</u> is:
                    value ⎨operator value⎬

5. A <u>value</u> is one of the following:
                    a. variable
                    b. integer

6. An <u>operator</u> is: + or -

7. A <u>variable</u> is: A or B or C ... or Z

8. An <u>integer</u> is: 0 or 1 or 2 ... or 9

9. A <u>literal</u> is: ' ⎨any non-quote character⎬'

Our syntax rules specify the allowed forms of PPS/3 programs. Rule 2 specifies that the only allowed statements are WRITELN, assignment and WHILE ... END. Since other statements such as READ and IF are not specified in the syntax, they are not allowed in PPS/3. Rule 2 specifies that a WHILE loop contains a list of statements enclosed in BEGIN and END; since a WHILE loop is itself a statement, rule 2 implies that WHILE loops can be nested inside WHILE loops. Rule 2 is almost a circular definition, in that a WHILE loop is specified to be a "statement" and yet a WHILE loop can contain "statements". We say such a definition is recursive; recursive definitions provide a concise way of stating that a particular construct, such as a WHILE loop, can be nested inside a construct of the same type.

USING SYNTAX RULES TO PRODUCE A PROGRAM

A PPS/3 program is considered to be syntactically correct if it can be produced or developed using the syntax rules. We start with rule 1 and produce a "program" of the form

```
PROGRAM T (INPUT,OUTPUT);
    VAR variable |,variable| : INTEGER;
    BEGIN
        statement|;statement|
    END.
```

The symbols written in small letters, "variable" and "statement", will not be a part of the final program. Instead, they represent a set of possibilities. By contrast, symbols such as "T", "PROGRAM", ";" and "END" are a part of the final program. Symbols like "variable" and "statement" that do not appear in the final program are called non-terminal symbols. Symbols such as "T", "PROGRAM", ";" and "END" are called terminal symbols because they appear in the final program.

We can produce a PPS/3 program using our syntax rules by starting with rule 1 and successively using rules to replace non-terminal symbols, such as "statement", until we are left with nothing but terminal symbols. In previous chapters, we have shown how to develop programs by step-by-step refinement. Producing programs using syntax rules is analogous to step-by-step refinement, but serves an entirely different purpose. We use step-by-step refinement as a method of designing programs. By contrast, we check the syntax of a given program by trying to produce it using the syntax rules. We will illustrate this process by using the PPS/3 syntax rules to verify that an example program is syntactically correct. We will use as our example the program from the last chapter that prints powers of 2:

```
PROGRAM T (INPUT,OUTPUT);
   VAR I: INTEGER;
   BEGIN
      WRITELN(' POWERS OF 2');
      I:=1;
      WHILE I<=8 DO
         BEGIN
            WRITELN(I);
            I:=I+I
         END
   END.
```

We start with rule 1 and produce

```
PROGRAM T (INPUT,OUTPUT);
   VAR variable |,variable| : INTEGER;
   BEGIN
      statement|;statement|
   END.
```

In order to produce the desired final program we replace the parts

```
variable |,variable|
```

and

```
statement|;statement|
```

by the corresponding parts

```
variable
```

and

```
statement;
statement;
statement
```

Our program has now become

```
PROGRAM T (INPUT,OUTPUT);
   VAR variable: INTEGER;
   BEGIN
      statement;
      statement;
      statement
   END.
```

We can now use rule 7 to produce I from "variable", making the declaration become

```
VAR I: INTEGER;
```

We can produce the first WRITELN statement in our example program by applying rules 2a, 3b and 9 in succession to the "statement" immediately following the BEGIN:

```
statement;
WRITELN(output item);      (produced using rule 2a)
WRITELN(literal);          (produced using rule 3b)
WRITELN(' POWERS OF 2');   (produced using rule 9)
```

Up to now, we have used the syntax rules to produce

```
PROGRAM T (INPUT,OUTPUT);
   VAR I: INTEGER;
   BEGIN
      WRITELN(' POWERS OF 2');
      statement;
      statement
   END.
```

We can apply rules 2b, 7, 4, 5b and 8 to transform the "statement"; following WRITELN to the desired form:

```
statement;
variable:=expression;   (produced using rule 2b)
I:=expression;          (produced using rule 7)
I:=value;               (produced using rule 4)
I:=1;                   (produced using rules 5b,8)
```

We can now transform the last "statement" to the desired WHILE loop:

```
statement

WHILE expression<=expression DO    (rule 2c)
   BEGIN
      statement;
      statement
   END

WHILE I<=8 DO        (rules 2a, 2b, 3a, 4, 5, 6, 7 and 8)
   BEGIN
      WRITELN(I);
      I:=I+I
   END
```

We have now used the syntax rules to produce the example program that prints powers of 2. Since this program can be produced using the syntax rules, it is syntactically correct.

Syntax rules provide a concise way of describing a language. They do not completely describe a language. For example, the syntax rules for PPS/3 do not imply that every variable used in the program must be declared. The syntax rules for PPS/3 describe all legal PPS/3 programs, but they describe some illegal ones as well, in particular the ones with undeclared variables.

One of the most important uses of syntax rules is for specifying a high-level language so that a compiler can be written for the language. In the next sections we develop a complete compiler for PPS/3. Because of the level of detail in these sections, some readers may choose to skim them or to skip them altogether.

ACTIONS OF THE COMPILER

To keep our compiler simple, we will make several assumptions about PPS/3 programs. We will assume that <u>PPS/3 programs never contain errors</u>, so our compiler will not need to check for such errors. In the real world of programming, this would be a disastrous assumption; we are making it only so the example compiler can be smaller.

We will assume that every PPS/3 program is surrounded by the control cards %JOB and %DATA in this manner:

```
%JOB
    PPS/3 program
%DATA
```

Our compiler will use the %DATA card to detect the end of a PPS/3 job; it will ignore the %JOB card.

To present the compiler we will consider each of the following seven types of lines separately; they will appear on separate cards in a PPS/3 program. Whether or not there is a semi-colon or period will be ignored.

```
PROGRAM T (INPUT,OUTPUT);
VAR ...: INTEGER;
BEGIN
WRITELN(...)
variable:=expression
WHILE...DO
END
```

We will assume there are no cards that are all blank. Since every PPS/3 program begins with the same line,

```
PROGRAM T (INPUT,OUTPUT);
```

this line can be ignored by our compiler.

A real Pascal compiler analyzes declarations to determine the types of variables and to see that memory space is set aside to represent the variables. Our compiler takes advantage of the fact that all PPS/3 variables are INTEGER and must be named A, B, C, ... or Z. Our compiler always sets aside enough memory for all 26 possible PPS/3 variables, regardless of whether they are used in the particular program. This wastes memory, but it makes

our compiler simpler. The only purpose of the declarations in
PPS/3 is so that PPS/3 programs are legal PS/k programs.

The PPS/3 compiler can simply ignore the first four cards:

```
%JOB
 PROGRAM T (INPUT,OUTPUT);
    VAR ...: INTEGER;
    BEGIN
```

Having skipped these four cards, the compiler must translate each
of the following five types of cards to machine language:

```
    WRITELN(...)
    variable:=expression
    WHILE...DO
    BEGIN
    END
```

When the compiler reads each of these cards, it should take these
actions:

Type of Card	Action by Compiler
WRITELN(output item)	If the output item is a literal, then an instruction is generated to print the literal. Otherwise instructions are generated to find the value of the expression and print it.
variable:=expression	Instructions are generated to find the value of the expression and to store it in the variable's memory location.
WHILE expr<=expr DO	Instructions are generated to find the values of the two expressions. Then instructions are generated to compare their values, and either to execute the body of the loop or to jump beyond the body of the loop.
BEGIN	This is ignored.
END	If the END is for a WHILE loop, then a JUMP instruction is generated to repeat the loop. If it is the final END of the program, a HALT instruction is generated.

We can modularize our compiler by defining four procedures to
carry out the above actions:

```
COMPILEWRITELN
COMPILEASSIGNMENT
COMPILEWHILE
COMPILEEND
```

After reading a card, the compiler can decide which of these procedures to call by inspecting the first word on the card. We will define the procedure:

> SCANWORD - skips blanks and finds the first (or next) word
>   on a card and records it in NEXTWORD and its
>   length in LENGTH

Since each PPS/3 identifier consists of one letter, our compiler can recognize an assignment statement by seeing if the length of the first word on the card is 1. Using these procedures, we can now give the structure of our compiler:

```
Do any required initialization;
Read and print four cards (%JOB, PROGRAM T...,VAR..., and BEGIN)
WHILE CARD[1]<>'%' DO
    BEGIN
        Read and print card;
        SCANWORD;
        CASE LENGTH OF
            7:COMPILEWRITELN;
            1:COMPILEASSIGNMENT;
            5:IF CARD[1]='W' THEN
                    COMPILEWHILE;
            3:COMPILEEND
        END
    END;
```

Note that the word BEGIN has five letters but its first letter is not W so that nothing happens.

SCANNING WORDS AND CHARACTERS

Within a compiler, it is often necessary to determine the next word or character on a card. The part of the compiler that does this work is called the scanner. Our scanner includes the SCANWORD procedure and the two procedures:

> SCANCHAR - sets NEXTCHAR to the next character on the card.
>   (NEXTCHAR may be set to a blank).

> SCANNONBLANKCHAR - sets NEXTCHAR to the next non-blank
>   character on the card.

COMPILING ASSIGNMENT STATEMENTS

We will now explain how the COMPILEASSIGNMENT procedure works. Given a card such as

    I:=1;

this procedure must generate machine language:

    1   91   (LOAD ONE)
    2   59   (STORE I)

We set aside memory locations 51 through 76 to hold variables A through Z, so variable I corresponds to 59. We set aside memory locations 90 through 99 to hold the allowed PPS/3 constants 0 through 9. We record this use of memory locations by named constants.

    CONST FIRSTVARIABLE=51;
       FIRSTDIGIT=90;

There is no special significance to locations 51 to 76 and 90 to 99; we could have used other locations.

If PPS/3 allowed constants other than 0 to 9, our compiler would need to reserve locations for each new constant it encountered. We have avoided this complication by allowing only constants 0 to 9. If you wish, you can augment our compiler so it could accept other constants.

To generate machine language for assignment statements, the COMPILEASSIGNMENT procedure uses three other procedures or functions:

COMPILEEXPRESSION - generates instructions to find the value of an expression and leave that value in the accumulator.

COMPILEVARIABLE - determines the location corresponding to a given variable. For example, 59 is returned for variable I. Note that this is a function.

EMITINSTRUCTION - places one machine instruction in memory. This procedure accepts two parameters, an operator and an operand, and places these in two memory locations just after the last generated machine instruction. This procedure uses a variable called INSTRUCTIONPOINTER to keep track of the next location to receive an instruction. INSTRUCTIONPOINTER is initialized to zero. Do not confuse this INSTRUCTIONPOINTER with the one used by the simulator in the last chapter. They are two quite different things.

When the COMPILEASSIGNMENT procedure is entered, NEXTWORD holds the name of the variable to be assigned a value. The procedure will do the following:

    Skip over the ':=' sign;
    Find the beginning of the expression;
    Generate instructions to place the value of the expression
        in the accumulator;
    Generate a STORE instruction to assign the accumulator
        to the location corresponding to the variable
        in NEXTWORD;

When we write this in Pascal, we get the COMPILEASSIGNMENT procedure.

    PROCEDURE COMPILEASSIGNMENT;
        (* SKIP ':=' AND FIND START OF EXPRESSION *)
        BEGIN
            SCANNONBLANKCHAR;
            SCANNONBLANKCHAR;
            SCANNONBLANKCHAR;
            COMPILEEXPRESSION;
            EMITINSTRUCTION(STORE,COMPILEVARIABLE(NEXTWORD))
        END;

As was done in the last chapter, the names of the machine instructions, LOAD, STORE, and so on are declared as named constants with their appropriate numeric values. This allows us to write STORE in the call to EMITINSTRUCTION when we want to specify operator 2.

COMPILING WRITELN STATEMENTS

The COMPILEWRITELN procedure is not much more complicated than COMPILEASSIGNMENT. If the output item to be printed is an expression, then the COMPILEEXPRESSION procedure is called to generate instructions to place the expression's value in the accumulator. The PUTINTEGER instruction will print the value in the accumulator; this instruction is generated by executing:

    EMITINSTRUCTION(PUTINTEGER,0);

Since the PUTINTEGER instruction uses no operand, a dummy operand of zero is used.

If the output item is a literal, then the characters of the literal are collected and placed in the next available string location in the VS computer's special string memory. Then the PUTSTRING instruction is generated by

    EMITINSTRUCTION(PUTSTRING,STRINGNUMBER);

The variable STRINGNUMBER gives the location of the literal.

COMPILING WHILE AND END

There are two complications in compiling WHILE and END. The first has to do with using the accumulator to evaluate two different expressions, without losing the value of either. The second has to do with making JUMP instructions transfer control to appropriate locations. We will now consider the first of these complications.

When our compiler encounters a card such as

WHILE I+1 <= J-K DO

it must see that instructions are generated to evaluate both expressions, I+1 and J-K, before the comparison is made. The difficulty is that both evaluations use the accumulator. After I+1 is evaluated, its result, which will reside in the accumulator, is _temporarily_ saved while J-K is evaluated in the accumulator. The following sequence of instructions performs the evaluations, the temporary saving of one value, the comparison and the conditional jump beyond the end of the WHILE loop.

```
LOAD      I
ADD       ONE
STORE     TEMPORARY        (save value of I+1)
LOAD      J
SUBTRACT  K
SKIPLE    TEMPORARY        (compare values of I+1 and J-K)
JUMP      LOOPEND
```

These instructions are followed immediately by the body of the loop. The value I+1 is saved in the location called TEMPORARY. We will arbitrarily choose location 80; our compiler will use a named constant TEMPORARY with value 80.

The COMPILEWHILE procedure can generate the above sequence of instructions by first executing

```
COMPILEEXPRESSION;    (generates LOAD I and ADD ONE)
EMITINSTRUCTION(STORE,TEMPORARY);
```

Next, '<=' is skipped over and this is executed:

```
COMPILEEXPRESSION;    (generates LOAD J and SUBTRACT K)
EMITINSTRUCTION(SKIPLE,TEMPORARY);
```

Finally, this is executed:

```
EMITINSTRUCTION(JUMP,0);
```

This leads us to the second complication in compiling WHILE and END. When the JUMP instruction for WHILE is generated, the compiler does not yet know where the end of the loop will be. The operand of the JUMP is temporarily set to the dummy value of zero.

Our compiler records the location of this JUMP instruction, so its operand can be corrected when the END of the loop is found. The COMPILEEND procedure corrects the operand of this JUMP. It also generates a JUMP instruction to return to the beginning of the loop. The COMPILEEND procedure must know the location of the beginning of the loop so it can make the JUMP instruction transfer to the correct location.

If PPS/3 programs were allowed to contain at most a single un-nested WHILE loop, then we could easily produce the required JUMP operands by using two variables:

WHILESTART - records location of beginning of loop.
WHILEJUMP - records location of operand of JUMP at
      beginning of loop.

The COMPILEWHILE procedure would set WHILESTART to INSTRUCTIONPOINTER, which gives the location of the instruction to be generated next, before generating instructions to evaluate the left expression of the comparison. The COMPILEWHILE procedure would set WHILEJUMP to INSTRUCTIONPOINTER+1 just before generating the instruction JUMP 0. The COMPILEEND procedure would then execute

EMITINSTRUCTION(JUMP,WHILESTART);
MEMORY[WHILEJUMP]:=INSTRUCTIONPOINTER;

This generates a JUMP to the start of the loop and then corrects the JUMP instruction at the beginning of the loop to transfer control beyond the just generated JUMP instruction.

Things are not this simple in PPS/3, because WHILE loops can be nested inside WHILE loops. Whenever our compiler encounters the END of a loop, it must match it with the nearest preceding WHILE. It needs to keep track of the locations of the WHILEs on a last-in-first-out basis. The last encountered WHILE is the next one to be matched with an END. Once the compiler matches a WHILE to an END and produces the appropriate JUMPs, it can discard the location of that WHILE.

We need a data structure that allows us to save the locations of WHILEs until they are needed. What we need is a stack, as was described in Chapter 17. We can establish a stack by the declaration

CONST MAXWHILEDEPTH=20,
VAR STACK: ARRAY[1..MAXWHILEDEPTH]OF INTEGER;
    STACKTOP: 0..MAXWHILEDEPTH;

We will initialize STACKTOP to zero to indicate that the stack is empty.

Before the COMPILEWHILE procedure generates any instructions, it places the value of the INSTRUCTIONPOINTER on top of the stack. Just before it generates the JUMP instruction that transfers control beyond the end of the loop, it places the value

of INSTRUCTIONPOINTER+1 on top of the stack. The COMPILEEND
procedure uses these stacked locations in this way:

```
(* CORRECT OPERAND OF JUMP AT BEGINNING OF LOOP *)
MEMORY[STACK[STACKTOP]]:=INSTRUCTIONPOINTER+2;
STACKTOP:=STACKTOP-1;
(* EMIT JUMP TO GO BACK TO BEGINNING OF LOOP *)
EMITINSTRUCTION(JUMP,STACK[STACKTOP]);
STACKTOP:=STACKTOP-1;
```

Before executing these statements, the COMPILEEND procedure
checks to see if the stack is empty. If it is empty, this
indicates that the END does not correspond to a WHILE. Instead,
it is the final END of the PPS/3 program, and a HALT instruction
is generated.

THE COMPILER

We have now described the modules of our compiler. We can
put these modules together to make a procedure that compiles
PPS/3 programs. Our compiler has this overall structure:

```
PROCEDURE COMPILER;
    (declare the named constants FIRSTVARIABLE, TEMPORARY, FIRSTDIGIT
        MAXWHILEDEPTH and CARDSIZE)
    (declare the type CARDTYPE)
    (declare the variables INSTRUCTIONPOINTER, STRINGNUMBER,
        LENGTH, POS, I, STACK, STACKTOP,
        CARD, BLANKS, NEXTWORD, NEXTCHAR and ALPHABET)
    (declare the procedure READANDPRINTCARD)
    (declare the scanner procedures SCANWORD, SCANCHAR
        and SCANNONBLANKCHAR)
    (declare the procedure EMITINSTRUCTION)
    (declare the procedures COMPILEVARIABLE, COMPILEVALUE,
        COMPILEEXPRESSION, COMPILEWRITELN,
        COMPILEASSIGNMENT, COMPILEWHILE and COMPILEEND)
    BEGIN
        Initialize INSTRUCTIONPOINTER, STRINGNUMBER and STACKTOP;
        Initialize BLANKS and ALPHABET;
        Initialize constants 0 to 9 in MEMORY;
        Read and print four cards (%JOB, PROGRAM T..., VAR..., BEGIN)
        Read and print another card;
        WHILE CARD[1]<>'%' DO
            BEGIN
                SCANWORD;
                Call appropriate procedure among
                    COMPILEWRITELN,COMPILEASSIGNMENT,
                    COMPILEWHILE and COMPILEEND;
                Read and print a card
            END
    END;
```

Our compiler must have access to arrays representing the regular and string memory of the VS computer. These arrays can be declared to be global to the compiler procedure via

```
CONST MEMORYSIZE=99;
    STRINGSIZE=80;
    NUMBEROFSTRINGS=10;
VAR MEMORY: ARRAY[0..MEMORYSIZE] OF INTEGER;
    STRING: ARRAY[1..NUMBEROFSTRINGS] OF
        PACKED ARRAY[1..STRINGSIZE] OF CHAR;
```

As we have explained, our compiler uses the words in the VS computer's memory as follows:

```
Locations 0 to 50 - used for instructions.
Locations 51 to 76 - used for variables A to Z.
Location 80 - used for TEMPORARY (saves the value of the left
         expression in a comparison).
Locations 90 to 99 - used for constants 0 to 9.
```

We use named constants to record this layout of memory:

```
FIRSTINSTRUCTION=0;
FIRSTVARIABLE=51;
TEMPORARY=80;
FIRSTDIGIT=90;
```

And each of the VS instructions are named:

```
LOAD=1;
STORE=2;
...
HALT=9;
```

We put all the parts together and we have a complete procedure that translates PPS/3 programs into VS machine language:

```
(* THIS PROCEDURE COMPILES A CORRECT PPS/3 PROGRAM *)
PROCEDURE COMPILER;
    CONST FIRSTVARIABLE=51;   (* Where A,B,...,Z BEGIN *)
        TEMPORARY=80;         (* HOLDS EXPRESSIONS TEMPORARILY *)
        FIRSTDIGIT=90;        (* WHERE 0,1,...,9 BEGIN *)
        MAXWHILEDEPTH=20;     (* MAXIMUM NESTING OF LOOPS *)
        CARDSIZE=81;          (* MAX INPUT LINE LENGTH IS 80 *)
                              (* THE 81-ST IS A DUMMY FOR EOLN *)

    TYPE CARDTYPE=PACKED ARRAY [1..CARDSIZE] OF CHAR;
    VAR INSTRUCTIONPOINTER: 0..MEMORYSIZE;
        STRINGNUMBER: 0..NUMBEROFSTRINGS;  (* INITIALLY 0 *)
        LENGTH: 0..CARDSIZE;   (* IDENTIFIER OR KEYWORD LENGTH *)
        POS: INTEGER;        (* POSITION ON CARD AFTER NEXTCHAR *)
        I: INTEGER;        (* INDEX USED DURING INITIALIZATION *)
        STACKTOP: INTEGER;
        STACK: ARRAY[1..MAXWHILEDEPTH] OF 0..MEMORYSIZE;
        CARD,BLANKS,NEXTWORD: CARDTYPE;
```

```
                NEXTCHAR: CHAR;
                ALPHABET: ARRAY[1..26] OF CHAR;  (* MAPS 'A'..'Z' TO *)
                                                 (* INTEGERS *)

        PROCEDURE READANDPRINTCARD;
           VAR I: 0..CARDSIZE;
           BEGIN
              CARD:=BLANKS;
              I:=0;
              WHILE NOT EOLN DO
                 BEGIN
                    I:=I+1;
                    READ(CARD[I])
                 END;
              READLN;
              POS:=1;
              WRITELN(CARD);
              CARD[I+1]:='$' (* MARK EOLN SO SCANNONBLANK STOPS *)
           END;

        PROCEDURE SCANWORD;
           BEGIN
              NEXTWORD:=BLANKS;
              LENGTH:=0;
              WHILE CARD[POS]=' ' DO
                 POS:=POS+1;
              WHILE(CARD[POS]>='A') AND (CARD[POS]<='Z') DO
                 BEGIN
                    LENGTH:=LENGTH+1;
                    NEXTWORD[LENGTH]:=CARD[POS];
                    POS:=POS+1
                 END
           END;

    PROCEDURE SCANCHAR;
       BEGIN
          NEXTCHAR:=CARD[POS];
          POS:=POS+1
       END;

    PROCEDURE SCANNONBLANKCHAR;
       BEGIN
          SCANCHAR;
          WHILE NEXTCHAR=' ' DO
             SCANCHAR
       END;

    (* PUT AN INSTRUCTION INTO THE MEMORY *)
    PROCEDURE EMITINSTRUCTION(OPERATOR,OPERAND: INTEGER);
       BEGIN
          MEMORY[INSTRUCTIONPOINTER]:=OPERATOR;
          MEMORY[INSTRUCTIONPOINTER+1]:=OPERAND;
          INSTRUCTIONPOINTER:=INSTRUCTIONPOINTER+2
       END;

    (* FOR IDENTIFIERS A TO Z, THIS WILL RETURN 51 TO 76, *)
```

```
(* RESPECTIVELY, ASSUMING FIRSTVARIABLE=51            *)
FUNCTION COMPILEVARIABLE(LETTER:CHAR): INTEGER;
    VAR J: 1..26;
    BEGIN
        J:=1;
        WHILE ALPHABET[J]<>LETTER DO
            J:=J+1;
        COMPILEVARIABLE:=FIRSTVARIABLE+J-1
    END;

(* FIND MEMORY LOCATION OF NEXT VARIABLE OR INTEGER ON *)
(* CARD                                                *)
FUNCTION COMPILEVALUE: INTEGER;
    VAR LOCATION: 0..MEMORYSIZE;
    BEGIN
        IF(NEXTCHAR>='A') AND (NEXTCHAR<='Z')THEN
            LOCATION:=COMPILEVARIABLE(NEXTCHAR)
        ELSE (* VALUES 0,1,...9 START IN LOCATION FIRSTDIGIT *)
            LOCATION:=ORD(NEXTCHAR)-ORD('0')+FIRSTDIGIT;
            (* ASSUMES CONTIGUOUS ASCENDING DIGIT VALUES *)
        COMPILEVALUE:=LOCATION
    END;

(* GENERATE CODE FOR NEXT EXPRESSION ON CARD *)
PROCEDURE COMPILEEXPRESSION;
    VAR PLUSMINUS: CHAR;
    BEGIN
        EMITINSTRUCTION(LOAD,COMPILEVALUE);
        SCANNONBLANKCHAR;
        WHILE(NEXTCHAR='+')OR(NEXTCHAR='-') DO
            BEGIN
                PLUSMINUS:=NEXTCHAR;
                SCANNONBLANKCHAR;
                IF PLUSMINUS='+' THEN
                    EMITINSTRUCTION(ADD,COMPILEVALUE)
                ELSE
                    EMITINSTRUCTION(SUBTRACT,COMPILEVALUE);
                SCANNONBLANKCHAR
            END
    END;

PROCEDURE COMPILEWRITELN;
    CONST QUOTE='''';
    VAR POSITION:1..CARDSIZE;
    BEGIN
        (* SKIP '(' AND FIND START OF EXPRESSION *)
        SCANNONBLANKCHAR;
        SCANNONBLANKCHAR;
        (* SEE IF NEXT CHARACTER IS A QUOTE *)
        IF NEXTCHAR=QUOTE THEN
            BEGIN
                STRINGNUMBER:=STRINGNUMBER+1;
                FOR POSITION:=1 TO STRINGSIZE DO
                    STRING[STRINGNUMBER][POSITION]:=' ';
                SCANCHAR;
                POSITION:=1;
```

```
                    WHILE NEXTCHAR<>QUOTE DO
                       BEGIN
                          STRING[STRINGNUMBER][POSITION]:=NEXTCHAR;
                          POSITION:=POSITION+1;
                          SCANCHAR
                       END;
                    EMITINSTRUCTION(PUTSTRING,STRINGNUMBER)
              END
           ELSE
              BEGIN
                 COMPILEEXPRESSION;
                 EMITINSTRUCTION(PUTINTEGER,0)
              END
     END;

PROCEDURE COMPILEASSIGNMENT;
   (* SKIP ':=' AND FIND START OF EXPRESSION *)
   BEGIN
      SCANNONBLANKCHAR;
      SCANNONBLANKCHAR;
      SCANNONBLANKCHAR;
      COMPILEEXPRESSION;
      EMITINSTRUCTION(STORE,COMPILEVARIABLE(NEXTWORD[1]))
   END;

PROCEDURE COMPILEWHILE;
   BEGIN
      SCANNONBLANKCHAR;   (* FIND START OF LEFT EXPRESSION *)
      (* RECORD LOCATION OF BEGINNING OF LOOP ON TOP OF STACK *)
      STACKTOP:=STACKTOP+1;
      STACK[STACKTOP]:=INSTRUCTIONPOINTER;
      COMPILEEXPRESSION;
      EMITINSTRUCTION(STORE,TEMPORARY);
      (* SKIP OVER '<=' *)
      SCANNONBLANKCHAR;
      SCANNONBLANKCHAR;
      COMPILEEXPRESSION;
      EMITINSTRUCTION(SKIPLE,TEMPORARY);
      (* RECORD JUMP LOCATION SO ITS OPERAND CAN BE CORRECTED *)
      STACKTOP:=STACKTOP+1;
      STACK[STACKTOP]:=INSTRUCTIONPOINTER+1;
      EMITINSTRUCTION(JUMP,0)
   END;
```

```
PROCEDURE COMPILEEND;
   (* SEE IF STACK HOLDS LOCATION OF 1 OR MORE WHILE'S *)
   BEGIN
      IF STACKTOP>0 THEN
         BEGIN
            (* CORRECT OPERAND OF JUMP AT BEGINNING OF LOOP *)
            MEMORY[STACK[STACKTOP]]:=INSTRUCTIONPOINTER+2;
            STACKTOP:=STACKTOP-1;
            (* EMIT JUMP TO GO BACK TO BEGINNING OF LOOP. *)
            EMITINSTRUCTION(JUMP,STACK[STACKTOP]);
            STACKTOP:=STACKTOP-1
         END
      ELSE
         (* THIS IS THE FINAL 'END' OF THE PPS/3 PROGRAM *)
         EMITINSTRUCTION(HALT,0)
   END;

(* BODY OF PROCEDURE THAT COMPILES PPS/3 PROGRAMS *)
BEGIN
   FOR I:=1 TO CARDSIZE DO
      BLANKS[I]:=' ';
   ALPHABET:='ABCDEFGHIJKLMNOPQRSTUVWXYZ';
   FOR I:=0 TO 9 DO  (* INITIALIZE CONSTANTS 0 TO 9 *)
      MEMORY[FIRSTDIGIT+I]:=I;
   (* INITIALIZE INSTRUCTIONPOINTER, STRINGNUMBER, STACKTOP *)
   INSTRUCTIONPOINTER:=0;
   STRINGNUMBER:=0;
   STACKTOP:=0;
   (* SKIP %JOB, PROGRAM T..., VAR... AND BEGIN *)
   READANDPRINTCARD;
   READANDPRINTCARD;
   READANDPRINTCARD;
   READANDPRINTCARD;
   (* GET FIRST CARD TO BE COMPILED *)
   READANDPRINTCARD;
   WHILE CARD[1]<>'%' DO
      BEGIN
         SCANWORD;
         CASE LENGTH OF
            7:COMPILEWRITELN;
            1:COMPILEASSIGNMENT;
            5:IF NEXTWORD[1]='W' THEN
                  COMPILEWHILE;
            3:COMPILEEND
         END;
         READANDPRINTCARD
      END

END (* OF COMPILER *);
```

RUNNING THE COMPILED PROGRAM

We can have a PPS/3 program executed by translating it using
our compiler, and then placing the machine language version of

our program in the memory of a VS computer. The electronic circuitry of the VS computer would carry out the machine instructions corresponding to our program.

Unfortunately, we do not have a VS computer. But we do have a simulator for VS machine language, which we developed in the last chapter, and we could use it to execute our translated PPS/3 program. This is accomplished by the following job, which both compiles and executes a PPS/3 program:

```
$JOB 'MARG KIMBALL'
 (* COMPILE AND EXECUTE A PPS/3 PROGRAM *)
 PROGRAM RUNPPS3 (INPUT,OUTPUT);
    CONST MEMORYSIZE=99;
       STRINGSIZE=80;
       NUMBEROFSTRINGS=10;
       FIRSTINSTRUCTION=0;   (* WHERE EXECUTION BEGINS *)
       LOAD=1;
       STORE=2;
       ADD=3;
       SUBTRACT=4;
       JUMP=5;
       SKIPLE=6;
       PUTINTEGER=7;
       PUTSTRING=8;
       HALT=9;
    VAR MEMORY: ARRAY[0..MEMORYSIZE] OF INTEGER;
       STRING: ARRAY[1..NUMBEROFSTRINGS] OF
          PACKED ARRAY[1..STRINGSIZE] OF CHAR;
    PROCEDURE COMPILER;
       (PPS/3 compiler as given in this chapter)
       END;
    PROCEDURE SIMULATOR;
       (simulator for VS computer as given in last chapter)
       END;
    BEGIN
       COMPILER;
       SIMULATOR
    END.
$DATA
%JOB
PROGRAM T (INPUT,OUTPUT);
   VAR I: INTEGER;
   BEGIN
      WRITELN(' POWERS OF 2');
      I:=1;
      WHILE I<=8 DO
         BEGIN
            WRITELN(I);
            I:=I+I
         END
   END.
%DATA
```

If you want to run a PPS/3 program, make sure that your PPS/3 program has no errors. Remember, the compiler was simplified by

ignoring the possibility of errors; it may fail miserably if it
encounters a syntax error in a PPS/3 program.

CHAPTER 22 SUMMARY

In this chapter we showed how a program, called a compiler,
can translate from a high-level language like Pascal to machine
language. A simple language called PPS/3 was defined to
illustrate points about syntax, language specification and
translation. We presented a compiler written in Pascal that
translates error-free PPS/3 programs to the machine language for
the VS computer described in the last chapter. If this compiler
is combined with the VS computer simulator given in the last
chapter, we have a program that compiles and executes PPS/3
programs. The following important terms were discussed in this
chapter:

Syntax (or grammar) - a set of rules that specify the legal
forms of programs in a particular programming language.

Non-terminal symbol - a symbol such as "statement" used in
syntax rules to represent a set of possibilities. Non-
terminal symbols do not appear in the final program.

Terminal symbol - a symbol such as "PROGRAM", ";" or "I" that
appears in the final program.

Producing a program - using the syntax rules to create a
program by successively replacing non-terminal symbols
until only terminal symbols remain.

Recursive definition - defining a term in a way that uses the
term. For example, in PPS/3 a WHILE loop is defined
recursively as a statement with the form

```
WHILE expression<=expression DO
   BEGIN
       statement⌊;statement⌋
   END
```

This is recursive because a statement inside a WHILE
loop can be a WHILE loop.

Stack - a data structure providing last-in-first-out
manipulation of data, as described in Chapter 17.
Stacks are used in compilers for keeping track of nested
structures, including WHILE loops and parenthesized
expressions.

CHAPTER 22 EXERCISES

1. The PPS/3 compiler given in this chapter requires the following seven types of lines to be on separate cards:

```
(1) PROGRAM T (INPUT,OUTPUT);
(2) VAR ...: INTEGER;
(3) WRITELN(...)
(4) WHILE..DO
(5) END
(6) variable:=expression
(7) BEGIN
```

Modify the PPS/3 compiler so that more than one of these can appear on a card.

2. Modify the PPS/3 compiler and VS simulator so that any attempt to use an uninitialized variable is detected. For example, the following job should be stopped by the simulator in line 5 when the uninitialized value of J is accessed.

```
1       %JOB
2        PROGRAM T (INPUT,OUTPUT);
3           VAR I,J: INTEGER;
4            BEGIN
5               I:=J;
6               WRITELN(I)
7            END.
8       %DATA
```

The use of an uninitialized variable can be detected in the following manner. Before the program begins execution, the values of all variables are set to some special value, say 99999. When the simulator executes the LOAD instruction, it checks to see if the loaded value is 99999. If so, the program is stopped and an error message is printed.

3. Modify the PPS/3 compiler as given in this chapter so that it prints an error message if a variable is used but not declared. This can be done in the following manner. A Boolean array having 26 elements is declared and initialized so that all elements are FALSE. When the compiler reads the declaration, the elements of the array corresponding to declared variables are set from FALSE to TRUE. Whenever a variable is encountered in the remainder of the PPS/3 program, a check is made to see if the corresponding array element is FALSE or TRUE. If it is FALSE, an error message is printed.

4. The compiler given in this chapter was made simpler by omitting certain checks. The absence of these checks makes it is very poor for handling actual programs. Improve it to handle the following problems gracefully.
   (a) If the generated code requires more than 50 words, the instructions overlap with the variables.

(b) If WHILE loops are nested to a depth of greater than MAXWHILEDEPTH, the compiler fails to work properly

(c) If a string is missing its right quote, the compiler runs off the end of a card.

(d) If an input line is longer than 80 characters, perhaps it was typed on a terminal, the compiler makes an error.

(e) If the PPS/3 program contains more than 10 literals, the compiler makes an error.

5. There is no limit on the amount of execution time for a PPS/3 program. Modify the simulator to stop a program when it executes too many instructions.

6. The compiler given in this chapter can be made a little smaller by using a recursive procedure that compiles a compound statement (BEGIN...END).

The procedure can have the form:

```
PROCEDURE COMPILEBEGIN;
    (Declare here procedures to compile
        WRITELN,ASSIGNMENT and WHILE)
    BEGIN
        compile the statements WRITELN,
            ASSIGNMENT and WHILE until END is found
    END;
```

The procedure to compile WHILE will call COMPILEBEGIN to handle statements within the loop. Since the procedure to compile WHILE is recursive, it gets new copies of local variables which can hold locations of jumps to be corrected from the loop beginning. This means that the stack previously used to record these locations is no longer needed.

Appendix 1
SPECIFICATIONS FOR
THE PS/k LANGUAGE

PS/k is a sequence of subsets of the Pascal language that has been developed for the purpose of teaching computer programming. PS/k is based on the SP/k subsets of PL/1 designed at the University of Toronto, and this appendix is an adaption of a technical report by Richard C. Holt and David B. Wortman for the SP/k subset.

Since PS/k is a compatible subset of Pascal, PS/k programs can be run under any compiler that supports Standard Pascal as defined by Jensen and Wirth in the "Pascal User Manual and Report".

In the interest of making Pascal more suitable for pedagogic purposes, PS/k restricts or eliminates some Pascal features. The following features are eliminated: GOTO statements, sets (powersets), variant records and subprograms as parameters.

We will specify PS/k by giving a list of included features. Language features introduced by subsets PS/1 to PS/8 are summarized in the following table.

Subset   Features Introduced

PS/1   Characters: letters, digits and special characters
          Constants: integer, real and character string
          Expressions: +, -, *, /, div, mod, trunc, round
          Simple output: write, writeln
          Predeclared functions: abs, sin, cos,
                    arctan, ln, exp, sqrt.

PS/2   Identifiers and variables
          Declarations: integer and real
          Assignment statements (with integer to real conversion)
          Simple input: read
          Real to integer conversion: trunc, round

PS/3   Comparisons: <, >, =, <=, >=, <>
Logical expressions: AND, OR, and NOT
Selection: if-then-else, case
Repetition: while, repeat and for loops
Paragraphing
Boolean variables and constants
Type definitions

PS/4   Arrays (including multiple dimensions)
Subranges
Named types

PS/5   Characters and strings
Character string comparison
Enumerated types
Predeclared functions: eof, eoln, ord, chr, succ, pred

PS/6   Procedures and functions
Calling and returning
Actual and formal parameters
Global and local variables
Arrays and character strings as parameters

PS/7   Records
Files with read, write and eof

PS/8   Pointers
Dynamic allocation: new and dispose
File buffers

    The   following sections give detailed specifications for each
subset. In describing the subsets, we will use this notation:

    [item] means the item is optional
    |item| means the item can appear zero or more times

Note that square brackets are used around the index of an array
in the language itself and here are used as non-terminal symbols
to indicate that an item is optional. You will just have to try
not to confuse these two uses as we have run out of different
kinds of brackets.   Sometimes we call a non-terminal symbol a
meta-symbol. A meta-symbol is part of the meta-language which is
used to describe the syntax of the actual language, which in our
case is PS/k. When presenting the syntax of language constructs,
items written in upper case letters, for example,

       PROGRAM

denote keywords; these items must appear in PS/k jobs exactly as
presented. Items written in lower case letters, for example,

       statement

denote one of a class of constructs; each such item is defined
below as it is introduced.

PS/1: EXPRESSIONS AND OUTPUT

We now begin the specification of the first subset.

A <u>character</u> is a letter or a digit or a special character.

A <u>letter</u> is one of the following:

A B C D E F G H I J K L M N O P Q R S T U V W X Y Z
a b c d e f g h i j k l m n o p q r s t u v w x y z

Some implementations do not have lower case letters.

A <u>digit</u> is one of the following:

0 1 2 3 4 5 6 7 8 9

A <u>special</u> <u>character</u> is one of the following:

+ - * / ( ) = < > . : ; , [ ] | | ↑ ? %
b (blank)
' (apostrophe or single quote)

Implementations may make the following substitutions for these
special characters:

[becomes   (.
]   becomes   .)
| becomes   (*
| becomes   *)
↑   becomes   a

Some implementations may not have all these special characters or
may have additional special characters.

An <u>unsigned</u> <u>integer</u> is one or more digits (without embedded
blanks), for example:

4   19   243   92153

An <u>unsigned</u> <u>real</u> can take two forms. One form consists of two or
more digits with a decimal point. At least one digit, which may
be 0, must precede and must follow the decimal point. The other
form consists of a mantissa followed by an exponent part (without
embedded blanks). The <u>mantissa</u> must be one or more digits with
an optional decimal point. If there is a decimal point, at least
one digit must precede it and follow it. The <u>exponent</u> part must
have the letter E, followed by an optional plus or minus sign
followed by one or more digits. The following are examples of
real constants.

5.16   50E0   0.9418E24   1.0E-2

An underlined number is an unsigned integer or an unsigned real.
Unsigned numbers cannot contain blanks and cannot be split across
lines (cards).

A literal (or character string) is a single quote (an
apostrophe), followed by one or more occurrences of non-single-
quote characters or twice repeated single quotes, followed by a
single quote. The following are examples of literals:

    'FRED' 'X=24' 'MR. O''REILLY'

In PS/1, an expression is one of the following:

        unsigned integer
        unsigned real
        literal
        +expression
        -expression
        expression + expression
        expression - expression
        expression * expression
        expression / expression
        expression DIV expression
        expression MOD expression
        (expression)
        predeclared function designator

    Real and integer values may be combined in expressions. When
an integer value is combined with a real value using +, - or *
the result is a real value. Two integers combined with +, - or *
yield an integer result.

    The / operation can have real and integer operands and always
returns a real result. The DIV and MOD operations must have
integer operands. DIV produces an integer result, which is
division with truncation toward zero. MOD produces an integer
result which is the remainder of the DIV operation.

    Evaluation of expressions proceeds from left to right, with
the exceptions that multiplications and divisions have higher
precedence than (i.e., are evaluated before) additions and
subtractions and that parenthesized sub-expressions are evaluated
before being used in arithmetic operations. The following are
examples of legal expressions.

    -4+20   2*8.5E+00   (4.0E+01-12.0E+01)/-2

The values of these three expressions are, respectively, 16,
17.0E+00, and 4.0E+01.

    Character strings cannot be used in arithmetic operations.

A PS/1 predeclared function designator is one of the following:

        ABS(expression) $\propto$

```
SQR( expression )
SIN( expression )
COS( expression )
ARCTAN( expression )
LN( expression )
EXP( expression )
SQRT( expression )
ROUND( expression )
TRUNC( expression )
```

The ABS, SQR, SIN, COS, ARCTAN, LN, EXP, and SQRT mathematical functions accept a single integer or real expression as an argument and except for ABS and SQR produce a real result. For ABS and SQR the result has the same type as the parameter. ROUND and TRUNC accept a real expression and produce an integer result. Appendix 3 gives a more detailed description of PS/k predeclared functions.

A PS/1 <u>statement</u> is one of the following:

```
WRITE(output-item |,output-item|)
WRITELN|(output-item |,output-item| )|
PAGE
```

A PS/1 <u>program</u> is: PROGRAM identifier (INPUT,OUTPUT);
                            BEGIN
                                statement |;statement|
                            END.

Remember that the notation |item| means optional repeats, so statement |;statement| means one or more statements separated by semicolons. The following is an example of a PS/1 program:

```
PROGRAM DEMO (INPUT,OUTPUT);
   BEGIN
      WRITELN(2, '    PLUS', 3, '    MAKES', 2+3)
   END.
```

The output from this example is: 2   PLUS   3   MAKES   5

Each <u>output-expression</u> is one of the following:

    (a) e
    (b) e:width
    (c) e:width:fractional digits   (only for REAL value "e")

where "e" is an expression value to be printed and "width" is the field width to hold the printed value.

If e is a literal (string) and the width is not given, then the width is taken to be the number of characters in the string. If the width is given then the printed item is the string value padded with blanks on the left to the specified width.

If e is an integer value then it is printed right-justified in a field of "width" characters. If width is not given then the field width depends on the implementation, but a width of 10 is typical.

If e is a REAL value then it is printed right-justified in a field of "width" characters, where the default width is implementation dependent, but 22 is typical. Forms (a) and (b) cause the REAL value to be printed with its exponent value. Form (c) causes printing without the exponent in fixed point form; for example, 1.7324E1:6:2 causes this to be printed: b17.32.

There will be a slight difference in the handling of certain aspects of the PS/1 subset by different implementations. The maximum number of characters on a print line may be as small, say as 72, or as large, say as 136. The maximum magnitude of integers depends on the implementation but is usually at least 32767, which is common for minicomputers and microcomputers. The maximum magnitude of real numbers depends on the implementation, but is probably at least 1E36. The maximum number of digits in the mantissa of a real number depends on the implementation, but is probably at least 6 even for microcomputers. Some implementations notably Pascal 6000, use the first character of each printed line for carriage control; for such systems, the first character of each line can be a blank.

PAGE starts a new page in the output.

PS/2: VARIABLES, CONSTANTS, INPUT AND ASSIGNMENT

We now begin the specifications of the second subset, PS/2.

An identifier is a letter followed by letters or digits. An identifier cannot contain embedded blanks. Some compilers use only the first eight characters of each identifier (or more depending on the compiler). With these compilers, identifiers can be longer than eight characters, but characters after the first eight are ignored. Identifiers cannot contain blanks and cannot be split across lines (cards).

An identifier cannot be the same as one of the Pascal keywords:

AND	END	NIL	SET
ARRAY	FILE	NOT	THEN
BEGIN	FOR	OF	TO
CASE	FUNCTION	OR	TYPE
CONST	GOTO	PACKED	UNTIL
DIV	IF	PROCEDURE	VAR
DO	IN	PROGRAM	WHILE
DOWNTO	LABEL	RECORD	WITH
ELSE	MOD	REPEAT	

Predeclared identifiers including REAL, INTEGER and WRITE can be redeclared to have new meanings, but this is poor programming style which causes confusion.

A PS/2 program is: PROGRAM identifier (INPUT,OUTPUT);
                    [constant declaration]
                    [variable declaration]
                    BEGIN
                        statement |;statement|
                    END.

A constant declaration is: CONST identifier = constant;
                    |identifier = constant;|

A variable declaration is: VAR identifier |,identifier| : type;
                    |identifier |,identifier| : type;|

A type is one of the following:
                  INTEGER
                  REAL

A statement is one of the following:
                  WRITE(output-item |,output-item|)
                  WRITELN[(output-item |,output-item|)]
                  PAGE
                  variable := expression
                  READ(variable |,variable|)

An identifier declared using the CONST construct is a <u>named constant</u>. It takes the value of the <u>constant</u> which must be a literal (string) or an optionally signed value, The value is an unsigned number or a named constant representing a number.

An identifier declared using the VAR construct is a variable. (There are no arrays in PS/2.)

In Pascal all variables must be declared.

In PS/2 an expression may contain variables as well as constants.

Real values may not be directly assigned to or read into integer variables. Real values may be converted to integer values in order to be assigned to integer variables by using either the ROUND or TRUNC functions. Integer values may be assigned to or read into real variables with automatic conversion.

In PS/2 each item in the data (the input stream) read by the READ statement must be an unsigned number optionally preceded by + or -. Consecutive items must be separated by blanks or ends of lines (cards). One number is read for each item in the READ statement.

Any number (real or integer) can be read (and will be automatically converted if necessary) into a real variable. Only an integer can be read into an integer variable.

Any number of blanks and line (card) ends can appear between symbols, e.g., between constants, keywords, identifiers, operators +, -, *, / and the parentheses (and). When constants, keywords or identifiers are adjacent, for example, the adjacent keywords WHILE and NOT, they must be separated by at least one blank or end of line (card).

A <u>comment</u> consists of the characters (* followed by any characters except the combination *) followed by the characters *). A blank cannot appear between the (and * or between the * and). Comments can appear wherever blanks can appear. In general, it is good practice for comments to appear on separate lines or at the ends of lines. Comments cannot appear in the data. Some compilers allow braces {...} to enclose comments as well as the convention (*...*) used in this book.

PS/3: LOGICAL EXPRESSIONS, SELECTION AND REPETITION

A <u>condition</u> is one of the following:

                    TRUE
                    FALSE
              NOT condition
        condition AND condition
        condition OR condition
             comparison
            (condition)
          Boolean variable

A condition is sometimes called a <u>BOOLEAN</u> <u>expression</u>.

A <u>comparison</u> is one of the following:

        expression < expression
        expression > expression
        expression = expression
        expression <= expression
        expression >= expression
        expression <> expression (<> means "not equal to")

A PS/3 <u>type</u> is one of the following:

        INTEGER
        REAL
        BOOLEAN

    Variables declared to have the BOOLEAN type are called
<u>BOOLEAN</u> <u>variables</u>. BOOLEAN variables can be operands in the
logical operations of AND, OR and NOT. Real or integer values
cannot be operands in logical operations. The AND operator has
higher priority than the OR operator. Boolean variables can be
compared, assigned and printed. Boolean values cannot
participate in numeric operations. They cannot be read in but
can be written out.

    The operations are evaluated in order according to these four
precedence classes:

    first: NOT
    second: * / DIV MOD AND
    third: + - OR
    fourth: = < > >= <= <>

    Operations in the same class are evaluated from left to
right. Parenthesized subexpressions are evaluated first.

    Unfortunately, the Boolean operations (AND, OR, NOT) have
higher precedence than comparisons, so comparisons should be
parenthesized when Boolean operations are involved, as in

```
IF (J>=1) AND (J<=12) THEN...
```

A PS/3 <u>statement</u> is one of the following:

```
WRITE(expression |,expression| )
WRITELN[(expression |,expression| )]
PAGE
variable := expression
READ(variable |,variable| )

IF condition THEN
   statement
[ELSE
   statement]

WHILE condition DO
   statement

FOR identifier := expression TO expression DO
   statement

FOR identifier := expression DOWNTO expression DO
   statement

BEGIN
   statement |;statement|
END

CASE expression OF
   case-label|,case-label|:statement
     |;case-label|,case-label|:statement|
END
```

If a list of statements is wanted in a THEN, ELSE or CASE clause or as the body of a loop, these must be enclosed in BEGIN...END. The list of statements inside BEGIN...END are separated by semicolons. Note that THEN, ELSE, DO, BEGIN and OF are <u>not</u> followed by semicolons.

Each label for a case statement must be an optionally signed integer constant; this constant can be an identifier defined as a CONST. (In a later subset, PS/5, case labels will be allowed to have character or enumerated-type labels.) The expression in the CASE statement must evaluate to one of the case labels (otherwise the meaning of the case statement depends on the particular implementation).

In the FOR loop, the index variable (identifier) must have been declared as an integer variable. Each expression is evaluated once before execution of the loop begins. The body (statement) of the loop is executed once for each value in the range defined by the two expressions in increasing order for TO and decreasing order for DOWNTO. There are zero repetitions if the first expression exceeds the last for TO (or the last exceeds the first for DOWNTO). (In a later subset, PS/5, FOR loop index variables are allowed to be of character or enumerated types.) The value of the index variable must not be changed during the loop's execution. After the execution of the loop the value of the index variable should not be used (the remaining value if any depends on the particular implementation).

The following is an example of a PS/3 program.

```
PROGRAM PS3 (INPUT,OUTPUT);
    VAR N,X,TOTAL: INTEGER;
    BEGIN
        TOTAL:=0;
        READ(N);
        WHILE N>0 DO
            BEGIN
                READ(X);
                TOTAL:=TOTAL+X;
                N:=N-1
            END;
        WRITELN(' TOTAL IS',TOTAL)
    END.
```

<u>Paragraphing rules</u> are standard conventions for indenting program lines. Some compilers provide automatic paragraphing of programs. If this feature is available, it should be used.

A set of paragraphing rules can be inferred from the method used to present PS/k constructs.

Comments that are on separate lines should be indented to the same level as their corresponding program lines. The continuation(s) of a long program line should be indented beyond the line's original indentation. If the level of indentation becomes too deep, it may be necessary to abandon indentation rules temporarily, maintaining a vertical positioning of lines.

PS/4: ARRAYS, SUBRANGES AND NAMED TYPES

Named types (type identifiers) can be defined following the keyword TYPE in an expanded definition of "program".

A PS/4 <u>program</u> is: PROGRAM identifier(INPUT,OUTPUT);
                          [constant declaration]
                          [type declaration]
                          [variable declaration]
                          BEGIN
                               statement|;statement|
                          END.

A <u>type</u> <u>declaration</u> is: TYPE identifier=type;
                          |identifier=type;|

Each declared identifier in a type declaration names a type.

The definition of "type" is expanded to include arrays, subranges and named types (type identifiers).

A <u>type</u> is one of the following:

     INTEGER
     REAL
     BOOLEAN
     type-identifier
     constant..constant   (subrange type)
     ARRAY[type|,type|] OF type

A <u>type-identifier</u> is an identifier declared to name a type in a type declaration.

A <u>subrange</u> <u>type</u> has the form constant..constant. For PS/4, each <u>constant</u> is an optionally signed value, the value being an unsigned integer or a named constant that has an integer value. (In PS/5, subranges are expanded to allow constants that are characters, Booleans and enumerated values.)

An <u>array</u> <u>type</u> has the form ARRAY[type|,type|] OF type. The square brackets here are special symbols that must appear in the Pascal program; they are not meta brackets. The type appearing in brackets must be a subrange type (possibly named). The type appearing after OF can be any type including an array.

An element of an array A is referred to as A[expression|,expression|] where the square brackets are Pascal special symbols. Each expression must be within the subrange of the corresponding type in the array's type definition.

Entire arrays may be assigned, but comparison, reading and writing are only possible element by element.

PS/5: CHARACTERS, ENUMERATED TYPES AND STRINGS

The definition of "type" is expanded to include:

CHAR
(identifier|,identifier|)   (enumerated type)
PACKED ARRAY[type] OF type

The predeclared type CHAR is introduced. A CHAR variable has as its values a character (a letter, digit or special character). Such a value is written as a literal string containing a single character, that is, a single quote, followed by the character, followed by another single quote, for example 'A'. If the character value is a quote, it is written a four quotes, namely ''''. CHAR values can be compared and assigned.

Each CHAR value C has a unique corresponding ordinal value ORD(C) which is a non-negative integer. If I is the integer value ORD(C) then CHR(I) has the character value C. In most implementations,

ORD('0')=ORD('1')-1=ORD('2')-2...=ORD('9')-9.

SUCC(C) of character value C is the next character value, if any, after C. PRED(C) is the previous character value if any.

An <u>enumerated type</u> has the form (identifier|,identifier|). Each identifier is a newly defined value; it names a member of an enumerated set. For example (BLEU,BLANC,ROUGE) defines the type whose values are the three colors in the French flag. Enumerated types can be assigned and compared but not read or written. ORD, CHR, SUCC and PRED can be applied to enumerated types. For example, ORD(BLEU) is 0 and SUCC(BLEU) is BLANC. These functions can also be applied to Boolean; ORD(FALSE)=0 and SUCC(FALSE)=TRUE.

The following are <u>scalar types</u>: INTEGER, BOOLEAN, CHAR and enumerated types. Scalar types can have subranges; these can be array index types. Case labels can be of scalar types. FOR loop index variables can be of scalar types.

Arrays can be PACKED meaning that the implementation may try to use less space for the array at the possible cost of slower access time. In some implementations, PACKED has no effect on either space or type.

A literal (string) of length n, where n is two or more characters, e.g., 'ABC', has the special type

PACKED ARRAY [1..n] OF CHAR

Values of this array type for a particular n can be compared (=, >, <, >=, <=, <>) according to the alphabetic ordering of the collating sequence of the underlying character set. No other arrays can be compared.

The input stream read by the predeclared procedure READ is a
file of characters, divided into lines. When there are no more
characters to be read in the file, EOF becomes true. When there
are no characters to be read on a particular line, EOLN becomes
true. A character variable C can be read, for example by

    READ(C)

In contrast to reading numbers, this does not skip preceding
blanks and ends of lines. If the next character is a blank then
C is assigned the value blank. If the last character on the line
is read, then EOLN becomes true and the READLN predeclared
procedure should be called.   When READLN is called without
parameters, it skips any remaining characters on the line and the
end of line allowing the next line to be read.

    Note that READ(I) when reading the last number in the data
does not make EOF become true when the integer is followed by
blanks.

    READLN can have parameters:

    READLN(variable|,variable|)

This is defined to mean

    |READ(variable); READLN

This reads each of the variables, then skips the remaining
characters of the line and skips the end of line, allowing the
next line to be read.

PS/6: PROCEDURES AND FUNCTIONS

A <u>subprogram</u> is a procedure or function. The form of a program is extended to allow the definition of these.

A PS/6 <u>program</u> is: PROGRAM identifier(INPUT,OUTPUT);
             [constant declaration]
             [type declaration]
             [variable declaration]
             |subprogram declaration|
             BEGIN
                statement|;statement|
             END.

A <u>subprogram</u> <u>declaration</u> is one of the following:
             procedure declaration
             function declaration

A <u>procedure</u> <u>declaration</u> is:
                PROCEDURE identifier
                 [([VAR]identifier|,identifier|:type-identifier
                 |;[VAR]identifier|,identifier|:type-identifier|)];
                 [constant declaration]
                 [type declaration]
                 [variable declaration]
                 |subprogram declaration|
                 BEGIN
                    statement|;statement|
                 END;

A <u>function</u> <u>declaration</u> is:
                FUNCTION identifier
                 [(identifier|;identifier|:type-identifier
                 |;identifier|,identifier|:type-identifier|)]:
                    type-identifier;
                 [constant declaration]
                 [type declaration]
                 [variable declaration]
                 |subprogram declaration|
                 BEGIN
                    statement|;statement|
                 END;

The identifiers declared in the optional list following the subprogram name are <u>formal</u> parameters. The call to a subprogram consists of the subprogram's identifier followed optionally by a parenthesized list of expressions (no parenthesized list occurs when the subprogram has no formal parameters). These expressions are the <u>actual</u> <u>parameters</u>. The number and type of actual parameters must correspond to the formal parameters.

A formal parameter declared with VAR is a <u>variable</u> formal parameter; those declared without are <u>value</u> formal parameters. Functions may have value formal parameters but not variable formal parameters. A value formal parameter behaves like a variable local to the subprogram that is initialized to the value of the actual parameter. A variable formal parameter behaves like the actual parameter with a new name; the corresponding actual parameter must be a variable (i.e., it must be able to change its values). It cannot be a constant or a result of an operation or a function call. If the actual parameter is an array element, the array indices are evaluated at call time and do not change.

Functions should not have side effects, meaning they should not change (or cause to change) any but local variables or variables local to subprograms that they call directly or indirectly. No reading or writing should be done.

A function is called when its identifier with actual parameter list appears in an expression. A procedure is called when its identifier with actual parameter list appears as a statement.

A function is given a value by an assignment within it that assigns a value to its identifier. (Full Pascal but not PS/k allows names of subprograms to be parameters.)

PS/7: RECORDS AND FILES

The definition of <u>type</u> is expanded to include records and files:

```
RECORD
    identifier|,identifier|: type
    |;identifier|,identifier|: type|
END

FILE OF type
```

A record is an aggregate consisting of several fields, with an identifier defined for each field. The types of the fields are not restricted to be scalar and can be previously defined records and arrays. Arrays of records are also allowed. (Full Pascal but not PS/k allows records to have variants.) A variable V of a record type with field F has this field referred to as V.F. <u>A record can be PACKED.</u>

A new statement allows fields in records to be referenced by field name only:

```
WITH variable|,variable| DO
    statement
```

Each <u>variable</u> must be of a record type. Usually the statement will be BEGIN...END. Within the statement references to fields of the record are by field name only. For example, if R is the record variable and R.F is a field, then within the statement F can be written instead of R.F.

A file is a sequence of values of its type that can be read or written. If F is a variable whose type is FILE OF T then

```
WRITE(F,e)
```

appends a value e of type T to the end of F and

```
READ(F,v)
```

reads the next (or first) value of F into variable v of type T. Before a file is written it must be cleared to be an empty file:

```
REWRITE(F)
```

Before a file can be read, it must be reset to its beginning:

```
RESET(F)
```

REWRITE and RESET are predeclared procedures.

Files that exist beyond the execution of a program are called <u>external</u>. Files created by a program and not kept afterwards are called <u>local</u>. External files are listed in the program header which has the form

    PROGRAM identifier(identifier|,identifier|);

The parenthesized list usually contains INPUT and OUTPUT as these are the standard files for reading and writing. For example, if INPUT, OUTPUT and F are to be used then the header is

    PROGRAM identifier(INPUT,OUTPUT,F);

There is a predeclared function EOF that takes a file variable as its parameter. When reading file F, EOF(F) is true when there are no more items beyond the item most recently read from the file. When a file is RESET, EOF(F) becomes false unless the file is empty. After REWRITE(F) and WRITE(F), EOF(F) is true. Reading when EOF is true is undefined (depends on the implementation).

There is a predeclared type TEXT that is defined as FILE OF CHAR. INPUT and OUTPUT are predeclared TEXT files. There is an implicit RESET(INPUT) and REWRITE(OUTPUT) before a program begins execution. INPUT and OUTPUT must have no other RESET or REWRITE operations.

TEXT files other than INPUT and OUTPUT can have the same READ, READLN, WRITE and WRITELN procedure usages as do INPUT and OUTPUT, except that the file identifier is the first parameter in the procedure call. These files can be reset and rewritten.

Files other than TEXT files can only be read or written using the forms

    READ(file name,variable of type T)
    WRITE(file name,expression of type T)

where the file's type is FILE OF T.

Implementations do not usually support files of files, records of files, pointers to files or arrays of files.

PS/8: POINTERS AND FILE BUFFERS

The definition of type is expanded to include pointers:

↑type-identifier

For example, variables P and Q are pointers to record type R.

        TYPE R=RECORD...END;
        VAR P,Q: ↑R

P is made to point to a <u>dynamically</u> created variable of type R by executing the statement

        NEW(P)

P can be made to point to no variable by assigning it the NIL value:

        P:=NIL

When P is pointing to a variable, this variable has its space released by the statement

        DISPOSE(P)

When P has value NIL or points to a variable, Q can be assigned the same pointer value:

        Q:=P

P↑ denotes the variable pointed to by P. For example, when P and Q are pointing to variables, Q↑:=P↑ assigns the variable pointed to by P to the variable pointed to by Q. If P is not pointing to a variable then P↑ is meaningless. Most implementations do not allow pointers to files.

        Pointers can be used to create recursive data structures. For example, NEXT in a PERSON record type points to another variable of type PERSON.

        TYPE LINK=↑PERSON;
            PERSON=
                RECORD
                  ...
                    NEXT: LINK
                END;

        For each file variable F, there is a <u>buffer variable</u> for F that is denoted F↑. When file F is being read, F↑ gives the value of the next item that will be READ. When file F is being written, F↑ gives the next value to be appended to the file. The definition of READ(F,v) for FILE OF T and v of type T is:

```
v:=F↑;
GET(F)
```

The GET procedure advances the file so that F↑ locates the next
value in the file if any exists.   If there are no more items   in
the file then F↑ becomes undefined (implementation dependent) and
EOF(F) becomes true.   When a file is RESET, F↑ locates the first
value (if any) in the file.   Attempting to GET(F) when EOF(F) is
true is undefined.

The   definition   of   WRITE(F,e) for FILE OF T and e of type T
is:

```
F↑:=e;
PUT(F)
```

The PUT procedure appends the value in F↑ to the end of the file;
F↑ becomes undefined.   PUT is defined only when EOF(F) is true.

Appendix 2
SYNTAX OF PS/k

This is the syntax of full Pascal with expressions omitted and these Pascal features eliminated: GOTO statements, label declarations, sets, variant records and subprograms as parameters.

Notation: [item] means the item is optional
          |item| means the item repeated zero or more times.

A <u>program</u> is: PROGRAM identifier(identifier|,identifier|);
                 [constant declaration]
                 [type declaration]
                 [variable declaration]
                 |subprogram declaration|
                 BEGIN
                     statement |;statement|
                 END.

A <u>subprogram declaration</u> is one of the following:
                 procedure declaration
                 function declaration

A <u>procedure declaration</u> is:
                 PROCEDURE identifier
                     [([VAR]identifier |,identifier|: type-identifier
                     |;[VAR]identifier |,identifier|: type-identifier|)];
                 [constant declaration]
                 [type declaration]
                 [variable declaration]
                 |subprogram declaration|
                 BEGIN
                     statement |;statement|
                 END;

A <u>function</u> <u>declaration</u> is:
```
              FUNCTION identifier
                   [(identifier |,identifier|: type-identifier
                    |;identifier |,identifier|: type-identifier|)]
                         type-identifier;
                 [constant declaration]
                 [type declaration]
                 [variable declaration]
                 |subprogram declaration|
                 BEGIN
                     statement |;statement|
                 END;
```

A <u>constant</u> <u>declaration</u> is: CONST identifier=constant;
```
                         |identifier=constant;|
```

A <u>type</u> <u>declaration</u> is: TYPE identifier=type;
```
                     |identifier=type;|
```

A <u>variable</u> <u>declaration</u> is: VAR identifier |,identifier|: type;
```
                         |identifier |,identifier|: type;|
```

A <u>type</u> is one of the following:

```
    INTEGER
    REAL
    BOOLEAN
    CHAR
    (identifier |,identifier|)            (enumerated type)
    constant..constant                    (subrange type)
    [PACKED] array-type
    [PACKED] record-type
    [PACKED] FILE OF type
    ↑ type
    type-identifier
```

An <u>array-type</u> is:

    ARRAY[type|,type|] OF type (square brackets are special symbols her⟩

A <u>record-type</u> is:
```
    RECORD
        identifier |,identifier|: type
        |;identifier |,identifier|: type|
    END
```

A <u>statement</u> is one of the following:
```
    WRITE( [file name,] output-item |,output-item| )
    WRITELN|([file name,]output-item |,output-item| )|
    READ( [file name,] variable |,variable| )
    READLN|( [file name,] variable |,variable| )|
    PAGE
    variable:=expression

    BEGIN
        statement|;statement|
    END
```

```
IF condition THEN
    statement
[ELSE
    statement]

CASE expression OF
    constant |,constant|: statement
    |;constant |,constant|: statement|
END

WHILE expression DO
    statement

REPEAT
    statement |;statement|
UNTIL expression

FOR variable-identifier:=expression TO expression DO
    statement

FOR variable-identifier:=expression DOWNTO expression DO
    statement

WITH variable |,variable| DO
    statement

procedure-identifier[(expression |,expression| )]

(empty statement--contains nothing)
```

Appendix 3
PREDECLARED
PASCAL FUNCTIONS

For these predeclared functions, the parameter may be real or
integer. The result is real.

    SIN(x)   - sine of x radians.
    COS(x)   - cosine of x radians.
    ARCTAN(x)- arctangent of x in radians.
    LN(x)   - natural logarithm of x.
    EXP(x)   - e to the x power.
    SQRT(x) - square root of x.

For these functions a real parameter produces a real result; an
integer parameter produces an integer result

    ABS(x) - absolute value of x.
    SQR(x) - x squared (x*x).   (but not x^y

For these functions the arguments must be real; the result is
integer.

    ROUND(x) - the integer part of the number rounded.
    TRUNC(x) - the integer part of the number truncated.

These functions have a Boolean value.

    EOF [(file name)] - value is false unless the end of the
            file has been reached.
    EOLN [(file name)] - value is false unless the end of the
            current line of the file has been reached.

If no parameter is given for these two functions the INPUT file
is the one that they refer to.

This Boolean function requires an integer parameter:

    ODD(x) - value is true if x is an odd integer.

For these functions the parameter must be a <u>scalar</u> <u>type</u>, that is, integer, Boolean, char, or enumerated type (or any subrange of such a type):

> SUCC(x) - has a value which is the successor to x in the
>   ordering.
>
> PRED(x) - has a value which is the predecessor of x in the
>   ordering.

The ORD function is used with parameter of a <u>scalar</u> <u>type</u>.

> ORD(x) - yields an integer value corresponding to the ordinal
>   value of the character in the set of characters.
>   The actual value of a character may vary from one
>   compiler to another but alphabetic characters are
>   always in alphabetical order.
>
> CHR(x) - yields a character value corresponding to the integer
>   x. This is the inverse function of ORD, so CHR(ORD(C))=C
>   for any character C.

Appendix 4
SUMMARY OF PASCAL INPUT/OUTPUT FEATURES

BASIC FILE HANDLING

PUT(f) appends the value of buffer variable f↑ to the file f. EOF(f) must be true before the PUT and remains true after. The value of f↑ becomes undefined.

GET(f) advances the file position; buffer variable f↑ is assigned the next value in the file if any. If none exists, f↑ is undefined. EOF(f) must be false before the GET.

RESET(f) resets the file position to the first position; file buffer f↑ is assigned the first value in the file if any. If none exists, f↑ is undefined. EOF(f) becomes false unless the file is empty in which case EOF(f) becomes true.

REWRITE(f) discards the present contents of the file if any. EOF(f) becomes true. A PUT(f) but not a GET(f) can be executed next.

Note: The standard text files INPUT and OUTPUT are implicitly declared and RESET(INPUT) and REWRITE(OUTPUT) are performed automatically. The Pascal program must not RESET or REWRITE the INPUT or OUTPUT files.

BASIC READING AND WRITING

For a file variable f declared as FILE OF t, READ and WRITE are defined as:

```
READ([f,]v):    (variable v is of type t)
   v:=f↑;
   GET(f)
```

```
WRITE([f,]e):   (expression e is of type t)
   f↑:=e;
   PUT(f)
```

If the first parameter of READ is omitted, INPUT is assumed.   If
the first parameter of WRITE is omitted, OUTPUT is assumed.

                              TEXT FILES

     There is a predeclared type TEXT defined as FILE OF CHAR.
The standard files INPUT and OUTPUT are TEXT files.   Generalized
forms of READ and WRITE including READLN and WRITELN can be used
with TEXT files.

TEXT files are divided into lines. If when reading file f the
last character of a line of the file is read, EOLN(f) becomes
true.

     WRITELN[(f)] completes the current line of file f; the next
               line can then be written.

     READLN[(f)] skips the rest of the current line of file f; the
               next line can then be read.

When f is omitted, OUTPUT is assumed for WRITELN, INPUT for
READLN.

     READLN and WRITELN can have multiple parameters.

     WRITELN(f|,output-item|) is defined as:

          |WRITE(f,output-item);| WRITELN(f)

     READLN(f|,variable|) is defined as:

          |READ(variable);| READLN(f)

As before the file parameter f is optional.

     For TEXT files the variable of a read must be of type CHAR,
REAL or (subrange of) INTEGER. If REAL, preceding blanks and
line ends are skipped and an optionally signed number value
(unsigned integer or unsigned real) is read.   If INTEGER, the
same action is taken but the input value must be an integer.

     For TEXT files the <u>output-item</u> must have one of the forms

     (a) e
     (b) e:width
     (c) e:width:fractional digits (only for REAL value "e")

where "e" is an expression value to be printed and "width" is the
field width to hold the printed value.

If e is a literal (string) and the width is not given, then
the width is taken to be the number of characters in the string.
If the width is given then the printed item is the string value
padded with blanks on the left to the specified width.
If e is an integer value then it is printed right-justified
in a field of "width" characters. If width is not given then the
field width depends on the implementation, but a width of 10 is
typical.

If e is a REAL value then it is printed right-justified in a
field of "width" characters. Where the default width is
implementation dependent, but 22 is typical. Forms (a) and (b)
cause the REAL value to be printed with its exponent value. Form
(c) causes printing without the exponent in fixed point form with
the specified number of fractional digits. For example,
1.7324E1:6:2 causes this to be printed: b17.32 (where b means
blank).

PAGE[(f)]   starts a new page in file f (assumes
               OUTPUT file when f is omitted).

Appendix 5
COLLATING SEQUENCE

The order determining comparisons among character values is determined by the character collating sequence of the implementation. For most implementations, ORD(C) for character value C returns the numeric value of the representation of C. For most implementations

    ORD('0')=ORD('1')-1=ORD('2')-2...=ORD('9')-9

The EBCDIC collating sequence used, for example, on the IBM 360 computer and its successors, does not have contiguous values for letters. For example, a 360 Pascal implementation should have:

    ORD('A')=ORD('B') -1 but ORD('R')<>ORD('S') -1

Fortunately, the following holds for most collating sequences including EBCDIC.

    'A'<'B'<'C'...<'Z'
    ORD('A')<ORD('B')<ORD('C')...<ORD('Z')

We will give three common encodings of the characters. Most unprintable characters are not given. Various characters may vary from implementation to implementation.

ASCII: Used on most microcomputers and minicomputers, including PDP-11, 8080 and successors, 6800 and successors.

0:		(null character)
4:		(EOT: end of transmission)
8:		(backspace)
9:		(tab)
10:		(line feed)
12:		(form feed)
13:		(carriage return)
32:	b	(blank)
33:	!	
34:	"	
35:	#	
36:	$	

```
37:          %
38:          &
39:          '                    (apostrophe)
40:          (
41:          )
42:          *
43:          +
44:          ,                    (comma)
45:          -
46:          .
47:          /
48-57:       0 to 9
58:          :
59:          ;
60:          <
61:          =
62:          >
63:          ?
64:          @
65-90:       A-Z
91:          [
92:          \
93:          ]
94:          ^
95:          _                    (underscore)
96:          `                    (reverse quote)
97-122:      a to z
123:         {
124:         |
125:         }
126:         ~
```

CDC Scientific Character Set: Used in Pascal 6000.

```
0:           :                    (or unprintable)
1-26:        A to Z
27-36:       0 to 9
37:          +
38:          -
39:          *
40:          /
41:          (
42:          )
43:          $
44:          =
45:          b                    (blank)
46:          ,                    (comma)
47:          .
48:          ≡                    (equivalence, or #)
49:          [
50:          ]
51:          %
52:          ≠                    (or ")
53:          ↦                    (or _)
54:          ∨                    ("or‾, or !)
55:          ∧                    ("and", or †)
```

```
56:        ↑           (up arrow, or ')
57:        ↓           (down arrow, or question mark)
58:        <
59:        >
60:        ≤           (or ə)
61:        ≥           (or *)
62:        ¬           (or question mark)
63:        ;
```

EBCDIC: Used on IBM 360 and successors and various other computers.

```
64:        b           (blank)
74:        ¢
75:        .
76:        <
77:        (
78:        +
79:        |
80:        &
90:        !
91:        $
92:        *
93:        )
94:        ;
95:        ¬           ("not")
96:        -
97:        /
107:       ,           (comma)
108:       %
109:       _           (underscore)
110:       >
111:       ?           (question mark)
122:       :
123:       #
124:       ə
125:       '           (single quote)
126:       =
127:       "
129-137:   a-l
145-153:   j-r
162-169:   s-z
193-201:   A to I
209-217:   J to R
226-233:   S to Z
240-249:   0 to 9
```

Appendix 6
SYNTAX DIAGRAMS
FOR FULL PASCAL

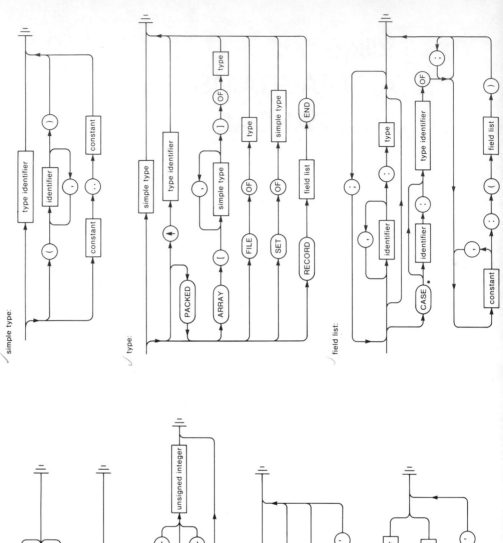

simple type:

type:

field list:

identifier:

unsigned integer:

unsigned number:

unsigned constant:

constant:

*Variant records not in PS/k

simple expression:

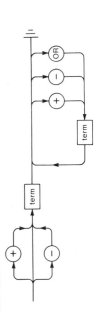

expression:

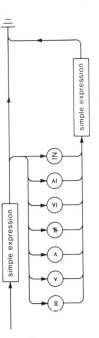

parameter list:

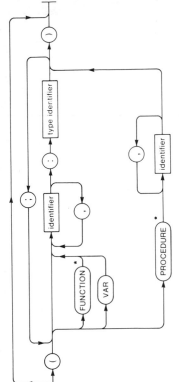

*Subroutines as parameters not in PS/k

variable:

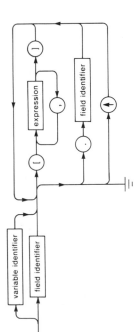

factor:

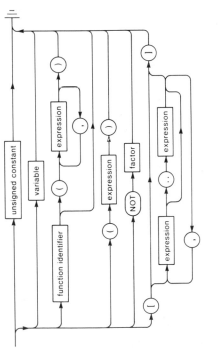

term:

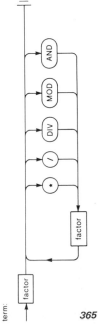

statement:

block:

program:

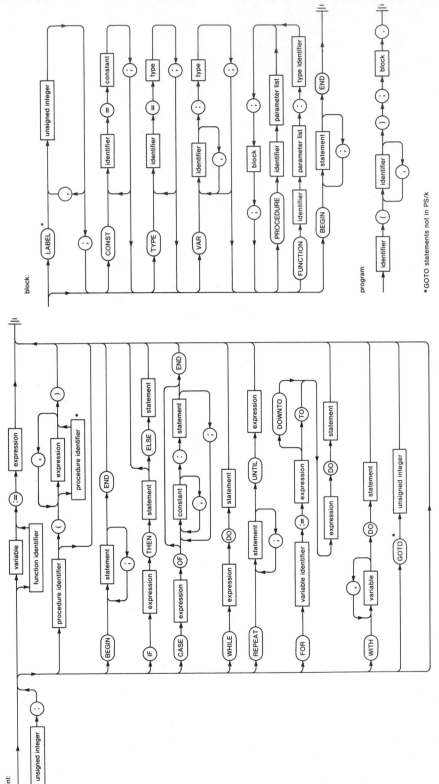

*GOTO statements not in PS/k

INDEX

ABS, 353
Accumulator, 12, 291
Accuracy, 257, 270
Actual parameter, 154, 159,
    165, 343
Adding, to tree, 229
Address, of word in memory, 11,
    294
Address calculation, search by,
    187
Algol-60, 286, 290
Algorithm, 130, 232
    developing of, 132
    sorting, 137
Allocation, 240
    dynamic, 240
    of memory, 240
Alphabetical information, 103
Alphabetical order, 112
AND operator, 55
Approximation, 257
ARCTAN, 353
Area, computation of, 258, 260
Arithmetic expression, 23, 30
Arithmetic unit, 12
ARRAY, 91
Array, 91
    of arrays, 97, 100
    bounds of, 100
    as data structure, 98
    declaration of, 100
    index of, 100
    of records, 205, 213
    of strings, 113
    two-dimensional, 93
    type, 340
Artificial intelligence, 143
ASCII collating sequence, 121,
    359
Aspects of good programming,
    129

Assembler, 303
Assembly language, 295, 303
Assigning records, 213
Assignment statement, 35, 49,
        335
Automatic conversion of numbers,
        336
Automatic error repair, 200

Batch processing, 14
BEGIN, 28, 54, 338
Bin, 187
Binary digit, 9
Binary search, 183, 190
Binary tree, 228, 233
Bit, 9
Blank as separator, 144
Body of loop, 57
BOOLEAN, 337
    expression, 337
    type, 55
    variable, 337
Boolean operator, 55
Boolean variable, 56
Bottom-up testing, 198
Branch, 64
    in control flow, 64
    of tree, 99, 229
Bubble sort, 188
Bucket, 187
Buffer, file, 242, 245, 347
    file merge using, 243
Bug, in program, 197
Building block, 79
Byte, 9

Calling a procedure, 164
Card, punched, 14
Card deck, 15
Carriage control character, 30

Carriage return, 107
CASE statement, 67, 72, 338
Cathode ray tube screen, 14
CDC scientific character set,
      Pascal 6000, 360
Central processing unit, 17
CHAR, 104, 123, 341
Character, 19, 29, 331
Character string, 103, 110, 332
Character string constant, 22
Character variable, 33
Chip, silicon, 13
CHR, 118, 124, 341, 354
Cobol, 287
Coded information, 18
Collating sequence, 359
    ASCII, 121
    EBCDIC, 120
Command line, 28
Comment, 41, 50, 195, 336
    use of, 139
Communication among modules, 171
Comparison, 71, 337
    of strings, 110
Compatible subsets, 289
Compilation, 18
    of programs, 1, 318
Compiler, 305, 318
Compiling, 311-325
    of assigment statement, 314
    of WHILE and END, 316
    of WRITELN statement, 315
Complex roots, 256
Compound condition, 85
Compound statement, 54, 56
Computer, speed of, 2
Condition, 54, 71, 337
    compound, 85
    test of, 57
Conditional loop, 56, 63
    flow chart for, 80
Constant, 335
    declaration of, 48, 335
Control card, 28
Control flow, 53
    branch in, 64
    structuring of, 77
Control phrase, 77
Control register, 13
Control unit, 13
Convergence, 270, 277
Conversion between characters
    and numbers, 117
Conversion between
    INTEGER and REAL, 40
Core, magnetic, 11

Correctness of programs, 5,
    6, 194
COS, 353
Cosine, series for, 266
Counted loop, 53
Counting variable,
   final value of, 61
CPU, 17
Credit exception report, 177
CRT, 14
Curve fitting, 255, 260

DATA control card, 28, 39
Data, 49
   input of, 39
   reduction of, 247
   retrieval of, 181
Data bank, 230
Data card, 39
Data processor, 2
Data structure, 131, 217
   choosing of, 131
Data type, 33
(see also Type)
Dataset, 208, 213
Debugging, 197, 199, 202
Decimal digit, 9
Declaration, 34
   of array, 91
   of constant, 48, 335
   of function, 164
   of procedure, 163
   of type, 97
   of variable, 48
Defensive programming, 194
Deleting from linked list, 223
Deleting from tree, 230
Deviation, 255
Digit, 20, 331
   significant, 249, 260
Disk, magnetic, 10
DISPOSE, 240, 245, 347
DIV, 38
Division, 23
Documentation, 50
Double precision, 268, 277
DOWNTO, 54
Drum, magnetic, 10
Dummy card, 58
Dummy operand, 297
Dynamic allocation, 240

EBCDIC collating sequence,
    120, 361
Efficiency of program, 135
Efficiency of searching, 230

Empirical fit, 256
END, 28, 54
End conditions, 197
End-of-file, 46, 71, 107
   marker for, 58, 172
End of line, 106
Enumerated type, 121, 124
EOF, 123, 212, 242, 353
EOLN, 106, 123, 353
Error, 50
   automatic repair of, 200
   in program, 47
   in program design, 199
   semantic, 46
   syntax, 45
Error message, 46, 200
Evaluating formula, 248, 260
Exception reporting, 177
Executable statement, 35
Execution of instructions, 13
   tracing of, 37
Exit from loop, 78, 87
EXP, 353
Exponent, 21, 331
Exponential, series for, 266
Expression, 23, 331
(see also Arithmetic expression)
Extension to a language, 290
External file, 345

False, 54
Field, 25, 30, 39, 181
   size of, 172
   width of, 27, 333
FILE, 345
File, 181
   declaration of, 214
   maintenance of, 210, 214
   merge of, using buffers, 243
   in secondary memory, 208
   sequential, 208
   TEXT, 212
File buffer, 242, 245, 347
Fitting, least-squares, 256
Flow of control, 53
Flowchart, 79, 87
   for conditional loop, 80
   for IF...THEN...ELSE, 80
FOR loop, 54, 70, 338
Formal language, 143
Formal parameter, 153, 159,
      165, 343
Format for printing, 26, 30
Fortran, 282
Fraction part, 21
   truncation of, 38

Fractional digit, 27, 333
Function, 155, 343
    declaration of, 164
    designator for, 332
    predeclared, 353

Generated error, 265, 276
GET, 242, 246, 348, 355
Global variable, 162
GOTO statement, 78, 87, 293
Grammar, 306
(see also Syntax)
Graphing a function, 250, 260

Hard copy, 14
Hash code, 187, 190
Hierarchical structure, 229
High-level language, 3, 6,
      16, 305
Histogram, 148
Horner's rule, 264, 276
Hypothetical computer, 302

Identifier, 12, 33, 48
    good choice of, 196
IF...THEN...ELSE statement, 64,
      72, 338
    example of, 68
    flow chart for, 80
    with multiple conditions, 86
    nesting of, 67
Incompatible dialects, 289
Indentation of program, 70
Index, 54
    of array, 91
    of loop, 57
    range of, 91
Indexed FOR loop, 54
Infinite loop, 63
Infinite series, evaluation of,
      266, 277
Information, 2
    alphabetical, 103
    coded, 8
    retrieval of, 230
    retrieval system for, 143
Information explosion, 247
Information processor, 2
Initialization of loop, 57, 77
INPUT, 212
Input, 17, 333
Input device, 14
Input and output for Pascal, 355
Input and output of records, 206
Inserting into linked list,
      219-220

Instruction pointer, 13, 297
Instruction repertoire, 1
INTEGER type, 34, 335
Integer, 331
Integer constant, 21, 29
Integer character, printing of,
      357
INTEGER and REAL, conversion
      between, 40
Integer variable, 33
Integration, numerical, 271
Interactive system, 14
Interval-halving method, 269,
      277

JOB card, 28
Jump instruction, 13, 292

Key, of file, 181
Keyboard, 15
Keypunch, 15
Keyword, 50
    in Pascal, 335

Label, 78, 303
    instruction, 292
Labeling of output, 43
Language, 3
    assembly, 295, 303
    construct in, 330
    formal, 143
    high-level, 3
    machine, 16, 295, 303
    natural, 143
    peculiarities of, 200
    translation of, 150
Layout of record, 204
Leaf node, 229
Leaf of tree, 229
Least squares approximation, 256,
      274, 278
Length of line, 107
Length of string, 106, 123
Letter, 331
Line, reading and printing of,
      106
Linear equations, 258, 260,
      273, 278
Linear flow of control, 77
Linear search, 181, 190
Link, 99, 218
Linked list, 217, 232
    inserting into, 219-220
Literal, 22, 30, 332
    printing of, 25, 356
LN, 353

Local variable, 157, 162
Location in computer, 33
Logarithm, series for, 266
Logical expression, 337
Logical sequence, 218
Loop, 70
    body of, 71
    conditional, 56
    counted, 53
    examples of, 60
    FOR, 54, 70, 338
    infinite, 63
    with multiple conditions, 85
    nested, 81
    problems with, 81
    REPEAT...UNTIL, 63, 71
    WHILE, 56, 70

Machine instruction, 12, 291
Machine language, 16, 295, 303
Machine, sequential, 13
Magnetic core, 11
Magnetic disk, 10
Magnetic drum, 10
Magnetic tape, 9
Maintenance of file, 210
Maintenance of program, 177
Mantissa, 331
Mark sense card, 15
Marker, end-of-file, 58
Mathematical software, 275, 278
Matrix, 94
Maximum magnitude of
      real number, 334
Measurement error, 259
Memory, 9, 17
    management of with lists, 219
    management of with pointers,
      239
Memory allocation, 296
Merging, sorting by, 188, 191
Meta-language, 330
Meta-symbol, 330
Microcomputer, 106
Microprocessor, 13
Minicomputer, 106
Mixed number, 21
Mnemonic name, 295, 302
MOD, 38, 118
Modular programming, 130, 169
Module, 169
    prefabricated, 138
    use of, 176
Moving records, 204
Multiple conditions, 88
Multiplication, 23

Multiply-dimensioned array, 100

Named constant, 336
Named type, 97, 100
Natural language, 143
Nesting, 67
    of IF...THEN...ELSE
        statements, 67
    of loops, 81
    of statements, 88
    of subprograms, 157
NEW, 239, 245, 347
Newton-Raphson method, 270, 277
NIL, 237, 245, 347
Node, 223
    of tree, 99
Non-terminal symbol, 308, 325
Null string, 104
Number conversion, 49
Number, mixed, 21
Numerical analyst, 249
Numerical integration, 271, 277
Numerical method, 257, 263

ODD, 353
Off-line program preparation, 14
Online computer input terminal,
        15
Operand of instruction, 292
Operating system, 227
Operator of an instruction, 292
OR, 55
ORD, 117, 124, 341, 354, 359
Order, alphabetical, 112
Out-of-bounds array index, 100,
        116
OUTPUT, 212
Output, 17, 31, 331, 333
    expression for, 333
    item of, 356
    labeling of, 43

PACKED, 123
PACKED ARRAY, 110, 341
Packed array of characters, 110
Padding with blanks, 113
PAGE, 27, 333, 357
Paragraphing of program, 69,
        71, 338
Parameter, 154
    actual, 154
    formal, 154
    value, 154
    variable, 154
Parentheses, precedence rule
        for, 23

Pascal, 3, 6
    keyword in, 35, 335
    syntax diagrams for, 363
Percentage error, 265
Phases of loop, 57
Physical sequence, 218
PL/1, 282, 290
Plotting a graph, 252
Pointer, 99, 218, 347
    dangling, 240, 245
    instruction, 13, 297
    type, 237
Polynomial equation, 256
Polynomial evaluation, 263
Pop from stack, 225
Portable program, 290
Posting of file, 210
PPS/3, 305
    syntax for, 307
Precedence, rule of, 23, 30
    for Boolean operators, 55
Precision, 257
    loss of, 274
PRED, 121, 124, 341, 354
Predeclared function, 249, 353
Predefined enumerated type, 122
Prefabricated module, 138
Procedure, 153, 343
    declaration of, 163
    recursive, 225
    statement, 154
Production of program, 308, 325
PROGRAM heading, 27, 34, 333
Program, 6
    correctness of, 194, 202
    heading statement, 209, 214
    listing of, 46
    maintenance of, 177
    paragraphing of, 69
    production of, 308
    specification of, 201
    testing of, 45
Programming, 1, 6
    defensive, 194
    habits of, 202
    language of, 6
    modular, 130
    style of, 195, 202
Propagation of error, 265, 276
Printed output, 39
Printer, 15
Printing, 24
    of integer character, 357
    of literal, 356
    of REAL value, 357
    of tree, 231

Printout, 31
PS/k, 4, 6
   language specification for,
      329
   syntax of, 349
Pulse, 8
Punched card, 14
Punctuation mark, 20, 147
Push on stack, 224
PUT, 243, 245, 348, 355

Quadratic equation, 256
Question-answering system, 143
Queue, 226, 233

Range of index, 91
READ, 50, 335, 345
   definition of, 355
Reading, 57
   of characters, 104
   of input, 57
   of lines, 106
   of Pascal, 150
   of value in file, 214
READLN, 106, 123, 342, 356
REAL, 34
   type, 335
   value, printing of, 357
Real, 331
Real constant, 21, 29
Real variable, 33
RECORD, 345
Record, 181, 203, 212
   array of, 205
   input and output of, 206
   layout of, 204
   sorting of, 206
   structure of, 204
RECORD type, 213
Recusive algorithm, 232
Recursive data structure, 238
Recursive definition, 325
Recursive procedure, 225, 233
Register, control, 13
Relational expression, 54
Relational operator, 55
Relative error, 265
Repair of error, 46
REPEAT...UNTIL loop, 63, 71
Repetition, 337
RESET, 208, 213, 345, 355
Returning from a procedure
     or function, 164
REWRITE, 209, 213, 345, 355
Root of equation, 256
   finding of, 269, 277

Root node, 229
Root of tree, 99, 229
ROUND, 39, 353
Rounding, 49
Round-off error, 259, 265, 276
Rule of precedence, 23, 30

Scalar type, 118, 124, 341
Scanning words and characters,
    313
Scope of a variable, 165
Search, 181-191
    by address calculation, 187
    binary, 183, 190
    efficiency of, 230
    linear, 181
    time taken for, 183
Secondary memory, file in, 208
Selection, 64, 337
Semantic error, 46
Semicolon, as statement
    separator, 28
Sequencing of strings, 112
Sequential control, 64
Sequential execution, 13
Sequential file, 208, 213
Sequential machine, 13
Silicon chip, 13
Significant digits, 249, 260
    loss of, 265, 277
Simpson's rule, 272, 277
Simulator, 299, 303
    uses for, 301
SIN, 353
Sine, series for, 266
Single precision, 268
Slope of function, 270
Software, mathematical, 275, 278
Solution tree, 130
    growing of, 131
Sorting, 188
    efficiency of, 189
    of list, 132
    by merging, 188
    of records, 206
Special character, 19, 331
    substitution for, 331
Special condition, 197
Specification for program, 193
SQR, 353
SQRT, 353
Square bracket, 330
Statement, 20, 338
    assignment, 35
    BEGIN...END, 28, 54
    CASE, 67

compound, 54
empty, 351
FOR loop, 54, 70
GOTO, 78
IF...THEN...ELSE, 64, 72
PAGE, 27, 333
procedure, 154
READ, 50, 335, 355
READLN, 106, 123, 342
REPEAT...UNTIL loop, 63, 71
WHILE loop, 56, 70
WITH, 208
WRITE, 26, 30, 333
WRITELN, 25, 30, 333
Structure, 77
  of control flow, 77
  of data, 131, 217
  of loop, 77
  of record, 204

Structured programming, 2, 6
Style, programming, 195
SUCC, 121, 124, 341, 354
Stack, 224, 233, 325
  top of, 224
  use of in recursive
    procedure, 226
Step-by-step refinement, 129, 139
Stored program calculator, 13
String, 19
  array of, 113
  of characters, 103, 110
  comparison of, 110, 124
  null, 104
Subprogram, 153-163, 343
  declaration of, 163
  name of as parameter, 344
  nesting of, 157
Subrange of enumerated type, 122
Subrange type, 96, 100, 340
Substitution for special
    characters, 331
Subtree, 229
Swapping process, 136
Symbol, 19
Syntax diagrams for full
    Pascal, 363
Syntax errors, 17, 45
Syntax rule, 306, 325

Terminal, 14
Terminal symbol, 308, 325
Testing, 202
  of condition, 57
  exhaustive, 6
  of program, 45, 197, 202

Text editor, 148
TEXT file, 212, 214, 346, 356
Three-way branch, 65
Time sharing, 14
TO, 54
Top-down approach to
    programming, 129, 138
Top of stack, 224
Tracing execution, 37
Transaction, 170
Translation of program, 1, 16, 18
Translation of programming
    languages, 150
Translator, 305
Tree, 228
    adding to, 229
    binary, 228
    printing, 231
Tree structure, 99
    to problem solution, 130, 139
True, 54
TRUNC, 353
Truncation error, 260
Truncation of fractional part,
    38, 49
Truncation of series, 268
Two-dimensional array, 93–95
Type, 48, 337
    ARRAY, 91
    BOOLEAN, 55
    CHAR, 104, 123, 341
    enumerated, 121, 124
    FILE, 345
    INTEGER, 34, 335
    named, 97
    pointer, 237
    REAL, 34, 335
    RECORD, 213
    scalar, 118
    subrange, 96, 100, 340

VAR, 34, 48
Variable, 33, 335
    Boolean, 56
    declaration of, 48, 335
    global, 162
    local, 157
    undeclared, 47
    uninitialized, 47
Value formal parameter, 154,
    165, 343
Value of variable, 33
Variable formal parameter, 154,
    165, 343
VS computer, 293

WHILE loop, 56, 70
    compiling of, 316
Width of field, 27
WITH statement, 208, 214, 345
Word, 9
    length of, in computer, 9
    in memory, 302
    recognition, 144
    statistics, 148
WRITE, 26, 30, 333, 345
    definition of, 355
    to file, 214
WRITELN, 25, 30, 333, 356

Zero of function, 269, 277